search for Business Decisions, No. 74

Richard N. Farmer, Series Editor

Professor of International Business
Indiana University

Other Titles in This Series

Re

Commercial Bank
Interstate Expa

Issues, Prospects, and

Commercial Banking and Interstate Expansion

Issues, Prospects, and Strategies

by
Larry A. Frieder
Florida A & M University

Vincent P. Apilado
University of Texas at Arlington

George J. Benston
University of Rochester

Jeffrey Davis
University of Florida

Robert A. Eisenbeis
University of North Carolina

Thomas G. Gies
University of Michigan

Paul M. Horvitz
University of Houston

Harvey Rosenblum
Federal Reserve Bank of Chicago

David D. Whitehead, III
Federal Reserve Bank of Atlanta

UMI RESEARCH PRESS

Ann Arbor, Michigan

Produced and distributed by
UMI Research Press
an imprint of
University Microfilms International
A Xerox Information Resources Company
Ann Arbor, Michigan 48106

Library of Congress Cataloging in Publication Data

Main entry under title:

Commercial banking and interstate expansion.

(Research for business decisions ; no. 74)
Bibliography: p.
Includes index.
1. Interstate banking—United States—Addresses,
essays, lectures. 2. Interstate banking—Law and
legislation—United States—Addresses, essays, lectures.
3. Banks and banking—United States—Addresses, essays,
lectures. 4. Banking law—Florida—Addresses, essays,
lectures. I. Frieder, Larry A. II. Series.

HG2491.C642 1985   322.1'6   84-28109
ISBN 0-8357-1621-X (alk. paper)

To Michele

Contents

Preface

Much of the specific content of this book is the result of the Florida Interstate Banking Study which was commissioned by the Florida House of Representatives Committee on Commerce. The study was directed by Dr. Larry A. Frieder, Professor of Banking and Finance, School of Business and Industry (SBI), Florida A&M University.

The investigation requested was of great magnitude and comprehensive in scope. We conducted detailed inquiries into the following areas: financial innovations, methods of providing interstate financial services, the impact of nonbank entry and competition, economic development, economies of scale and technical efficiency, implications of changes in the payments system for interstate banking, legal analysis of reciprocal interstate banking, policy issues, and alternative legislative solutions pertaining to interstate banking. The study is the product of work performed by a group of nine scholars who were selected based upon their special expertise related to the issues surrounding the interstate banking issue. The scholars who contributed are listed on pages xiii and xiv.

The following extract from the Legislature's initial charge highlights the substantive areas the group was requested to pursue:

> ...conduct a detailed study of the Interstate Banking issue for the Commerce Committee of the Florida House of Representatives. We very much wish to tap the excellent work you and your colleagues are doing in this evolving area. The members of the committee will be needing detailed and critical analyses related to this important matter as we deliberate on the public policy ramifications of this issue.

> ... We expect your report to analyze available research and empirical evidence in the bank structure area. In this regard, the committee would appreciate insights related to financial markets/institutions, competition, allocational and technical efficiency. Your work should culminate in a written report to the Commerce Committee which includes: (1) public policy implications and alternatives related to Interstate Banking; (2) an analysis of the extent of interstate financial activity now being carried on; and (3) the type of such activity that could be carried on under the different possible legal alternatives (modification or repeal by Congress of the Douglas amendment or the McFadden Act) and the impact of that activity on the Florida economy, its citizens, and Florida based financial institutions.

Although Florida is the focal point for the analysis contained in the report, the contents are applicable to banking throughout the country. The perspective of a state (and its region) are instructive to all of the other states that are presently deliberating upon the interstate banking issue. The comprehensive research and analysis performed can assist those involved in either public or private sector consideration of the issue. This point must be underscored given the fact that so little research and analysis has been performed to date by the states. The tendency by the various states to establish advisory councils or panels has for the most part not provided for underlying research and analysis as a basis for recommendations.

The literature reviewed and the subjects analyzed in the study are not specific to the State of Florida. The work on the following topics is applicable to all states and all bank observers: (1) analysis of the erosion of interstate banking restrictions and approaches to interstate banking; (2) inventory of 4(c)8 activities; (3) impact of nonbank entry on interstate banking; (4) relationship of interstate banking to economic development; (5) implications of economies of scale for interstate banking; (6) the policy issues and solutions related to geographic expansion; (7) implication of change in the payments system (EFT) for interstate banking; (8) legal analysis of reciprocal interstate banking; and (9) appraisal of possible legislative options.

The principal users of the preliminary findings have included senior management, strategists, and consultants of commercial banks; law firms who advise commercial banks; state legislators, policy makers, and commerce officials; and federal and state regulators for banking and financial affairs. Because of the broad scope and comprehensive nature of the study, libraries and classroom teachers can use the study either as a reference or textbook.

This study has been taking shape for the past two years. Meetings, conference calls, and exchange of drafts have been constant. A product like this could only result from the extensive contributions of the study's several talented authors. Each of these individuals has a dedicated commitment to a sound financial structure geared to the public interest. It certainly was a pleasure for me to work closely with the members of this group. Although I underscore their individual contributions, I fully accept final responsibility for any errors or omissions.

I want to acknowledge the encouragement of Speaker H. Lee Moffitt (Florida House of Representatives) and Dr. Sybil Mobley (SBI Dean) to pursue this effort. They are truly magnificent leaders. Also, our appreciation is extended to Mr. Wyatt Martin, Staff Director of the Committee on Commerce, who provided continual support for this project. Finally, we note the valuable financial support of the Florida Institute of Government.

Tallahassee, Florida   Larry A. Frieder
February, 1985

Contributors

Vincent P. Apilado, Ph.D., Professor of Finance and Chairman, Department of Finance and Real Estate, The University of Texas at Arlington. Dr. Apilado's works have appeared in the *Journal of Financial and Quantitative Analysis, Journal of Financial Research* and the *Journal of Bank Research.*

George J. Benston, Ph.D., Professor of Accounting, Finance and Economics, The University of Rochester: visiting scholar at the Federal Reserve Bank of Atlanta. Former consultant for the Federal Reserve Board, the Office of the Comptroller of the Currency, the FDIC, the Federal Home Loan Bank Board, and the National Commission on Consumer Finance.

Jeffrey Davis, J.D., Professor of Law, Holland Law Center, University of Florida. Member of the American Bar Association Section of Corporate, Banking, and Business Law.

Robert A. Eisenbeis, Ph.D., Wachovia Professor of Banking, School of Business Administration, University of North Carolina at Chapel Hill. Formerly senior deputy associate director in the Division of Research and Statistics of the Federal Reserve Board.

Larry A. Frieder, Ph.D., Professor of Banking and Finance, Florida A & M University. Author of "Commercial Banking and Holding Company Acquisitions: New Dimensions in Theory, Evaluation, and Practice," and articles in the *Journal of Bank Research, Journal of Financial Research, Bankers Magazine,* and *Journal of Corporation Law.*

Thomas G. Gies, Ph.D., Professor of Finance, The University of Michigan. Served as special consultant to the Securities & Exchange Commission, the U.S. Treasury and the Board of Governors of the Federal Reserve, the Senate Banking Committee and the Select Committee on Small Business. Author of *Utility Regulation: New Directions in Theory and Policy* (with Professor W.G. Shepherd).

Paul M. Horvitz, Ph.D., Judge James A. Elkins Professor of Banking and Finance, College of Business Administration, University of Houston. Member of President Reagan's Advisory Task Force on Small Business, and former consultant to the Treasury Department, FDIC, Federal Home Loan Bank Board, and Small Business Administration.

Harvey Rosenblum, Ph.D., Vice President and Economic Advisor, Federal Reserve Bank of Chicago.* Visiting professor of finance at DePaul University.

David D. Whitehead, III, Ph.D., Senior Research Economist, Federal Reserve Bank of Atlanta.* Publisher of two special issues of the Atlanta Bank's *Economic Review.*

* Note: The views of Dr. Rosenblum and Dr. Whitehead are their own, and do not necessarily represent the viewpoint of the Federal Reserve System.

1

An Overview of the Interstate Banking Issue

Larry A. Frieder

Introduction

The commercial banking industry has undergone great changes during the past decade. A number of reasons account for this change. Technological developments in electronic funds transfer have been dramatic. The large number of new financial products and services offered in the continuing inflationary environment has resulted in a rising level of consumer sophistication. Nonbanks are increasingly competing directly with commercial banks. The interest rate structure in the United States has been radically altered in terms of level and volatility. And, finally, the industry has been deregulated substantially.

For years various types of deregulation have constituted the major political-economic concerns of the nation's banks. *Price deregulation* involves the removal of legal restrictions on (1) the interest rates banks may pay for deposits and (2) the interest rates banks may charge on loans. Recently, banks have realized substantial price deregulation. The Garn-St. Germain bill allowed the introduction of money market demand accounts (MMDA) in December 1982. In October 1983, all rate ceilings on deposits with more than 31 days initial maturity were removed. Additionally, the Depository Institutions Deregulation and Monetary Control Act (DIDMCA) of 1980 removed some rate ceilings on bank loans. Specifically, state usury ceilings on first residential mortgages and business and agricultural loans above $25,000 were eliminated.

Product deregulation involves the removal or liberalization of legal restrictions on the types of products or services banks may offer. Investment banking and insurance underwriting represent present product constraints faced by banks.

Geographic deregulation involves the removal or liberalization of limitations on the geographical coverage over which banks may operate. Historically, controversies surrounding geographic deregulation have centered on intrastate branching and merging laws. Recently, this issue has increasingly surfaced along interstate lines. Geographic deregulation in banking is the subject of this book.

Intrastate geographic deregulation is governed by the individual states. In recent years, the states have tended to liberalize their bank structure laws. Unit banking states (those prohibiting all branching) are now a small minority. *Interstate* deregulation is governed by both the federal government and the states. To date, the federal government has given little consideration to interstate banking. Accordingly, the issue has been left to the states to resolve. The states are showing increasing interest in interstate banking legislation. Activity in the form of legislative interest has now surfaced in the majority of states and regions in the country. States in New England and the Southeast have enacted interstate banking laws which have already been utilized by a number of banks in these regions. The prospect of additional states and regions enacting interstate bills in the next few years appears very likely.

This book is based upon a two-year study of the interstate banking issue commissioned by the Florida legislature. Although Florida is the focal point for the analysis, the contents are applicable to banking throughout the country. The perspective of a state (and its region) will be instructive to other states that are presently deliberating the interstate banking issue. The comprehensive research and analysis performed can assist those involved in either public or private sector consideration of the issue. This point must be underscored given the fact that so little research and analysis has been performed to date by the states. The tendency of the various states to establish advisory councils or panels has for the most part not provided for underlying research and analysis as a basis for recommendations.

The literature reviewed and the subjects analyzed in the study are not specific to the State of Florida. The work on the following topics is applicable to all states and all bank observers:

1. Analysis of the erosion of interstate banking restrictions and approaches to interstate banking
2. Inventory of 4(c)8 activities
3. Impact of nonbank entry on interstate banking
4. Relationship of interstate banking to economic development
5. Implications of economies of scale for interstate banking
6. The policy issues and solutions related to geographic expansion
7. Implication of change in the payments system (EFT) for interstate banking

8. Legal analysis of reciprocal interstate banking
9. Appraisal of possible legislative options.

The remainder of this chapter will introduce the context of the Florida Interstate Banking Study and background on Florida's bank structure in relation to the interstate banking issue. Next, the 1984 legislative session is reviewed. The provisions of the enacted regional reciprocal interstate banking law are examined, and some broader interstate banking trends are discussed. Finally, the coverage of this book is indicated.

Context of Report

The interstate banking issue first surfaced in Florida in 1979. Termed the "Intersouth Bill," the legislation introduced a regional reciprocity approach and passed one chamber.[1] Since this early introduction of the interstate banking issue in the Florida legislature, the topic has become increasingly controversial. Financial structure questions have surfaced nearly every year since 1979. Although legislation has, is, and will be pursued, the impact of all the ramifications and policy options surrounding this issue has not been systematically analyzed. Accordingly, a detailed study of the interstate banking issue was commissioned by the Florida House of Representatives Committee on Commerce.

Because the study envisioned was large in scope and required a diversity of expertise, it was agreed that a study group would be necessary. Fortunately, several of the nation's top experts were willing to provide an objective and dispassionate analysis of the various questions related to the interstate banking issue.[2]

Background on Florida's Bank Structure[3]

Similar to the trend in several other states throughout the U.S., Florida's banking structure has been systematically liberalized over the past ten years. Florida was traditionally a unit banking state. However, since the early part of the century various groups and chains of banks had formed. The multi-bank holding company (MBHC) organizational form had been in existence in Florida before the national Bank Holding Company Act of 1956. Accordingly, Florida has never had a statute prohibiting multi-bank holding companies. Between 1968 and 1973 Florida bank holding companies (BHCs) aggressively acquired independent banks to avoid the restrictive effects of unit banking.

During the recent past (1975–81), the bank structure laws of Florida have been increasingly liberalized. Essentially, the state's bank structure has evolved full tilt away from unit banking.

In 1975 bank branching laws were liberalized to allow banks to have drive-in and walk-up facilities providing certain limited services even though banks were still forced to operate primarily at one location. Additionally, Chapter 75-217, the original branch banking law, was passed during the 1975 regular session. (It did not become effective, however, until January 1, 1977.) This law allowed county wide branching. Each bank was permitted to establish two branches per year within the county in which the parent bank was located. Also, this law allowed banks to establish branches by merging with any other bank located within the same county, with Department approval.

In 1977 the law was amended to specify that drive-in or walk-up facilities converted to branches were not to be considered as one of the two authorized per year branches.

As a result of pressures for expanded banking activity across county lines, the branching/merger law was again amended in 1979 to provide for merger with any other bank in the state that had been incorporated for at least three years. This bill also allowed for the merged bank to establish two branches per year within its county.

Finally, in 1981 the Florida banking laws removed the limitations on the number of branches that could be established per year within the county in which the parent bank was located. Branching across county lines, however, is still limited because it has to occur via merger with banks which have been incorporated for three or more years. This amendment will be in effect until 1986, when it will undergo legislative review.

The expanded merger and branching capabilities have been widely used by Florida banks—particularly Florida MBHCs. Southeast, for example, has merged all of its offices statewide into a single bank (OBHC). Others, such as Barnett and Sun, have also significantly merged and branched but remain as multi-bank holding companies.

Table 1.1 highlights some of the trends in Florida's banking structure. As a result of the more liberal branching and merging laws described previously, the number of banks in Florida has declined from 668 in 1977 to 458 in 1982. However, during the same period the number of offices has increased from 996 to 2004. Independent banks and small one-bank holding companies (OBHCs) have managed to maintain their market share of deposits in comparison to Florida MBHCs. In 1977 MBHCs held 71.4% of Florida's bank deposits, and in 1981 MBHCs controlled 71.3%.

Table 1.2 provides a listing of Florida bank holding companies (BHCs) as of December 31, 1980. This historical listing is revealing in terms of identifying the major consolidation occurring in Florida's banking markets. Note that nine of the 10 largest banking organizations in the state have either made major acquisitions of banking assets or have merged into a larger organization. Specifically, note the following:

Table 1.1.   Florida Bank Structure

Number of Banks	1977	1980*	1981	1982**
Total	668	556	494	458
Multi-BHCs	386	271	228	206
Independents and One BHC	282	285	266	252
Branch Offices	328	846	--	1544
Total Offices	996	1402	--	2004
Deposits (billions)				
Total (%)	$29.7 (100%)	$40.4 (100%)	$43.5 (100%)	$49.2 (100%)
MBHCs	21.2 (.714)	28.7 (.71)	31.0 (.713)	29.3 (.60)
Independents and OBHCs	8.5 (.286)	11.7 (.29)	12.5 (.287)	19.9 (.40)

Source: Annual Reports: Division of Banking, State of Florida.

*The published data are adjusted to classify large OBHCs that had been MBHCs previous to change in banking law as MBHCs.

**The reader should note that 1982 data is not comparable to prior years because larger Florida BHCs such as Southeast converted from being a MBHC to an OBHC and thus the "independents and OBHCs" classification is inflated vis-à-vis prior years.

Table 1.2.   Listing of Florida Holding Companies

Florida Banking Structure by Classification
As of December 31, 1980
(Figures in 000's)

HOLDING COMPANIES BY DEPOSIT SIZE (26 Multi-bank & 34 One-bank)	# OF BANKS	TOTAL OFFICES***	TOTAL DEPOSITS	ALL HCs (%)	STATE (%)
1. SOUTHEAST BANKING CORPORATION, MIAMI	24	83	$ 4,524,406	14.53	11.20
2. BARNETT BANKS OF FLORIDA, INC., JACKSONVILLE	31	134	3,700,859	11.89	9.16
3. SUN BANKS OF FLORIDA, INC., ORLANDO	15	15	2,921,903	9.38	7.23
4. FLORIDA NATIONAL BANKS OF FLORIDA, INC., JACKSONVILLE	25	84	1,995,280	6.41	4.94
5. FLAGSHIP BANKS INC., MIAMI	26	81	1,969,634	6.33	4.87
6. FIRST FLORIDA BANKS, INC., TAMPA	14	41	1,693,784	5.44	4.19
7. ATLANTIC BANCORPORATION, JACKSONVILLE	16	55	1,605,743	5.16	3.97
8. ELLIS BANKING CORPORATION, BRADENTON	26	34	1,059,567	3.40	2.62
9. LANDMARK BANKING CORPORATION OF FLORIDA, FORT LAUDERDALE	5	30	1,036,223	3.33	2.56
10. SOUTHWEST FLORIDA BANKS, INC., FORT MYERS	12	42	960,707	3.09	2.38
11. CENTURY BANKS, INC., FORT LAUDERDALE	11	34	917,676	2.95	2.27
12. EXCHANGE BANCORPORATION, INC., TAMPA	10	27	897,665	2.88	2.22
13. PAN AMERICAN BANCSHARES, INC., MIAMI	6	30	735,179	2.36	1.82
14. FLORIDA COMMERCIAL BANKS, INC., MIAMI	7	16	520,562	1.67	1.29
15. GULFSTREAM BANKS, INC., BOCA RATON	3	13	493,127	1.58	1.22
*16. FIRST MARINE BANKS, INC., RIVIERA BEACH	1	15	411,026	1.32	1.02
17. FIRST BANKERS CORPORATION OF FLORIDA, POMPANO BEACH	5	16	389,999	1.25	.97
18. GREAT AMERICAN BANKS, INC., NORTH MIAMI	8	11	375,538	1.21	.93
*19. CITY NATIONAL BANKING CORPORATION, MIAMI	1	4	368,698	1.18	.91
*20. FIRST STATE BANKING CORPORATION, MIAMI	1	8	353,503	1.14	.87
21. ROYAL TRUST BANK CORPORATION, MIAMI	7	17	338,523	1.09	.84
*22. REBANK CORPORATION, MIAMI	1	5	317,294	1.02	.79
*23. COMMUNITY BANKS OF FLORIDA, INC., SEMINOLE	1	16	295,483	.95	.73
24. POPULAR BANCSHARES CORPORATION, MIAMI	2	8	269,836	.87	.67
25. METROPOLITAN BANCORPORATION, TAMPA	3	10	265,585	.85	.66
26. MFG INVESTMENTS, INC., HIALEAH	2	10	255,432	.82	.63
27. COMBANKS CORPORATION, WINTER PARK	6	13	234,188	.75	.58
28. FLORIDA COAST BANKS, INC., POMPANO BEACH	2	10	232,929	.75	.58
29. CENTRAL BANCORP, INC., MIAMI BEACH	2	6	201,111	.65	.50
*30. MICKLER CORPORATION, TAMPA	1	2	152,695	.49	.38
31. AMERICAN BANKS OF FLORIDA, INC., JACKSONVILLE	2	5	145,684	.47	.36
32. JEFFERSON BANCORP, INC., MIAMI BEACH	3	7	130,094	.42	.32
*33. MULTI-LINE, INC., TAMPA	1	4	129,189	.41	.32
*34. JACKSONVILLE NATIONAL CORPORATION, JACKSONVILLE	1	1	127,377	.41	.32
*35. TOTALBANK CORPORATION OF FLORIDA, MIAMI	1	4	88,049	.28	.22
*36. NATIONAL BANKING CORPORATION OF FLORIDA, MIAMI	1	3	73,380	.24	.18
*37. N & W CORPORATION, CHICAGO	1	1	69,014	.22	.17
*38. EAGLE NATIONAL HOLDING COMPANY, INC., MIAMI	1	2	68,604	.22	.17
*39. CHARTER BANKING CORPORATION, ST. PETERSBURG BEACH	1	2	64,691	.21	.16
*40. SUMMIT BANKING CORPORATION, TAMARAC	1	3	62,287	.20	.15
*41. CREWS BANKING CORPORATION, WAUCHULA	1	2	59,019	.19	.15
*42. CITRUS & CHEMICAL BANCORPORATION, BARTOW	1	1	53,309	.17	.13
*43. BANK OF FLORIDA CORPORATION, ST. PETERSBURG	1	3	52,227	.17	.13
*44. D.J. INVESTMENTS, INC., DELAND	1	1	47,332	.15	.12
*45. TRI-STATE INVESTMENT CORPORATION, PENSACOLA	1	4	45,363	.15	.11
*46. UNITED BANK CORPORATION, COCOA BEACH	1	2	36,369	.12	.09
*47. NORTHWEST BANKING CORPORATION, QUINCY	1	3	36,064	.12	.09
*48. FLORIDA SHARES, INC., MIAMI	1	1	35,561	.11	.09
*49. SUWANEE COUNTY BANCORPORATION, LIVE OAK	1	2	31,734	.10	.08
*50. AMERICAN BANCORPORATION, MERRITT ISLAND	1	4	31,449	.10	.08
*51. LEVY COUNTY BANCORPORATION, CHIEFLAND	1	3	29,528	.09	.07
*52. CARIBANK CORPORATION, CORAL GABLES	1	1	28,432	.09	.07
*53. STRACHAN CONSTRUCTION CO., INC., FORT WALTON BEACH	1	1	27,612	.08	.07
*54. FLORIDA BANK CORPORATION, INC., CLEARWATER	1	1	26,218	.08	.06
*55. TRANS FLORIDA BANCSHARES, INC., SARASOTA	1	3	26,155	.08	.06
*56. AVON SECURITIES, INC., SEBRING	1	1	25,492	.08	.06
*57. SOUTHERN BANKS OF FLORIDA, INC., HIGH SPRINGS	1	3	24,466	.08	.06
*58. MANUFACTURERS BANCSHARES, INC., MIAMI	1	2	23,680	.08	.06
*59. DESOTO BANKING CORPORATION, ARCADIA	1	1	21,642	.07	.05
*60. SEMINOLE BANCORPORATION, CASSELBERRY	1	3	20,804	.07	.05
HOLDING COMPANY TOTALS	307	944	$31,134,960	100.00	77.05
INDEPENDENT BANKS	249	458	$ 9,275,169	-	22.95
STATE TOTALS**	556	1402	$40,410,129	-	-

*One-bank holding company.

**Does not include 3 trust banks and 8 trust companies (without deposits); 19 international agencies/representative offices and 22 edge act corporations.

***Office count reflects only facilities reporting deposits to Florida Bankers Association.

Source: Florida Bankers Association.

1. Southeast acquired a number of banks from Florida National in resolution of a failed takeover bid of Florida National.
2. Barnett acquired a large fraction of Great American Banks, First Marine Banks, and has recently bid for Florida Coast Banks.
3. Sun has acquired Century Banks and Flagship banks.
4. Florida National has bought Royal Trust and at the same time is working out details of being acquired itself by Chemical Bank of New York on a "when and if" interstate banking is legal basis.
5. NCNB has purchased Ellis Banking Corporation.
6. Landmark and Southwest Florida Banks have agreed to a merger.

Only five of the banks listed 11-20 in table 1.2 still remain. NCNB has purchased Exchange and Gulfstream while Barnett has purchased First Marine. We mentioned the acquisitions of Century and Great American earlier. The remaining MBHCs are also being pursued. Royal Trust has been bought by Florida National and ComBanks was bought by Freedom Savings.

This consolidation activity has reduced the number of large MBHCs which compete in Florida, increased the size of the survivors, and escalated the state's concentration ratios—the percentage of deposits controlled by the state's largest banking organizations. Although a few more consolidations are expected, it is believed that market share limits from the regulatory viewpoint are being approached.[4] Since published data on Florida bank structure for year-end 1983 are not yet available, we estimated the share of total banking deposits in Florida controlled (or to be controlled once announced mergers are consummated) by the 10 largest banking organizations to approximate 70% to 75% versus about 53% in 1980.

Background on the Interstate Banking Issue

Present restrictions on interstate banking emanate primarily from the Douglas Amendment to the Bank Holding Company Act and the McFadden Act. The Douglas Amendment prohibits BHCs from acquiring banks in other states unless the entered state expressly permits such entry by statute. The McFadden Act essentially prohibits interstate branching by national or state member banks. The federal government has not to date addressed the fundamental interstate banking issue. Accordingly, state action revolving around the Douglas Amendment has become the central focus in Florida as well as in several other states or regions.[5]

Florida has become a state with a great amount of interstate banking attention. Numerous national and regional financial and non-financial institutions have entered or anticipate entrance into Florida via the numerous *de facto* or *de jure* approaches to interstate banking.[6] Florida's population growth, wealth, and commerce potentials are extremely attractive to all types of financial organizations.

After the 1979 introduction of a regional reciprocal bill in Florida (mentioned previously), political attention shifted to the loan production offices (LPOs) in Florida of BHCs headquartered in other states. The entire banking code which had just been rewritten by the Legislature was vetoed by Governor Robert Graham because it prohibited LPOs. In 1981 the removal of the limitation on the number of branches that could be established per year within the county in which the parent bank is located was the focus of attention. However, the interstate banking issue was highlighted by the fact that NCNB Corporation convinced the Federal Reserve Board that their entry into Florida banking was provided via a loophole in a Florida statute designed to keep out-of-state banks out of Florida.

In 1982 the House Commerce Committee approved a regional reciprocal interstate banking bill, which after a three year adjustment period would have authorized interstate banking on a reciprocal basis nationwide (see exhibit 1).[7] This bill did not go beyond the Commerce Committee. In 1983 a proposed regional banking bill was widely opposed in a Commerce Committee hearing (see exhibit 2). A nationwide reciprocity bill was opposed in the Florida Senate (see exhibit 3).

The 1984 Florida Legislature

The two bills presented in exhibits 4 and 5 were entertained by the 1984 Florida Legislature. Governor Robert Graham had set regional banking as a 1984 legislative priority and established an Advisory Committee on Regional Interstate Banking chaired by Joel Wells, Chief Executive Officer of Sun Banks of Florida, Inc. The bill outlined in exhibit 4 emanated from the initiative of Governor Graham and the strong endorsement of the committee. The committee recommended several definitions, provisions, and limitations that were deemed necessary to satisfy the coalition assembled to support the bill politically (see exhibit 4 and discussion below). The main groups in this coalition include the Florida Bankers Association (FBA) and the Florida Registered Bank Holding Companies Association. The proponents of the regional bill maintained that this approach would allow banks in the state to obtain the size necessary to survive and thus preserve some regional institutions.

Opponents to the regional reciprocity bill included the (Florida) Independent Bankers Association (IBA) as well as the money center banks. The IBA is opposed to any form of interstate banking. Underlying its opposition is the fear that interstate banking will concentrate financial resources and threaten the preservation of community banks. The money center banks oppose the regional reciprocity approach because it does not provide for eventual entry by out-of-region banks. Citicorp and Chemical Bank were the major money center opponents. They stressed that regional reciprocity is valid only as an adjustment to nationwide banking. And, unless a trigger allowing nationwide banking is included, the bill is protectionist and, thus, undesirable. The bill set forth in exhibit 4 (regional reciprocity) eventually passed and became law despite this significant opposition.

The alternative bill (see exhibit 5) allowed for: (1) regional reciprocity; (2) immediate nationwide reciprocity, allowing banks outside the region to acquire one bank smaller than $400 million in assets per year; and (3) a nationwide reciprocity trigger after five years (no limitation on size of bank or the number of banks acquired each year). Although this bill had the support of money center banks, it was opposed by all Florida banking groups (IBA, FBA, and BHCs). As a result, it was dropped from consideration in both the Florida House and Senate.

Provisions of the Florida Regional Reciprocal Interstate Banking Bill[8]

As mentioned earlier, several definitions, provisions, and limitations were deemed necessary to satisfy the coalition of bank interest groups assembled to support the Florida bill politically. The regional reciprocity bill enacted in Florida includes nine important provisions (see exhibit 4).

1. Structure of the Bill

The Bank Holding Company Act prohibits interstate acquisitions by bank holding companies unless the laws of a state expressly authorize it. The legal basis for the regional reciprocal concept is that each state has the authority to determine which bank holding companies may acquire institutions within its borders and the conditions upon which they may do so. The bill identifies those institutions that will be permitted to make acquisitions and defines the terms and conditions upon which they may do so.

2. Institutions Making Acquisitions

The Act authorizes certain bank holding companies to make acquisitions in Florida. The statute is a relaxation of the prohibition against interstate banking contained in the Douglas Amendment. The bill does not authorize acquisitions of Florida institutions by out-of-state savings and loans, industrial savings banks, or the so-called nonbank banks.

3. Regional Bank Holding Companies

Acquisitions in Florida would be permitted only by "regional bank holding companies." A regional bank holding company is one whose principal place of business is in a state within the region, and has 80% of its deposits in the region. The regional bank holding company may not be controlled by a bank holding company outside the region. Up to 20% of the bank holding company's deposits may be in institutions outside the region. This allows some leeway for a bank holding company to have interests outside its region, but compels that its center of interest be within the states comprising the region.

4. The Region

The region is defined as Alabama, Arkansas, Florida, Georgia, Louisiana, Maryland, Mississippi, North Carolina, South Carolina, Tennessee, Virginia, West Virginia and the District of Columbia. They are the states that make up the Fifth and Sixth Federal Reserve Districts (with the exception of Arkansas).

5. Reciprocity

For a regional bank holding company to make acquisitions in Florida, the laws of the state in which it has its principal place of business must extend reciprocity to Florida bank holding companies. On seeking to acquire a Florida bank or holding company, approval must be obtained from the Florida Department of Banking. Reciprocity involves a three-part test.

   A. The laws of the other state must generally permit Florida bank holding companies to acquire banks or bank holding companies in that state.
   B. Any discriminatory laws in the other state restricting a Florida company's entry would apply to the acquisition in Florida.
   C. The Florida bank holding company sought to be acquired could legally acquire the holding company that seeks to acquire it.

The purpose of the reciprocity requirement is to assure that Florida bank holding companies have an equal opportunity to transact business in the state where the incoming holding company has its principal place of business.

6. No De Novo Entry

The statute requires that in order for a Florida bank to be acquired, it must have been organized and operating for two years or more. All banks owned by a bank holding company must meet that same test. An out-of-state bank holding company, therefore, could not acquire a newly chartered bank or charter one itself and then acquire it.

7. *Nonseverability*

If any of the provisions relating to reciprocity or which establish the limited regional framework were declared invalid, then the entire statute would become void. Transactions which had occurred prior to that determination, however, would be effective.

8. *Anti-Leapfrogging*

If a regional bank holding company ceased to qualify as such under the statute, it would be required to divest itself of its banking subsidiaries in Florida within one year. Thus, if a bank holding company whose principal place of business was in the region was acquired by or acquired a bank holding company outside the region, and this caused more than 20% of the combined deposits of the resulting institution to be outside the region, then it would be required to divest its Florida bank subsidiaries. In order to avoid possible constitutional questions, exceptions are made for failing bank acquisitions pursuant to the Garn-St. Germain Act.

9. *No National Trigger*

The bill does not set a date that would open Florida to acquisitions by companies located in states outside the region. The so-called "trigger to national."

Limitation of Indefinite Regional Reciprocity

The Florida legislature's preference for the regional reciprocity option in 1984 is consistent with the analysis contained in this book. As an interim step or transition to provision for diverse entry into the state and region, the option is pro-competitive. However, to the extent that regional reciprocity is protectionist and serves to prevent the possibility of out-of-region bank entry into the state or the region after a short transition period, the public interest would not be served. The state and the region would most likely consolidate rapidly and the resulting concentration would need to be addressed. Such concentration, along with the lack of actual or potential entry, would tend to have undesirable public policy effects in terms of lower credit availability, service offerings, and/or less attractive prices (borrowing or savings rates).

Since entry into the region in the near future is important, a "trigger" provision is necessary. Conceptually, whether the present bill has a trigger or not appears academic. That is, if a bill has no trigger, it remains as a future legislative option. Correspondingly, if a trigger were in a bill, it could be removed or delayed by the legislature at a later date. However, in a political context, these options may be more transparent than real, i.e., can you really add or delete a trigger in the near future given political realities? Since regional reciprocity is desirable only in the transitional context and a "trigger" is not politically feasible presently, then it is important that the matter be meaningfully revisited in future state legislative sessions or addressed at the federal level.[9]

Fundamental Aspects of Interstate Banking and Trends

In regards to a framework for our interstate banking discussion, consider the following:[10]

1. The public interest should be central to all modifications of financial structure. Although interstate banking will affect specific bank economics, the effects on the users of financial services should be our focus.
2. Liberalization of geographical restrictions evolves in a political economy. Political forces often dominate economic theory. Interstate banking in general is not a consumer or even a business sector political issue.
3. There exist a very large number (if not an infinite number) of interstate banking alternatives. The interstate banking choices are unlimited when one considers that 50 states can possess different preferences regarding effective dates for various liberalization provisions, reciprocity versus unrestricted entry, *de novo* entry versus by acquisition only, varying trigger points and phase-in plans, varying anti-leapfrogging approaches, and different definitions of which states are included in a region.
4. There is uncertainty regarding the eventual role of the federal government in the interstate banking debate. Will the government wait a long period and then act to ratify whatever amalgamation the various states and regions devise? Or will it enter soon in response to the present trend to regional banking zones and the interstate activities of non-banks and bank holding companies forming non-bank banks in the post U.S. Trust decision period?
5. Are the present anti-trust laws adequate to guide the consolidation movement? Do the definitions of lines of commerce and relevant market need revisitation?

The Florida experience suggests that given the fact that interstate activity is taking place at the state level, it is either the dominant bank political force in a state or a coalition of important bank groups that most influences legislation. These groups will tend to advocate protectionist interstate banking bills. This accounts for the widespread absence of *de novo* provisions in most state deliberations to date. The stipulation of "no trigger" to nationwide entry into a state or region also emanates from this reality. Accordingly, specific bank economics and interests tend to dominate the public interest.

The Southeast regional reciprocity framework has been adopted by Georgia, North Carolina, and South Carolina in addition to Florida. Mergers between banks in these states have already occurred. Given New England's earlier adoption of the model, it appears that more bank regions may surface as a result of legislative activity in 1985 and 1986. Three other possible bank regions have been explored. A group of Southwestern states including Arizona, New Mexico, and Utah appears likely to consummate regional reciprocity legislation soon. Utah, of course, enacted regional reciprocal legislation in 1984. Five states in the Midwest considered regional proposals in 1984 to no avail. However, it is believed that some of these states will be more receptive in 1985. The Mid-Atlantic states have also given regional reciprocity attention. Another part of the Southwest led by Texas has suggested yet another region. Finally, the Far West could similarly restructure.

Although regional reciprocity is clearly the national trend, the political landscape of the states include other structure variations. States such as Rhode Island and Kentucky have enacted defined phase-in legislation that allows nationwide interstate banking after a certain time period. Several other states have expressed interest in nationwide phase-in plans.

The activities of the states to date clearly indicate that banks from four states—New York, California, Illinois, and Texas—will be excluded from participating in the interstate banking movement. That is, no states have included these states in their region. Yet, other states are included in more than one region. Maryland has been included in three different regional proposals. Inconsistencies have developed in state selection of regional partners. For example, Georgia would allow entry by Kentucky banks, but Kentucky allows entry only by banks in states immediately adjacent to Kentucky.

Regional banking states can be expected to resist further liberalization efforts such as those aimed at nationwide entry. This likelihood, along with the phase-in periods involved in the plans of other states, suggests that regional banking zones will dominate U.S. bank structure for at least the rest of the decade. Major shifting from this strong trend would have to come from action by the federal government. Although action on interstate banking policy has been basically nonexistent to date, there have been indications of federal concerns against the regional reciprocity trend. Federal Reserve Chairman

Paul Volcker expressed the Board's concerns about this in his September 13, 1983 congressional testimony. Besides the issues discussed above, Volcker warned against a new form of Balkanization of the banking industry.[11]

All of the issues surrounding the interstate banking debate are the subject of this book. It is believed that the analysis presented will prove valuable to both private and public sector participants in the banking industry, particularly those involved in public policy and strategic formulation.

Coverage of this Report

The material in the following chapters is organized around the specific topics requested by the Florida House of Representatives Committee on Commerce. The issues addressed, however, are of fundamental importance in any state considering the question of interstate banking.

Chapter 2 provides a thorough discussion of the changing realities of financial markets and institutions. Innovations to avoid interstate banking are explored. Policy issues pertaining to interstate banking proposals are examined.

Chapter 3 discusses the various methods of providing interstate financial services, grandfathered interstate banks, and the Garn-St. Germain legislation. The data provided on interstate 4(c)8 activity in Florida are the most exhaustive to date.

Nonbank competition is thoroughly explored in chapter 4. Again, the most exhaustive data base on nonbank banking activities which exists to date is offered.

Chapter 5 explores the country's changing financial structure and its implication for the economic development of Florida. Particular attention is given to the user of financial services.

Chapter 6 covers the research evidence produced to date on economies of scale and operational efficiency. Inferences regarding interstate banking are based upon this evidence.

A thorough analysis of the research literature involving geographic restrictions/expansions is presented in chapter 7. The evidence pertaining to the economic benefits and costs of financial structure liberalization is presented.

Chapter 8 examines the implications of electronic funds transfer for the interstate banking issue.

Most legal issues revolve around the regional reciprocity approach to interstate banking. Accordingly, a thorough legal analysis of the regional reciprocity notion is presented in chapter 9.

Chapter 10 synthesizes the findings of our research. An analysis of the implications of interstate banking is presented.

Exhibit 1. Regional Reciprocity Bill (1982) with Nationwide Reciprocity Trigger

170-398-2-2

```
 1|              A bill to be entitled               1:btc
 2|     An act relating to banking; adding paragraphs   1.3
 3|     (f) and (g) to s. 658.29(3), Florida Statutes;
 4|     providing exceptions to the prohibition against  1.5
 5|     out-of-state bank holding companies owning
 6|     banks or bank holding companies in this state;   1.6
 7|     providing effective dates.                       1.7
 8|
 9| Be It Enacted by the Legislature of the State of Florida:   1:enc
10|
11|       Section 1.  Paragraph (f) is added to subsection (3) of   1.7
12| section 658.29, Florida Statutes, to read:            1.8
13|       658.29  Certain ownership and control prohibited.--   1.10
14|       (3)  Notwithstanding any other provisions of this   1.11
15| section, the restrictions and prohibitions of this section   1.13
16| shall not apply:
17|       (f)  After January 1, 1984, to the ownership of voting   1:lus
18| shares of, interests in, or all or substantially all of the   1.15
19| assets of banks and bank holding companies located in this
20| state which have been conducting the business of a bank or   1.16
21| bank holding company for not less than 3 years by a bank   1.17
22| holding company located in Alabama, Georgia, Louisiana,   1.18
23| Mississippi, North Carolina, South Carolina, Tennessee or
24| Virginia, and such ownership is hereby specifically   1.19
25| authorized; but only if the statute laws of the state in which   1.20
26| that bank holding company is located specifically authorize   1.21
27| this same privilege of owning voting shares of, interests in,   1.23
28| or all or substantially all of the assets of banks and bank   1.24
29| holding companies located in that state to bank holding   1.26
30| companies located in Florida.  For the purpose of this   1.27
31| paragraph, a bank or bank holding company is "located" in the   1.29
```

1

(Exhibit 1 continued)

170-398-2-2

1	state in which its bank or bank holding company operations are	
2	principally conducted.	1.13/16
3	Section 2. Paragraph (g) is added to subsection (3) of	1.31
4	section 658.29, Florida Statutes, to read:	1.31/1
5	658.29 Certain ownership and control prohibited.--	1.34
6	(3) Notwithstanding any other provisions of this	1.35
7	section, the restrictions and prohibitions of this section	1.37
8	shall not apply:	
9	(g) After January 1, 1987, to the ownership of voting	1:lus
10	shares of, interests in, or all or substantially all of the	1.39
11	assets of banks and bank holding companies located in this	
12	state which have been conducting the business of a bank or	1.40
13	bank holding company for not less than 3 years by a bank	1.41
14	holding company located in any other state, and such ownership	
15	is hereby specifically authorized; but only if the statute	1.42
16	laws of the state in which that bank holding company is	
17	located specifically authorize this same privilege of owning	1.43
18	voting shares of, interests in, or all or substantially all of	1.43/1
19	the assets of banks and bank holding companies located in that	
20	state to bank holding companies located in Florida. For the	1.43/3
21	purpose of this paragraph, a bank or bank holding company is	
22	"located" in the state in which its bank or bank holding	1.43/4
23	company operations are principally conducted.	1.43/5
24	Section 3. Section 1 of this act shall take effect	1.43/5
25	January 1, 1984, and section 2 of this act shall take effect	1.48
26	January 1, 1987.	
27		
28		
29		
30		
31		

2

Exhibit 2. Regional Reciprocity Followed by Nationwide Reciprocity (1983)

A bill to be entitled

1   An act relating to banking; amending subsection

2   (1) of s. 658.29, Florida Statutes, changing a

3   cross-reference; adding a new subsection (4) to

4   section 658.29, Florida Statutes, providing

5   exceptions to the prohibition against out-of-

6   state bank holding companies owning banks or

7   bank holding companies located in this state;

8   providing an effective date.

9

10

11 Be It Enacted by the Legislature of the State of Florida:

12

13   Section 1. Subsection (1) of section 658.29, Florida

14 Statutes, is amended, and a new subsection (4) is added to

15 said section to read:

16   (1) Except as provided in subsections (3) and (4)

17 subsection (3), no bank, trust company, or bank holding

18 company, the operations of which are principally conducted

19 outside this state, shall acquire, retain, or own, directly or

20 indirectly, all, or substantially all, of the assets of, or

21 control over, any bank or trust company having a place of

22 business in this state where the business of banking or trust

23 business or functions are conducted, or acquire, retain, or

24 own all, or substantially all, of the assets of, or control

25 over, any business organization having a place of business in

26 this state where or from which it furnishes investment

27 advisory services in this state. However, if a bank, trust

28 company, or bank holding company directly or indirectly owning

29 all, or substantially all, the assets of, or having control

30 over, a bank or a trust company or business organization to

31 which the restrictions and prohibitions of this section apply,

1

CODING: Words in struck through type are deletions from existing law; words *underlined* are additions.

(Exhibit 2 continued)

PCB 83-31

1 having acquired such assets or control prior to becoming

2 disqualified hereunder, shall, on or after December 20, 1972,

3 the effective date of former s. 659.141(1), as amended, be or

4 become disqualified hereunder to acquire, retain, or own the

5 same, the restrictions and prohibitions of this section shall

6 not be enforced against it for a period which, under all the

7 circumstances, is determined by the department to be

8 reasonable, not exceeding 2 years from December 20, 1972, the

9 effective date of former s. 659.141(1), as amended, or from

10 the date it becomes disqualified hereunder, whichever is

11 later, unless said period of 2 years is extended by the

12 department as herein provided. The department is authorized,

13 upon a showing of undue hardship, to extend the 2-year period

14 from time to time if it determines that any such extension

15 would not be detrimental to the public interest; but any such

16 extension shall not exceed 1 year, and all extensions shall

17 not in the aggregate exceed 3 years.

18   (4) Notwithstanding any other provision of this

19 section:

20   (a) A bank holding company located in Alabama,

21 Georgia, Louisiana, Mississippi, North Carolina, South

22 Carolina, Tennessee or Virginia which is not controlled by a

23 bank holding company located in any state other than one of

24 the states mentioned herein may acquire, directly or

25 indirectly, voting shares of, interests in, or all or

26 substantially all of the assets of banks located in this state

27 which have been conducting the business of banking for not

28 less than 3 years, or bank holding companies located in this

29 state, provided that the statute laws of the state in which

30 such bank holding company is located extend the same privilege

31 of acquiring voting shares of, interests in, or all or

2

(Exhibit 2 continued)

PCB 83-31

1 substantially all of the assets of banks or bank holding

2 companies located in that state to bank holding companies

3 located in Florida.

4   (b) Five years after the date on which statute laws

5 have become effective in any one of the states named in

6 paragraph (a) authorizing bank holding companies located in

7 Florida to acquire the voting shares of, interests in, or all

8 or substantially all of the assets of banks or bank holding

9 companies located in that state, a bank holding company

10 located in any other state may acquire voting shares of,

11 interests in, or all or substantially all of the assets of

12 banks located in this state which have been conducting the

13 business of banking for not less than 3 years, or bank holding

14 companies located in this state, provided that the statute

15 laws of the state in which such bank holding company is

16 located extend the same privilege of acquiring voting shares

17 of, interests in, or all or substantially all of the assets of

18 banks or bank holding companies located in that state to banks

19 or bank holding companies located in Florida.

20   (c) For the purposes of this subsection, a bank

21 holding company is located in the state in which the total

22 deposits of all its banking subsidiaries are largest.

23   Section 2. This act shall take effect October 1, 1983.

24

25

26

27

28

29

30

31

3

Exhibit 3. Nationwide Reciprocity Bill Introduced in Florida Senate (1983)

```
 1              A bill to be entitled
 2         An act relating to banks and trust companies;
 3         amending s. 658.29, Florida Statutes;
 4         permitting sale of ownership or control of a
 5         bank, trust company, or bank holding company in
 6         this state to a bank, trust company, or bank
 7         holding company, the operations of which are
 8         principally conducted outside this state, if
 9         the laws of the jurisdiction in which such
10         operations are principally conducted
11         specifically authorize the acquisition of
12         control of a bank, trust company, or bank
13         holding company in such jurisdiction by a bank,
14         trust company, or bank holding company the
15         operations of which are principally conducted
16         in this state; providing for review and repeal
17         in accordance with the Regulatory Sunset Act;
18         providing an effective date.
19
20  Be It Enacted by the Legislature of the State of Florida:
21
22         Section 1.  Section 658.29, Florida Statutes, is
23  amended to read:
24         658.29  Certain ownership and control prohibited.--
25         (1)  Except as provided in subsections subsection (3)
26  and (4), no bank, trust company, or bank holding company, the
27  operations of which are principally conducted outside this
28  state, shall acquire, retain, or own, directly or indirectly,
29  all, or substantially all, of the assets of, or control over,
30  any bank or trust company having a place of business in this
31  state where the business of banking or trust business or
```

1

(Exhibit 3 continued)

35-370A-83   See HB

1 functions are conducted, or acquire, retain, or own all, or

2 substantially all, of the assets of, or control over, any

3 business organization having a place of business in this state

4 where or from which it furnishes investment advisory services

5 in this state. However, if a bank, trust company, or bank

6 holding company directly or indirectly owning all, or

7 substantially all, the assets of, or having control over, a

8 bank or a trust company or business organization to which the

9 restrictions and prohibitions of this section apply, having

10 acquired such assets or control prior to becoming disqualified

11 hereunder, shall, on or after December 20, 1972, the effective

12 date of former s. 659.141(1), as amended, be or become

13 disqualified hereunder to acquire, retain, or own the same,

14 the restrictions and prohibitions of this section shall not be

15 enforced against it for a period which, under all the

16 circumstances, is determined by the department to be

17 reasonable, not exceeding 2 years from December 20, 1972, the

18 effective date of former s. 659.141(1), as amended, or from

19 the date it becomes disqualified hereunder, whichever is

20 later, unless said period of 2 years is extended by the

21 department as herein provided. The department is authorized,

22 upon a showing of undue hardship, to extend the 2-year period

23 from time to time if it determines that any such extension

24 would not be detrimental to the public interest; but any such

25 extension shall not exceed 1 year, and all extensions shall

26 not in the aggregate exceed 3 years.

27   (2) Except as provided in subsection (4) (3), for the

28 purposes of this section, the operations of a bank, trust

29 company, or bank holding company are principally conducted

30 outside this state if:

31

2

(Exhibit 3 continued)

35-370A-83   See HB

```
 1        (a)  In the case of a bank, the largest amount of its
 2  total deposits is held outside this state.
 3        (b)  In the case of a trust company, the largest amount
 4  of its total trust assets is held or administered outside this
 5  state.
 6        (c)  In the case of a bank holding company, the largest
 7  amount of the total deposits of all banks controlled by the
 8  bank holding company is held outside this state or the largest
 9  amount of the total trust assets held by all trust companies
10  controlled by the bank holding company is held or administered
11  outside this state.
12        (3)(a)  A bank, trust company, or bank holding company,
13  the operations of which are principally conducted outside this
14  state, may acquire shares of or control over any bank, trust
15  company, or bank holding company having a place of business in
16  this state if the statute laws of the jurisdiction in which
17  such operations are principally conducted specifically
18  authorize the acquisition of control of a bank, trust company,
19  or bank holding company in such jurisdiction by a bank, trust
20  company, or bank holding company the operations of which are
21  principally conducted in this state.
22        (b)  Any acquisition of shares or control authorized
23  under paragraph (a) shall not affect the powers or privileges
24  of the bank, trust company, or bank holding company so
25  acquired.
26        (4) (3)  Notwithstanding any other provisions of this
27  section, the restrictions and prohibitions of this section
28  shall not apply:
29        (a)  To the ownership or control of shares acquired by
30  a bank, trust company, or bank holding company prior to
31  January 1, 1972.
```

3

CODING: Words in struck through type are deletions from existing law; words *underlined* are additions.

(Exhibit 3 continued)

1   (b) To any acquisition of a bank, trust company, or

2 investment advisory business organization if an application

3 for approval of such acquisition or notice of proposed

4 investment advisory activities was filed with the Department

5 of Banking and Finance, or the Board of Governors of the

6 Federal Reserve System or other appropriate federal regulatory

7 agency having jurisdiction, prior to June 1, 1972.

8   (c) To the establishment of one investment advisory

9 office in this state by a bank or business organization which,

10 on March 1, 1972, and for a period of 1 year prior thereto,

11 rendered investment advisory services to trust companies or

12 banks in this state from an office outside the state.

13   (d) To any bank, trust company, or bank holding

14 company, the operations of which are principally conducted

15 outside this state, which, on December 20, 1972, owned all the

16 assets of, or control over, a bank or trust company located

17 within and doing business within this state.

18   (e) To the acquisition, retention, or ownership of an

19 Edge Act corporation when the Edge Act corporation is

20 performing functions authorized by the act under which it was

21 organized.

22   Section 2. Each section within chapter 658, Florida

23 Statutes, which is added or amended by this act, is repealed

24 on October 1, 1991, and shall be reviewed by the Legislature

25 pursuant to s. 11.61, Florida Statutes.

26   Section 3. This act shall take effect upon becoming a

27 law.

28

29

30

31

4

(Exhibit 3 continued)

35-370A-83   See 11B

1	▲▲
2	LEGISLATIVE SUMMARY
3	Permits sale of control of a Florida-based bank, trust
4	company, or bank holding company to a bank, trust company, or bank holding company having its principal operations outside the state if the jurisdiction in which
5	the acquiring entity has its principal operations affords Florida institutions reciprocal privileges.
6	
7	
8	
9	
10	
11	
12	
13	
14	
15	
16	
17	
18	
19	
20	
21	
22	
23	
24	
25	
26	
27	
28	
29	
30	
31	

5

Exhibit 4. Regional Reciprocity Bill Enacted May, 1984

CHAPTER 84-42

Committee Substitute for House Bill No. 795

An act relating to banking; creating s. 658.295, F.S.; creating the "Regional Reciprocal Banking Act of 1984"; providing definitions; authorizing bank holding companies whose operations are principally conducted in certain states to acquire banks and bank holding companies located in Florida; providing certain conditions and limitations; requiring divestiture in certain circumstances; providing applicable law and regulatory supervision; providing for nonseverability of provisions; amending s. 658.73, F.S.; providing for an application fee; providing for conditional repeal; providing for sunset review and repeal; providing effective dates.

Be It Enacted by the Legislature of the State of Florida:

Section 1. Section 658.295, Florida Statutes, is created to read:

658.295 Regional reciprocal banking.--

(1) TITLE.--This section may be cited as the "Regional Reciprocal Banking Act of 1984."

(2) DEFINITIONS.--For the purposes of this section:

(a) "Acquire" means:

1. The merger or consolidation of one bank holding company with another bank holding company;

2. The acquisition by a bank holding company of the direct or indirect ownership or control of voting shares of a bank or of another bank holding company if, after such acquisition, such bank holding company will directly or indirectly own or control more than 5 percent of any class of voting shares of such bank holding company or bank;

3. The direct or indirect acquisition by a bank holding company of all or substantially all of the assets of a bank or of another bank holding company; or

4. Any other action that would result in the direct or indirect control by a bank holding company of a bank or of another bank holding company.

(b) "Bank" means any "insured bank" as such term is defined in Section 3(h) of the Federal Deposit Insurance Act, 12 U.S.C. s. 1813(h), or any institution eligible to become an insured bank as such term is defined therein, which, in either event:

1. Accepts deposits that the depositor has a legal right to withdraw on demand; and

2. Engages in the business of making commercial loans.

(c) "Banking office" means any bank, branch of a bank, or any other office at which a bank accepts deposits; however, the term banking office shall not include:

1. Unmanned automatic teller machines, point of sale terminals, or other similar unmanned electronic banking facilities at which deposits may be accepted;

2. Offices located outside the United States; or

1

(Exhibit 4 continued)

3. Loan production offices, representative offices, or other offices at which deposits are not accepted.

(d) "Bank holding company" means any company which is a bank holding company under the federal Bank Holding Company Act of 1956, as amended, 12 U.S.C. s. 1841(a).

(e) "Control" has the meaning set forth in Section 2(a)(2) of the federal Bank Holding Company Act of 1956, as amended, 12 U.S.C. s. 1841.

(f) "Deposits" means all demand, time, and savings deposits of individuals, partnerships, corporations, the United States, and states and political subdivisions in the United States, but does not include deposits of banks or foreign governments or institutions or deposits held by foreign banking offices or corporations organized pursuant to Section 25 or Section 25(a) of the Federal Reserve Act, as amended, 12 U.S.C. ss. 601 through 604a or 12 U.S.C. ss. 611 through 631. Determinations of deposits shall be made by reference to regulatory reports of condition or similar reports filed by banks with state or federal regulatory agencies pursuant to rules established by the department.

(g) "Florida bank" means a bank organized under the laws of this state or the United States and having banking offices located only in Florida.

(h) "Florida bank holding company" means a bank holding company:

1. That has its principal place of business in this state;

2. More than 80 percent of the total deposits of the bank subsidiaries of which are held by bank subsidiaries located within the region; and

3. Which is not controlled by a bank holding company other than a Florida bank holding company.

(i) The "principal place of business" of a bank holding company is the state in which the total deposits of the bank subsidiaries of the bank holding company are the largest.

(j) "Region" means the states of Alabama, Arkansas, Florida, Georgia, Louisiana, Maryland, Mississippi, North Carolina, South Carolina, Tennessee, Virginia, West Virginia, and the District of Columbia.

(k) "Regional bank" means a bank organized under the laws of the United States or of one of the states in the region other than Florida and having banking offices located only in states within the region.

(l) "Regional bank holding company" means a bank holding company other than a Florida bank holding company:

1. That has its principal place of business in a state within the region;

2. More than 80 percent of the total deposits of the bank subsidiaries of which are held by regional bank subsidiaries located within the region;

3. Which is not controlled by a bank holding company other than a regional bank holding company; and

4. Which is not, and is not controlled by, a foreign bank as defined in the International Banking Act of 1978, 12 U.S.C. s. 3101(7).

(Exhibit 4 continued)

(m) "Subsidiary" means that which is set forth in Section 2 of the federal Bank Holding Company Act of 1956, as amended, 12 U.S.C. s. 1841.

(3) ACQUISITION OF CONTROL.--

(a) A regional bank holding company is authorized to acquire a Florida bank or Florida bank holding company upon approval by the department, which approval:

1. Determines that the laws of the state in which the regional bank holding company has its principal place of business permit Florida bank holding companies to acquire banks and bank holding companies in that state;

2. Determines that the laws of the state in which the regional bank holding company has its principal place of business permit the regional bank holding company to be acquired by the Florida bank holding company, or Florida bank, sought to be acquired. For the purposes of this subsection, the Florida bank shall be considered as if it were a Florida bank holding company;

3. Determines that the Florida bank sought to be acquired has been in existence and continuously operating for more than 2 years or that all of the bank subsidiaries of the Florida bank holding company sought to be acquired have been in existence and continuously operating for more than 2 years; and

4. Determines that notice of intent to acquire has been published in a newspaper of general paid circulation in the county or counties in which the bank to be acquired is located, or that a notice of intent to acquire has been mailed via certified mail to each person owning stock in the bank to be acquired.

5. Makes the acquisition subject to any conditions, restrictions, and requirements that would apply to the acquisition by a Florida bank holding company of a bank or bank holding company in the state where the regional bank holding company has its principal place of business, which conditions, restrictions, and requirements would not apply to acquisitions by bank holding companies all of whose bank subsidiaries are located in that state.

(b) A bank holding company controlling a Florida bank or Florida bank holding company prior to the date of enactment of this section, or a regional bank holding company having a Florida bank subsidiary or Florida bank holding company subsidiary which was not acquired pursuant to the provisions of Sections 116 or 123 of the Garn-St Germain Depository Institutions Act of 1982, 12 U.S.C. s. 1730a(m) or 12 U.S.C. s. 1823(f), or was not acquired in the regular course of securing or collecting a debt previously contracted in good faith as provided in Section 3(a) of the federal Bank Holding Company Act of 1956, as amended, 12 U.S.C. s. 1842(a), is authorized to acquire a Florida bank or Florida bank holding company pursuant to the laws and rules applicable to acquisitions of Florida banks and Florida bank holding companies by a bank holding company all of whose bank subsidiaries are located in this state. Control of a bank or corporation organized under the laws of the United States or of any state and operating under Section 25 or Section 25(a) of the Federal Reserve Act, as amended, 12 U.S.C. ss. 601 through 604A or 12 U.S.C. ss. 611 through 631, shall not constitute control of a Florida bank for the purposes of this paragraph. An acquisition authorized by this paragraph shall not require the approval of the department as provided in paragraph (a).

(c) Nothing in this subsection shall prohibit the acquisition by a regional bank holding company of all or substantially all of the shares of a bank organized solely for the purpose of facilitating the

(Exhibit 4 continued)

acquisition of a bank which has been in existence and continuously
operated as a bank for more than 2 years, if the acquisition has
otherwise been approved pursuant to this section.

(4) PROHIBITED TRANSACTIONS; DIVESTITURE.--

(a) Except as expressly permitted by federal law, no bank holding
company that is not a Florida bank holding company or is not a regional
bank holding company shall acquire a Florida bank or Florida bank holding
company.

(b) A Florida bank holding company or regional bank holding company
that ceases to be a Florida bank holding company or regional bank holding
company, as defined in this section, shall within 2 years divest itself
of all Florida banks and Florida bank holding companies. However, a
regional bank holding company or Florida bank holding company shall not
be required to divest its Florida banks or bank holding companies because
of:

1. Its acquisition of institutions in another state not within the
region, if such acquisition has been consummated pursuant to the
provisions of Sections 116 or 123 of the Garn-St Germain Depository
Institutions Act of 1982, 12 U.S.C. s. 1730a(m) or 12 U.S.C. s. 1823(f);

2. Its acquisition of a bank having banking offices in a state other
than within the region, if such acquisition has been consummated in the
regular course of securing or collecting a debt previously contracted in
good faith, as provided in Section 3(a) of the federal Bank Holding
Company Act of 1956, as amended, 12 U.S.C. s. 1842(a), if the bank or
bank holding company divests the securities or assets acquired within 2
years of the date of acquisition;

3. Its acquisition of a bank or corporation organized under the laws
of the United States or of any state and operating under Section 25 or
Section 25(a) of the Federal Reserve Act, as amended, 12 U.S.C. ss. 601
through 604a or 12 U.S.C. ss. 611 through 631, or a bank or bank holding
company organized under the laws of a foreign country that is principally
engaged in business outside the United States and which either has no
banking office in the United States or has banking offices in the United
States that are engaged only in business activities permissible for a
bank or corporation operating under Sections 25 or 25(a) of the Federal
Reserve Act, as amended; or

4. An increase in deposits in bank subsidiaries not within the
region, provided that such increase is not the result of acquisition of a
bank or bank holding company.

(c) The department shall have the power to enforce the prohibition of
this section through the imposition of fines and penalties, the issuance
of cease and desist orders, and such other remedies as are provided by
law.

(5) APPLICABLE LAW.--Any regional bank holding company which controls
a Florida bank or a Florida bank holding company shall be subject to such
laws of this state and such rules of its agencies relating to the
acquisition, ownership, and operation of banks and bank holding companies
as are applicable to Florida bank holding companies.

(6) REGULATORY SUPERVISION.--The department is authorized to enter
into cooperative agreements with other bank regulatory agencies to
facilitate the regulation of banks and bank holding companies doing
business in this state. The department may accept reports of
examinations and other records from such other agencies in lieu of
conducting its own examinations of banks controlled by bank holding
companies located in other states. The department may take any action

CODING: Words in struck through type are deletions from existing law; words *underlined* are
additions.

(Exhibit 4 continued)

jointly with other regulatory agencies having concurrent jurisdiction over banks and bank holding companies doing business in this state or may take such actions independently in order to carry out its responsibilities.

(7) NONSEVERABILITY.--It is the purpose of this section to permit orderly development of banking institutions on a regional basis. It is not the purpose of this section to authorize interstate banking on any basis other than as provided in this section. To that end, if any provision of this section pertaining to the terms, conditions, and limitations of interstate acquisition of Florida banks and bank holding companies is declared invalid for any reason by any Florida or federal court of competent jurisdiction, or if any federal agency construes this section to authorize the acquisition of a bank or bank holding company located in Florida by a bank or bank holding company located outside this state other than a regional bank holding company authorized to acquire a bank or bank holding company pursuant to this section and if such authorization is sustained by a Florida or federal court of competent jurisdiction, then, upon the entry of a final, nonappealable order or the expiration of time for appeal, this section shall be null and void in its entirety and shall cease to be of any force or effect from the effective date of such order or the expiration of such time; provided, however, that any transaction which has been lawfully consummated pursuant to this section prior to a determination of invalidity shall be unaffected by such determination.

Section 2. Paragraph (i) is added to subsection (2) of section 658.73, Florida Statutes, to read:

658.73 Examination fees and assessments.--

(2) Applications filed with the department shall be accompanied by payment of the following fees:

(i) Two thousand five hundred dollars for each application by a regional bank holding company to make an acquisition pursuant to s. 658.295.

Section 3. Section 658.295, Florida Statutes, shall stand repealed and be of no force or effect if, within 5 years from the date this act becomes a law, no other state within the region has in effect reciprocal laws permitting Florida bank holding companies to acquire banks or bank holding companies in that state.

Section 4. Each section which is added to chapter 658, Florida Statutes, by this act is repealed on October 1, 1991, and shall be reviewed by the Legislature pursuant to s. 11.61, Florida Statutes.

Section 5. This act shall take effect July 1, 1985, or on the date on which the state or states having 20 percent or more of the total deposits of banks within the region, excluding Florida, have enacted and have in effect statutes which permit Florida bank holding companies to acquire banks and bank holding companies in such state, whichever occurs sooner; except that section 3 of this act shall take effect upon becoming a law. For purposes of this section, the total deposits of banks within the region shall be determined by reference to the Spring 1984 issue of Polk's World Bank Directory, published by R. L. Polk and Company.

Approved by the Governor May 22, 1984.

Filed in Office Secretary of State May 22, 1984.

CODING: Words in struck through type are deletions from existing law; words *underlined* are additions.

Exhibit 5. Regional Reciprocity with Immediate Phase-In (1984)

35-614-84

```
 1                A bill to be entitled
 2        An act relating to banks and trust companies;
 3        amending s. 658.29, F.S.; defining "region";
 4        permitting sale of ownership or control of a
 5        bank, trust company, or bank holding company in
 6        this state to a bank, trust company, or bank
 7        holding company, the operations of which are
 8        principally conducted outside this state but in
 9        this region, if the laws of the jurisdiction in
10        which such operations are principally conducted
11        specifically authorize the acquisition of
12        control of a bank, trust company, or bank
13        holding company the operations of which are
14        principally conducted in this state; providing
15        that banks, trust companies or bank holding
16        companies, the operations of which are
17        principally conducted outside this state and
18        region may only acquire shares of or control of
19        a bank with less than $400 million in assets;
20        providing that banks, trust companies, or bank
21        holding companies outside the state and region
22        may only acquire one bank per calendar year for
23        5 years after enactment of this act; providing
24        that such acquisitions shall not affect the
25        powers and privileges of the bank so acquired;
26        providing that a bank, trust company, or bank
27        holding company so acquired shall have
28        conducted business in Florida for no less than
29        5 years prior to acquisition; providing for
30        publication of notice of intent to acquire;
31
```

1

(Exhibit 5 continued)

35-614-84

```
 1        providing for a uniform price for all shares of
 2        stock; providing an effective date.
 3
 4        WHEREAS, Florida has experienced a rapid growth rate in
 5   recent years, and
 6        WHEREAS, the existing financial structure is not
 7   equipped to meet the capital demands to fund this above
 8   average growth, and
 9        WHEREAS, it is the Legislature's belief that the
10   interests of the people of this state are best served by
11   allowing the widest possible range of banking services to be
12   made available through full interstate banking, and
13        WHEREAS, it is the Legislature's intent to preserve and
14   protect the rights of customers and shareholders during the
15   expansion of banking services by promoting stable growth and
16   preventing profiteering by allowing only those Florida banks
17   that have been doing business for no less than 5 years to be
18   acquired and by requiring that all shares of stock be
19   purchased at the same rate of payment, NOW, THEREFORE,
20
21   Be It Enacted by the Legislature of the State of Florida:
22
23        Section 1.  Subsection (1) of section 658.29, Florida
24   Statutes, is amended and a new subsection (4) is added to said
25   section to read:
26        658.29  Certain ownership and control prohibited.--
27        (1)  Except as provided in subsections subsection (3)
28   and (4), no bank, trust company, or bank holding company, the
29   operations of which are principally conducted outside this
30   state, shall acquire, retain, or own, directly or indirectly,
31   all, or substantially all, of the assets of, or control over,
```

2

CODING: Words in struck through type are deletions from existing law; words *underlined* are
         additions.

(Exhibit 5 continued)

35-614-84

1   any bank or trust company having a place of business in this
2   state where the business of banking or trust business or
3   functions are conducted, or acquire, retain, or own all, or
4   substantially all, of the assets of, or control over, any
5   business organization having a place of business in this state
6   where or from which it furnishes investment advisory services
7   in this state. However, if a bank, trust company, or bank
8   holding company directly or indirectly owning all, or
9   substantially all, the assets of, or having control over, a
10 bank or a trust company or business organization to which the
11 restrictions and prohibitions of this section apply, having
12 acquired such assets or control prior to becoming disqualified
13 hereunder, becomes disqualified hereunder to acquire, retain,
14 or own the same, the restrictions and prohibitions of this
15 section shall not be enforced against it for a period which,
16 under all the circumstances, is determined by the department
17 to be reasonable, not exceeding 2 years from the date it
18 becomes disqualified hereunder, unless such period of 2 years
19 is extended by the department as herein provided. The
20 department is authorized, upon a showing of undue hardship, to
21 extend the 2-year period from time to time if it determines
22 that any such extension would not be detrimental to the public
23 interest; but any such extension shall not exceed 1 year, and
24 all extensions shall not in the aggregate exceed 3 years.
25   (4)(a) For the purposes of this subsection, the term
26 "region" means the states of Alabama, Florida, Georgia,
27 Louisiana, Maryland, Mississippi, North Carolina, South
28 Carolina, Tennessee, Virginia, and West Virginia and the
29 District of Columbia.
30   (b) A bank, trust company, or bank holding company,
31 the operations of which are principally conducted outside this

3

(Exhibit 5 continued)

35-614-84

1 | state but within the region, may acquire shares of or direct
2 | or indirect control over any bank, trust company, or bank
3 | holding company having a place of business in this state if
4 | the statute laws of the jurisdiction in which such operations
5 | are principally conducted specifically authorize the
6 | acquisition of control of a bank, trust company, or bank
7 | holding company in such jurisdiction by a bank, trust company,
8 | or bank holding company the operations of which are
9 | principally conducted in this state.
10 | (c)1. A bank, trust company, or bank holding company,
11 | the operations of which are principally located outside this
12 | state and region, may acquire shares of or control over any
13 | bank, trust company, or bank holding company having a place of
14 | business in this state, if that bank has assets of under $400
15 | million, and if the statute laws of the jurisidiction in which
16 | such operations are principally conducted specifically
17 | authorize the acquisition of control of a bank, trust company,
18 | or bank holding company in such jurisdiction by a bank, trust
19 | company, or bank holding company, the operations of which are
20 | principally conducted in this state. The asset limitation
21 | shall not apply to acquisitions made pursuant to agreements in
22 | principle entered into prior to January 1, 1984.
23 | 2. A bank, trust company, or bank holding company, the
24 | operations of which are principally located outside this state
25 | and region may only acquire the shares of or control of one
26 | bank, trust company, or bank holding company in the state for
27 | each calendar year for 5 years after the enactment of this
28 | act, at which time any regional limitations shall no longer
29 | exist.
30 | (d) Any acquisitions of shares or control authorized
31 | under this subsection shall not affect the powers or

4

(Exhibit 5 continued)

35-614-84

1 privileges of the bank, trust company, or bank holding company
2 so acquired.
3   (e) A bank, trust company, or bank holding company,
4 which is acquired pursuant to this subsection shall have been
5 conducting business in this state for a period of at least 5
6 years prior to its acquisition.
7   (f) A bank, trust company, or bank holding company,
8 the operations of which are principally conducted outside this
9 state shall comply with the following procedures before
10 acquiring a bank, trust company, or bank holding company, the
11 operations of which are principally conducted in this state:
12   1. Notice of intent to acquire shall be published by
13 purchasing an advertisement of no less than one-quarter page
14 in a standard-size or a tabloid-size newspaper. The headline
15 of the advertisement shall be in a type no smaller than 18
16 point, and the advertisement shall not be placed in that
17 portion of the newspaper where legal notices and classified
18 advertisements appear. The advertisement shall be published
19 in a newspaper of general paid circulation in the county or
20 counties in which the bank, trust company, or bank holding
21 company to be acquired and its branches are located, and not
22 in a limited subject matter publication. The advertisement
23 shall appear in a newspaper that is published at least 5 days
24 a week and it shall be published at least once a week for 5
25 consecutive weeks before the acquisition.
26   2. In lieu of publishing the advertisement set out
27 above, the acquiring bank may mail a notice to each person
28 owning stock in the Florida bank to be acquired. Such notice
29 shall announce the intent to acquire and shall be sent via
30 certified mail, at least 5 weeks before acquisition.
31

5

CODING: Words in struck through type are deletions from existing law; words *underlined* are additions.

(Exhibit 5 continued)

35-614-84

1   (g) All acquisition agreements shall contain a

2   provision for a uniform price to be paid for all shares of

3   preferred stock and a uniform price to be paid for all shares

4   of common stock. The offer of purchase shall be available to

5   all shareholders upon request.

6   Section 2. This act shall take effect upon becoming a

7   law.

8

9

10

11   **

12   SENATE SUMMARY

13   Amends the Banking Code to allow regional interstate
      banking for 5 years. Defines what a region means, and
14   prescribes conditions under which a bank, trust company,
      or bank holding company outside the state but in the
15   region as well as a bank, trust company, or bank holding
      company outside the state and region may acquire a bank,
16   trust company, or bank holding company in Florida.

17

18

19

20

21

22

23

24

25

26

27

28

29

30

31

Notes

1. See Larry A. Frieder "Regional Interstate Banking: Transitional Progress," (1978), unpublished paper presented before Southern Finance Association for an early discussion of the case for regional interstate banking. Also, see 1979 Annual Report of Barnett Banks of Florida, Inc. for a discussion of "A Regional Approach to Interstate Banking: The Case for an Orderly Transition," by Guy Botts, then Barnett Chairman of the Board.

2. See pp. xiii and xiv for a listing of study group members.

3. See revised Banking Code: chapters 80-260, Laws of Florida, Section 658.26. Also, amendment to Section 658.26 in chapter 81-215, Laws of Florida.

4. Prior to 1981, it was commonly believed that Florida's MBHCs were at market share limits. However, regulatory authorities have since liberalized their notion of what these limits should be; i.e., a few years ago, it would not have been possible for the state's largest BHCs to combine.

5. See page 45, "States Permitting Outside Entry by Banking Organizations" for a listing of states permitting outside entry of banking organizations. Also, note that the New England region has pursued the regional notion to the greatest extent. The Southwest region is also exploring this approach.

6. See chapters 3 and 4 for more extensive documentation and discussion of both out-of-state bank and nonbank entry into Florida.

7. Exhibits 1, 2, and 3 illustrate the key language of bills previously considered in Florida.

8. The material in this section is adapted from a public handout prepared by J. Thomas Cardwell, of Akerman, Senterfitt, and Edison, Orlando, Florida, May 1, 1984.

9. See B. Frank King, "Interstate Banking: Issues and Evidence," *Economic Review,* Federal Reserve Bank of Atlanta, pp. 36-45, for a discussion of the transitional-interim value of regional reciprocity and the eventual desirability of the nationwide "trigger."

10. The material in this section is adapted from Larry A. Frieder "A Framework for Discussion of Interstate Banking," *Conference on Bank Structure,* Federal Reserve Bank of Chicago, 1984, in press.

11. See Donald T. Savage, "Regional Interstate Banking—Better Than the Alternatives," *Issues in Bank Regulation* (in press), for a critical review of the regional interstate alternative. Savage concludes that nationwide banking is a more desirable change than regional banking.

2

An Analysis of Regional Approaches to Interstate Banking

Robert A. Eisenbeis

Introduction

It is now widely recognized that market pressures are significantly changing the structure and regulation of the financial service industry. Financial innovations, such as NOW accounts and money market mutual funds, for example, were certainly important catalytic factors leading to the Monetary Control Act of 1980 and the Garn-St. Germain Act of 1982. This legislation not only mandated the phase-out of deposit interest rate ceilings but also significantly broadened the powers of thrift institutions, enabling them to expand further into both the consumer and corporate financial service business. Similar financial innovations and market forces are causing a reassessment by bankers, legislators and regulators of the desirability of maintaining the existing restrictions on interstate banking in the 1927 McFadden Act and 1956 Bank Holding Company Act.

This chapter briefly details these trends and explains why market forces may make it impossible in the long run for individual states to maintain existing interstate banking restrictions. We then discuss recent state efforts to promote regional approaches to interstate banking and evaluate some of the key policy issues that arise as these limitations are reexamined. The chapter concludes with an evaluation of some of the more likely options that have been proposed for states to make the transition to interstate banking.

Erosion of Interstate Banking Restrictions by Banking Organizations

Notwithstanding the 1927 McFadden Act prohibitions on interstate branching, table 2.1 shows banking organizations were very successful during

Summary Table 2.1. Summary of Interstate Activity

LOCATION	Domestic Holding* Companies	Banks	Branches	Grandfathered Holding* Companies	Foreign Banks	Branches
Alabama						
Alaska						
Arizona	1	1	181			
Arkansas						
California				8	8	148
Colorado	1	3	7			
Connecticut						
Delaware	12	12	40			
District of Columbia						
Florida	2	2	188			
Georgia						
Hawaii				1	1	15
Idaho	2	2	107			
Illinois	1	3	4	1	1	1
Indiana						
Iowa	1	11	50			
Kansas						
Kentucky						
Louisiana						
Maine						
Maryland	1	2	30			
Massachusetts						
Michigan						
Minnesota						
Mississippi						
Missouri						
Montana	3	25	48			
Nebraska	1	5	39			
Nevada	1	1	66			
New Hampshire						
New Jersey						
New Mexico	1	5	35			
New York	1	2	27	3	3	39
North Carolina						
North Dakota	3	34	110			
Ohio						
Oklahoma						
Oregon	1	1	169			
Pennsylvania						
Rhode Island						
South Carolina						
South Dakota	3	12	80			
Tennessee	2	2	27			
Texas						
Utah	1	1	35			
Vermont						
Virginia	1	6	63			
Washington	1	1	65			
West Virginia						
Wisconsin	3	6	22			
Wyoming	2	4	4			
TOTALS	45	141	1,397	13	13	203

Source: Whitehead, David D. "Interstate Banking: Taking Inventory," *Economic Review*, Federal Reserve Bank of Atlanta (May 1983), pp. 4-20.

Foreign Banks			States With Reciprocal Agreement	Preferred* Stock Deals Filed With Board	Interstate* S&Ls	Offices of 4(c)8 Subs	Loan Production Offices	Edge Act Corporations
Agency	Edge	Branch						
				1	1	107	1	
						4	1	
						159		
						3		
63	2	2			2	521	22	23
					1	158	14	
				1		64	1	
			()			27	3	5
		1			2	2	3	
22	6		()	1	7	372	6	25
10				1	2	253	8	5
2					2	39		
					1	47		
	3	36	()		1	132	21	11
						99	1	
			()	1		42	2	
					1	78		
					1	61		
1						164	4	1
				1		1		
					2	82	7	
				2	1	68	6	3
						56	2	
				1		34	5	4
						89		
					1	75	6	2
					2	28	1	
						28	2	
					1	21		
						20	1	
						110	2	
						44		
18	2	37		4	3	156	16	31
						367	3	
						23	1	
				2		310	8	4
				1		76	3	
		7			4	83	7	3
		6		2		320	7	2
						13		
				1		229		
			()			16		
						159	14	
	9			1	5	289	19	17
					1	37	1	
						4		
					1	227	1	
		10			2	114	3	0
						40		
						39		1
				1	1	10		
116	22	103	10	20	45	5,500	202	143

Notes: ()   These states allow entry of limited purpose banks.
These states allow expansion of interstate grandfathered banks.
*   These columns are not included in total number of offices.

the late 1960s and early 1970s in innovating methods to establish physical presences across state lines.[1] Banks have employed loan production offices, Edge Act Corporations, corporate calling officers, and EFT facilities to expand interstate.[2] Larger banks have adopted the bank holding company structure to facilitate the operation of nonbanking subsidiaries, such as consumer finance companies, industrial banks, mortgage banking firms and trust companies throughout the country.[3] Table 2.2 shows that of nine southern states, Florida has the largest number of out-of-state banking organizations operating within the state.[4]

Similarly, many key classes of customers—and especially large corporate customers—have found it profitable to incur the search and transactions costs to deal with nonlocally based suppliers of financial services. Large business loans have long been negotiated in national and international markets, and the establishment of such a corporate relationship has usually resulted in deposit balances flowing into the nonlocal market as well.

To a large extent, then, the prohibitions on intra- and interstate banking have become progressively eroded. But it is also significant that, except for the largest customers, most of these innovations have affected the lending activities of banking organizations. Retail deposit taking has remained less affected by these innovations.

Recently, however, important innovations and market developments have begun to break down the insulation of retail banking markets. For example, the Monetary Control Act of 1980 and the Garn-St. Germain Act of 1982 broadened the range of asset and liability powers of thrifts to enable them potentially to become full competitors with commercial banks for the retail consumer business. In addition, S&Ls have been permitted to branch nationwide as troubled S&Ls have been merged to form interstate networks. It is very likely that the Federal Home Bank Board will permit unrestricted interstate expansion. Lastly, numerous unregulated suppliers have sprung up, offering close substitutes to the services provided by commercial banks on an interstate basis.

Interstate Expansion by Unregulated Competitors

In the early 1980s the combination of extremely high interest rates and binding Regulation Q ceilings stimulated the entry of unregulated nondepository institutions into the financial service industry. These firms have pioneered ways (1) to take retail deposits across local markets and on an interstate basis at near market rates, and (2) to offer a wide range of financial, investment and insurance services not available from commercial banks.

The principal innovation that has evolved to collect consumer deposits on an interstate and national basis has been the money market mutual fund. At the

Table 2.2. Interstate Activities by Banking Organizations

LOCATION	GRANDFATHERED			FOREIGN BANKS			States with Reciprocal Agreement	Preferred[a] Stock Deals Filed with Board	Interstate[a] S&Ls	Offices of A(c)7 Subs	Loan Production Offices	Edge Act Corporations	Total Offices per State
	Holding Companies	Banks	Branches	Agency	Edge	Branch							
Alabama								1	1	107	1		108
Florida	2	2	188	22	6		□	1	7	372	6	25	621
Georgia				10				1	2	253	8	5	276
Louisiana				1						164	4	1	170
Mississippi								1	1	75	6	2	83
North Carolina										367	3		370
South Carolina								1		229			229
Tennessee	2	2	27							159	14		202
Texas						9		1	5	289	19	17	334

Notes: ° - These states allow entry of limited purpose banks
　　　 □ - These states allow expansion of interstate grandfathered banks
　　　 * - These columns are not included in total number of offices

Source: Whitehead, David D. "Interstate Banking: Taking Inventory," *Economic Review*, Federal Reserve Bank of Atlanta
　　　　(May 1983). pp. 4-20.

time of the Garn-St. Germain Depository Institutions Act of 1982, noninstitutional deposits in these funds approached $183 billion, or about 15% of bank and thrift institutions' small time and savings deposits. The real importance of money market mutual funds, however, is that they have broken down the dependence of previously locally limited customers on local depository institutions for financial services.

The rapid growth of these funds during the early 1980s indicates that, when the opportunity costs to consumers resulting from regulatory constraints are sufficiently high (1) to overcome the inconvenience and search costs associated with seeking higher rate alternatives, (2) to break down the resistance to dealing with nonlocal institutions, and (3) to compensate for holding a greater portion of their financial assets in the form of uninsured liabilities, consumers will shift their funds into alternative investment instruments.[5] Confirmation of this fact is the return of consumer funds to banks and thrifts following the offering of the MMDA and Super-Now accounts authorized by the Garn-St. Germain Act. In the lower rate environment of the first three quarters of 1983, these flow reversals resulted because the combination of convenience and deposit insurance was sufficient on the margin to overcome the relative rate advantage of the money market funds. One should not conclude, however, that these flow reversals are permanent.

As distinct from the market supply oriented methods banks have developed to avoid restrictions on interstate banking, the growth of money market mutual funds has affected the structure of both the market demand and supply for deposit funds. Clearly, the funds increased the number of alternative suppliers of deposit-type services offering near money market rates. In addition, their growth and customer acceptance signal a fundamental change in the nature of the demand for deposit and other financial services. Once customers are no longer dependent on local sources of supply for deposit service, the geographic market ceases to be local; and in this case it has become an interstate market. Under these circumstances, any benefits that might have accrued previously to in-state banks from prohibitions on intra- or interstate banking—by protecting local deposit markets from actual entry or the threat of entry by out-of-state banks—are completely dissipated.

Three other recent interrelated financial innovations should serve further to bring the efficacy of existing interstate banking restrictions into question by increasing the competitive presence of nonlocal suppliers in consumer markets. The first is the joining together of independent firms to provide services that the participants could not legally or economically provide individually (see Eisenbeis, 1981a). The classic example is the Merrill Lynch Cash Management Account, which combines a margin account at a brokerage firm, a captive money market mutual fund, a Visa debt card, and a servicing arrangement through BankOne of Ohio. Variants and refinements of this service are being offered by numerous other brokerage firms. Not only do these services capitalize on the fact that consumers have learned they can obtain financial services from nonlocal and nontraditional firms, but also some of these firms have an extensive interstate presence which could serve as additional consumer service centers.

The second financial innovation was the creation of the broker-bankers. Recent combinations of American Express-Shearson, Bache-Prudential, and Sears-Dean Witter-Coldwell Banker, just to name a few, have resulted in a whole new class of financial service firms.[6] These firms are internalizing certain symbiotic financial arrangements to take advantage of potential synergistic or scope economies. The broker-bankers are also positioning themselves to offer a wide range of consumer and corporate financial, brokerage and insurance services.[7] Thus the potential competitive threat of these unregulated broker-bankers and other unregulated competitors spreads far beyond their immediate activities with money market mutual funds and cash management accounts.

The third recent financial innovation that heightens the interstate competitive threat to commercial banks has been the recent wave of acquisitions of nonbank banks. Brokerage firms, insurance companies, retailers, money market funds and financial conglomerates have discovered that they can diversify into either the commercial banking or consumer banking business outside the present scope and jurisdiction of the Bank Holding Company Act by acquiring insured commercial banks and divesting either the demand deposit or commercial loan business. Such an entity—although federally insured and regulated as a commercial bank—does not meet the technical legal definition of a bank for purposes of the Bank Holding Company Act. Therefore, it may be acquired by any nonbanking or nonfinancial firm, and still not subject the acquiring firm to the restrictions of the Bank Holding Company Act or to regulation or supervision by the Federal Reserve.[8] Because of the potential for linking brokerage, commercial and industrial activities with interstate deposit taking, the expansion of nonbank bank acquisitions should be perceived as a real competitive concern to banks under the present regulatory system.

Analysis of Innovations to Avoid Interstate Banking Prohibitions

Several important observations emerge from this brief analysis of recent financial innovations to avoid branching constraints. First, banks, thrifts, and nondepository institutions have evolved numerous ways to supply bank-type services across state boundaries to nearly all significant classes of customers. Second, the unexploited potential of the broker-banker, the nonbank banks and other similar devices suggests that further expansion of nontraditional suppliers into the banking business is extremely likely. Third, the growth of money market mutual funds—and to a lesser extent of cash management type accounts—indicates that, like the large corporate customers, significant groups of consumers are no longer limited to local markets for many of their financial services. Fourth, the main parties likely to be adversely affected by the existing restrictions on geographical expansion are the commercial banks. Banks are forced to compete with institutions not subject to geographic restraints on their operations. Existing limitations are no longer protecting banks from outside competition. Instead, they are preventing banks from following their customers or attracting new customers over the same geographic range as their competitors, except by resorting to less efficient, more costly methods. Finally, for those banks preferring consolidation to independent status, the limitations on interstate banking restrict the number of outside bidders and thus reduce the prices shareholders are likely to realize by selling out. It may be concluded that interstate banking prohibitions are no longer limiting nationwide flows of funds or significantly reducing competition in local markets to the extent they once did. Indeed, they are harming those very banks they were once designed to protect.

Changing Attitudes

Competitive inequities are beginning to force the realization that it may no longer be in the long run interests of banks and their shareholders or of the states in which these institutions are located to maintain the status quo. A few states have recently liberalized their policies toward intrastate expansion. This includes Illinois, Florida, Oklahoma and Arkansas; more importantly, 12 states have also enacted legislation allowing out-of-state banking organizations to enter.[9] These 12 states may be divided roughly into three categories, based on the type of outside entry permitted (see table 2.3).

South Dakota, Delaware, Virginia, Maryland and Nebraska allow the acquisition of only single-office, limited-purpose banks by out-of-state bank holding companies. In each state, however, minimum initial capital requirements are specified. These limited-purpose banks also must employ a minimum number of employees. There are additional restrictions to prevent these institutions from conducting a general purpose banking business, thereby posing a competitive threat to indigenous banks. Several of these states (especially, Delaware and South Dakota) are attractive for entry by outside bank holding companies because of favorable usury ceilings and accommodating tax laws, and as a result banking organizations, such as those in New York and Pennsylvania, have relocated their credit card and certain other activities. Another motivation for attracting outside entry was the

Table 2.3. States Permitting Outside Entry by Banking Organizations

Limited Purpose Laws

Delaware. Allows acquisition of a single office, limited purpose, *de novo* bank with initial capitalization of $10 million and at least 100 employees must be hired. Competition with indigenous banks must be minimal.

South Dakota. Similar to Delaware in that it allows acquisition of single office, limited purpose bank subject to initial capitalization, employment and competitive restrictions. Existing state chartered banks may be acquired provided the retail activities are not expanded. One of the "limited purposes" is the full range of insurance business.

Virginia. As of July 1, 1983, permits out-of-state bank holding companies to set up a single office credit-card subsidiary, subject to capitalization and employment restrictions.

Maryland. As of July 1, 1983, permits out-of-state bank holding companies to establish a single office bank, subject to capitalization and employment requirements and restrictions on attracting local customers from existing banks.

Nebraska. As of August 26, 1983, permits out-of-state bank holding companies to set up a single office credit-card subsidiary, subject to capitalization and employment restrictions.

Reciprocity Laws

Maine. Permits out-of-state financial institution companies to acquire in-state financial institutions on a reciprocal basis, that is, provided the other state allows its own financial institutions to be acquired under no more restrictive conditions.

New York. Permits out-of-state bank holding companies to acquire in-state banks on a reciprocal basis, provided the other state has enabling legislation.

Massachusetts. Permits depository institution holding companies located in other New England states to acquire Massachusetts depository institutions on a reciprocal basis. Also permits branching on a reciprocal basis.

Rhode Island. To take effect on July 1, 1984. Permits out-of-state bank holding companies located in other New England states to acquire in-state banks on a reciprocal basis. Extends reciprocity beyond New England effective July 1, 1986.

Connecticut. As of June 8, 1983, permits depository institution holding companies located in other New England states to acquire Connecticut depository institutions on a reciprocal basis.

(Table 2.3 continued)

Unrestricted Laws

Alaska. Permits out-of-state bank holding companies to acquire, with few restrictions, in-state banks that were founded three or more years ago.

Troubled Institutions

Washington. Permits state banking superintendent to allow takeover of a banking organization that is in danger of closing, failing or becoming insolvent by an out-of-state organization.

Grandfather Laws

Iowa. Permits one out-of-state bank holding company whose operations were grandfathered--that is, the bank holding company was registered with the Fed on January 1, 1971 and owned two or more in-state banks--to acquire other in-state banks, so long as all banks controlled by the holding company have 8 percent or less of total state deposits.

Florida. Permits three out-of-state bank holding companies (two U.S., and one Canadian), whose operations were grandfathered as of December 20, 1972, to acquire other in-state banks and trust companies.

Illinois. Permits one out-of-state bank holding company, whose operations were grandfathered as of December 31, 1981, to acquire other in-state banks.

Source: *Banking Expansion Reporter*, June 20, 1983 vol. 2, no. 12 and Moulton (1983).

attempt to spur lagging local economic development and employment (see Moulton, 1983).

The second group, consisting only of the State of Washington, resulted from an effort to facilitate the takeover of SeaFirst, which was in financial distress. Washington's legislation cannot be interpreted as a change in policy toward interstate banking, but rather is an attempt to avoid the attendant costs—both explicit and implicit—of a bank failure.[10]

The remaining six states, Maine, New York, Massachusetts, Rhode Island, Connecticut[11] and Alaska, place no restrictions on the kinds of banking business that may be conducted. But each does restrict either the type of entry and/or the locations of those companies seeking to enter. For example, Alaska prohibits the acquisition of *de novo* banks and requires that entry be accomplished by acquisition of banks having been in existence for at least three years. The Alaska law, however, does not mandate reciprocal entry legislation on the part of the entering holding company's state. Maine and New York permit banking acquisitions by out-of-state bank holding companies provided these holding companies are located in states with reciprocal legislation permitting entry by Maine or New York bank holding companies, respectively. Massachusetts, Rhode Island and Connecticut, the most recent states to permit outside entry, have a similar reciprocal clause but only for bank holding companies headquartered in other New England states.

Limiting entry to institutions from particular geographic areas is a forerunner, and may be symptomatic, of a growing trend toward cooperative regional approaches to the problem of relaxing interstate banking restrictions. Unfortunately, part of the rationale for such regional approaches lies in the desire to avoid significant changes that may affect adversely the competitive positions of local banks or that may result in outflows of funds (especially core deposits) from the area.[12] This view ignores the significant developments in financial markets in recent years that are eliminating core deposits and that have evolved to efficiently collect and reallocate funds throughout the country.

Policy Issues Pertaining to Proposals for Regional Interstate Banking

The Carter Administration's report on interstate banking identified several policy issues to be considered when modifications in interstate banking restrictions are proposed.[13] These include the implications of any proposed changes for:

1. the level and quality of services to local communities,
2. the viability of smaller banks,
3. safety and stability of the system,
4. the division of supervisory and regulatory responsibilities among state and federal authorities, and
5. competition and concentration of resources.

The consequences for the first three of these areas are largely the same, almost regardless of the alternative methods proposed for liberalizing branching and interstate bank expansion. Therefore, these issues will be treated in general terms, before moving to a discussion of the other issues and to particular policy options.

Level and Quality of Service

In evaluating the effects of liberalizing interstate banking restrictions on the level and quality of services, it is useful to focus on three classes of customers: consumers and small businesses, middle market firms, and municipalities.[14]

Generalizing on the evidence from intrastate banking studies, interstate banking would not be expected to reduce significantly the number of organizations in metropolitan areas (presuming entry is not limited to *de novo* expansion), and in the longer run the number of offices in rural and nonmetropolitan markets should increase slightly.[15] These conclusions follow because most interstate expansion (entry) would take place by acquisition of banks in metropolitan markets, simply replacing locally based banks with nonlocal firms. Over the long run, since these new entrants would tend to be larger organizations, greater branch expansion would be expected in adjacent nonmetropolitan and rural areas, increasing the number of competitive alternatives and consumer convenience in these smaller markets.[16] Also, because of the larger relative size of these new entrants, the range of services would increase.[17]

More importantly, the research evidence suggests that the availability of credit, both in the aggregate and to small and middle-market businesses and to consumers, would increase, as would the allocation of funds to municipalities. Larger banks tend to have higher lending limits and loan-to-deposit ratios than smaller banks and hold a greater proportion of state and local obligations. Furthermore, there is no evidence to support the contention that multi-office banking would tend to syphon funds from rural or more local metropolitan markets into the national money markets.[18] Horvitz (1983) suggests that a smaller local bank acquired by a larger outside organization may become less locally oriented, but at this time there is no systematic evidence to support this possibility. Finally, it is also worth noting that smaller banks tend to have relatively lower loan-to-deposit ratios and greater proportions of Fed Funds sold and investments in Treasury obligations than do larger banks. In fact, small banks are net suppliers of federal funds and represent one of the principal channels by which funds are collected from local markets and directed into the national market.

Although these general net benefits of interstate banking may exist, the critical question for any state considering the issue is the incremental value of relaxing existing restrictions. In Florida, for example, given the recent expansion of powers of thrift institutions, the numerous methods that out-of-state organizations have exploited to enter its markets, and the relatively unconcentrated situation in most Florida markets, one must conclude that the incremental public benefits of permitting entry by outside bank holding companies, while positive, are probably very small.

Viability of Small Banks

Notwithstanding the widespread fears of smaller banking organizations, interstate branching or bank holding company expansion does not generally pose a threat to the viability of small banks. In many major metropolitan markets, numerous small banks already operate in head-to-head competition with large banks. Moreover, there is no evidence that these large banks enjoy cost or scale economic advantages over small banks.[19] Furthermore, small banks have tended to outperform large banks in recent years[20] in terms of return on assets or equity, and this holds even in the most competitive markets.[21] In fact, the research results imply that entry of large banks by acquisition of large banks within a market tend to result in declining market shares rather than market dominance.[22]

Safety and Soundness

Safety and soundness issues also do not appear to be determining factors in considering interstate banking issues. To the extent that competition, loan-to-deposit ratios and leverage are increased, then one might conclude that bank risk would be increased. This increased risk, however, is counterbalanced by a number of factors, including the opportunities for greater product and geographic diversification and the ease in facilitating the takeover of weak or failing institutions.[23] Studies reveal little effect of expanded geographic expansion opportunities on bank closings and, overall, fewer multi-office banks or bank holding companies appear on the regulatory agencies' problem lists than unit banks.[24]

It has been suggested that the foreign debt problems in money center banks could be transferred to local banks that affiliated with these money center banks.[25] Existing law, however, requires the Federal Reserve or other responsible federal agency to consider the effects of a proposed bank holding company acquisition or merger on safety and soundness. In addition, this increased risk exposure should also affect the willingness of the shareholders of small banks to swap their shares and suggests they should voluntarily demand increased compensation for any increased risk they would assume.

State and Federal Supervision

The proposals adopted to liberalize interstate banking laws can have important impacts on regulatory policies and structure and on the division of authority among state and federal agencies. In general, the wider the branching powers of banking organizations, the more difficult it will be for individual states to impose differential regulations on firms operating within their states or on their own state chartered banks. Similarly, state banking departments might be hard pressed to examine all their own institutions plus those operating within their state boundaries. Most likely, wide geographical expansion would force uniformity of state policies, and because of regulatory burdens, tend to favor conversion to national charter as opposed to remaining a state chartered bank.[26]

These problems would be somewhat reduced if expansion were by way of separately chartered bank holding subsidiaries in each state. In that case, the individual states would need to be concerned primarily with only those subsidiaries operating within their boundaries, which would facilitate examinations for compliance with individual state laws. On the other hand, to the extent it is impossible to separate the riskiness of individual bank subsidiaries from the health of the entire organizations, multi-office interstate holding companies would still make state examination for safety and soundness costly to state authorities and burdensome to the organizations. It seems inevitable, therefore, that the state's role in banking supervision is likely to decline over time.

Competition and Concentration

Perhaps the most controversial area is the effects of liberalized interstate banking on competition and concentration of banking resources. There is little doubt that restrictions on geographic expansion have, in the past, insulated many local markets from competition and restricted economic growth. Moreover, concentration in local markets tends to be less in states with more liberal state branching laws, and market performance, therefore, tends to result in lower prices and greater availability of services. On the other hand, there is also the legitimate concern that wider geographic expansion will be associated with increased consolidation of the banking system. And this consolidation is likely to take place—as has already begun in Pennsylvania and in New England—by first combining the largest competitors rather than assuring that a large number of more equal sized competitors are formed and then allowed to compete head to head.[27]

The Carter Administration expressed the fear that existing anti-trust laws and policies might not be adequate to guide the transition from a regional and local banking system to one that permits wide geographic expansion, and this is a concern that deserves careful consideration. Some regional approaches to liberalizing interstate banking would assure that several larger organizations would exist to compete at the national level, but the cost may be at increased concentration of resources and economic power within those regions. It is this issue that suggests any interstate banking proposals be given careful consideration and constitutes the principal focus of the analysis of the four policy proposals which follow.

Alternative Policies to Interstate Banking

Because of McFadden Act prohibitions on interstate branching, the most practical policy options for an individual state considering interstate banking center around whether or not to enact state legislation, as permitted under the Douglas Amendment to the Bank Holding Company Act of 1956, authorizing out-of-state organizations to operate banks within the state. There are, in fact, an infinite number of possibilities for controlling such activity, and the recent actions of the states in table 2.3 provide a reasonable menu of the practical alternatives. These include permitting (1) regional reciprocity, as in Massachusetts; (2) nationwide reciprocity, as in Maine; (3) unrestricted entry, as in Alaska; and (4) maintaining the status quo. Each of these alternatives is discussed below.

Maintaining the Status Quo

Opting for the status quo in a state such as Florida would mean that present trends in the evolution of banking structure would continue. Out-of-state organizations, especially foreign organizations and money center banks, would maintain and expand their existing strategies in the form of nonbanking activities by bank holding companies, LPOs, and Edge Act Companies. Competitively, they would concentrate on providing services to the major nonlocally limited business firms, foreign trade related commerce, and consumer credit. Most of this activity would be centered in the major metropolitan areas. In Florida, maintaining the status quo would not significantly impact the competitive situation in local markets, especially in the short run. The state is relatively unconcentrated and numerous nonbank and thrift competitors would remain. The latter would be especially important as they seek to expand into new product areas as a result of the Monetary Control Act and Garn-St. Germain Act.

The trend toward continued consolidation and concentration of banks within the state would continue. The main beneficiaries of this policy would be those aggressive instate organizations seeking to grow by consolidation and those grandfathered out-of-state firms able to continue to expand by acquisition. The principal benefits these firms would receive would be somewhat reduced competition for acquisitions and somewhat lower prices for acquisitions that were accomplished successfully.

Maintaining the status quo would not prevent, as some have argued, New York and other money center banks from making stake-out acquisitions to be consummated whenever state or federal law was changed in the future. In Florida, Chemical Bank has entered into such an agreement with Florida National Bank, and others could clearly be arranged if the parties could agree upon the terms.

Nationwide Reciprocity or Unrestricted Nationwide Entry

There is little substantive difference in terms of their likely effects between a policy of nationwide reciprocity, such as enacted by Maine, or one of unrestricted entry, such as permitted by Alaska. The principal effects would be to increase the demand for acquisitions of local banking organizations. And, if the patterns set in Maine continue to be followed, then these acquisitions would first involve the state's largest organizations. Even if such entry were limited to newly chartered banks, these *de novo* institutions could then merge with instate banks.[28] Of course under either policy local banks could expand outside their state into those few states that permitted entry, but the greater pressure would be on local banks to be acquired.

Either policy would likely lead to a banking structure dominated by out-of-state organizations, but a structure that would be less concentrated and hence relatively more competitive in its performance than the structure which would result in a "status quo" policy. This follows because there would be few incentives for consolidations among instate banking organizations whose shareholders would likely receive higher prices by accepting offers from out-of-state organizations.[29] In such circumstances, the nationwide unrestricted policy would be preferable to a reciprocal policy for two reasons. First, it would assure a more geographically dispersed representation of out-of-state organizations operating in local markets. This presumably would lead to greater competition and better market performance, since the same set of major firms would not be facing each other in major markets. It would also enhance the availability of alternative sources of credit to those middle market firms who could easily move throughout a state. Secondly, the nationwide policy would increase the number of bidders for local banks and lead to higher share prices in acquisitions.

Regional Reciprocity[30]

Regional reciprocity (among southern states, for example) seems to be a middle ground between maintaining the status quo and the nationwide options.[31] The short run effects of regional reciprocity on a state such as Florida would be similar to those of the "status quo" policy. Given that no other states in the region presently have reciprocity statutes, no entry into Florida or out-of-state expansion by Florida banking organizations could take place. If, however, other southern states were to pass regional reciprocity statutes, then the New England experience would suggest that the major organizations within the region would consolidate.

The main advantages of this policy would be to preserve regional control of banking organizations, permit the major organizations within the region to grow to a size to compete with money center organizations, and to integrate southern financial and commercial markets.[32] Also, regional banking organizations might possibly be more locally oriented regarding their accommodation of middle market firms and municipalities, but there is no empirical evidence to support such a contention. Regional reciprocity would also permit firms to expand their representation in natural markets which cross state boundaries. This would increase convenience to local customers. In general, however, regional reciprocity would have little important competitive impact in local consumer and small business markets for the reasons noted when discussing the nationwide reciprocity proposals. Bank shareholders would gain from appreciation in their stock as competition for acquisitions increased, but this appreciation would not be as great as with the nationwide options.

Conclusions

From the long run point of view of improving competition, enhancing the quantity and quality of services, and providing for more efficient allocation of financial resources, a persuasive argument can be made that limitations on interstate banking are unduly restrictive. On the other hand, the press of market forces and the evolution of ways to avoid these restrictions have facilitated the collection of funds at the local level and their reallocation nationally, making the additional benefits from a more liberal policy toward interstate banking smaller than they would have been several years ago. These developments, combined with recent changes in federal law broadening the powers of thrifts, have significantly increased competition in financial markets, be they national, regional or local in scope.

Despite these reduced benefits, however, it is still clear that maintaining existing restrictions is not now working to the best interests of commercial banks and their ability to compete against less regulated competitors. Nor are restrictive policies in the interest of those shareholders who wish to sell their stock to the highest bidder. And on these grounds, consideration should be given to relaxing the restrictions on interstate banking. The choice of which policy option to select hinges mainly on the tradeoffs between the interests of managers and their desire to maintain control of their institutions and the interests of shareholders, rather than on overriding public benefits or competitive considerations favoring one option over another.

Notes

1. See for example Eisenbeis (1980), Whitehead (1983), Department of the Treasury (1981), Peter Merrill Associates (1981) and Golembe Associates (1979).

2. There are now over 100 shared and proprietary EFT systems that allow a customer to obtain cash by drawing funds in an account across state lines.

3. Even the subsequent authorization of the $2500 minimum deposit Super NOW accounts and the MMDA December 14th account, both free of interest rate ceilings, did not reduce the importance of money market funds. To be sure the phenomenal growth of these two new accounts to over $290 billion (as of February 16, 1983) in a very short period suggests that, ceteris paribus, consumers prefer insured to uninsured accounts. However, only $10 billion of these funds probably came from money market funds, which still stand at $204.6 billion.

4. Florida is second only to California in the number of out-of-state subsidiaries of banking organizations operating within the state.

5. Not discussed in this section are the implications of the 24 interstate supervisory mergers of S&Ls. During 1982 and 1983, 24 interstate consolidations were approved (involving many more than 24 S&Ls because of multiple acquisitions in a single application). This includes the acquisition by Citicorp of a failing S&L in California. These acquisitions have created a number of interstate S&Ls, but the competitive significance will depend upon whether the industry weathers its financial crisis. Also not discussed is the potential expansion of single S&L holding companies which are not subject to as stringent limitations on permissible nonbanking activities as are multiple S&L holding companies and bank holding companies. (For further discussion see Federal Reserve [1981].)

6. For a detailed listing of such combinations see Rosenblum and Siegel (1982). Sears has most recently announced its intention to use its Sears World Trade, Inc. subsidiary to market financial services worldwide.

7. See Murphy and Brunner (1981).

8. Acquisition of more than 10% of such a bank's stock must still be approved by the appropriate federal bank regulator under the Change in Bank Control Act. To date such approvals have been given by both the FDIC and the Comptroller of the Currency.
   Of course, such banks would still be prohibited by the McFadden Act from branching interstate.

9. Iowa, Illinois and Florida are often included as states which permit out-of-state bank holding companies to acquire in-state banks. But in each instance, the applicable statute merely grandfathered existing out-of-state operations. Only one bank holding company in Iowa and Illinois and only three (one Canadian) in Florida are affected. In each instance, however, the grandfather companies have expanded through additional acquisitions.
   The Douglas Amendment to the Bank Holding Company Act of 1956 prohibits interstate acquisitions of banks unless the acquired bank's state has explicitly enacted legislation permitting such acquisitions.
   South Dakota recently passed legislation permitting banks to engage in insurance activities that they would be prohibited from engaging in through subsidiaries of bank holding companies. This will kindle additional interest in outside entry by banking organizations into South Dakota.

10. Minnesota passed a similar law to permit the acquisition of a troubled savings bank which was subsequently acquired by an in-state institution. Since only one savings bank existed in Minnesota, the law is not moot.

11. The constitutionality of the Connecticut law is under consideration by the courts. Northwest Bancorp Inc. v. Woolf, NO. H-83-654 (D.C. Conn., filed July 29, 1983).

12. In New England, a strong desire remains to exclude the large New York banks from possible expansion throughout New England. While New York banks can presently expand into Maine, the new Massachusetts law explicitly excludes New York banks from using their subsidiaries in Maine to expand into Massachusetts.

13. See Department of the Treasury (1981).

14. National market firms would be unaffected since they are not confined in their search for services to the State of Florida. See also Horvitz (1983).

15. For reviews of these studies see Gilbert and Longbrake (1974) and McCall (1980).

16. For evidence supporting these conclusions see Guttentag (1976) and Jessup and Stolz (1975).

17. Whether these services would be demanded or used is another matter.

18. One of the studies which failed to find evidence of parasitic behavior was by Kohn, Carlo and Kaye (1973) which looked at the effects of entry by large banks into local markets in New York State.

19. For a review of the scale economies literature see Benston, Humphrey and Hanweck (1982).

20. See Opper (1981-83) and Wall (1983).

21. Savage and Rhoades (1981) have examined the performance of small banks in major metropolitan markets.

22. See Rhoades (1978).

23. In large banking organizations, the Garn-St. Germain bill now provides for a suspension of interstate banking limitations by permitting the acquisition of large qualifying institutions in financial difficulty by out-of-state banking organizations.

24. See McCall and Lane (1980).

25. Rivard (1983).

26. In the extreme, a state chartered bank operating in 50 states might be examined by 50 state banking departments whereas a national bank would only be examined by the Comptroller of the Currency.

27. Similar patterns seem to be emerging in Florida as well.

28. The recent change in the Florida law permitting the consolidation of holding company affiliates into a state-wide branching network could facilitate the acquisition of Florida banks by out-of-state organizations operating under a *de novo* entry rule.

29. It has been reported in the financial press that bank share values in New England states have appreciated in value by as much as 40% since the reciprocal laws have been passed.

30. This discussion leaves aside the constitutionality issues of such legislation presently in the courts. For a review and analysis of these issues, see Davis (1983). See footnote 11. It also does not explore the variety of regional options that might be considered, such as contiguous state expansion, EFT expansion or expansion entry into SMSAs crossing state boundaries. For discussion of these options see Department of the Treasury (1981).

31. Regional reciprocity was the approach recommended by the Southern Regional Banking Committee of the Southern Growth Policies Board. As part of a broader program to foster economic development in member states, the SGPB formed the Southern Regional Banking Committee and charged it with making recommendations to the 12 member states of possible changes in the banking structure to improve performance and enhance the ability of southern banks to compete for funds. Committee members proposed the elimination of state usury ceilings, the liberalization of intrastate branching restrictions, and a phased relaxation of limitations on bank holding company expansion. While the committee did suggest a regional, reciprocal approach to holding company expansion, it argued that such agreements should be in place for only a limited time before nationwide agreements could be pursued. To date, however, these recommendations have received little consideration among the Southern Growth Policy states.

32. It was for these reasons that the Southern Growth Policies Board recommended that regional reciprocity be used as a transition to national reciprocity. The SGPB stated, "To provide for a greater accumulation of capital to enhance economic development and to facilitate more effective allocation of financial services to individuals and businesses of all sizes, the SGPB states should enact legislation to permit entry of out-of-state bank holding companies on a reciprocal basis. To allow regional bank holding companies an opportunity to position franchises to compete in national markets, reciprocal banking agreements should be limited to the states of the SGPB region for a specified period of time with provisions for nationwide agreements beyond the limiting interval" (see Skinner (1982). Rhode Island has also adopted this model.

References

Benston, George J., Gerald A. Hanweck and David B. Humphrey, "Operating Costs in Commercial Banking," *Economic Review,* Federal Reserve Bank of Atlanta, November 1982.

Davis, Jeffrey, "A Legal Analysis of Regional Interstate Banking," Holland Law Center, University of Florida (unpublished), Gainesville Florida.

Department of the Treasury, *Geographical Restrictions on Commercial Banking in the United States,* The Report of the President, Department of the Treasury, 1981.

Eisenbeis, Robert A., "Financial Innovation and The Role of Regulation: Implications for Banking Organization, Structure and Regulations," Board of Governors of the Federal Reserve System, February 1980.

––––––. "Interstate Banking: Federal Perspectives and Prospects," *Proceedings of a Conference on Bank Structure and Competition,* Federal Reserve Bank of Chicago, May 1981a.

––––––. "Regulation and Financial Innovation: Implications for Financial Structure and Competition Among Depository and Non-Depository Institutions," *Issues in Bank Regulation,* vol. 4, no. 3, Winter, 1981b.

Federal Reserve, "Bank Holding Company Acquisition of Thrift Institutions," a study by the Staff of the Board of Governors of the Federal Reserve System, September 1981.

Forde, John P., "Drive for Regional Banking Gains in New England States," *American Banker,* Tuesday, February 8, 1983.

Golembe Associates, "A Study of Interstate Banking by Bank Holding Companies," prepared for the Association of Bank Holding Companies, May 25, 1979.

Guttentag, Jack M., "Branch Banking in Alabama," mimeo, February 1976.

Horvitz, Paul M., "Alternative Approaches to Interstate Banking," *Economic Review,* Federal Reserve Bank of Atlanta, May 1983.

Jessup, Paul F. and Richard Stalz," Customer Alternative Among Rural Banks," *Journal of Bank Research,* Summer 1975.

Kane, E.J., "Accelerating Inflation, Technological Innovation, and the Decreasing Effectiveness of Bank Regulation," *Journal of Finance,* May 1981.

Kohn, Ernest, Carmen J. Carlo and Bernard Kaye, *Meeting Local Credit Needs,* New York State Banking Department, 1973.

McCall, Alan S., "The Impact of Bank Structure on Bank Service to Local Communities," *Journal of Bank Research,* Summer 1980.

McCall, Alan S. and John T. Lane, "Multi-Office Banking and the Safety and Soundness of Commercial Banks," *Journal of Bank Research,* Summer 1980.

McNeil, Charles R. and Denise M. Rechter, "The Depository Institutions Deregulation and Monetary Control Act of 1980," Federal Reserve *Bulletin,* June 1980.

Moulton, Janice M., "Delaware Moved Toward Interstate Banking: A Look at the FCDA," *Business Review,* Federal Reserve Bank of Philadelphia, July-August 1983.

Murphy, C. Westbrook and Thomas W. Brunner, "Will Anyone Try to Block Amexco?", *American Banker,* Thursday, April 23, 1981.

Opper, Barbara Negri, "Profitability of Insured Commercial Banks in 1980," Federal Reserve *Bulletin,* September 1981.

_____. "Profitability of Insured Commercial Banks in 1981," Federal Reserve *Bulletin,* August 1982.

_____. "Profitability of Insured Commercial Banks in 1982," Federal Reserve *Bulletin,* July 1983.

Peter Merrill Associates, "The Environment for Non-Local Competition in U.S. Banking Markets," prepared for the American Bankers Association, January 1981.

Rhoades, Stephen A., "The Effect of Bank Holding Companies on Competition," *The Bank Holding Company Movement to 1978: A Compendium,* Board of Governors of the Federal Reserve System, September 1978.

Rivard, Richard J., "An Independent Analysis of the Implications of Interstate Banking for Florida," *Florida Banking,* April 1983.

Rosenblum, Harvey and Diane Siegel, "Competition in Financial Services: The Impact of Nonbank Entry," Federal Reserve Bank of Chicago, 1982.

Savage, Donald T. and Steven A. Rhoades, "Can Small Banks Compete," *Bankers Magazine,* January-February 1981.

Skinner, Alton, "Report of the Southern Regional Banking Committee to the Executive Committee of the Southern Growth Policies Board," Southern Growth Policies Board, November 14, 1982.

Wall, Larry D., "Will Bank Capital Adequacy Restrictions Slow the Development of Interstate Banking?," *Economic Review,* Federal Reserve Bank of Atlanta, May 1983.

Whitehead, David D., "Interstate Banking: Taking Inventory," *Economic Review,* Federal Reserve Bank of Atlanta, May 1983.

3

Interstate Banking: An Inventory of the Florida Connection

David D. Whitehead, III

Interstate banking, defined as banking organizations outside the state supplying financial services inside the state, is already a reality in Florida. Florida's mild climate, pollution free environment, relatively low cost of living, and thriving business environment have established the state as one of the fastest growing in the nation. Florida was the third fastest growing state during the 1970s in terms of actual population growth. This made Florida one of the most attractive markets in the nation, especially for banking organizations seeking to expand their geographic coverage in supplying financial services. Although interstate banking is prohibited by Federal law, banking organizations throughout the country have found various ways to tap the lucrative Florida market. There are in fact very few banking type services that are not being supplied in Florida by out-of-state banking organizations. The purpose of this chapter is to document the extent to which banking organizations throughout the nation have already established their presence in Florida.

Methods of Providing Interstate Financial Services

The combined provisions of the McFadden Act and the Douglas Amendment to the Bank Holding Company Act prohibit interstate banking. But banking organizations are providing financial services on an interstate basis and have been for some time. There are basically five gateways through which commercial banking organizations may offer financial services on an interstate basis. First, "grandfather" provisions in banking legislation allow some banking organizations to maintain full-service commercial banks in more than one state. Second, the Garn-St. Germain Depository Institutions Act of 1982 allows banks and savings and loan associations to acquire failing institutions across state lines. Third, and perhaps most importantly, the 4(c)8 provisions of the Bank Holding Company Act allow bank holding companies to establish or acquire nonbank subsidiaries that offer financial services not subject to the prohibition on interstate banking. Fourth, banking organizations may establish other nonbank subsidiaries, such as loan production offices and Edge Act corporations, across state lines. And fifth, provisions of the Douglas Amendment allow bank holding companies to acquire or establish banking subsidiaries in states which explicitly permit such entry. To date Florida does not allow this type of entry. The following sections discuss the first four of these gateways individually and document the extent to which each has been used by banking organizations headquartered outside the state to offer financial services in Florida. The numbers represent the best available information but may not include all activities or offices. Therefore, the figures should be viewed as a bare minimum.

Grandfathered Interstate Banks

It should be recognized that this study deals only with the number of *offices* of out-of-state banking institutions providing financial services in Florida. Banks are capable of providing financial services across state lines without establishing a physical presence. Nothing prevents a bank in one state from accepting demand deposits and savings deposits from consumers in another state. Many large banks aggressively sell large CDs on an interstate basis and actively market credit cards nationwide. Banks also send calling officers, and offer cash management services, electronic fund transfers, loan participation and correspondent banking services across state lines. Although we know these services are provided, we are unable to document the extent to which they are being provided in Florida.

Florida is one of the few states that has grandfather provisions allowing a limited number of out-of-state banking organizations to acquire banks in the state. Out-of-state banking organizations that controlled trust companies in Florida on December 20, 1972 are permitted to acquire banks and trust companies in the state. Two of the three organizations enjoying grandfather privileges in Florida are domestic organizations, NCNB Corporation of North Carolina and Northern Trust Corporation of Illinois, and the third is a foreign organization, Royal Trust Company of Canada. Currently, an application by Florida National Bank of Florida, Inc. to acquire Royal Trust Company's Florida subsidiaries is pending with the Federal Reserve. Completion of this transaction would eliminate Royal Trust's presence in Florida but might not nullify grandfather status. Table 3.1 shows the banking subsidiaries of all three organizations enjoying "grandfathered" positions in Florida and the number of offices each subsidiary controls.

Table 3.1. Bank Holding Companies with Grandfathered Banks in Florida

(as of December 31, 1982)

Parent Organization	Subsidiary Banks in Florida	Number of Offices
NCNB Corporation	First National Bank of Lake City	2
	NCNB National Bank of Florida, Tampa	47
	NCNB National Bank of Florida, Boca Raton	24
Northern Trust Corporation	Security Trust Company of Sarasota, N.A.	1
Royal Trust Bank Corporation	Royal Trust Bank, Gulfport	10
	Royal Trust Bank of Jacksonville	1
	Royal Trust Bank of Pinellas County	6
	Royal Trust Bank of Miami	12
	Royal Trust Bank of Palm Beach	6

* NCNB Corporation has announced an agreement to acquire Ellis Banking Corporation. However, no application for approval had been made to the Federal Reserve Board as of 11-1-83. The Ellis system includes 17 banks and 52 branches (69 offices).

** Application pending by Florida National Banks of Florida, Inc. to acquire all Royal Trust Company's Florida subsidiaries.

Source: Board of Governors of the Federal Reserve System.

Garn-St. Germain

The Garn-St. Germain Depository Institutions Act of 1982 allows a potential gateway for full service interstate bank expansion. The act allows out-of-state organizations to acquire troubled banks and insured mutual savings banks under certain circumstances. Although these provisions have not been used to allow interstate bank acquisitions to date, they do provide a potential avenue for interstate expansion. In addition, the Federal Home Loan Bank Board began allowing interstate mergers of savings and loans in 1981. To date, more than 30 such mergers have been allowed nationwide including nine Florida savings and loans merged into six California S&Ls and three New Jersey S&Ls (see table 3.2). Four Florida savings and loans have also been permitted to acquire a total of six out-of-state S&Ls.

Interstate 4(c)8 Subsidiaries in Florida

Although banks may not establish banking offices across state lines, they may establish offices of nonbank subsidiaries capable of offering financial services similar to those provided by banks. Legally, a commercial bank is an entity that

Table 3.2. Interstate Mergers of Florida Savings and Loan Associations

Date	Institution Merged	Resulting Organization
8/81	Washington FS&LA, Miami Beach, FL	Citizens FS&LA[1], San Francisco, CA
11/81	First FS&LA, Ft. Lauderdale, FL	Glendale FS&LA, Glendale, CA
12/81	Boca Raton FS&LA, Boca Raton, FL	City FS&LA, Elizabeth, NJ
12/81	Southern FS&LA, Pompano Beach, FL	Home S&LA of America, a FS&LA, Los Angeles, CA
2/82	United FS&LA, Ft. Lauderdale, FL	California FS&LA, Los Angeles, CA
9/82	First FS&LA, Delray Beach, FL	Carteret S&LA, Newark, NJ
12/82	Tampa FS&LA, Tampa, FL	Glendale FS&LA, Glendale, CA
1/83	Fidelity FS&LA, Ocala, FL	California FS&LA, Los Angeles, CA
6/83	Home FS&LA, Palm Beach, FL	City FS&LA, Elizabeth, NJ

MERGERS RESULTING IN FLORIDA BASED SAVINGS AND LOAN ASSOCIATIONS
OUT OF STATE SAVINGS AND LOAN ASSOCIATIONS

6/82	Harris County FS&LA, Baytown, TX	First FS&LA of Mid-Florida[2], Deland, FL
11/82	Island FS&LA, Hempstead, NY and South Shore FS&LA, Massapequa, NY	Empire of America FSA, Deland, FL
12/82	Tarrant SA, Fort Worth, TX	Empire of America FSA, Deland, FL
8/83	Mount Vernon S&LA, VA and Middle Peninsula—Northern Neck FS&LA, Gloucester, VA	First Florida Federal Savings Bank, Gainesville, FL

1. Corporate Title as of 1/2/82—First Nationwide Savings, a Federal Savings and Loan Association.
2. Resulting Association: Empire Savings, F.A.

Source: Federal Home Loan Bank Board.

both offers demand deposits and makes commercial loans. Therefore any organization that both offers demand deposits and makes commercial loans may be declared a commercial bank and, as such, will be subject to the prohibition against establishing offices across state lines. By simply separating the lending and deposit functions, banking organizations may circumvent interstate restrictions and provide financial services on an interstate basis.

One way to accomplish this is through the creation or acquisition of nonbank subsidiaries by bank holding companies. Nonbank subsidiaries offer a more limited array of financial services than commercial banks and do not offer both demand deposits and commercial loans. The nonbank subsidiary would not, therefore, constitute a commercial bank and, hence, would be free to open offices on an interstate basis. This in turn allows the bank holding company to establish its name, its expertise and contacts in geographic areas prohibited to its banking subsidiaries. Besides the profit and risk diversification motives, the establishment of nonbank subsidiaries across state lines is a good indication that a given holding company may consider a state a desirable market for purposes of interstate bank expansion if and when the law permits.

Section 4(c)8 of the Bank Holding Company Act states the criteria the Board must apply before allowing bank holding companies to engage in certain nonbank activities. To be considered a permissible nonbank activity for bank holding companies, the activity must pass two tests. First, it must be closely related to the activities in which banks engage. This is a rather vague criterion in light of the "incidental powers" accorded banks through Section 8 of the National Bank Act of 1864, which states that banks may "exercise . . . all such incidental powers as shall be necessary to carry on the business of banking . . . " Given this vagueness it is not surprising that the Board of Governors has no published statement of the criteria it uses to determine activities closely related to banking. Researchers have observed, however, that the Board has approved activities in which banks have historically engaged, or activities complementing services normally provided by banks or activities in which banks clearly possess technical skills.[1] If the activity satisfies at least one of these criteria, it may be proclaimed a permissible activity if it also passes the second test: that providing the service through a nonbank subsidiary may reasonably be expected to produce net public benefits. Nonbank subsidiaries do not constitute a commercial bank and, hence, are free to open offices on an interstate basis. National banks may undertake a number of the same 4(c)8 type activities allowed to bank holding companies (see table 3.3). For the most part, however, activities of national banks are constrained to the state in which the parent bank is located.

The Board of Governors may approve a 4(c)8 application in one of two ways. First, it may approve the activity and add it to the "laundry list" that bank holding companies may offer. In this case, the given activity is by regulation appropriate for holding companies, but an application and approval by the Board to undertake the activity is still required. The second way an activity may be approved is by an order of the Board of Governors. Approval by order is on a case-by-case basis and does not declare the activity to be generally appropriate for all bank holding companies. Other proposed activities are simply denied. Table 3.3 lists all 4(c)8 activities permitted by regulation, permitted by order, and denied. The activities permitted by regulation and permitted by order constitute the available types of nonbank subsidiaries bank holding companies may establish on an interstate basis.

With the assistance of the 11 other Federal Reserve District Banks, we were able to piece together a composite picture of holding companies throughout the nation that controlled interstate 4(c)8 subsidiaries and the number of interstate offices each controlled. Although an application is required prior to a 4(c)8 subsidiary opening a new office, no consolidated records were available. Each District Federal Reserve Bank compiled a list of holding companies with interstate 4(c)8 offices and provided the office locations on a state-by-state basis. In a few instances it was necessary to contact holding companies directly to obtain the desired information. This study presents the best information available on 4(c)8 interstate activity, but the data may not be 100 percent inclusive. The numbers represent an actual count of those institutions and office locations of those institutions we identified as being involved in providing 4(c)8 services on an interstate basis. Therefore, the numbers may understate the extent of interstate activity.

In total we identified 139 bank holding companies controlling at least one 4(c)8 subsidiary which has interstate offices. The 139 holding companies controlled 382 4(c)8 subsidiaries with a total of 5,500 interstate offices. Map 3.1 shows the number of 4(c)8 subsidiaries with interstate offices by the state in which their parent holding company was domiciled. For instance, map 3.1 shows that bank holding companies headquartered in New York controlled 96 4(c)8 subsidiaries which operate interstate offices. As would be expected, bank holding companies located in the money centers are the most active in providing interstate financial services through their 4(c)8 subsidiaries.

The location of each of the 5,500 interstate offices of the 4(c)8 subsidiaries is shown in map 3.2. The primary activity of offices is the focus of map 3.2 because more than one 4(c)8 activity may be provided through a single office of a 4(c)8 subsidiary. Many activities are low profile and normally provide a complementary service to some other 4(c)8 activity. For example, the insurance agent activity is provided at 2,440 locations, although the interstate offices of 4(c)8 subsidiaries primarily engaged in this activity number only 40. The same is true for underwriting credit life insurance, which is provided through 1,118 offices of 4(c)8 subsidiaries but only 56 are primarily engaged in this activity. Therefore, to assess the geographic extent to which bank holding

Table 3.3. Permissible Nonbank Activities for Bank Holding Companies Under Section 4(c)8 of Regulation Y

February, 1983

Activities permitted by regulation

1. Extensions of credit[2]
   Mortgage banking
   Finance companies: consumer, sales, and commercial
   Credit cards
   Factoring
2. Industrial bank, Morris Plan bank, industrial loan company
3. Servicing loans and other extensions of credit[2]
4. Trust company[2]
5. Investment or financial advising[2]
6. Full-payout leasing of personal or real property[2]
7. Investments in community welfare projects[2]
8. Providing bookkeeping or data processing services[2]
9. Acting as insurance agent or broker primarily in connection with credit extensions[2]
10. Underwriting credit life, accident and health insurance
11. Providing courier services[2]
12. Management consulting to all depository institutions
13. Sale at retail of money orders with a face value of not more than $1000, travelers checks and savings bonds[1,2]
14. Performing appraisals of real estate[1]
15. Issuance and sale of travelers checks

Activities permitted by order

1. Issuance and sale of travelers checks[2,6]
2. Buying and selling gold and silver bullion and silver coin[2,4]
3. Issuing money orders and general-purpose variable denominated payment instruments[1,2,4]
4. Futures commission merchant to cover gold and silver bullion and coins[1,2]
5. Underwriting certain federal, state and municipal securities[1,2]
6. Check verification[1,2,4]
7. Financial advice to consumers[1,2]
8. Issuance of small denomination debt instruments[1]
9. Arranging for equity financing of real estate
10. Acting as futures commission merchant
11. Discount brokerage
12. Operating a distressed savings and loan association
13. Operating an Article XII Investment Co.
14. Executing foreign banking unsolicited purchases and sales of securities
15. Engaging in commercial banking activities abroad through a limited purpose Delaware bank
16. Performing appraisal of real estate and real estate advisor and real estate brokerage on nonresidential properties.
17. Operating a Pool Reserve Plan for loss reserves of banks for loans to small businesses
18. Operating a thrift institution in Rhode Island
19. Operating a guarantee savings bank in New Hampshire
20. Offering informational advice and transactional services for foreign exchange services

Activities denied by the Board

1. Insurance premium funding (combined sales of mutual funds and insurance)
2. Underwriting life insurance not related to credit extension
3. Sale of level-term credit life
4. Real estate brokerage (residential)
5. Armored car
6. Land development
7. Real estate syndication
8. General management consulting
9. Property management
10. Computer output microfilm services
11. Underwriting mortgage guaranty insurance[3]
12. Operating a savings and loan association[1,5]
13. Operating a travel agency[1,2]
14. Underwriting property and casualty insurance[1]
15. Underwriting home loan life mortgage insurance[1]
16. Investment note issue with transactional characteristics
17. Real estate advisory services

1. Added to list since January 1, 1975.
2. Activities permissible to national banks.
3. Board orders found these activities closely related to banking but denied proposed acquisitions as part of its "go slow" policy.
4. To be decided on a case-by-case basis.
5. Operating a thrift institution has been permitted by order in Rhode Island, New Hampshire and California.
6. Subsequently permitted by regulation.

Source: Federal Reserve Board of Governors.

Map 3.1.   Number of Interstate 4(c)8 Subsidiaries of Holding Companies
Home Officed in the State

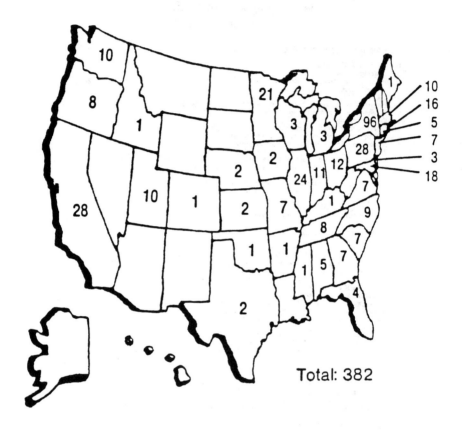

Total: 382

companies are establishing a physical presence on an interstate basis, one
should focus on the number of 4(c)8 offices by primary activity.

Three of the 139 holding companies with interstate 4(c)8 activities are
Florida based holding companies; Barnett Banks of Florida, Inc., Florida
National Banks of Florida, Inc. and Southeast Banking Corporation. Table 3.4
shows the interstate 4(c)8 subsidiaries of each of these organizations and the
number of offices each controls by state. Barnett is engaging only in check
verification on an interstate basis, while both Florida National Bank of
Florida, Inc. and Southeast Banking Corporation engage in mortgage
banking. Florida National is also engaging in finance company activities,
industrial banking and leasing on an interstate basis. Comparatively, Florida
banking organizations are providing few financial services on an interstate
basis.

Map 3.2. Total Number of Offices by Primary Activity of Interstate 4(c)8 Subsidiaries

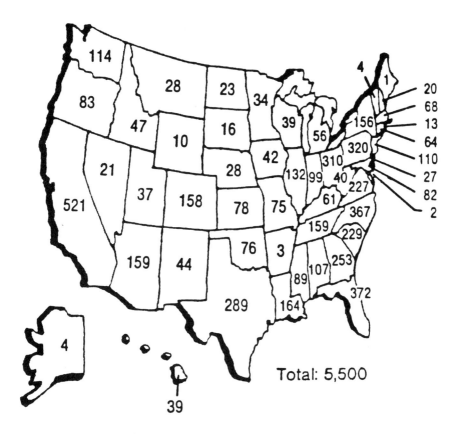

Of the remaining 136 non-Florida bank holding companies with interstate 4(c)8 subsidiaries, 51 or 38% of the total have subsidiaries with offices located in Florida. In total these 51 non-Florida holding companies operate 5,003 interstate offices through their 4(c)8 subsidiaries, 372 or 7.4% of which are located in Florida as shown by map 3.2. Appendix A gives the name of each holding company controlling a 4(c)8 subsidiary that operates a Florida office, the name of its 4(c)8 subsidiary, the number of offices that it operates in Florida, the primary and secondary activities these offices engage in and the home office state of the holding company.

Table 3.5 is a summary table of holding companies with 4(c)8 subsidiaries operating in Florida, their state of residence and the number of offices each operates in Florida. Of the 372 4(c)8 offices in Florida operated by out-of-state

Table 3.4.   Interstate 4(c)8 Subsidiaries of Florida Bank Holding
Companies

	Mortgage Banking	Financial Company	Credit Cards	Factoring	Industrial Bank	Servicing Loans	Leasing	Check Verification	
Barnett Banks of Florida, Inc.									
Verifications, Inc.								x	GA(1),AL(1),NC(1)
Florida National Banks of Florida, Inc.									AL(3),CA(1),GA(3),KY(1)
Charter Mortgage Corporation	x	x[1]				x[2]			MD(1),SC(2),TN(2),VA(1)
Florida National Credit Corporation					x[3]	x			GA(9),NC(12),SC(7)
Southeast Banking Corporation									
Southeast Mortgage Corporation									
of Atlanta	x								GA(1),TX(2)

x[1]   AL(2)

x[2]   AL(1),CA(1)

x[3]   The twelve offices of Florida National Credit Corporation located in North Carolina are empowered to function as industrial banks—however, under North Carolina state law industry banks are not allowed—therefore, these offices do not provide all the services associated with industrial banks.

holding companies, 87 are offices of subsidiaries of New York holding companies. They account for almost one fourth of all interstate 4(c)8 offices located in Florida. The propensity for New York holding companies to offer financial services in Florida is shown in table 3.6. Of the 51 holding companies with 4(c)8 subsidiaries operating interstate offices in Florida 11 are New York based holding companies.

In total these 51 out-of-state holding companies control 4(c)8 subsidiaries that operate 281 finance company offices, 55 mortgage banking offices, 20 trust companies, 1 industrial bank office and 5 leasing offices and 10 offices that offer other 4(c)8 services (see table 3.7).

Other Nonbank Interstate Subsidiaries

In addition to interstate 4(c)8 subsidiaries, banking organizations are permitted to establish loan production offices and Edge Act Corporations on an interstate basis. Loan production offices can do little more than calling officers, but they are useful in establishing a wholesale presence in an area. Edge Act offices also are aimed at wholesale customers but are limited to dealing with organizations engaged in international trade.

Since regulatory agencies do not track data on loan production offices, it was necessary to survey banking organizations directly. Only the largest

Table 3.5. Holding Companies with Interstate 4(c)8 Offices in Florida

Bank Holding Company	Home State	Total Number of Offices	Number of Offices In Florida
AmSouth Bancorpoation	Alabama	9	2
BankAmerica	California	287	29
Security Pacific Corporation	California	273	15
CBT Corporation	Connecticut	12	1
Beneficial Corporation	Delaware	1171	38
C&S Georgia Corporation	Georgia	17	6
First Atlanta Corporation	Georgia	110	14
Trust Company of Georgia	Geogia	1	1
Continental Illinois Corporation	Illinois	13	4
First Chicago Corporation	Illinois	8	1
Northern Trust Corporation	Illinois	5	4
Walter E. Heller International Corporation	Illinois	43	3
American Fletcher Corporation	Indiana	24	1
Merchants National Corporation	Indiana	13	2
Citizens Fidelity Corporation	Kentucky	5	1
Maryland National Corporation	Maryland	28	1
Union Trust Bancorp	Maryland	65	4
First National Boston Corporation	Massachusetts	26	5
UST Corporation	Massachusetts	1	1
NBD Bancorp, Inc.	Michigan	6	1
First Bank System	Minnesota	29	2
Northwest Bancorporation	Minnesota	537	23
Deposit Guaranty Corporation	Mississippi	2	1
Heritage Bancorporation	New Jersey	4	1
Horizon Bancorp	New Jersey	7	3
Midlantic Banks	New Jersey	3	2
Bank of New York Company	New York	14	1
Bankers Trust New York Corporation	New York	7	2
Barclays Bank Limited	New York	557	16
Chase Manhattan	New York	53	14
Chemical New York Corporation	New York	108	7
Citicorp	New York	262	28
JP Morgan	New York	2	1
Lincoln First Banks	New York	3	2
Manufacturers Hanover Corporation	New York	562	14
Marine Midland Banks	New York	3	1
US Trust Corporation	New York	1	1
First Union Corporation	North Carolina	36	3
NCNB Corporation	North Carolina	182	37
Wachovia Corporation	North Carolina	6	1
National City Corporation	Ohio	2	1
Orbanco Financial Services, Inc.	Oregon	17	1
Mellon National Corporation	Pennsylvania	140	11
The Girard Company	Pennsylvania	2	1
Philadelphia National Corporation	Pennsylvania	76	1

(continued on page 70)

(Table 3.5 continued)

Pittsburg National Corporation	Pennsylvania	48	1
Fleet Financial Group	Rhode Island	142	36
Hospital Trust Corporation	Rhode Island	1	1
Old Stone Corporation	Rhode Island	24	18
United Virginia Bankshares	Virginia	17	4
Virginia National Bankshares	Virginia	39	3
		5003	372

Source: Federal Reserve Bank of Atlanta.

Table 3.6.   Holding Companies with 4(c)8 Subsidiary Offices Located in Florida

Parent States	Number of Holding Companies
Alabama	1
California	2
Connecticut	1
Delaware	1
Georgia	3
Illinois	4
Indiana	2
Kentucky	1
Maryland	2
Michigan	1
Minnesota	2
Mississippi	1
New Jersey	3
New York	11
North Carolina	3
Ohio	1
Oregon	1
Pennsylvania	4
Rhode Island	3
Virginia	2
	51

Source: Federal Reserve Bank of Atlanta.

banking organizations are likely to commit resources to loan production offices, especially in light of the fact that calling officers may provide the same services without a physical presence in an area. Therefore we surveyed the top 200 banking organizations in the country and found that they controlled a total of 202 loan production offices. Map 3.3 shows the location of loan production offices by state. It should be noted, however, that these loan production offices

Table 3.7.   Interstate 4(c)8 Offices Located in Florida

Type of Activity	Number of Offices
Mortgage Banking	55
Financial Company	281
Industrial Bank	1
Servicing Loans	1
Trust Company	20
Financial Advisor	4
Leasing	5
Data Processing	2
Underwriting Credit Life	2
Management Consulting	1
Total	372

Source: Federal Reserve Bank of Atlanta.

Map 3.3.   Interstate Loan Production Offices Located in Each State

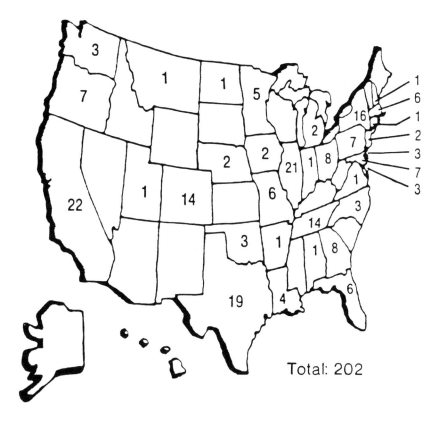

Total: 202

service not only the state in which they are located but also surrounding states. They are in many cases servicing a given region of the country.

Table 3.8 shows the parent organizations of each of the six loan production offices located in Florida. Two North Carolina organizations, two Illinois organizations and one organization each from California and Kentucky controlled loan production offices in Florida. In addition to these Florida offices, there are 8 loan production offices of out-of-state organizations in Georgia and 14 in Tennessee that may be servicing the entire Southeast.

Table 3.8.   Interstate Loan Production Offices Located in Florida

Parent Company	Loan Production Office	Number of Offices
BankAmerica Corporation, CA	Corporate LPO	1
Continental Illinois Corporation, IL	Continental Bank-Regional Office	1
First Chicago Corporation, IL	First Chicago LPO	1
Citizens Fidelity Corporation, KY	Citizens Fidelity LPO	1
NCNB Corporation, NC	NCNB Corporate Services, Inc.	1
The Wachovia Corporation, NC	Wachovia Financial Corporation	1

Source: Federal Reserve Bank of Atlanta Survey

Edge Act Corporations are another type of nonbank subsidiary that are not geographically restricted. They are established in order to follow the geographic distribution of one's customers engaged in international trade. There are 143 interstate Edge Act offices of 49 domestic banking organizations located in the United States (see map 3.4). Predictably, states with international trade centers have attracted the most Edge Act offices. New York attracted the largest number, 31, closely followed by Florida with 25 offices. California follows with 23, Texas with 17 and Illinois is a distant fifth with 11 Edge Act offices. Florida is a prime target for this type of wholesale banking. Since only the largest banks may offer services needed by international corporations, banking organizations in the money centers have established 10 Edge Act offices in Florida (see table 3.9). Interstate banking would allow these organizations to provide little more in the way of wholesale services than they are providing today.

To round out the picture, foreign banking organizations are capable of locating agency and Edge Act offices in Florida. There are 22 agency offices and 6 Edge Act offices of foreign banking organizations currently operating in Florida. (See table 3.10 for details.)

Map 3.4. Interstate Edge Act Offices of Domestic Banking
Organizations

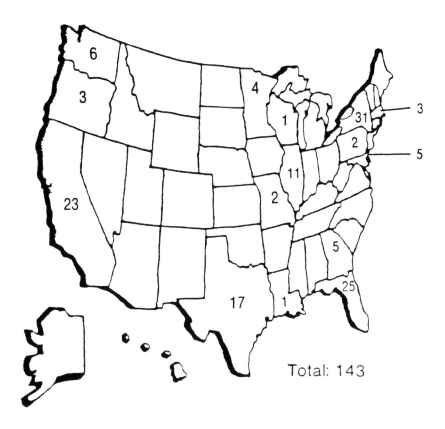

Total: 143

Source: Federal Reserve Bank of New York (As of Oct. 1982).

Conclusion

The number of interstate offices of subsidiaries of banking institutions located
in Florida is truly impressive. Florida is one of the most attractive markets in
the country if attractiveness can be measured by the number of out-of-state
banking institutions establishing offices in Florida through their nonbank
subsidiaries. Out-of-state bank holding companies have already established
372 4(c)8 offices, 6 loan production offices and 25 Edge Act offices not to
mention the presence of foreign banks and domestic banks which enjoy
grandfathered provisions to acquire Florida banks. On the wholesale side or

retail side there are very few services out-of-state holding companies cannot provide to Florida customers today. The competition within the financial services industry in Florida is intense. Should interstate banking laws be changed either at the state or national level, Florida will be a prime target for entry.

Table 3.9.   Interstate Edge Offices of Domestic Organizations in Florida by Home State

(as of October, 1982)

BankAmerica International	CA	1
First Interstate International	CA	1
Security Pacific International Bank	CA	1
Wells Fargo Bank International	CA	1
American Security Bank International	DC	1
Riggs International Banking Corporation	DC	1
Citizens & Southern International Bank	GA	1
Continental Bank International	IL	1
First Chicago International	IL	1
Northern Trust InterAmerican Corporation	IL	1
Bank of Boston	MA	1
New England Merchants Bank International	MA	1
Shawmut Boston International Banking Corporation	MA	1
Bankers Trust New York Corporation	NY	1
Bank of New York International Corporation	NY	1
BNY International Investment Inc.*	NY	1
Chase Bank International	NY	1
Chemical Bank International	NY	1
Citibank International	NY	1
Irving Trust International Bank	NY	1
Manufacturers Hanover International Banking Corporation	NY	1
Morgan Guaranty International Bank	NY	1
Republic International Bank of New York	NY	1
Girard International Bank	NY	1
Mellon Bank International*	NY	1
Total		25

* Non-banking edge
Source: Federal Reserve Bank of New York.

Table 3.10.   Foreign Bank Offices Located in Florida

(as of June 30, 1982)

FOREIGN BANK	U.S. OFFICE	AGENCY	EDGE
Credit Suisse	Credit Suisse	1	
Chartered Bank	Standard Chartered Bank	1	
Lloyds Group	Lloyds Bank International Ltd.	1	
Banco do Brazil	Banco de Brazil SA Agency	1	
Bank Leumi Le-Israel	Bank Leumi Le-Israel Agency	1	
Bank Hapoalim	Bank Hapoalim BM Agency	1	
Algemene Bank Nederland	Algemene Bank Nederland NV	1	
Banco de la Nacion	Banco de la Nacion Argentina Agency	1	
Banco Real	Banco Real SA Agency	1	
Banco de Bogata	Banco de Bogata International Corporation		1
Banco Union	Union Chelsea International Banking Corporation		1
Banco de Venezuela	Banco de Venezuela International		1
Hong Kong & Shanghai Bank	Marine Midland Interam Bank		1
European American Group	European American Bank International		1
Scotiabank	Bank of Nova Scotia Agency	1	
Royal Bank of Canada	Royal Bank of Canada Agency	2	
Banca Nazionale del Lavoro	Banca Nazionale del Lavoro	1	
Banco de Bilbao	Banco de Bilbao	1	
Banco de Vizcaya	Banco de Vizcaya SA Agency	1	
Banco Exte de Espana	Bank of Exterior de Espana	1	
Barclays Group	Barclays Bank International Ltd.	1	
Schroder Group	J. Henry Schroder International Bank		1
Israel Discount Bank	Israel Discount Bank Ltd.	2	
Banco Prov Buenos Aires	Banco de la Prov de Buenos Aires	1	
Banco de Estado de Sao Paulo	Banco de Estado de Sao Paulo	1	
Banco Industrial de Venezuela	Banco Industrial de Venezuela CA	1	
Total Number of Offices		22	6

Source: Federal Reserve Bank of Atlanta.

Notes

1.   The Depository Institutions Act of 1982 allows closed insured commercial banks with assets of $500 million or more and insured mutual savings banks with assets of $500 million or more and in danger of failing to be acquired by an out-of-state bank or bank holding company with priority given in the following order: acquisition of similar institutions in the same state; acquisition by same type of institution in different states; acquisition by different types of institutions in the same state; and acquisition by different types of institutions in different states.

Appendix A

Holding Companies with Interstate 4(c)8 Subsidiaries with Offices in
Florida, Activities Permitted and Number of Offices

Holding Companies with Interstate 4(c)8 Subsidiaries in Florida, Activities Permitted and Number of Offices. (x indicates secondary activity)	Mortgage Banking	Financial Company	Credit Cards	Factoring	Industrial Bank	Servicing Loans	Trust Company	Financial Advisor	Leasing	Investment in Community Welfare	Data Processing	Insurance Agent	Underwriting Credit Life	Courier Service	Management Consulting	Money Order $1000, Travelers Checks	Check Verification
Alabama																	
AmSouth Bancorporation																	
Engel Mortgage Company	2																
California																	
BankAmerica Corporation																	
BA Mortgage and International Realty Corporation	1							x	x								
FinanceAmerica		28															
Security Pacific Corporation																	
Security Pacific Finance Systems	15					x			x			x					
Connecticut																	
CBT Corporation																	
Lazerre Financial Corporation	1																
Delaware																	
Beneficial Corporation																	
Beneficial Finance Company		37															
Southern Industrial Savings Bank of Orlando					1												
Georgia																	
C&S Georgia Corporation																	
Family Credit		5															
Citizens & Southern Mortgage Company	1	x															
First Atlanta Corporation																	
Gulf Finance		14										x					
Trust Company of Georgia																	
Trust Company Mortgage	1											x					
Illinois																	
Continental Illinois Corporation																	
CI Leasing Corporation									2								
Continental Illinois of Florida							2	x									
First Chicago Corporation																	
Real Estate Research Corporation								1									
Northern Trust Corporation																	
Security Trust Company							4										
Walter E. Heller International Corporation																	
General Capital Corporation	1																
Walter E. Heller & Company	2		x						x								

	Mortgage Banking	Financial Company	Credit Cards	Factoring	Industrial Bank	Servicing Loans	Trust Company	Financial Advisor	Leasing	Investment in Community Welfare	Data Processing	Insurance Agent	Underwriting Credit Life	Courier Service	Management Consulting	Money Order $1000, Travelers Checks	Check Verification
Indiana																	
American Fletcher Corporation																	
American Fletcher Mortgage Company, Inc.	1					x											
Merchants National Corporation																	
Circle Leasing Corporation		x							1								
Merchants National of Indiana, Inc.					1												
Kentucky																	
Citizens Fidelity Corporation																	
Citizens Fidelity Leasing Corporation									1								
Maryland																	
Maryland National Corporation																	
Maryland National Mortgage Corporation	1					x							x				
Union Trust Bancorp																	
Landmark Financial Services		4				x						x	x				
Massachusetts																	
First National Boston Corporation																	
FBC Inc.											1						
First of Boston Mortgage Corporation	1							x									
FNB Financial Company		1	x														
Old Colony Trust Company							2										
UST Corporation																	
FCA Corporation								1									
Michigan																	
NBD Bancorp																	
NBD Financial Services of Florida															1		
Minnesota																	
First Bank System																	
FBS Mortgage Corporation	1																
First Trust Florida					1												
Northwest Bancorporation																	
Banco Mortgage Company	1																
Dial Corporation		22										x	x				
Mississippi																	
Deposit Guaranty Corporation																	
Deposit Guaranty Mortgage Company	1											x					

	Mortgage Banking	Financial Company	Credit Cards	Factoring	Industrial Bank	Servicing Loans	Trust Company	Financial Advisor	Leasing	Investment in Community Welfare	Data Processing	Insurance Agent	Underwriting Credit Life	Courier Service	Management Consulting	Money Order $1000, Travelers Checks	Check Verification
New Jersey																	
Heritage Bancorporation																	
Heritage Mortgage Finance Company	1																
Horizon Bancorporation																	
Horizon Credit Corporation	3					x			x			x					
Midlantic Banks, Inc.																	
Midlantic Mortgage Company	2																
New York																	
Bank of New York Company																	
ARCS Mortgage, Inc.	1					x											
Bankers Trust New York Corporation																	
Bankers Trust Company of Florida							1										
Bankers Trust Investment Managers								1									
Barclays Bank Limited																	
American Credit Corporation	16											x					
Chase Manhattan Corporation																	
Chase Commercial Corporation of New York	3					x			x								
Chase Home Mortgage Corporation	7					x		x				x					
Chase Manhattan Financial Services	4					x						x				x	
Chemical New York Corporation																	
Chemical Business Credit Corporation	1					x			x			x					
Chemical Trust Company of Florida							1										
SunAmerica Corporation	5											x					
Citicorp																	
Citicorp Homeowners, Inc.	13					x							x				
Citicorp Industrial Credit, Inc.	1					x			x								
Citicorp Person-to-Person Financial Centers, Inc.	13					x							x				
Citicorp USA, Inc.	1					x			x								
J. P. Morgan & Company, Inc.																	
Morgan Trust Company of Florida							1										
Lincoln First Banks Inc.																	
Lincoln First of Florida, Inc.								1									
Lincoln First Trust Company of Florida, N. A.							1										
Manufacturers Hanover Corporation																	
Finance One, Inc.	6											x					
Finance One Credit of Florida, Inc.	3												x				
Manufacturers Hanover Leasing	x					x			1								
Finance One Mortgage, Inc.	2					x						x					
Manufacturers Hanover Mortgage Corporation	2					x											

	Mortgage Banking	Financial Company	Credit Cards	Factoring	Industrial Bank	Servicing Loans	Trust Company	Financial Advisor	Leasing	Investment in Community Welfare	Data Processing	Insurance Agent	Underwriting Credit Life	Courier Service	Management Consulting	Money Order $1000, Travelers Checks	Check Verification
New York—Continued																	
Marine Midland Banks																	
Marine Midland Trust Company of Florida, N. A.							1	x									
U. S. Trust Corporation																	
U. S. Trust Company of Florida							1										
North Carolina																	
First Union Corporation																	
Cameron-Brown Company		3															
NCNB Corporation																	
NCNB Mortgage Corporation	2												x				
Transouth Financial Corporation		34											x			x	
Trust Company of Florida							1										
The Wachovia Corporation																	
Wachovia Mortgage Company	1																
Ohio																	
National City Corporation																	
National City of Florida							1										
Oregon																	
Orbanco Financial Services Corporation																	
Ft. Wayne Mortgage Company	1					x											
Pennsylvania																	
Mellon National Corporation																	
Mellon Bank, N. A.							1										
Mellon Financial Services Corporation		9															
Mellon Mortgage, Inc.	1																
Philadelphia National Corporation																	
Colonial Mortgage Service Corporation	1					x											
The Girard Company																	
GTC Management, Inc.							1										
Pittsburg National Corporation																	
Kissell Company	1																

	Mortgage Banking	Financial Company	Credit Cards	Factoring	Industrial Bank	Servicing Loans	Trust Company	Financial Advisor	Leasing	Investment in Community Welfare	Data Processing	Insurance Agent	Underwriting Credit Life	Courier Service	Management Consulting	Money Order $1000, Travelers Checks	Check Verification
Rhode Island																	
Fleet Financial Group, Inc.																	
Amortized Mortgage Inc.	1												x				
Mortgage Associates	1	x				x							x				
Southern Discount Company	34											x	x				
Hospital Trust Corporation																	
Hospital Trust of Florida, N. A.							1										
Old Stone Corporation																	
American Standard Insurance Agency													1				
DAC Computer Services											1						
DAC Corporation of Florida	13					x											
Motor Life Insurance Company													1				
Unicredit Corporation of Florida		1															
Unifinancial Corporation	x	1															
Virginia																	
United Virginia Bankshares																	
United Virginia Mortgage Corporation	4					x						x					
Virginia National Bankshares																	
VNB Equity Corporation	3					x						x					

4

Impact of Nonbank Entry

Harvey Rosenblum

Introduction

As discussed in chapter 2, states considering interstate banking legislation have three options: (1) do nothing, thus maintaining the status quo; (2) adopt a reciprocal agreement with one or more other states, allowing in-state banks to own or control banks in these other states and vice versa; or (3) avoid the reciprocity requirement and allow out-of-state banks, irrespective of the home state in which they are domiciled, to enter either through the formation of *de novo* banks and/or through acquisition of existing banks chartered in Florida. Ironically, these three alternatives make distinctions where there are few differences, at least from the point of view of residents who are business and household consumers of commercial banking services.

The reason for this lack of real legislative choice is that interstate banking—at least in the generic sense of the term—is in many states already a reality. It is present in substance if not in the form of interstate brick and mortar commercial bank branches. In Florida, for example, *de facto* banking services are offered by out-of-state commercial banks or their affiliated bank holding company sister subsidiaries. Most of the major bank holding companies entered Florida beginning in the early 1970s through acquisition of trust companies, consumer finance companies and other vendors of financial and related services.

However, many, if not all, services offered by commercial banks can be provided without a commercial bank charter. Many of these same services can be offered by savings and loan associations as a result of their expanded asset powers in the last few years, including a wide range of consumer and commercial lending; furthermore, many S&Ls have begun operating on an interstate basis since 1981 when interstate acquisitions of failing thrifts became a necessity. The provision of deposit and credit services is not limited to depository institutions. These services are also offered by department stores such as Sears; by captive finance subsidiaries of manufacturers such as General Motors Acceptance Corporation or Ford Motor Credit which essentially long ago turned every one of their dealers into a supplier or distributor of automobile credit; by insurance companies, brokers and security dealers (or some combination thereof) which offer a wide range of investment vehicles, including federally insured bank deposits; and by finance companies that offer a wide range of consumer or commercial credit. Many of these finance companies are affiliated with large manufacturers and they offer a wide range of commercial and consumer loans unrelated to the products made by their parent company. General Electric Credit and Westinghouse Credit are but two examples of prototypes of manufacturers-turned-bankers.

This research has uncovered 32 of these companies whose primary base of operations involves neither commercial banking nor the taking of federally insured deposits. On a nationwide basis these companies have made significant inroads into lines of business served by commercial banks.

The next section highlights the results of the research on the penetration of nonbank competitors into financial services. The following section explores the general policy implications. Conclusions and implications are stated in the final section.

Financial Services in Transition: The Effects of Nonbank Competitors

During the last two years, I have undertaken research designed to quantify the extent of penetration into commercial bank product lines achieved by manufacturers, retailers, insurance companies and other firms whose primary business activity does not involve the taking of federally insured deposits. This research has culminated in two studies published by the Federal Reserve Bank of Chicago (2,3) which cover the period 1962-1982, with special emphasis on 1981 and 1982.

To explore the prevailing degree of competition between banks and nonbank companies, the financial activities of 32 major U.S.-based companies were analyzed and compared with the 15 largest bank holding companies as of year-end 1981 and 1982 by utilizing company Annual Reports and 10-k statements filed with the Securities and Exchange Commission. Additional information was obtained from recent articles that have appeared in *American Banker, The Wall Street Journal, Business Week, Fortune, Moody's Bank and Finance Manual,* and other current periodicals and publications believed to be reliable sources.

Companies were chosen on the basis of their being the most frequently mentioned nonbanking-based competitors of commercial banks. Several diversified financial service companies were also studied. Many other financial companies (in particular, many large insurance companies) were, for the most part, excluded because they have demonstrated little or no inclination to invade the turf of commercial banks during the last few years.

The list of companies that were analyzed includes many well known companies whose activities and acquisitions in the last few years have focused the public's attention on their bank-like nature. Among these firms are Sears, Merrill Lynch, American Express and Prudential. Included among the companies studied were many that have established a truly significant presence in one or more product lines generally considered to be dominated by banks. Among these companies are Ford Motor Credit, General Electric Corp., General Motors Acceptance Corp. and Greyhound Financial Group. A complete list of the companies that were analyzed can be found in table 4.1.

These companies do not provide their financial and related information on a state-by-state basis. Consequently, the findings of this research represent data aggregated on a national basis. (By and large, foreign business has been excluded and the totals for each company represent domestic business only.)

Among the highlights of the findings are the following points (for further documentation, see tables 4.2 to 4.17):

1. The interest of nondepository-based companies in financial services that overlapped with commercial banks was very minor until the second half of the 1960s.
   a) In 1962 only two companies—General Motors and Sears—had significant earnings attributable to their financial service activities.
   b) By 1972, 10 such manufacturers or retailers could be identified.
   c) By 1982, the financial service earnings of these same 10 companies (which totaled $2.4 billion) was about equal to the total worldwide earnings of the seven largest bank holding companies ranked by earnings.
   d) And in 1982, 32 companies could be identified that had one or more product line that overlapped with commercial banks and established those firms with a significant regional or nationwide presence in one or more financial services.
2. Among the top 17 companies in earnings from financial services in 1982 (i.e., those with financial service profits exceeding $200 million), about half were bank holding companies and half were nondepository-based firms. Among the top six, only one was a bank holding company and among the top 10, only 3 were banking based firms.
3. Many of the manufacturing companies' financial activities involve captive lending to finance the sale of goods they manufacture; nonetheless, the finance subsidiaries of several companies such as General Electric, Borg Warner and Westinghouse devote over 90% of

the credit they issue to financing consumer and business borrowing totally unrelated to the parent company's products.

4. In consumer installment credit, nondepository institutions dominate the list of the largest 15 lenders, occupying 10 of the top 15 positions; bank holding companies have 5 positions within the top 15 and only 3 positions in the top 10.

5. In automobile credit, General Motors is far and away the largest lender with over one-fourth of all auto loans outstanding, having doubled its share from 13% in 1978. By contrast, the entire commercial banking industry holds 45% of domestic auto loans, down from 60% in 1978. The captive auto finance companies have simply dominated the auto lending business since 1979 due to a number of special circumstances. The growth of GMAC and Ford Motor Credit was primarily defensive in nature and is likely to be reversible.

6. The commercial banking industry has done quite well in the credit card business with Visa and Mastercard having taken the lead over Sears according to most or all of the more commonly used measures of business volume. A decade ago, Sears had a commanding lead over both bank cards. In spite of the banking *industry's* current lead in the area, the two single largest issuers of consumer credit through a card are Sears and American Express who together issue more consumer credit through their charge cards than the largest eight bank issuers of credit cards combined.

7. a) Commercial banks are still the dominant business lenders in the country, particularly in short-term commercial and industrial (C&I) lending. The 32 companies sampled issued combined short-term loans of $42.5 billion in 1982, slightly more than one-fourth the amount of domestic C&I loans of the 15 largest bank holding companies and about 6.6% of the total for all commercial banks. These proportions appear to have changed little in the last 7-8 years.

    b) A different picture emerges in commercial mortgage lending where the four insurance based companies in the sample make more commercial mortgage loans than the largest 15 bank holding companies and about 27 per cent as much as the nation's almost 15,000 banks.

    c) The business lease financing market is dominated by industrial companies. The 15 such companies in the sample had greater lease receivables than that of the domestic offices of all insured U.S. banks.

8. Ten of the 32 companies sampled have sponsored one or more money market mutual funds and account for about 38% of all money market

fund assets. They clearly compete to some extent with commercial banks on the deposit side of the balance sheet.

9. A number of these same companies, however, have acted as brokers for retail deposits and have helped numerous banks and S&Ls extend their market for insured retail deposits to a nationwide area.

10. Most of the nondeposit based firms provide their financial services on a national basis through offices located in most if not all 50 states. Several of the larger bank holding companies have a national network of offices that resembles that of their nonbank competitors. By and large, the sheer size of many of the nonbanking based firms— particularly in consumer lending—in comparison with banks is attributable to the former's nationwide presence while most banks provide retail services in one state.

Policy Implications

Given the findings in the preceding section, it seems readily apparent that local commercial banks presently compete not only with other in-state commercial banks but also with credit granting manufacturers, retailers, insurance companies, locally based S&Ls and credit unions, and out-of-state banks and bank holding companies operating through nonbank subsidiaries, Edge Act affiliates and loan production offices. In many states, trying to prevent entry by out-of-state banks in this day and age is worse than closing the barn door after the horses have gotten out; it is akin to arguing whether a red door or a green door would have been more effective in keeping the horses in the barn.

In the 1960s and 1970s an important part of banking involved deposit gathering at less than market rates. The combined forces of technological advances, high interest rates and inflation, and deposit-rate deregulation have transformed the banking business from a deposit-driven business to a credit-driven business (see 1). In the 1980s, banks have to pay market rates to attract deposits; as a result there are fewer characteristics of banks that make them distinguishable from other credit grantors or rely on commercial paper and other open market debt as a source of funding.

Legislation cannot prevent nonbanking based companies from competing against in-state banks in the markets for household and business credit. Nor can legislation prevent out-of-state entities from gathering local deposits. In Florida, there presently exist several million *de facto* branches of out-of-state financial institutions; they are called telephones, radios, newspapers, TV, and mailboxes. In combination, they allow money market mutual funds, brokers and securities dealers, and out-of-state banks to attract deposits from Florida residents and businesses. It is well recognized that one cannot prevent the use and abuse of certain drugs by legislating a prohibition of their sale. Similarly, one may prohibit out-of-state banks from doing business in one's state, but technology allows other out-of-state firms to do roughly the same business anyway. The only difference is that these firms do not call themselves banks. It would seem preferable and more effective to try to control the expansion of out-of-state institutions through open regulation than through prohibition.

Conclusions and Implications

Given that interstate banking is already a reality, it would seem that the most appropriate public policy would be to openly recognize the situation by amending the law. If a state is an attractive market for conducting a banking business, then U.S. business enterprises will find some way to penetrate that market. This will hold true, and the ultimate results will be the same, whether the state establishes reciprocal branching laws with other states in its region, whether it seeks reciprocity with a few selected states, or even whether it tries to prohibit any entry by out-of-state banks. In short, the form of prohibition is largely an irrelevancy; it will only affect the form of competition, not its extent or substance.

Under these circumstances, attempts to hold back the tide of new entry are simply not practical. They may even be counterproductive if incumbent banks are deluded into thinking they are protected from such entry. If local banks do operate on such a premise, they will avoid making the strategic preparations and decisions necessary to compete successfully in the environment of the remainder of the 1980s. The most appropriate public policy in this situation may well be to announce that in, say, two years, the state will be open to all banks.

Whether it would be beneficial to impose restrictions on which states these banks can come from is an open question. To be fair to local banks, reciprocal agreements should be made with any and all states that wish to enter into such agreements. Then, at least, banks could do business in other states that look attractive or where their current customers do business. However, such reciprocal agreements will not prevent banks located in states that have not entered into a reciprocal agreement from doing business in the state, or indirectly doing business with its residents. Nor will such reciprocity agreements prevent nonbanking firms from offering hybrid forms of banking services.

In short, legislative discussion of the various alternatives is somewhat academic, because interstate banking will continue to expand in many states, irrespective of any action or inaction on the part of the Legislature. The only choice centers on whether the business is done by banks or by nonbanks.

References

Kaufman, George, Larry R. Mote, and Harvey Rosenblum, "The Future of Commercial Banks in the Financial Services Industry," *Staff Memoranda* 83-5, Federal Reserve Bank of Chicago, May 1983.

Rosenblum, Harvey and Diane Siegel, "Competition in Financial Services: The Impact of Nonbank Entry," *Staff Study* 83-1, Federal Reserve Bank of Chicago, 1983.

Rosenblum, Harvey and Christine Pavel, "Financial Services in Transition: The Effects of Nonbank Competitors," Federal Reserve Bank of Chicago, October 1983.

Table 4.1. List of the 32 Companies Analyzed

15 Industrial/Communication/Transportation-Based Companies

Associated First Capital (Gulf & Western)
Armco Financial Services
Borg-Warner Acceptance Corp.
Chrysler Financial Corp.
CIT Financial Corp. (RCA)
Commercial Credit Co. (Control Data)
Diamond Financial Holdings (Dana)
FN Financial Corporation (National Steel)
Ford Motor Credit Company
General Electric Credit Corp.
General Motors Acceptance Corp.
Greyhound Financial Group
IBM
ITT
Westinghouse Credit Corp.

10 Diversified Financial Service Companies

American Express
Avco Financial Services
Baldwin-United Corp.
Beneficial Corp.
Walter E. Heller International
Household International
E.F. Hutton Group
Loews Corp.
Merrill Lynch
Transamerica

4 Insurance-Based Companies

Aetna Life & Casualty
American General Corp./Credithrift Financial
Equitable Life Assurance Society
Prudential (and Bache)

3 Retail-Based Companies

Montgomery Ward
J.C. Penney
Sears

Table 4.2. Estimated Financial Service Earnings of Nonfinancial-Based
Companies

	1962		1972		1982	
	Million dollars	Percent of total earnings	Million dollars	Percent of total earnings	Million dollars	Percent of total earnings
Borg-Warner	$0.5	1.5%	$6.3	10.6%	$37	21.5%
Control Data	nil	nil	55.6	96.2	46	29.7
Ford Motor	0.4	nil	44.1	5.1	229	n.a.
General Electric	8.7	3.3	41.1	7.8	205	11.3
General Motors	40.9	2.8	96.4	4.5	688	71.4
Gulf & Western	nil	nil	29.3	42.1	89	53.4
ITT	1.2	2.9	160.2	33.6	350	51.7
Marcor	nil	nil	9.0	12.4	85	n.a.
Sears	50.4	21.6	209.0	34.0	580	89.2
Westinghouse	0.9	2.0	15.2	7.6	51	11.4
	103.0		666.2		2,360	

Table 4.3 Earnings from Financial Activities, 1981 and 1982:
Manufacturers, Retailers, Diversified Finance Companies, Insurance-Based
Companies, and Bank Holding Companies
($ millions)

Company	Earnings	
	1982	1981
Prudential	2,014	1,576
Citicorp	723	531
General Motors	688	365
Equitable Life Assurance	584	651
American Express	581	518
Sears	580	385
BankAmerica Corp.	447	445
Aetna Life & Casualty	427	462
J.P. Morgan & Co.	394	375
ITT	350	387
Merrill Lynch	309	203
Chase Manhattan Corp.	307	412
Manufacturers Hanover Corp.	295	252
Chemical New York Corp.	241	215
Bankers Trust New York Corp.	239	188
Security Pacific Corp.	234	206
First Interstate Bancorp	221	236

Table 4.4. Percent of Financing in Conjunction with Sales of Parent's Products

Company	1972	1981	1982
General Electric Credit Corp.	9	5	virtually none
Borg-Warner Acceptance Corp.	not available	9	9
Westinghouse Credit Corp.	43	less than 1	less than 1
Associates/G&W	2	1	1
Commercial Credit/Control Data	8	11	11

Table 4.5. Total Domestic Finance Receivables of 30 Selected
Companies Having Over $5 Billion in Receivables: 1981 and 1982
($ billions)

Company	Receivables	
	1982	1981
BankAmerica Corp.	52.4	52.0
Citicorp	49.8	40.6
General Motors	48.2	45.1
Manufacturers Hanover Corp.	26.7	23.1
Prudential/Bache/PruCapital	25.1	23.0
First Interstate Bancorp	23.7	21.3
Continental Illinois Corp.	23.5	23.7
Security Pacific Corp	23.0	19.2
Chase Manhattan Corp.	21.8	21.2
Chemical New York Corp.	20.9	20.3
Ford Motor	17.6	19.5
Wells Fargo & Co.	17.0	16.1
First Chicago Corp.	15.4	14.5
Sears	14.8	13.8
Bankers Trust New York Corp.	14.5	13.0
Equitable Life Assurance	14.0	13.7
General Electric	13.2	11.1
Crocker National Corp.	12.9	12.7
J.P. Morgan & Co.	12.8	12.9
Aetna Life & Casualty	11.2	10.8
Merrill Lynch	10.9	5.1
American Express	10.5	9.5
Mellon National Corp.	9.4	8.1
Marine Midland Banks, Inc.	8.7	7.9
CIT Financial	7.3	7.2
Gulf & Western	6.0	5.9
National Steel	6.0	5.9
Walter Heller	5.5	5.1
ITT	5.2	4.8
IBM	5.2	4.6

Table 4.6. Top 15 Consumer Installment and Revolving Credit Lenders:
1981 and 1982
($ millions)

Company	Installment and Revolving Credit	
	1982	1981
General Motors	35,623	31,077
Citicorp	11,213	9,556
Ford Motor	10,542	11,892
Sears	10,109	9,528
BankAmerica Corp.	9,506	9,703
Prudential/Bache/Prucapital	5,887	5,142
American Express	5,608	5,035
Merrill Lynch	4,778	4,725
First Interstate Bancorp	4,591	4,418
General Electric	4,459	2,792
Security Pacific Corp.	4,354	3,799
J.C. Penney	3,450	3,183
Montgomery Ward	3,291	3,623
Chase Manhattan Corp.	3,085	2,726
Equitable Life Assurance	2,911	2,692

Table 4.7. Domestic Automobile Loans Outstanding as of year-end:
1978-1982

	1982	1981	1980	1979	1978
	(- $ millions - - - - - - - - - - - - - - - - - - -)				
General Motors Acceptance Corp.	$ 33,520	$ 28,545	$ 20,298	$ 17,526	$ 13,519
Percent of total	26%	23%	17%	15%	13%
Ford Motor Credit Co.	$ 9,321	$ 10,450	$ 8,977	$ 7,678	$ 6,527
Percent of total	7%	8%	8%	7%	6%
Chrysler Financial Corp.	$ 1,665	$ 1,948	$ 1,742	$ 1,472	$ 1,728
Percent of total	1%	2%	2%	1%	2%
Total of three auto finance companies	$ 44,506	$ 40,943	$ 31,017	$ 26,676	$ 21,774
Percent of total	34%	32%	27%	23%	21%
Commercial banks	$ 58,851	$ 59,181	$ 61,536	$ 67,367	$ 60,510
Percent of total	45%	47%	53%	58%	60%
Other	$ 26,870	$ 26,307	$ 24,285	$ 22,319	$ 19,363
Percent of total	21%	21%	20%	19%	19%
Total auto loans outstanding	$130,227	$126,431	$116,838	$116,362	$101,647

Table 4.8.   Automobile Credit by Holder
($ billions)

	Amount Outstanding			Net Change During Year			New Loans		
	1978	1981	1982	1978	1981	1982	1978	1981	1982
Commercial Banks	60.5	58.1	58.9	10.9	- 3.5	0.8	53.0	41.6	45.3
Finance Companies	19.9	45.3	48.8	4.7	11.0	3.5	16.5	33.5	32.4
Credit Unions	21.2	22.0	22.6	3.1	0.9	0.6	18.5	18.1	18.3
Total	101.6	125.3	130.3	18.7	8.4	4.9	88.0	93.2	96.0

Table 4.9. Sources of New Consumer Installment Credit to Households

	1978		1981		1982	
	$ billion	percent	$ billion	percent	$ billion	percent
Commercial banks	23.6	55	.6	3	4.4	33
S&Ls	*	*	1.7	9	2.3	18
Finance companies	9.4	22	13.1	72	4.5	34
Credit Unions	6.7	16	1.9	11	1.3	10
Others	3.4	7	.9	5	.6	5
Total	43.1	100	18.2	100	13.1	100

Table 4.10a. Consumer Credit Card Programs of Major Card Issuers

	1972	1981	1982
Number of Active Accounts at Year-End (millions)			
Sears	18.5	24.5	24.8
MasterCard	10.3	22.1	n.a.
Visa	10.0	25.8	28.0
American Express	—	10.0	n.a.
Customer Charge Volume ($ billions)			
Sears	6.3	9.8	10.5
MasterCard	5.9	26.1	30.7
Visa	4.4	29.3	35.3
American Express	—	n.a.	up 17%
Total Customer Account Balances at Year-End ($ billions)			
Sears	4.3	6.8	7.1
MasterCard	2.8	12.3	n.a.
Visa	2.3	15.2	17.6
American Express	—	4.2	4.7

Table 4.10b. Leading Issuers of Credit Cards—1982. Ranked by Customer Account Receivables ($ billions)

Company	Receivables
Sears	7.10
American Express	4.70
Citibank (South Dakota & Buffalo)*	3.28
Bank of America	2.77
First National Bank of Chicago	1.73
Chase Manhattan Bank	0.96
Continental Bank	0.74
Manufacturers Hanover Trust Co.	0.72
Wells Fargo Bank	0.48
Marine Midland Bank	0.47

*Citicorp, the parent of Citibank, has other credit-card-issuing subsidiaries which do not provide detailed information on credit card receivables for three heavily promoted credit cards: Diners Club, Carte Blanche, and the Choice Card.

Table 4.11. Business Lending by Selected Nonbanking-Based Firms and
Banking Holding Companies at Year-End 1981 and 1982
($ millions)

	C&I Loans		Commercial Mortgage Loans		Lease Financing		Total Business Lending	
	1981	1982	1981	1982	1981	1982	1981	1982
Industrial/ Communications/ Transportation	39,365	36,365	1,768	2,036	14,417	15,924	55,550	54,325
Diversified Financial	3,602	4,705	3,054	3,451	1,581	1,419	8,237	9,575
Insurance-Based	399	827	35,506	36,419	892	737	36,797	37,983
Retail-Based	606	605	—	—	—	—	606	605
	43,972	42,502	40,328	41,906	16,890	18,080	101,190	101,883
15 Largest BHCs								
Domestic	141,582	155,527	19,481	20,069	14,279	15,066	175,342	190,662
International	118,021	126,307	5,046	6,462	—	—	123,067	129,655
Total	259,603	281,834	24,527	26,531	14,279	15,066	298,409	320,317
Domestic Offices, All Insured Commercial Banks	327,101	379,566	120,333	132,685	13,168	13,738	460,602	525,989

Table 4.12a. Top 10 Commercial and Industrial Lenders
($ millions)

	1982	1981
Citicorp	18,627	16,442
BankAmerica Corp.	17,580	16,187
Chemical New York Corp.	14,605	14,322
Continental Illinois Corp.	13,715	12,862
Manufacturers Hanover Corp.	12,961	9,866
Chase Manhattan Corp.	11,522	10,563
Security Pacific Corp.	10,051	9,866
General Motors	9,259	10,824
First Interstate Bancorp	8,766	10,464
Bankers Trust New York Corp.	7,694	6,549

Table 4.12b. Top Commercial Mortgage Lenders
($ millions)

Bank Holding Companies	Commercial Mortgage Loans	
	1982	1981
BankAmerica Corp.	4,402	4,643
Continental Illinois Corp.	3,145	3,043
Citicorp	2,915	2,635
First Interstate Bancorp	2,472	n.a.
Wells Fargo & Co.	1,221	1,165
	14,155	11,486
Nonbank Companies		
Prudential	14,675	14,928
Aetna Life & Casualty	10,662	10,219
Equitable Life Assurance	9,399	9,357
American General	1,683	1,002
Transamerica Corp.	1,423	1,329
	37,842	36,835
Bank Holding Cos. & Nonbanks		
Prudential	14,675	14,928
Aetna Life & Casualty	10,662	10,219
Equitable Life Assurance	9,399	9,357
BankAmerica Corp.	4,402	4,643
Continental Illinois Corp.	3,145	3,043
Citicorp	2,915	2,635
First Interstate Bancorp	2,472	n.a.
American General Corp	1,683	1,002
TransAmerica Corp.	1,423	1,329
Wells Fargo & Co.	1,221	1,165

Table 4.13.   Top 15 Lessors
($ millions)

	1982	1981
General Electric	4,188	3,019
Manufacturers Hanover Corp.	3,882	3,601
General Motors	2,910	3,209
Greyhound	2,236	2,044
Ford Motor	2,059	2,088
BankAmerica Corp.	1,925	1,883
Citicorp	1,848	2,044
Security Pacific Corp	1,465	1,195
Continental Illinois Corp.	1,172	1,123
Control Data	1,160	1,211
Chemical New York Corp.	1,148	1,117
First Interstate Bancorp	999	910
Wells Fargo & Co.	920	887
Prudential	737	892
RCA	652	706
Borg-Warner	651	528

Table 4.14. C&I Loan Comparison: Banks vs. Nonbanks

	All Insured Commercial Banks	Top 15 Banks in C&I Lending[b]	Bank Subsidiaries of 15 Largest BHCs[c]
1975	8.5%	23.5%	23.7%
1976	9.5	28.0	28.0
1981	9.6	28.4	28.6
1982	7.8	22.9	23.1

Notes: a. The nine nonbanking companies included ITT, Control Data, RCA, Borg-Warner Acceptance, Chrysler Financial, Ford Motor Credit, GMAC, Gulf & Western, and General Electric Credit.
  b. Ranked by C&I loans.
  c. Ranked by total assets.

Table 4.15. Money Market Fund Assets of Selected Nonbank
Institutions
($ billions)

Company	Net Money Market Fund Assets	
	12/1/82	6/29/83
Merrill Lynch	50.4	33.6
Shearson/American Express	15.5	11.7
Sears/Dean Witter	11.9	8.2
E.F. Hutton	7.7	8.1
Prudential/Bache	4.3	5.2
American General Corp.	0.4	0.3
Transamerica Corp.	0.3	0.3
Equitable Life Assurance	0.4	0.3
Aetna Life & Casualty	0.03	0.0
Ford Motor	not available	not available
Total	90.9	67.7
Total Assets of All MMFs	242.5	178.2

Table 4.16. Depository Institution-Broker Relationships in the Distribution of Insured Retail Deposits as of August 1982

MERRILL LYNCH (475 offices)
ALL-SAVERS CERTIFICATES for 15 thrifts nationwide
RETAIL CDs* for 20 banks and thrifts nationwide including Bank of America
SECONDARY MARKET IN RETAIL CDs of 2 banks and 2 thrifts
91-DAY NEGOTIABLE CDs for Great Western Federal Savings and Loan, Beverly Hills

DEAN WITTER (8 Sears stores with financial center pilot programs and 320 Dean Witter offices nationwide)
RETAIL CDs* for 2 thrifts including Allstate Federal Savings and Loan
SECONDARY MARKET IN RETAIL CDs for City Federal Savings and Loan, New Jersey

BACHE (200 offices in 32 states)
ALL-SAVERS CERTIFICATES for City Federal Savings and Loan
RETAIL CDs* for City Federal Savings and Loan and one S&L in Los Angeles

SHEARSON/AMERICAN EXPRESS (330 domestic offices)
ALL-SAVERS CERTIFICATES for Boston Safe-Deposit & Trust Company
RETAIL CDs* for selected banks and thrifts

FIDELITY MANAGEMENT GROUP (29 offices in 50 states)
ALL-SAVERS CERTIFICATES for 6 banks including Security Pacific National Bank and First National Bank of Chicago

E.F. HUTTON (300 offices in 50 states)
ALL-SAVERS CERTIFICATES for 15 regional banking companies

EDWARD D. JONES & COMPANY (435 offices in 33 states)
ALL-SAVERS CERTIFICATES for Merchants Trust Company, St. Louis

MANLEY, BENNETT, McDONALD & COMPANY (10 offices in 2 states)
ALL-SAVERS CERTIFICATES for First Federal Savings & Loan, Detroit

PAINE WEBBER (240 offices)
ALL-SAVERS CERTIFICATES for 2 banks in California, including Bank of America

CHARLES SCHWAB & CO. (offices in 38 states)
ALL-SAVERS CERTIFICATES for First Nationwide Savings and Loan, San Francisco

THE VANGUARD GROUP (offices in 50 states)
ALL-SAVERS CERTIFICATES for Bradford Trust Company, Boston

---

*3 1/2-, 4-, 5-year, and zero coupon certificates of deposit.

Source: Various issues of *American Banker* and other general business periodicals.

Table 4.17. Geographic Locations of Major Financial Firms that Provide Credit: 1981

Bank Holding Companies

		Offices	
	States	Nonbanking	Banking*
Citicorp	40 & D.C.	422	25
BankAmerica Corp.	40 & D.C.	360	38
Chase Manhattan Corp.	15 & D.C.	42	4
Manufacturers Hanover Corp.	32	471	28
Continental Illinois Corp.	14	20	28
Chemical New York Corp.	23	135	6
J.P. Morgan & Co.	6	7	5
First Interstate Bancorp	13	19	24
Security Pacific Corp.	39	427	7
Bankers Trust New York Corp.	4	2	8
First Chicago Corp.	27	23	14
Wells Fargo & Co.	16	52	6
Crocker National Corp.	6	15	5
Marine Midland Banks, Inc.	5	14	not available
Mellon National Corp.	13 & D.C.	151	11

Other Major Creditors

	States	Offices**
American Express	50	1400 Plus
American General's Credithrift Financial	24	524
Avco Corp.	47	694
Beneficial Corp.	36	1468
Control Data's Commercial Credit	50	900
Ford Motor Credit Co.	50	200
General Electric Credit Corp.	50	480
General Motors Acceptance Corp.	50	310
G&W's Associates First Capital Corp.	50	670
Household International	47	1260
ITT	31	590
Merrill Lynch	50	475
Sears	50	1260

*These figures are exclusive of banking branches in their home states but include offices of bank subsidiaries.

**Avco Financial closed 539 offices in 1981; Beneficial has closed 576 offices since 1980, stopped making loans in 12 states, and sold its operations in Alabama and Tennessee; Household International closed 271 consumer finance offices in 1981; and the Associates consolidated 240 domestic offices in 1981.

Source: Annual Reports and 10-K forms.

Changing Financial Structure and Economic Development

Thomas G. Gies

Introduction

Much of this analysis of interstate banking necessarily focuses on the impact of potential change in the law governing interstate banking on the banking institutions themselves. For example, in other chapters we consider economies of scale to the bank, the structure and development of banking organizations, and the intensity of competition among banks. These are relevant and necessary considerations. *But underlying the legislative interest in this topic is the impact of regional interstate banking on the user of credit.* Present legislative attention *is not focused primarily on the success and survival of banks per se, but on the ability to establish an environment in which users of credit and other financial services will best be served.* It is this topic which will be addressed in the pages that follow, using the state of Florida as a case study.

Present Credit Structure in Florida Markets

Out-of-state financial institutions already have a significant presence in Florida financial markets. It has been reported that major non-Florida based financial institutions operate in major Florida markets in the forms shown in Table 5.1.[1]

Retail Credit

The firms involved in these activities are major out-of-state banks, out-of-state nonbank financial institutions, and out-of-state nonfinance based firms. Based upon a study at the Federal Reserve Bank of Chicago (4) setting forth the penetration of major suppliers of credit on a multi-state basis, it can reasonably

Table 5.1

Type of Credit	Type of Institution	No. of Offices
Retail Credit	Finance Companies	260
	Mortgage Companies	52
	Trust Companies	19
Commercial Credit	Loan Servicing Offices	72
	Leasing	44
	Insurance	72
	Loan Production Offices	6
	Edge Act Corporations	45
	International Banking Facilities	71

be assumed that Florida retail markets either now or in the near future will be offered credit from such firms as the following, regardless of what decision is made on the reciprocal interstate banking question:

Table 5.2

Type of Firm	Name of Firm
Industrial-Communication-Transportation	G.M.A.C.
	Ford Motor Credit
	General Electric Credit
	CIT Financial Associates (Gulf & Western)
	ITT Financial Corporation
	Chrysler Finance Company
	Borg Warner Acceptance
	Westinghouse Credit
	IBM Credit
Diversified Finance Companies	American Express
	Beneficial
	Merrill Lynch
	Walter E. Heller
	Household
	E.F. Hutton
	Transamerica
	Baldwin United
Insurance Based Finance Companies	Prudential-Bache
	Equitable
	American General

Source: Rosenblum, H. and D. Siegel, *Competition in Financial Services: The Impact of Non Bank Entry*. Federal Reserve Bank of Chicago, Staff Study, 83-1.

Wholesale Credit

A similar set of facts can be offered with regard to business credit either presently available from non-Florida based financial and non-financial firms or which can reasonably be expected to become available in the near future. The data supplied below are based upon national markets, but the favorable position held by Florida in the ranking of markets nationally, virtually assures that this state will not be overlooked in the competition for market share.

Table 5.3. Business-Type Credits Provided by Nonfinancial Firms and by Bank Holding Companies—Year End 1981 (000,000)

Type of Firm	Total Business Credit
Industrial, Communication, Transportation	55,550
Diversified Financial Companies	8,237
Insurance Based Companies	36,797
Retail-Based Companies	606
Total	101,190
15 Largest BHC	298,409
	399,599
All Insured Commercial Banks	460,602

Source: Rosenblum, H. and Siegel, D. *Competition in Financial Services: The Impact of Non Bank Entry.* Federal Reserve Bank of Chicago, Staff Study, 83-1.

The volume of business credit offered by nonbanks in the U.S. (and presumably a corresponding proportion in Florida) was slightly over $100 billion at year end 1981 or more than 10% of all commercial credit. In addition the big bank holding companies, many of whom have loan production and loan servicing operations in Florida, provided almost $300 billion more, for a total of business credit by firms which are able to operate freely across state boundaries of approximately $400 billion, *nearly half of all commercial credit provided in the U.S.* By comparison, total commercial lending by all domestic offices of U.S. commercial banks was approximately $460 billion. If the data for Florida are in rough proportion to the national data offered here, it means that Florida business borrowers have about as easy access to credit—and in fact do obtain credit as frequently—from out-of-state sources as from in-state banks. This is a very broad generalization, obviously, and circumstances for borrowing and access to out-of-state sources of credit vary greatly from one borrower to another. Nevertheless, these data are strongly indicative of the extent of an already existing infrastructure of credit facilities supplied in major part from out-of-state sources.

Competition for Deposit Funds in Florida Markets

In the past two years, competition for the roughly $100 billion in Florida deposit funds has taken on a significantly different dimension. Until fairly recently, deposit funds were subject to competition almost entirely from local commercial banks and, for time deposits, from local thrift institutions. Second, the competition was largely nonprice in character. Most commonly, competition took the form of convenience of location for the depositor-customer, and favorable branch locations were prime competitive tools. However, with the advent of the aggressive, unregulated money market funds and the virtual demise of Regulation Q, local market competition has changed radically.

The money market fund quickly became a household institution in the U.S. between 1978 and 1983 and nationally now exceeds $200 billion in volume. These funds permit individuals to deposit, withdraw on demand with little delay or transaction cost, and receive interest rates highly superior to the old bank rates under Regulation Q. The differences between money market fund yields and bank rates on deposit funds have been as much as 10-15 percentage points in the past four years. No wonder depositors in Florida and elsewhere have flocked to the funds. But aggressive bankers under the new deregulation mode have responded with counter offers for depositors' attention, and it is now commonplace to find advertised rates in the *Wall Street Journal* and local dailies offering depositors convenient deposit service at money market rates. Commonly, contact is as easy as banking locally, simply by dialing an 800 number. Citibank recently invited readers of the *Wall Street Journal* to contact a representative about rates and terms. Their ad ran alongside that of a prominent money market fund.

Moreover, new affiliations have been formed which make former competitors into cooperating out-of-state financial institutions effectively reaching local Florida markets. Merrill Lynch now markets an all-savers certificate in Florida through its extensive network of retail offices. The certificates are issued by Bank of America and Crocker National Bank in California. Merrill Lynch is not unique in this type of joint product. Sears/Dean Witter, Shearson/American Express and E.F. Hutton—who collectively operate scores of offices in Florida—also now compete with local banks and thrifts for deposit funds.

Ability of Out-of-State Banks to Serve and Compete in Florida Markets

There are now 50 out-of-state banking offices operating in Florida through bank holding companies (BHCs). This was the number at the time of the latest count published by the Federal Reserve Bank of Atlanta. It is likely that the number is now larger.

How does this happen? In a number of ways. An out-of-state BHC is permitted to provide financial services through a brick and mortar presence as long as the operation is not legally a bank—that is, does not make commercial loans *and* accept demand deposits. In other words, it can do one or the other, as long as it does not do both. Major out-of-state banks are now operating in Florida, as well as in other non home-office states, and providing interstate banking services. At present there is no legal prohibition against a bank holding company in one state advertising and accepting demand and saving deposits from customers in another state. Out-of-state bank holding companies are now offering credit cards, debit cards, cash management accounts, electronic funds transfers and other financial services in Florida.

Altogether, Florida had 621 offices of out-of-state financial organizations offering a wide variety of banking services as of the most recent survey by the Federal Reserve Bank of Atlanta.

Imbalance in Supply-Demand Relationships in Florida Financial Markets

We have presented evidence in the preceding sections of this chapter showing that there is currently a substantial and growing out-of-state bank and nonbank financial presence in the Florida market. Out-of-state financial firms now provide billions of dollars of credit to the Florida market from more than 600 offices.

With this combination of domestically based banks plus several score out-of-state financial firms, how well is the state's economy served? Florida's economy must be well-served in a financial sense because it has enjoyed a vigorous growth rate—population, income, and employment gains have substantially exceeded the national average during the past decade. Further, financial indexes for Florida—deposits and loans per capita and per employed person—are close to the national averages, characteristically within one or two percentage points of national figures. Of course, we can speculate on how much higher Florida growth might have been had the state's local financial resources been supplemented even more extensively from nonstate funds.

Table 5.4 provides a striking comparison of the high growth Florida has enjoyed in the past decade, with population expanding almost four times as

Table 5.4. Population, Employment, and Income Growth 1970-82
(change in percent)

	Florida	U.S.	Florida: U.S.
Population	52.2	13.6	3.8:1
Employment	74.8	27.1	2.8:1
Income	338	218	1.6:1

rapidly as the U.S. as a whole; employment increased nearly three times as fast as for the U.S.; and income at 1-1/2 times the national rate of gain. This has been a truly impressive performance and would lead to corresponding expectation for financial development. Florida has in fact increased, both in deposits and loans, but the growth has not produced corresponding superiority in the per capita level of deposits and loans. The accompanying data in table 5.5 indicate that Florida continues to be slightly *below* the national average.

Table 5.5.   Deposits and Loans: Florida vs. U.S.—1982

	Per Capita Deposits	Relative to U.S.	Per Capita Loans	Relative to U.S.
Florida	$8,977	98%	$6,538	91%
U.S.	9,119	100	7,181	100

Would a more extensive supply of deposits and a more liberal volume of credit have generated even higher growth in the state? There is a presumptive relationship between financial resources and economic development, but we do not at present have models which make clear whether financial developments lead, coincide with, or follow general economic growth. That is, we do not have clear evidence that Florida's favorable general economic development occurred because of a favorable financial infrastructure, or whether its deposit-loan growth followed and was a result of general economic development; or, third, whether the two types of growth occurred more-or-less simultaneously.

It would be nice to be able to offer a definite answer for these questions; if financial growth *precedes* general growth and is a necessary precondition, then we would wish to establish a functional banking relationship with states or regions which were rich in banking facilities and deposit volume. If the reverse is true, that is, that a high rate of general economic development is necessary to deposit accumulation, then affiliation with high growth states or regions would seem desirable, regardless of financial wealth.

The southeastern group of states currently mentioned as candidates for a regional interstate group are Alabama, Georgia, Louisiana, Mississippi, North Carolina, South Carolina, Tennessee, and Virginia. What are the facts regarding general economic development and financial development for this group of southeastern states?

Tables 5.6 and 5.7 are designed to summarize this information.

Clearly, the southeastern region is an area of comparatively high population growth, high employment growth, and high income growth in the 1971-81 period. By all three measures, the southeastern group exceeds the performance of the U.S. as a whole—and by a wide margin. However, it is

Table 5.6.   Growth Measured by Selected Demographic and Economic Changes of the Southeast*, 1971-81

	Southeast Region	U.S. Total
Population	15.2%	10.5%
Employment	36.3	29.0
Income	302	208

*Includes: Alabama, Georgia, Louisiana, Mississippi, North Carolina, South Carolina, Tennessee, and Virginia.

Table 5.7.   Deposits and Loans: Southeastern Region*, Relative to U.S. 1982

Per Capita Deposits	Relative to U.S.	Per Capita Loans	Relative to U.S.
$5,904	65%	$4,119	57%

* Includes: Alabama, Georgia, Louisiana, Mississippi, North Carolina, South Carolina, Tennessee, and Virginia.

similarly evident that, apart from Florida, the southeastern group falls below the U.S. levels on a per capita deposit and loan measurement—again, by a wide margin.

For the policy question at hand, should Florida adopt a regionally oriented interstate banking posture, the answer should turn on the impact which such a change would have, not on the banking-financial institution industry in Florida, but upon the state's economy more broadly. On the basis of the facts available and our knowledge of their relationship, it appears that (1) the attractive general economic growth of the southeastern states would provide a strong loan market for Florida banks. However, by the same type of reasoning, the southeastern region does not appear to be a potentially rich source of deposit funds—which may fully offset the beneficial effects of the southeast as a loan market. From a broader economic viewpoint, Florida may well have little to gain from affiliating with a group of "financial have nots". There is relatively little likelihood of the southeastern region serving as a rich source of deposit funds to be drawn into Florida and there may be high likelihood that these financial "have not" states would look to Florida banks for financing and, tend to siphon off loan funds from the Florida market.

Implications and Conclusions of Recent Financial Innovations for Local Florida Banking Markets

The facts of the local Florida banking market have changed radically in the past three years and represent an irreversible break with the past.

1. Both out-of-state BHCs and nonbank suppliers of financial services have developed new, innovative networks for providing services including traditional loan and deposit services across state lines.

2. The growth of both BHC offices and nonbank offices into contact with virtually all Florida markets—literally anywhere telephone and postal service exist—indicates that users of financial services are no longer limited to local bank sources.

3. As a significant, though not central conclusion, we should note that present interstate banking limitations are probably affecting the economics of banking in Florida more sharply than the development of the Florida economy. That is, the changes we have outlined in the form of financial firms in the Florida market represent a competitive threat to existing Florida based banks. However, the new competitors may have positive beneficial effects on nonfinancial sectors of the Florida economy—agriculture, industry, and trade.

4. It should be unequivocally clear that a regional interstate banking prescription is unlikely to afford Florida banks protection from interstate competition. The out-of-state competition is already present in Florida, is strong and growing stronger. A regional interstate banking statute will have no perceptible effect on this wave of new services being offered the Florida public by out-of-state bank and non-bank sources.

5. There is always some danger that any geographic "opening up" of financial markets will cause a net outflow rather than inflow of funds, and this has been used as a basis for resisting intrastate branch banking legislation, in earlier years, regional interstate banking, and national interstate banking. However, the combination of statutory deregulation of the financial firms at the Federal level and the rapid advance of technology in the field of financial information transmission, processing, and storage is making interstate banking an accomplished fact in the United States. *Florida could not avoid this rapid evolutionary change, even if it appeared desirable, and there is no clear reason for believing that it would be desirable for this rapidly growing state.*

Notes

1.   John M. Godfrey, "Reciprocity and Florida Banking", unpublished memorandum, April 4, 1983, p. 4.

References

Federal Reserve Bank of Atlanta, *Monthly Review,* September 1982, May 1983.

Kaufman, George, Larry R. Mote, Harvey Rosenblum. *The Future of Commercial Banks in the Financial Services Industry,* Occasional Paper 83-5, Federal Reserve Bank of Chicago.

Proceedings of a Conference on Bank Structure and Competition, Federal Reserve Bank of Chicago, 1981.

Rosenblum, Harvey and Diane Siegel, *Competition in Financial Services: The Impact of the Non Bank Entry.* Staff Study 83-1, Federal Reserve Bank of Chicago.

Southern Growth Policies Board, *Report of the 1980 Commission on the Future of the South.* 1981.

Spellman, L.J., *The Depository Firm and Industry.* Academic Press, 1983.

Youle, J.J., *Competitive Analysis of the Banking Industry and its Implications for the Future.* University of Michigan, 1983, unpublished thesis.

6

The Cost of Banking Operations and Interstate Banking

George J. Benston

Issues and Concerns

The removal of constraints on interstate banking, either regionally or nationally, is likely to lead to the development of larger banks. This, in turn, has implications for the costs of banking operations, if it were the case that the costs incurred by larger banks differed from those incurred by the smaller banks that they might compete with and possibly displace.

In this regard, two principal concerns might be distinguished: (1) efficiency and (2) competition. If it were the case that larger banks could be operated more efficiently than smaller banks, all other things equal, the cost of providing services to consumers could be less. Consequently, the amounts consumers paid for the services could be lower and/or the quality of the services provided could be greater. At the same time, if larger banks had a significant operating cost advantage over smaller banks, the result of permitting the development of larger national or regional banks might be the demise of smaller banks. This could have serious implications for consumers of banking services as well as for the bankers who provide those services.

Fortunately, some recent studies have provided some estimates of the costs incurred by banks of different sizes and with differing numbers of branches. While these analyses are not perfect, they are informative. Before these findings are described, it is best to specify some of the principal assumptions and shortcomings of the studies so that the results can be meaningfully interpreted.

Conceptual and Measurement Problems

Any study of costs depends critically on how "cost" and "output" are measured. Each is discussed briefly in turn.

Cost

Cost in the research reviewed refers to the costs of banking operations, as recorded in the accounting records of the banks studied. Fortunately, the annual accounting-based costs of banks generally provide good measures of their economic (opportunity) costs. Accounting numbers, such as depreciation, that yield poor representations of economic values are of relatively small importance for banks.

But several important aspects of costs are not well measured in the research. The two most important of these are consumer-borne costs and risk. Consumer-borne costs include the costs of inconvenience and search. In particular, branches usually offer consumers savings in travel time. Unit banks, on the other hand, may offer consumers efficiencies in providing information if decisions were made more directly. These advantages are reflected largely in the revenues of the banks rather than in their costs. The risk of bank failure is likely to be lower when a bank's portfolio of loans and deposit sources is geographically diversified. This advantage of national and regional banks also is not captured in the cost studies.

Output

For the purpose of measuring bank operations cost, output is best measured in terms of the things that banks do that cause costs to be incurred. Consequently, output is defined as the number of transactions that a bank processes. The studies reviewed measure output as the number of loans and deposit accounts a bank services and as the average balances in these accounts (since larger accounts tend to be more expensive to service.) These measures are preferable to total dollars of deposits or assets. Since a $1,000 check doesn't cost 10 times more to process than a $100 check or a $100,000 loan 10 times more to service than a $10,000 loan, were these measures used banks that serviced customers with larger balances would seem to be more efficient than banks that dealt mostly with individuals and small businesses. This would be equivalent to concluding that wholesaling was cheaper per item than retailing. While this is true, it could lead to the incorrect inference that retailing is inefficient.

The Evidence[1]

Studies of bank costs conducted with data from the 1950s through the late 1960s generally revealed some economies of scale. In general banks were found to have operating costs that were about 93% of the costs of banks half their size. The banks that appeared to have been at an operating cost disadvantage were those with less than about $150 million in deposits (in 1983 dollars.) These studies, however, suffered from some limitations, including only partial measures of output and a form of the estimating equation that did not allow for the possibility that costs might first decrease and then increase as bank output increased. In addition, the widespread availability of computers for even the smallest of banks have changed the nature of operating costs since these earlier studies were conducted.

The most recent study used Federal Reserve Functional Cost Analysis (FCA) data reported by from 747 to 852 banks for the years 1975 through 1978. Since the FCA program is voluntary, it is likely to include banks that are more conscious than most of the value of cost control. The banks studied range in size up to $1 billion in deposits. A measure of total bank output was constructed that, in effect, is a weighted total of the numbers of loans and deposit accounts serviced by each bank (the weights are in proportion to the bank's direct costs of each type of account.) Operating costs exclude the cost of other banking functions, such as safe deposit box, trust, customer computer services and investments. Other factors that cause costs to differ among banks, such as labor and capital costs that vary by area, holding company affiliation, and number of branch offices operated, were accounted for. Since branch banks tend to expand by adding branches rather than by just adding customers, increases in output for these banks were assumed to be accompanied by additional branches. In addition banks in states that permit branching were analyzed separately from banks in unit banking states.

Among the findings that are relevant to Florida (a branch banking state) and to the issue of national or regional interstate banking, the research revealed the following:

- Banks with more than $25 million in deposits experienced statistically significant diseconomies of scale. For example, banks with from $25 to $50 million in deposits had operating costs that averaged 9% more than banks half their size, while the costs of banks with deposits over $400 million averaged 16% more than banks half their size. (As noted above, output is measured by the weighted number of deposit and loan accounts, with factors other than the number of branches operated held constant. Bank size is described by dollars of deposits for the convenience of readers who are more used to thinking of banks in this way.)

- The economies of scale are about the same for each of the four years studied, 1975-78.
- Not surprisingly, larger-sized accounts were proportionately less costly to process than smaller accounts. These costs probably reflect the cost of monitoring larger loans and of paying interest on demand deposits in the form of "free" services. However, the smaller banks had almost no additional costs associated with larger account sizes, but the costs of the largest deposit size banks almost doubled when their average account sizes doubled. These higher costs might reflect the greater range of services that large banks typically provide.
- Holding company affiliation was not associated with significantly higher or lower operating costs.
- The costs of operating branches appear to be slightly greater than the costs of operating unit banks of the same size. However, larger banks experience relatively higher branching costs than do smaller banks.

Implications of the Evidence

The research indicates that most smaller banks are not at an operating cost disadvantage with respect to larger banks. Nor are the branches of larger banks likely to be operated at lower cost than are the branches of smaller banks or of unit banks. Thus, with respect to operating costs, the evidence gives no grounds for fears that national or regional interstate banking would result in the domination of local banks by banks headquartered elsewhere that expand into the state.

However, the evidence does not imply that consumers might not benefit from interstate banking. As is noted above, consumer-borne costs are not included in the studies. Hence, consumers could benefit from banks that offer them more convenient outlets, including offices in other states. In addition, the studies did not include consideration of the value to consumers of specialized services, such as import-export banking, corporate and personal trust, and regional and national account collection and check disbursement. Larger, national or regional banks might be able to provide such services more efficiently than can smaller banks. On the other hand, the smaller banks probably have a competitive advantage in being able to offer their customers more direct, personalized service.

Local bankers also could benefit from national or regional interstate banking. Some bankers could serve their customers better if they were permitted to open branch offices in other states. The public in other states might find such bankers better able to meet their needs than are their present bankers. And some bankers might find selling out to or merging with banks headquartered in other states preferable to continuing to operate independently. Last, but not least, the risk of bank failure would be reduced if local banks were offered the opportunity of greater geographic diversification.

In summary, were a state such as Florida to permit national or regional interstate banking, there is little reason to believe that local banks would not be able to compete with the banks that might seek to enter the state. Consumers, both businesses and individuals, are likely to benefit from having a wider range of institutions that want their business. Some of these institutions are likely to provide some specialized services that present banks are not now offering (or offer at higher prices.) Or it may be that locally based institutions will develop these services in response to competition. Or the local institutions might be more effective providers of financial services to consumers in other states than are the institutions in those states. Though the available data and studies cannot speak directly to these possibilities, they do indicate that neither banks or consumers are likely to be damaged from national or regional interstate banking.

Notes

1.   For a review of this evidence and references to the published studies, see George J. Benston, Gerald A. Hanweck, and David B. Humphrey, "Operating Costs in Commercial Banking," *Economic Review* (Federal Reserve Bank of Atlanta), November 1982, pp. 6-21.

7

Geographic Expansion in Banking: An Analysis of Issues and Alternative Solutions

Vincent P. Apilado

Introduction

The ability of commercial banks to expand geographically has been regulated for many decades. Because of dual chartering and the presence of state boundaries, the regulation has been dichotomized into a set of rules for each of the respective states with regard to their state-chartered banks and a set of federal rules with regard to nationally-chartered banks.

Generally, the federal rules make national banks in the various states largely subservient to rules for state banks. This subservience reflects the tenaciously held belief of local governments that each state should have the unfettered right to dictate its own banking structure. Thus, geographic expansion on the part of individual banks, where allowed, has been predominantly an intrastate phenomenon.

The question at hand is whether the commercial banking industry should continue to be geographically restricted in its expansionary efforts. As will be seen, several factors have developed over the years that call for a current assessment of these restrictions. The assessment would consider not only the possibility of interstate expansion, but also whether any remaining intrastate restrictions on the part of individual states should be further loosened. In addition, the assessment would consider the method of expansion, whether through *de novo* entry or acquisition as well as via a bank holding company.

This chapter first describes the legislative framework regulating the geographic expansion of banks. It then explains why this framework may be incongruous with reality. The major issues regarding bank expansion are given in the next section, with a summary of related empirical evidence. Finally, the conclusions and implications are presented, including a discussion of the methods—and their feasibility—of easing the branching restrictions on the banking industry.

Background

Legislative Framework

Historically, federal regulations have deferred to state regulations concerning the geographic expansion of banking. Since a bank would typically expand through the setting up of a branch, these regulations are generically referred to as branching regulations.

The current federal restrictions on branching are embodied in the McFadden Act of 1927. Prior to this, national banks, wherever located, could operate only one full-service office. As our nation's population grew and became more spatially distributed, the limitation to one office created a competitive disadvantage for national banks. State banks were often free to branch within their city limits in accordance with their state regulations. To forestall the resultant increasing conversion of national banks to state charters, the McFadden Act was passed giving national banks similar branching rights within city limits as granted state banks in their respective states. And the Banking Act of 1933 amended the McFadden Act by extending the branching privilege of national banks to beyond the city limits if state law permitted state banks this freedom.

Thus, all national banks are restrained by the assorted branching laws of the 50 states as a result of the McFadden Act. The controlling factor in branch banking, therefore, is the framework of state branching regulations. Among the states, these regulations range from the allowance of statewide branching (22 states presently) or limited branching (18 states) to unit banking (10 states). Not only can the states vary at any one time as to which category of branching is allowed, an individual state can change its category over time. For example, Florida was a unit banking state until 1977 when it changed to countywide branching; and in 1980, it became a statewide branching state.

Up until the 1950s, the multi-bank holding company (BHC) was frequently used by innovative bankers as a mechanism to branch in disregard of intrastate branching restrictions, as well as to establish interstate banking networks not covered by state or federal laws. Pressure to restrict such growth resulted in the Holding Company Act of 1956. Section 3(d) of the Act, referred to as the Douglas Amendment, prohibited a BHC from acquiring a bank in any but its home state unless specifically allowed by state law. In 1970 the Act was extended to cover one-bank holding companies and to provide for certain restrictions on the "nonbanking" activities of BHCs.

In summary, the McFadden Act and the Douglas Amendment set the broad parameters for the geographic expansion of banking. The first parameter is that a bank or BHC generally may not have a full-service office in other than its home state. Second, national banks and state banks are subject to the same geographic restrictions on expansion within a state. Third, each state has the right and responsibility to determine its position on multi-office banking and what the structural details will be.

Erosion of Geographic Barriers

Regulatory loopholes, unregulated competition, and technological innovations have served to weaken the effectiveness and relevance of legal restrictions on the geographic expansion of banking.

Regulatory Loopholes

There are many regulatory loopholes. The most important involve bank holding companies, loan production offices, Edge Act corporations, and foreign banks.

BHCs are allowed in many states that do not permit branching *per se.* Thus, the BHC device has been a legal way to establish a quasi-branching intrastate network of subsidiary banks. Further, the Douglas Amendment grandfathered 12 BHCs which continue to do banking business in other than their home state. In addition, BHCs are permitted to acquire nonbank subsidiaries in other states. Because these nonbank subsidiaries are generally free to open offices on an interstate basis, BHCs have used them as a means to evade interstate restrictions and provide interstate financial services. These services include, among others, consumer financing, insurance agency activity, credit life underwriting, loan servicing, mortgage banking, and leasing. Presently, BHCs control over 380 nonbank subsidiaries located in 37 states. These subsidiaries operate at least 5,500 offices outside the home state of the parent holding company.

Loan production offices, although they cannot make loans, accept deposits or pay checks, represent an important interstate activity of banks. An LPO operates at the commercial or retail level soliciting or originating loans for its bank. Presently, it is estimated that nearly 400 LPOs operate in about half the states.

Edge Act Corporations are organizational devices a bank can employ outside its home state to provide both loan and deposit services related to the international trade of the bank's customers. There are over 140 Edge Act offices of domestic organizations located in the United States, with the majority in regional financial and trade centers.

Until the International Banking Act of 1978 (IBA), foreign banks were able to open branches and/or agencies in more than one state. Further, foreign BHCs could have a subsidiary bank in one state and branches of the foreign parent bank and/or agency in other states where allowed. Although the IBA closed these loopholes, it grandfathered 30 foreign banking organizations conducting business in other than their home state. In addition, the IBA allowed foreign banks to create Edge Act Corporations, thereby allowing them to offer interstate banking services, albeit limited to international trade.

Unregulated Competition

Banks have many nonbank competitors in both the lending and deposit-taking areas. They include depository as well as nondepository institutions.

Depository institutions include mutual savings banks (MSBs), savings and loan associations (S&Ls) and credit unions (CUs). Generally, they are not subject to the regulatory framework governing the geographic expansion of banks. Further, the broadened asset and liability powers given them by the Depository Institutions Deregulation and Monetary Control Act of 1980 should increase their competitive stance, especially at the retail level, with commercial banks.

MSBs as of 1978 can convert from a state charter to a federal charter if they so wish. With approval of the Federal Home Loan Bank Board (FHLBB), a federally-chartered MSB can branch interstate anywhere regardless of more restrictive state law. Also, federally-chartered S&Ls in all states have been permitted by the FHLBB as of 1980 to pursue full intrastate branching. In addition, the common bond requirement of CUs allows them to conduct operations wherever their members are located. As their members disperse and/or the common bond requirement becomes more loosely defined, CU membership may become more broadly available geographically, thereby enhancing the possibilities of CUs for interstate and intrastate expansion.

From the standpoint of bank competition and geographic expansion, the most significant nondepository institutions are stock brokerage firms and money market mutual funds (MMFs). Many stock brokerage firms offer checking accounts, consumer loans and other financial services, and are free to locate throughout the United States. Where brokerage firms have merged with others to form financial conglomerates (e.g., Dean Witter with Sears, and Shearson Loeb Rhoades with American Express), the resultant competition with banks, both in product and geography, should be even more formidable. MMFs, by investing in short-term instruments, compete directly with bank retail deposits when money market yields are relatively high. Many MMFs also offer checking accounts to their investors. Because of the largely inverted yield curve prevalent over the last decade, MMFs have grown at a rate much faster than other financial intermediary. MMFs solicit funds throughout the United States, while the retail deposits of banks are largely local in origin. The growth in MMF deposits has been, at least in part, at the expense of commercial bank deposits.

Technological Innovations

Historically, the delivery of financial services by banks to their retail customers has been mostly a face-to-face matter. Households by necessity would have to go to the bank's premises to carry out most transactions. While the telephone and mail service have somewhat lessened the amount of personal interaction required to implement financial transactions, banks have still felt the need to provide conveniently located offices for the general population.

New technological innovations offer the opportunity to beneficially change the public's banking habits. The development of retail electronic banking services is decreasing the need for branch offices. Automated teller machines (ATMs) allow customers to deposit, withdraw, and transfer funds as well as make credit payments and obtain personal loans. Point-of-sale (POS) services, while not as widely available as ATMs, can allow customers check authorization/guarantee services, credit authorization services, direct debiting of account for immediate payment of purchases, and the same services of ATMs but at retail locations. Home banking via personal computer is still in the experimental stage but should eventually allow customers at home or office to access their accounts.

The components of an interstate retail electronic banking system are being fitted together, concentrating first on the formation of ATM networks. A current stumbling block has been the legal interpretation that an ATM constitutes a branch bank. Despite this, continuing technological developments will render geographical barriers to banking expansion increasingly archaic.

Major Issues

It is clear that the case for continued restrictions against the geographic expansion of banking warrants examination. This examination will concentrate on the major public policy issues that have been associated over the years with the branch banking-unit banking controversy and summarize related empirical research. The issues include: convenience and needs, safety and soundness, credit allocation, operating efficiency, competition and concentration, and preservation of the dual banking system. Where available, pertinent research findings on holding company banking will also be given. For the most part, they will contrast BHC-affiliated banks with independent (unit) banks. There are very few studies contrasting branch banks with BHC-affiliated banks. One reason for this is the somewhat plausible assumption, given that BHCs are commonly viewed as an interim step between unit banking and branch banking, that the net advantages (disadvantages) of branch banking are greater (less) than for holding company banking.

Convenience and Needs

Does branch banking better serve the convenience and needs of the public than unit banking? To answer this one must first define what is meant by convenience and needs. Convenience is usually defined in terms of the number of banking offices for a given size of population. Needs are usually defined in terms of the number of different banking services made available to the public.

Studies on convenience using the above definition usually assume that the number of banking facilities (normalized for population size) captures most of the aspects of convenience normally identified as important to customers. These other aspects include, for the most part, location, hours of operation, and adequacy of staffing. The assumption in part has been confirmed through other studies, i.e., that the greater the number of facilities, the greater the providing of desirable locations. The findings regarding hours of operation and adequacy of staffing are less clearcut. In general, these appear to be more a function of the local competitive environment and internal cost factors.

Empirical research clearly indicates that branch banking provides more offices per population than unit banking. This is strongly the case in metropolitan areas. A less favorable margin, nevertheless positive, also has been found to be the case for smaller towns or nonmetropolitan areas. On the other side, branch banking has tended to reduce the number of individual banks primarily because of the bank incentives associated with branching via merger or acquisition. The reduction in bank number has competitive implications and will be dealt with in the section on competition and concentration.

Regarding the availability of bank services (needs), related studies likewise establish the broader offerings of branch banks as compared to unit banks. This is also a finding, although less documented, for holding company affiliated banks relative to independent banks. In some cases, however, the greater availability is more nominal than real. Further, the studies are nebulous regarding whether or not the small unit or nonaffiliated banks would have made available additional services, as via a correspondent relationship, if customer demand so warranted.

Safety and Soundness

Does branch banking contribute to a higher rate of bank failure than unit banking? The consensus of related research is that branch banking states have lower failure rates than unit banking states. On the other hand, the average deposit size of failed banks in branch banking states is larger. Further, the proportion of banks on the FDIC Problem List is slightly larger for branch banking states relative to unit banking states, but slightly lower for BHC-affiliated banks compared to unit banks.

Branch banks and BHC-affiliated banks typically attain greater leverage and riskier portfolios than unit banks. It is not clear whether this apparent risk-taking is greater than is socially desirable. The argument is often given that multi-office banking systems are inherently capable of handling more risk than unit banks given their greater possibilities for geographic diversification. More broadly, bank failure studies indicate that the primary reasons for failure involve illegal managerial factors (fraud, defalcation, insider dealings, etc.) and not multi-office status. Thus, one must question the relevance of the issue of safety and soundness in considering the status of geographic restrictions against bank expansion, notwithstanding the fact of lower failure rates in branching states vis-à-vis unit banking states.

Credit Allocation

Does branch banking contribute to a better allocation of credit than unit banking? This question has several dimensions: (1) the transferring of funds from low demand areas to high demand areas; (2) the proportion of funds directed to meet local credit needs; (3) the relative priority given larger customers as compared to smaller ones; and (4) the relative priority given head office cities as compared to nonurban areas.

Regarding the first dimension, studies show that branch banks transfer a greater proportion of loanable funds to areas of higher credit demand. The likely reason for this is the lower level of transaction costs and other frictions associated with transfers between related branch banks as opposed to independent banks. In this regard, it is suggested that the transfer capabilities of unit-bank correspondent relationships do not equal that of branch banks.

Regarding the second dimension, branching has been found to result in a larger proportion of business loans going to local firms than is provided by unit banking. The research on this dimension, however, is sparse.

Regarding the third dimension, very little comprehensive research has been done. The few studies at the requisite level of detail reveal that while branch banks may allocate a smaller proportion of their loans to smaller customers than unit banks, that the absolute dollar amounts may not significantly differ. In short, more research is needed.

Regarding the fourth dimension, investigations to date do not indicate, on balance, a parasitic relationship where branch banks drain funds from nonurban areas for use in head office areas. Rather, the transfer of funds, when occurring, tends to be between nonurban areas.

To summarize, branch banks show superiority in transferring funds to areas of greater demand and in meeting local credit needs. Further, they do not appear to discriminate against smaller firms as compared to larger firms or against nonurban areas relative to head office cities.

The research done on credit allocation by BHC-affiliated banks has not examined all the dimensions noted above for branch banks versus unit banks. The general consensus, however, is that affiliated banks provide more credit to the local community than do nonaffiliated banks.

Operating Efficiency

Does branch banking result in a lower cost per unit of output when providing a financial service than unit banking? Even if such operating efficiencies were found to exist, and whether or not associated with branch banking or unit banking, they may or may not be passed on to the public depending on the degree of market competitiveness. Regardless, it is important for public policy purposes to determine whether multi-office banking affects scale economies and in what direction. For example, the existence of scale economies in banking would affect the social desirability of bank mergers. It would also affect the pervasiveness of branching in that more liberal banking laws result in fewer numbers of larger banks.

There have been many studies on operating efficiency. Until recently, most were plagued with definitional problems and unavailability of data at the required level of detail. Many of these problems have been mitigated.

The latest most comprehensive research indicates that: (1) banks with deposits exceeding $50-75 million in unit banking states experienced diseconomies of scale; (2) all sizes of banks in branch banking states experienced economies of scale in terms of number of deposits and loan accounts; (3) taking into account the mode of expansion (i.e., expanding the number of accounts or number of offices for branch banks, or the number of accounts for unit banks), banks with deposits exceeding $50-75 million in both unit banking and branching states experienced diseconomies of scale; (4) when considering the mode of expansion (i.e., increasing offices for branch banks, and increasing average account size for unit banks), average costs were generally the same among similar size banks in unit and branching states; (5) whether or not a bank is affiliated with a BHC has little effect on its costs; and

(6) it is unlikely that significant if any scale economies exist for the most important banking services (except perhaps for business loans).

In short, operating efficiency does not seem at this time to be a relevant factor in determining the case for more liberalized intrastate or interstate branching. Further, the results clearly suggest that smaller banks are, as a minimum, not at an operational disadvantage in their competition with larger banks.

Competition and Concentration

Concentration in banking is typically defined as the proportion of total bank deposits held by the largest bank(s) in a given market. The general presumption is that the greater the concentration the less the competition, unless offset by other factors. Less competition could be reflected in a number of ways such as higher interest costs on loans, lower interest rates for depositors, lower quality and less variety of services, and so on.

Does branch banking contribute to greater concentration and lower competition than unit banking? This is probably the most controversial issue concerning the geographic expansion of banking. In analyzing the issue, certain problems arise. First, the market is usually defined as a specific geographical area (e.g., state, SMSA, metropolitan area, nonmetropolitan area). This definition may not accurately fit a bank's multiplicity of products nor may it recognize that branching per se may determine a bank's market boundaries. Under unit banking, market areas are largely customer-determined. Under branch banking, market areas can be bank-determined to the extent that related branch offices are spread over wider areas than customer-determined markets and to the extent that these offices adopt uniform operating policies. Second, short-run versus long-run effects need to be isolated. Third, the effect of branching or unit banking on ease of entry needs to be incorporated in the analysis. Other things equal, the easier the entry, the greater the threat of potential competition to thwart anticompetitive behavior.

Empirical research leaves little question that greater branching authority contributes to greater concentration at the state and SMSA levels. This is mostly due to branch bank mergers and acquisitions. The SMSA level includes large metropolitan areas and is interpreted as a better, though still imperfect, proxy for bank markets than the state level. On the other hand, greater branching into nonmetropolitan areas tends to decrease concentration, at least in the short run. This is mostly due to *de novo* expansion by branch banks.

In addition, studies show that greater bank concentration is positively associated over time with less competition. However, it has also been found that greater branching authority facilitates easier entry, the potential competition of which may more than neutralize over the long run the anticompetitive effects of increased concentration. In short, the higher concentration accompanying wider branching need not be a problem where bank authorities follow a liberal entry policy. It is also feasible that the tendency toward higher concentration of wider branching might be eased at the outset of a stricter federal regulatory posture towards related mergers and acquisitions.

The research on BHCs indicates unimportant increases in concentration except in those states with low and moderate concentration. At the local level, there have been no significant systematic increases in concentration attributable to BHCs.

Preservation of Dual Banking System

Does branch banking undermine the dual banking system? Of all the issues, this is the most politically oriented. The dual banking system was essentially established with the first National Bank Act in 1863 when the federal government joined the states in providing a chartering alternative for banks. It was the intention then that the states and federal government have basically equal powers regarding chartering and related supervisory and examination activities. This principle of competitive equality has been reiterated several times over the last 120 years, most notably with the McFadden Act wherein Congress placed national banks under the control of state law with regard to restrictions on geographic expansion.

In reality complete competitive equality between federal regulation and state regulation does not exist. Federal dominance over state law is a typical feature of our dual banking system. This is especially the case with regard to the application of state-chartered banks for membership in the Federal Research System, for insurance by the Federal Deposit Insurance Corporation, and for mergers and acquisitions subject to the approval of the Justice Department. In the many cases involving these situations, the outcome is federally determined.

Branching policy is the only significant area of regulation in the dual banking system that has been state dominated. This is still largely the case despite the regulatory loopholes (discussed above) that banks have capitalized on attempting to circumvent state restrictions on geographic expansion. The real issue, therefore, is whether an easing of these restrictions (in particular, with regard to interstate expansion) will lessen the ability of states to adequately control their respective banking structures. This will depend on how the easing takes place, assuming the rationale for regulatory relief has been first established. The concluding section will discuss these dimensions.

Conclusions and Implications

Several factors suggest that the present impediments against further growth in branch banking be lessened. Geographical barriers have already been eroded. Banks have found many regulatory loopholes to establish and deepen intrastate and interstate operations, especially concerning commercial customers, despite restrictions to the contrary. By itself, this argument is not persuasive in that it could be posited that one "wrong" (legislative oversight) does not warrant another "wrong" (making the legislation less restrictive). On the other hand, the growing presence of near-banks and their largely unregulated status regarding geographical expansion call for some regulatory relief. Further, technological developments in electronic banking are starting to make spatial boundaries irrelevant in the providing of bank services. This trend should continue, particularly on behalf of retail customers.

In addition, the analysis of major public policy issues suggests that branch banking, on balance, may well provide more benefits than unit banking. This is mostly the case regarding convenience and needs, the credit allocation. Also, branch banking states have been found to have lower failure rates than unit banking states; however, it should be said that the applicability of the safety and soundness issue to the question of freer branching is open to question. Furthermore, branch banks do not generally appear to be any less efficient than unit banks. Although greater branching has been seen to increase concentration, the possible anticompetitive effects can be more than offset through the increase in potential competition from easier bank entry. Finally, the determination of whether greater bank expansion will undermine the dual banking system is largely dependent on how such expansion might take place.

Thus, it is concluded that the opportunities for wider geographic expansion of banking should be allowed, but in ways that will optimize net benefits. In general, these options do not include maintaining the status quo, as is sometimes recommended, or nationwide full-service branching. Maintenance of the status quo would deprive nonbranching areas from realizing greater convenience and needs as well as more credit availability. Also, it shuts its eyes to the competitive incquities presently caused by the limited regulation of geographic expansion on the part of nonbank financial intermediaries. Nationwide full-service branching is not politically realistic since it represents the greatest threat to states' rights under our dual banking system. Further, the number and complexity of reciprocal arrangements it would require among the federal and state regulatory bodies could be unworkable. Also, it would probably be the hardest alternative to deal with in trying to ensure that the potential anticompetitive effects of the resultant increase in concentration do not materialize.

Considering economic and political factors, the first recommendation in alleviating expansionary restraints would be for the 28 states not currently allowing statewide branching to consider doing so. Consumer benefits would be greater as well as more dispersed, especially when compared to the related alternative of marketwide branching. The strongest arguments against marketwide branching are its delimiting of potential competition from outside the market, its encouraging of local market entrenchment to the extent that preemptive branching is allowed, and its arbitrary definition (usually SMSA or county) of what geographically constitutes the market. Statewide branching, on the other hand, poses no threat to states' rights, and its possible promotion of anticompetitive behavior can be subject to the control of antitrust policy.

The second recommendation would be to allow branching in contiguous states or within a region, and to do so on a reciprocal basis. Reciprocity would allow each neighboring state to still maintain control of its banking structure in the sense that out-of-state banks would be allowed to branch in a state only if the latter's banks have a similar privilege in the other state(s). The implementation of this recommendation would require, among other things, that banks have interstate branching powers thereby necessitating a change in the McFadden Act. Given the issue of states' rights, the political likelihood of such a change in the near future is not high.

In the interim, a second best solution in progressing towards a regional interstate banking framework would be to use the bank holding company as the vehicle for expansion. This would require specific state action in light of the Douglas Amendment, a less onerous task than changing the McFadden Act. Under this option, out-of-state BHCs would be allowed to establish a subsidiary in a reciprocating state subject only to Federal Reserve Board approval and the chartering agency of the new or acquired bank. As a minimum, the subsidiary would continue to be subject to the branching regulations of the particular state, as is currently the case under the McFadden Act. Thus, the option would still allow the individual states to retain substantial control over the banking structure within their borders.

A regional approach to interstate banking would be preferred over a contiguous state approach because of the latter's uneven effects on peripheral states. A number of states, especially those on our nation's perimeter, interface but a few other states.

A regional approach would also be preferred, at least initially, to a nationwide approach, given the aforementioned caveats to nationwide branching, especially regarding potential anticompetitive effects. Some guidance would be required in optimally determining the particular regions and their components states.

The BHC option has other advantages besides the substantive preservation of states' rights. First, although the geographical expansion of bank organizations would be liberalized, the Federal Reserve Board must ensure that any BHC acquisition will not adversely affect competition. A state's authorization of a regional approach will not alter this requirement.

Second, it seems reasonable to presume that the BHC option will also provide greater consumer benefits, especially in the form of added convenience and needs as well as expanded credit availability locally. Although these benefits might be even greater with interstate branch banking as opposed to interstate BHC expansion, they should constitute nevertheless a net addition to those benefits currently available.

Third, the smaller banks would seemingly support interstate BHC expansion more so than interstate branch banking. Despite empirical studies attesting to the competitive strength of small banks vis-à-vis large banks, small bank representatives fear the possible low cost structures of branches and their potential for predatory pricing. With interstate BHC expansion, smaller banks might have the opportunity to affiliate with a potential or actual outside competitor or maintain their independent status.

The feasibility of greater expansion beyond that indicated in the previous recommendations seems more than conjectural at this time. It would be desirable to wait for additional empirical data, particularly in regard to the effects of any regional-reciprocal interstate banking arrangements, before examination of other possible alternatives. Left unanswered is the question of how to treat ATMs, the most highly developed component of electronic banking. This appears appropriate at this time given the debatable classification by federal court of ATMs as branch banks, and given the yet-to-be evaluated effects of ATM sharing arrangements on concentration, joint ventures, and antitrust law.

References

Bell, James F. and Arthur E. Weimarth, Jr. "The Interstate Banking Controversy: President Carter's McFadden Act Report." *Banking Law Journal,* September 1982, pp. 722-44.

Federal Reserve Bank of Atlanta. *Economic Review.* November 1982 (special issue on "Economies of Scale in Banking"). See especially articles by George Benston, Gerald Hanweck, and David Humphrey, pp. 6-21; and B. Frank King, pp. 35-40 and 41-47.

Federal Reserve Bank of Atlanta. *Economic Review.* May 1983 (special issue on "Interstate Banking"). See especially articles by David Whitehead, pp. 4-20; Alan Gart, pp. 21-33; Robert Eisenbeis, pp. 24-31; Paul Horvitz, pp. 32-39; B. Frank King, pp. 40-45; and Veronica Bennett and Charles Haywood, pp. 55-59.

Federal Reserve Bank of Chicago. *Proceedings of a Conference on Bank Structure and Competition,* 1981. See especially part 3 on "Interstate Banking."

Frieder, Larry A. and Vincent P. Apilado. "Bank Holding Company Expansion: A Refocus on its Financial Rationale." *Journal of Financial Research,* Spring 1983, pp. 67-81.

Frieder, Larry A. and Vincent P. Apilado. "Bank Holding Company Research: Classification, Synthesis and New Directions." *Journal of Bank Research,* Summer 1982, pp. 80-95.

Frodin, Joanna H. "Electronics: The Key to Breaking the Interstate Banking Barrier." *Business Review* (Federal Reserve Bank of Philadelphia), September/October 1982, pp. 3-11.

Godfrey, John M. "Deregulation: The Attack on Geographic Barriers." *Economic Review* (Federal Reserve Bank of Atlanta), February 1981, pp. 17-21.

Guttentag, Jack M. and Edward S. Herman. *Banking Structure and Performance* (Bulletin No. 41/43, Institute of Finance, New York University), February 1967.

McCall, Alan S. and Donald T. Savage. "Branching Policy: The Options." *Journal of Bank Research,* Summer 1980, pp. 122-26.

Rhoades, Stephen A. and Donald T. Savage. "The Relative Performance of Bank Holding Companies and Branch Banking Systems." *Journal of Economics and Business,* Winter 1981, pp. 132-41.

U.S. Board of Governors of the Federal Reserve System. *The Bank Holding Company Movement to 1978: A Compendium.* Washington, D.C.: Board of Governors of the Federal Reserve System, 1978.

U.S. Congress. Senate. Subcommittee on Financial Institutions of the Committee on Banking, Housing, and Urban Affairs. *Compendium of Issues Relating to Branching by Financial Institutions.* 94th Cong., 2d sess., 1976. See especially papers by Gary Gilbert, pp. 84-98; Jack Guttentag, pp. 99-112; Bernard Shull, pp. 113-53; Gerald Fischer and Raymond Davis, pp. 155-89; George Benston, pp. 455-73; and Gary Gilbert and William Longbrake, pp. 475-98.

U.S. Department of the Treasury. *Geographic Restrictions on Commercial Banking in the United States—The Report of the President.* Washington, D.C.: Department of the Treasury, 1981.

8

The Implications of Change in the Payments System for Interstate Banking

Paul M. Horvitz

Introduction

The payments system of the United States has been changing dramatically over the last several years. These changes are due to improvements in technology, deregulation, and increasing consumer sophistication. Some of these changes have been led by commercial banks, some by other suppliers of financial services, and others by vendors of equipment and systems. With few exceptions the motivation for these changes has not been an attempt to get around restrictions on interstate banking. Nevertheless many of these developments will have profound implications for interstate banking. This chapter summarizes the effect that future changes in the payments system can be expected to have on the traditional American restriction of banking to state boundaries. The first part describes the payment practices of the past, and the second part examines the future. The final section summarizes the implications of these developments for interstate banking.

Payments in the Past

It is helpful in analyzing these issues to consider separately the use of the payments system by consumers and by business firms. Consumer payments in the United States have traditionally been made with paper checks. It is not the function of this paper to consider the cost, efficiency, or convenience of the paper check system, but rather to focus on those aspects of the use of paper checks that have implications for interstate banking.

The use of checks virtually requires a local banking connection. Because a physical piece of paper is involved, deposits most conveniently can be made locally. It is possible to deal by mail with a distant bank, but that clearly involves additional time for checks to move through the mail. With the higher interest rates that have prevailed in recent years and increasing consumer awareness of the time value of money, banking by mail with a nonlocal bank is less appealing than it was in the past. Making payments and cashing checks are facilitated by having a local bank account. Some merchants will accept only local checks. This is a reasonable policy on their part since verification is more difficult for checks on distant banks and collection takes longer for nonlocal checks. If nonlocal checks will not be as readily accepted by merchants and cashing checks is more difficult, it is reasonable for consumers to prefer a local bank.

Large business firms have less need to be concerned with a local banking connection for their major payments activity. Large corporate fund transfers are primarily by wire or electronic means at the present time. Small business, however, still relies heavily or totally on the paper check system and needs a local supplier of payment services. Even the large firm that has its major banking connections with money center banks will still need a local banking connection for payroll accounts and other payments made locally.

In view of these considerations, it is not surprising that the payments system based on the paper check has been associated with a localized banking system. Consumers, small business, and to some extent large firms have needed a local banking connection.

Payments in the Future

The consumer is becoming less tied to local institutions because of several payment system developments that are lessening the reliance on the paper check. While these developments are occurring at the present time, it must be recognized that we are discussing long term trends. The paper check is not going to be replaced by other payments means within the next few years. It is worthwhile, however, to describe a few of these alternatives which are becoming increasingly important.

Credit Cards

Credit cards can be used anywhere. They are equally acceptable regardless of the location of the issuing bank. That is, a VISA card is equally acceptable in Tampa regardless of whether it is issued by a bank in Tampa, Miami, or San Francisco. Thus, the consumer who maintained a local checking account because local merchants would not accept out-of-state checks, no longer is constrained by that consideration. Another implication of this is that banks can solicit credit card customers on an interstate or national basis. Citicorp is doing a national credit card business from its base in South Dakota. Restrictions on interstate banking relate to physical facilities such as branches and subsidiary banks, and cannot protect local institutions from this competition.

Automated Teller Machines

Shared national ATM networks are developing. This allows a consumer to maintain a depository account with an out-of-state institution and to rely on the ATM for cash withdrawals. The reluctance of local merchants to cash checks on out-of-state banks no longer becomes a constraining factor. Combined with the credit card or check guarantee system, the consumer can deal with an out-of-state bank and be able to make payments or obtain cash locally with no significant problems. Deposits made at an ATM begin earning interest promptly, without the delay associated with deposits made by mail.

Automated Clearinghouse

The typical automated clearinghouse transaction would involve an employer preparing payroll information for its employees on magnetic tape which would be sent to the local automated clearinghouse. Funds will be distributed automatically to the bank of each employee. This resolves the first reason cited above for a consumer to need a local bank—the need to make deposits conveniently. Since the consumer does not have to physically carry or mail a check to the bank, he has less reason to be concerned about where his bank is located.

Point-of-Sale Terminals

Point-of-sale systems have developed more slowly than the systems previously described, but they are likely to grow in importance in the future. With a point-of-sale system, funds are electronically transferred from the account of a consumer to the account of a merchant at the time a sale is made (though a deferred payment option may be available). The technology exists for this to be done on a national basis, and when the economics and the volume make such systems viable, neither the consumer nor the merchant will be concerned about the physical location of the bank.

Home Banking

While some experiments are underway at the present time, home banking will not become a widespread means of doing business for some time (one exception to that is pay-by-phone systems). The technology already exists for consumers to conduct banking business and to originate payments through use of home computers or interactive cable TV systems. When such systems are widely used, the consumer will have little concern with the physical location of the bank he deals with. His choice of banks will be based on the quality and convenience of the programs offered and the prices charged. At the present time pay-by-phone systems are locally limited because of the cost of telephone service. There are various ways of dealing with this problem without the need for a physical bank building or charter to provide such service.

Conclusions and Implications

State lines have long been of little relevance to large corporations in choosing their principal banking connections. Payments system developments are making state lines less important even to consumers and small firms. Even if the current restrictions on interstate banking are strictly maintained, it will become more and more difficult to protect local institutions from interstate competition. The methods described in this chapter will eventually enable out-of-state banks to compete for banking business *regardless of state law concerning branching or holding company operations.* Even if it is possible indefinitely to keep the Georgia or California bank from establishing a branch or a subsidiary bank outside its state borders, it will not be possible to keep those institutions from competing with local banks in the provision of payments services, or in extending credit to consumers. Further, some of these services may be provided by nonbank institutions that may include savings and loan associations which can operate interstate under present law, but it may also include nondepository institutions, such as Sears Roebuck, Merrill Lynch, or a cable TV company.

It should be noted that the enhanced ability of out-of-state institutions to provide payments services in the future through electronic means is due to the new technology, and not to any advantage they may have because of their large size. Most studies of economies of scale in banking find that "smaller banks are... not at an operational disadvantage with respect to large banks: (cf. Benston, Hanweck and Humphrey, Federal Reserve Bank of Atlanta *Economic Review,* November 1982, p. 21). While these studies may not be relevant as technology changes, and they do not include the very largest banks, they do indicate that smaller banks have been able to remain competitive despite the major changes in the technology of banking that we have already witnessed. The issue is not of local versus nonlocal, rather than small versus large. The advantages enjoyed by all local institutions, both large and small banks, are what is likely to be eroded by changes in the payments system.

This chapter does not go into the merits of whether increasing interstate banking is desirable or undesirable. There may be good reasons for a state to desire to preserve a structure of local or in-state depository institutions. The purpose here is not to argue the merits of that desire, but only to point out that implementing it will become more and more difficult in the future.

References

Association of Reserve City Bankers, *Report on the Payments System*, 1982.

Bennett, Veronica M. and Charles R. Haywood, "Technology and Interstate Banking," Federal Reserve Bank of Atlanta *Economic Review*, May 1983, p. 55.

Benston, George, Gerald Hanweck, and David Humphrey, "Operating Costs in Commercial Banking," Federal Reserve Bank of Atlanta *Economic Review*, November 1982, p. 6.

Federal Reserve Bank of Boston, *The Economics of a National Electronic Funds Transfer System*, Conference Series No. 13, October 1974.

Horvitz, Paul M., "Payments System Developments and Public Policy," in *The Future of American Financial Services Institutions*, The American Assembly, George Benston, ed., 1983.

9

A Legal Analysis of Reciprocal Interstate Banking

Jeffrey Davis

Introduction

Present Florida law prohibits out-of-state banks or bank holding companies from acquiring control of Florida banks or bank holding companies.[1] This prohibition is authorized by the Douglas Amendment to the Bank Holding Company Act of 1956,[2] which states that the Federal Reserve Board may not approve a bank holding company's application to acquire a bank in another state unless the acquisition is "specifically authorized" by the statutory law of the state in which the bank to be acquired is located.[3]

The Florida legislature is currently considering amending this broad prohibition to permit the acquisition of Florida banks by banks located in any of eight specified southern states[4] provided the legislature of that state extends the same privilege to Florida banks. The objective, assuming the specified states adopt reciprocal legislation, is to create what has been called regional interstate banking. Since the effect is to preclude competition from banks outside the region, the question arises whether this discrimination is permitted under the United States Constitution. The primary threats to the constitutionality of such legislation arise under the commerce clause, the equal protection clause of the fourteenth amendment, and the interstate compacts clause. This chapter discusses each of these in order. While the matter is hardly free from doubt, existing authorities point toward constitutional validity.

The legislature is also considering enacting a nationwide reciprocal interstate banking statute. However, since there seems to be no legal difficulty with such an approach, this chapter will treat only the issues raised by the regional statute.

The Commerce Clause

The commerce clause provides that "the Congress shall have Power to Regulate Commerce...among the several States."[5] Though it contains no explicit limitation on the power of the states, a long line of cases establishes the implied limitation on the states' power to interfere with interstate commerce.[6] However, Congress may regulate interstate commerce indirectly by granting the states power to restrict the flow of interstate commerce that they would not otherwise enjoy.[7] "If Congress ordains that the states may freely regulate an aspect of interstate commerce, any action taken by a state within the scope of the congressional authority is rendered invulnerable to commerce clause challenge."[8] Moreover, since the commerce clause serves as no limit on the Congress' authority, Congress may, if it so chooses, eliminate all commerce clause limitations on state authority to regulate an aspect of interstate commerce.[9] Since the commerce clause would surely invalidate Florida's proposed legislation absent Congressional authorization,[10] the question becomes simply whether sufficient authorization has been given. More precisely, the question is whether, in requiring that states specifically authorize by statute interstate bank acquisitions, the Douglas Amendment was intended to permit Florida to discriminate against out-of-state banks on the basis of the state or region in which they are located.

Since the early thirties, the banking industry has been rigidly regulated. In order to assure safety and soundness, competition in the industry has been carefully monitored and controlled. With the growth of bank holding companies Congress became concerned about the adequacy of existing controls.[11] One of the stated objectives of the Bank Holding Company Act of 1956 was to better protect the competitive balance—to protect against "the concentration of commercial bank facilities in a particular area under a single control or management."[12] As proposed, the act required bank holding companies to obtain Federal Reserve Board approval of all bank acquisitions.[13] Unlike the House bill, which simply prohibited acquisitions across state lines,[14] the Senate bill contained no specific limit on interstate acquisitions. The Senate Committee on Banking and Currency believed the concerns of the states would be adequately protected by providing the states an opportunity to express an opinion on an application.[15] The Douglas Amendment, which was added on the Senate floor, gave the states concurrent authority to limit acquisitions by out-of-state holding companies. With the consent of the House, it became part of the act.

The Senate debate over the amendment shows the concern for state policy: "[c]ontrol of expansion of Bank Holding Companies across State lines into State banks is a matter of primary concern to the State governments and is an area best left to their discretion rather than to have it solely under the jurisdiction of the Federal Reserve Board."[16] While clearly intending to relieve the states of the strictures of the commerce clause,[17] the Senate scarcely discussed how states might exercise this discretion. One scenario that does appear to have been contemplated, as at least one court has held,[18] is that states would authorize specific bank holding companies to acquire in-state banks on an individual basis.[19] However, the requirement that the authorization be made by statute suggests that broader, categorical authorizations were contemplated as well. There was no discussion of any intended limits on state discretion; throughout the debate the concern for broad state discretion was evident, with frequent analogical reference to the states' unfettered discretion to regulate intrastate branching.[20] But the specific question of whether the states might permissibly discriminate on the basis of bank holding company location appears not to have been thought of at all.

In speculating as to how the United States Supreme Court might rule on this issue, one should resist the temptation to wonder what Congress would have done had it considered the matter. This adds an unhelpful analytical step and obscures the more appropriate inquiry into what, consistent with Congress' explicit intent, the meaning of the statute *should* be in this instance. Between the extremes of authorizing only specific acquisitions and erecting no barriers to acquisition at all lies a wide range of intermediate legislative approaches. Surely, there should be no objection to general statutory prerequisites to acquisition, such as size, capitalization, corporate structure, or perhaps even location of the acquiring bank holding company. Additionally, in making *ad hoc* decisions, it would seem clearly permissible to take account of location, at least insofar as it bears on the state's ability to regulate a distant holding company.[21] But the concern of the State of Florida is not inability to regulate. Its concern is to limit competition—what might be called regional protectionism. The Douglas Amendment specifically authorizes state protectionism, an abhorrent practice outside the banking industry. Perhaps at the heart of the permissibility of the proposed legislation is the question of whether regional protectionism is any more abhorrent to societal concerns than is state protectionism. Would it unduly complicate our economy to permit the development of self-regulating regional economic entities in addition to the states? Or, does the special need to strictly control competition in the banking industry justify permitting such a development? The Court would be forced to draw some exceedingly fine distinctions in order to decide that regional protectionism in banking is substantially more abhorrent than state protectionism. Given Congress' deliberate decision permitting the states completely to prevent interstate bank acquisitions, it seems unlikely that the Court would say the Douglas Amendment does not permit states to experiment with regional banking free of commerce clause restraints.

Equal Protection

The Fourteenth Amendment states: "(N)or shall any State deprive any person of life, liberty or property without due process of law; nor deny to any person within its jurisdiction the equal protection of the law."[22] Historically, both the due process and equal protection clauses have played important roles in limiting the scope of state authority to regulate business. However, in recent years, their impact has been severely lessened.[23] A substantive due process attack on state regulation must now overcome a virtually irrebuttable presumption of validity.[24] The equal protection clause has recently been used effectively to strike down economic regulation, but only in situations involving suspect classifications or fundamental interests.[25] The Court has explicitly indicated that economic rights standing alone are constitutionally significant under the equal protection clause; statutory discriminations are presumed constitutional, the Court requiring "only that the classification challenged be rationally related to a legitimate state interest."[26] In *City of New Orleans v. Dukes*,[27] the Court upheld an ordinance that prohibited vendors from selling food in the French Quarter but exempted the two vendors who had operated for more than eight years. The lower court had found irrational the hypothesis that an eight-year veteran of the pushcart hot dog market would operate in a manner more consistent with the traditions of the Quarter than any other operator.[28] In reversing the lower court, the Supreme Court disapproved an earlier case, the only one in the last half century to invalidate a wholly economic regulation solely on equal protection grounds.[29] The Court stated that inquiry into the statute's potential irrationality was a needlessly intrusive judicial infringement, and held:

> The city could reasonably decide that newer businesses were less likely to have built up substantial reliance interests in continued operation in the Vieux Carre and that the two vendors who qualified under the "grandfather clause"—both of whom had operated in the area for over 20 years rather than only eight—had themselves become part of the distinctive character and charm that distinguishes the Vieux Carre. We cannot say that these judgments so lack rationality that they constitute a constitutionally impermissible denial of equal protection.[30]

The specific question whether statutory discrimination in permitting out-of-state bank holding companies to acquire local banks violates the equal protection clause was recently taken up by the D.C. Circuit. In *Iowa Independent Bankers v. Board of Governors of the Federal Reserve System*,[31] the state of Iowa had passed a statute prohibiting out-of-state bank holding companies from acquiring Iowa banks. Specific exception was made for Northwest Bancorporation, the only out-of-state bank holding company that, at the time, owned any banks in Iowa. Referring to the committee report stating that Northwest Bancorporation had shown itself to be a good citizen of the Iowa business community, the court concluded the statute was rationally related to a legitimate state purpose and upheld its constitutionality.

> In short, the legislature intended to allow all pre-existing bank holding companies, whether in-state or out-of-state, to compete on an equal basis, while preventing a new influx of out-of-state bank holding companies into Iowa. We think that this is precisely the type of "grandfathering" that has been repeatedly approved by the Supreme Court.[32]

Unlike the familiar practice of grandfathering, the legislation under consideration in Florida would discriminate on a basis that is unique to existing jurisprudence.[33] However, the *Dukes* case illustrates the Court's extreme willingness to find that a statutory discrimination bears a rational relationship to a legitimate state purpose. While there may be strong arguments against the advisability of any particular legislative decision, states are accorded wide lattitude in regulating their economies, including the lattitude to proceed cautiously.

> When local economic regulation is challenged solely as violating the Equal Protection Clause, this Court consistently defers to legislative determination as to the desirability of the particular statutory discriminations ... (R)ational distinctions may be made with substantially less than mathematical exactitude. Legislatures may implement their program step by step in such economic areas, adopting regulations that only partially ameliorate a perceived evil and deferring complete elimination of the evil to future regulation.[34]

A number of authorities have suggested that a period of regional interstate banking would be a desirable prelude to national interstate banking.[35] Representatives of both the Carter and Reagan administrations have referred with approval to the usefulness of regional expansion of interstate banking.[36] The existence of these authorities would seem to establish that there is at least a rational basis for choosing the regional approach. Perhaps the legislative basis could be strengthened by providing explicitly that the period of regional protectionism will be only temporary[37] or by conducting a more careful inquiry into the makeup of the region.[38] But neither of these precautions seems essential. The fact that there may be sound arguments against regional banking generally, or that the legislation might have been more rationally conceived is constitutionally irrelevant. The legislation would appear nevertheless to be safe from equal protection attack.

The Interstate Compacts Clause

Article 1, §10 declares "No State shall, without the consent of Congress ... enter into any Agreement or Compact with another State...."

The clause poses two issues: first, whether the contemplated reciprocal pairs of legislation are "agreements or compacts" within the meaning of the clause; and second, if so, whether Congress has consented to such agreements.

While "agreements or compacts" need not be formally executed to fall within the clause, the Supreme Court has conceptualized them as contractual exchanges. "The legislative declaration will take the form of an agreement or compact when it recites some consideration for it from the other party affected by it, for example, as made upon a similar declaration of the . . . contracting state."[39] Such an exchange could, of course, take the form of simultaneous legislation by two states, as in the landmark case of *Virginia v. Tennessee*[40] in which two states ratified a joint commission's decision on the location of the boundary between them. Nevertheless, unlike simultaneous legislation, reciprocal statutes affording special privileges to the residents of the reciprocating states have never been treated as interstate compacts, although no conceptual basis for this distinction exists. In *Bode v. Barrett*,[41] for example, Illinois imposed a tax for the use of highways, but exempted nonresidents whose home states granted like exemptions to Illinois residents. The Court said simply, "[T]hat kind of reciprocal arrangement between states has never been thought to violate the Compact Clause. . . "[42] By the early twentieth century, these arrangements had become quite common;[43] Felix Frankfurter and James Landis characterized them as one of the "extra-constitutional forms of legal invention for the solution of problems touching more than one state."[44] However, in none of the cases to date have legislatures discriminated against other states in offering the benefits of reciprocity, and in a recent case, the Court specifically added,

> We are not called upon to decide in this case whether or at what point the diversionary effects upon trade occasioned by a given reciprocity agreement (even though voluntary and nondiscriminatory) between some but not all States might be such as to constitute an impermissible burdening of the national interests embodied in the Commerce Clause, or the Compact Clause.[45]

Obviously, if at some point the diversionary effect of a nondiscriminatory reciprocity agreement might become impermissible, that point would be reached more quickly by a discriminatory statute. The Court thus has left open the possibility of finding regional reciprocity violative of both the Commerce and Compacts Clauses.

Aside from its structure, courts look at the content of an agreement to determine whether it falls within the Compacts Clause. Not all matters upon which the states may agree concern the United States. Looking at the object of the clause, the Court in *Virginia v. Tennessee* articulated the amorphous but often quoted dictum that an agreement will fall within the clause if it "may lead . . . to the increase of the political power or influence of the States affected and thus encroach . . . upon the full and free exercise of Federal authority."[46]

Given the imprecision of this component, if the Court finds regional protectionism offensive enough to the precepts of federalism, the Compacts Clause could well be invoked.

If the clause is invoked, the legislation will stand only with Congress' consent. That consent may take the form of prior authorization as well as subsequent approval, so the key becomes whether consent may be inferred from the Bank Holding Company Act of 1956. The legislative history of the Douglas Amendment and the likelihood that the Court will find regional banking authorized have already been discussed. While the Court might conceivably conclude Congress intended to free the states from all Commerce Clause strictures yet did not intend to authorize the instant regional interstate compacts, such a conclusion would require extremely fine and fruitless distinctions. More probably, the Court will find either that the legislation was authorized and violates neither provision, or, if unauthorized, that it violates the Commerce Clause. Whether the Court goes on to declare that it also violates the Compacts Clause will be incidental.

Conclusion and Implications

There appear to be no legal barriers to the effectiveness of a statute providing for national reciprocal interstate banking. The constitutionality of a regional statute, however, is not so certain. The Commerce Clause poses the greatest threat to regional legislation, depending on the determination of the legislative intent of the Douglas Amendment. Since Congress seems not to have imagined the possibility of regional economic protectionism, this question could be decided either way. However, Congress' apparent strong concern for state policy in passing the Amendment lends solid support to the argument that permitting states to experiment with regional interstate banking is most consistent with the intent of the Douglas Amendment. Of course, since Congress is specifically empowered to regulate interstate commerce, the states may regulate interstate banking only so long as Congress continues to permit them to do so. Any changes Congress might make to the Douglas Amendment would change the analysis.

The due process clause requires only a rational basis for the legislative choice of regional interstate banking. Owing to the numerous authorities who have referred to the advantages of a regional approach and the extreme solicitousness of the Supreme Court in finding legislative rationality in business regulation, the due process clause poses little threat to the regional approach. The threat will be especially small if the Florida legislature expressly intends the period of regionalism to be experimental or temporary and if the legislature gives some thought to how the region should be defined. The interstate Compacts Clause also seems unlikely to serve as an independent basis for striking down a regional statute.

Notes

1. Fla. Stat. §658.29 (1981). The prohibition does not apply to the three out-of-state banks that owned Florida banks on December 20, 1972. Fla. Stat. §658.29(3)(d). They are: North Carolina National Bank; Northern Trust Company (Illinois); and Royal Trust (Canada).

2. 12 U.S.C. §§1841-50 (1980).

3. The Douglas Amendment added §3(d) to the Act, 12 U.S.C. §1842(d) (1980).

4. They are Alabama, Georgia, Louisiana, Mississippi, North Carolina, South Carolina, Tennessee, and Virginia.

5. U.S. Const., art. 1, §8, cl. 3.

6. See Western & Southern Life Ins. Co. v. State Board of Equalization, 451 U.S. 648, 652 (1980); Philadelphia v. New Jersey, 437 U.S. 617 (1978).

7. Lewis v. BT Investment Managers, Inc., 447 U.S. 27, 45 (1980).

8. Western & Southern Life Ins. Co. v. State Board of Equalization, 451 U.S. 648, 652 (1980).

9. In Western & Southern Life Ins. Co. v. State Board of Equalization, 451 U.S. 648 (1980), California had passed a "retaliatory tax" on out-of-state insurance companies if the insurer's state would impose taxes on a hypothetical California insurer exceeding those imposed by California. The insurer argued that the tax was anticompetitive and that it discriminated against out-of-state insurers. The Supreme Court's only concern was whether Congress had intended to grant states the broad authority to enact such a statute. After a lengthy discussion of the legislative history of the McCarran-Ferguson Act and the cases interpreting it, the Court concluded that Congress had removed all Commerce Clause limitations on the state's authority to regulate and tax the insurance business. *Id.* at 653-656. The strongly similar societal roles of the insurance and banking businesses leave little doubt that Congress has the power to grant the same immunity to the states in regulating banking.

10. The Supreme Court has consistently held that "where simple economic protectionism is involved, a virtually *per se* rule of validity has been erected." Lewis v. BT Inv. Managers, Inc., 447 U.S. 27, 36 (1980). Accordingly, Fla. Stat. §658.29, prohibiting all acquisitions by out-of-state bank holding companies, would surely be invalid absent the Douglas Amendment. Applying the prohibition in a discriminatory manner would hardly save it.

11. The Committee on Banking and Currency reported to the Senate: "Considerable care has been taken to provide regulatory control over individual banks by Federal and State authorities. Yet there is at present only a very limited control over the activities of bank holding companies that manage or control banks." S. Rep. No. 1095, 84th Cong., 2d Sess. 11, *reprinted in* (1956) U.S. Code Cong. & Ad. News 2482, 2482.

12. Id. at 2483.

13. 12 U.S.C. §1842(a) (1980).

14. H.R. Rep. No. 609, 84th Cong. 1st Sess. 15.24 (1955).

15. S. Rep. No. 1095, *supra* note 9, at 2492.

16. 121 Cong. Rec. 6862 (1956) (remarks of Sen. Payne).

17. 121 Cong. Rec. 6862 (1956) (remarks of Sen. Bennett).

18. Iowa Indep. Bankers v. Board of Governors of the Federal Reserve System, 511 F.2d 1288, 1296-97 (D.C. Cir. 1975).

19. For example, regarding concurrent state and Board approval, Senator Douglas stated, "If and when individual states permitted *a bank holding company* from another state to acquire across state lines, then the Federal Reserve Board would have final jurisdiction in those cases as well." 102 Cong. Rec. 6860 (1956) (emphasis added).

20. See, e.g., the remarks of Senator Douglas:

> I wish to repeat that, so far as interstate acquisition of banks is concerned, namely, purchase by bank holding companies of banks in other states, the provision in my amendment is in principle almost identical with the present provision which governs branch banking.
>
> Therefore, it is a logical continuation of the principles of the McFadden Act, which tried to prevent the Federal power from being used to permit national banks to expand across State lines in a way contrary to State policy and, of course, under the McFadden Act, even to expand within a State. 102 Cong. Rec. 6860 (1956).

21. For example, in Iowa Indep. Bankers v. Board of Governors of the Federal Reserve System, 511 F.2d 1288, 1294 (1975), the D.C. Circuit cited with apparent approval an Iowa legislative committee report stating:

> [The Northwest Bancorporation of Minnesota] has shown itself to be a good citizen of the Iowa business community, and should be allowed the same benefits of state law as the domestic bank holding companies. However, it is not considered desirable to leave the state's banking structure open to entry by outside bank holding companies generally, some of which might be too large and too far-flung to be effectively regulated by the Iowa Department of Banking.

22. U.S. Const. amend. XIV, § 1.

23. See, generally, Reznick, *The Constitutionality of Business Regulation in the Burger Court: Revival and Restraint*, 33 HASTINGS L.J., 1 (1981).

24. In North Dakota State Bd. of Pharmacy v. Snyder's Drug Stores, 414 U.S. 165 (1973), Justice Douglas quoted extensively from post-New Deal opinions, such as Ferguson v. Skrupa, 372 U.S. 726, 731-32 (1963):

> We refuse to sit as a "superlegislature to weigh the wisdom of legislation," and we emphatically refuse to go back to the time when courts used the Due Process Clause "to strike down state laws, regulation of business and industrial conditions, because they may be unwise, improvident, or out of harmony with a particular school of thought." Nor are we able or willing to draw lines by calling a law 'prohibitory' or "regulatory." Whether the legislature takes for its textbook Adam Smith, Herbert Spencer, Lord Keynes, or some other is no concern of ours...[R]elief, if any be needed, lies not with us but with the body constituted to pass laws....414 U.S. at 165-66.

25. See, e.g., In re Griffiths, 413 U.S. 717 (1973); Examining Board of Engineers, Architects and Surveyors v. Flores de Otero, 426 U.S. 572 (1976).

26. City of New Orleans v. Dukes, 427 U.S. 297, 303 (1976), hereinafter *Dukes*.

27. Id.

28.   Id. at 306.

29.   Morey v. Doud, 354 U.S. 457 (1957).

30.   *Dukes,* 427 U.S. 297, 305.

31.   511 F.2d 1288 (1975).

32.   Id. at 1295.

33.   Similar statutes have been passed by the New England states but the validity of these has not been litigated.

34.   *Dukes,* 427 U.S. 297, 303.

35.   For example, The Southern Growth Policies Board recommended:

> As a precursor to interstate banking, the Southern states should develop reciprocal banking agreements within the region as permitted under current federal law with an eye toward the eventual development of regional, multi-bank holding companies.

Report of the 1980 Commission on the Future of the South, 31 (1981). See also, Frieder, Regional Interstate Banking; Transitional Progress, paper prepared for Southern Finance Association Annual Meeting, Nov. 6, 1980, Wash., D.C.

36.   Referring to reservations about the efficacy of present antitrust law, the Treasury Department under the Carter administration stated:

> Such reservations suggest that it is undesirable to move immediately to unrestricted nationwide branching. A more moderate liberalization initially should include safeguards designed to complement existing antitrust laws, thereby allowing the pro-competitive aspects of intra- and interstate expansion to develop while minimizing the prospect of a significant increase in nationwide concentration. Such safeguards could include, for example, limits on regions or product markets to be entered....

Geographic Restrictions on Commercial Banking, the Report of the President, Department of the Treasury, 14 (1981).

The Secretary of the Treasury under President Reagan, in testimony before the Senate Committee on Banking, Housing, and Urban Affairs, stated:

> [M]any states are easing or eliminating their restrictions on the interstate activities of depository institutions. The New England experience is particularly interesting. Several states in that area have authorized interstate operation of institutions headquartered elsewhere in that region. Local governments familiar with local markets should be able to make sound decisions about their regional economy. Moreover, the strengthening of local institutions prior to a removal of all geographic restrictions nationwide facilitates the potential for development of more organizations able to compete nationally when the opportunity arises. This should enhance the diversity and competitive vitality of the future financial system.

Testimony of the Honorable Donald T. Regan, Secretary of the Treasury, before the Senate Committee on Banking, Housing, and Urban Affairs, Written Statement, 12 (April 6, 1983).

37.   One current concern is whether the statute should specify a date, say five years subsequent to passage, after which the benefits of reciprocity would be extended to the entire nation. This would make it clear that the legislature intends regional interstate banking to be only a step in the transition to national interstate banking. But there is no constitutional need for such a specific terminus, for two reasons. First, regional interstate banking as an end in itself may well be rationally based; it need not necessarily be a transition device. Second, the legislature may make clear its intention to make a transition to national interstate banking without specifying the transition point. Just as easily as the legislature could later nullify a point that turned out to be improvidently chosen, it could choose at the outset to wait until the proper time arrives to make the transition. The fact that there may be certain practical and political advantages to setting a prospective transition date should not make the failure to do so irrational.

38.   Obviously, the states selected for reciprocity must constitute a region. The rationale for regional reciprocity would not support the selection of Arizona, Maine and Hawaii. There could, of course, be no complaint about the selection of a group of states that have traditionally been treated as comprising an economic region, such as one or two Federal Reserve Districts. The danger of litigation would also be reduced if the Florida legislature were to inquire specifically into the nature of the economic interaction of the nearby states and to define the region on the basis of that inquiry. However, the question of what is an economic region is hardly well settled. The eight states selected have been traditionally thought of as the Deep South. While one might argue that the region more appropriately should include one or two additional or fewer states, it would be difficult to show that any group of contiguous states was selected so irrationally as to run afoul of the equal protection clause.

39.   Virginia v. Tennessee, 148 U.S. 503, 520 (1892).

40.   Id.

41.   433 U.S. 583 (1953).

42.   Id. at 586.

43.   See, e.g., Kane v. New Jersey, 242 U.S. 160, 167-68 (1916) in which Justice Brandeis stated:

The Maryland law contained a reciprocal provision by which non-residents whose cars are duly registered in their own States are given, for a limited period, free use of the highways in return for similar privileges granted to residents of Maryland. Such a provision promotes convenience of owners and prevents the relative hardship of having to pay the full registration fees for a brief use of the highways. It has become common in state legislation.

44.   Frankfurter and Landis, *The Compact Clause of the Constitution: A Study of Interstate Adjustments,* 34 YALE L.J. 685, 688-91 (1925).

45.   Great Atl. and Pac. Tea Co. v. Cottrell, 424 U.S. 366, 379 n. 13 (1976).

46.   Virginia v. Tennessee, 148 U.S. 503, 520 (1892).

10

Interstate Banking and the Public Interest: The Florida Case

Larry A. Frieder

Introduction

Although interstate banking legislation affects the specific economics of in-state banks, a legislature must establish a financial structure that best serves its citizens, the users of financial services. A great many observers believe that interstate banking is inevitable and that significant consolidation will continue to characterize the current deregulated environment. Nevertheless, the state does possess an ability to influence the process leading to a more national and integrated financial marketplace. This chapter summarizes: (1) the magnitude of interstate banking currently conducted in Florida; (2) the implications of technology, technical efficiency and economic development for interstate banking; and (3) the legal and public policy considerations of interstate banking. We also review the case for and against liberalization of geographical restrictions on interstate banking, and analyze possible legislative options. Finally, conclusions and implications are given.

A Synopsis of Evidence and Arguments Related to Interstate Banking

It is important to emphasize that the findings presented in this book were based upon an extensive body of literature related to bank structure. A study of this nature, fortunately, can draw upon numerous past studies which examine the impact of different bank (legal) structures and bank expansion(s), given geographical restrictions and/or geographical liberalization. For example, multi-bank holding company expansion by acquisition, and expansion by *de novo* market entry, which are two approaches to interstate banking,[1] have been researched. Thus, although interstate banking per se is a new development, a basis for analyzing its probable effects does exist.

Magnitude of Interstate Banking in Florida and Competition

The assessment of the magnitude of interstate banking activity in Florida at the present time proceeded along two lines. One examined the methods out-of-state commercial banking organizations have used to offer financial services on an interstate basis (see chapter 3). Another explored the degree to which nonbank competitors, such as manufacturers, retailers and insurance companies, have penetrated commercial bank product lines (see chapter 4).

Five gateways to interstate banking in Florida exist for banking organizations. These include (1) banks "grandfathered" by state statute; (2) Garn-St. Germain allowance for banks and savings and loans associations (S&Ls) to acquire failing institutions across state lines; (3) 4(c) 8 provisions of the Bank Holding Company Act allowance for bank holding companies (BHCs) to establish or acquire nonbank subsidiaries that offer financial services not subject to the prohibition on interstate banking; (4) banks may establish other nonbank subsidiaries such as Loan Production offices (LPOs) and Edge Act corporations across state lines; and (5) provisions of the Douglas Amendment allow BHCs to establish or acquire banking subsidiaries in states that explicitly permit such entry. These five gateways focus on establishing offices interstate. Accordingly, although a great amount of interstate financial activity could be documented much could not. Out-of-state banks currently accept deposits of Florida residents (although booked out-of-state), aggressively sell large CDs, market credit cards, send business loan calling officers, offer cash management and electronic fund transfer devices, and provide correspondent services across state lines into Florida.

Although Florida has not explicitly permitted out-of-state bank entry, three organizations were "grandfathered" in Florida via a 1972 Florida statute. Of the three—NCNB (North Carolina), Northern Trust (Chicago), and Royal Trust (Canada)—only NCNB has aggressively utilized its grandfathered status. It has moved to acquire three Florida MBHCs (Gulfstream, Exchange, and Ellis), as well as independent banks in Lake City and Miami. Royal Trust, after reversing its earlier decision to buy Flagship, has agreed to be acquired by Florida National. Northern Trust has moved to convert its trust office into a commercial bank. It has not moved to acquire any existing Florida organizations.

Florida S&Ls have constituted a major part of the interstate mergers of S&Ls. To date nine Florida S&Ls have merged into six California S&Ls and three New Jersey S&Ls. Four Florida S&Ls have acquired six out-of-state S&Ls. Only one banking organization (Citicorp) has used the Garn-St. Germain avenue for interstate expansion into Florida.[2]

Out-of-state banks have established 372 4(c) 8 offices, 6 LPOs, and 25 Edge Act offices in Florida. The loan production activity in Florida is probably understated due to the fact that several banks that have established LPOs in

Atlanta service Florida from these offices. Moreover, Florida is well covered by many out-of-state lenders who have not chosen to set up LPOs. It is interesting to note that only 3 Florida based BHCs are among the 139 BHCs that conduct interstate 4(c)8 activities. Barnett engages only in check verification, while Southeast and Florida National engage in mortgage banking. Florida National also has leasing, finance company, and industrial bank activities on an interstate basis. Of the remaining 136 BHCs with interstate 4(c)8 subsidiaries, 51 have located 372 offices in Florida.

Nonbank competition with commercial banks has increased dramatically over the past decade. The majority of firms with the largest earnings from financial services are now nonbanks (see 16, 35). Nondepository institutions were found to dominate the lists of the largest providers of consumer installment credit, automobile credit, commercial mortgage loans, and business lease financing.

Despite commercial bank dominance in business loans and credit cards, nonbanks have significant market share in these areas. Sears and American Express are the two largest issuers of consumer credit through a card and together issue more credit through charge cards than the largest eight bank issuers. The 32 nonbanks sampled issued $42.5 billion in short term business loans. These nonbank financial services competitors were found to be very active on the deposit/savings side via money market mutual funds. They account for about 38% of all money fund assets.[3] Moreover, these same institutions actively serve numerous depository institutions as broker (agents) for insured retail deposits, thus assisting depository institutions in reaching the nationwide deposit market. Most of the nonbank competitors operate in most or all 50 states, including Florida.[4]

In light of the preceding evidence, it is obvious that Florida banks must compete with credit granting manufacturers, retailers, insurance companies, security firms, Florida based S&Ls and credit unions, and out-of-state banks operating through 4(c)8 subsidiaries, Edge Acts, and LPOs. Policy making in this context must recognize that substantively interstate banking is a reality. Its existence, extent, and nature cannot be avoided, delayed, or modified by state action or inaction. (See also chapter 5.)

It should also be noted that the various types of interstate entry and nonbank competition are procompetitive. The result is more credit availability for the Florida credit user and more deposit services for the Florida saver. The resulting prices (interest rates) are also more favorable to both Florida savers and borrowers. These attributes, of course, are beneficial to the overall Florida economy.

These competitive realities also reinforce the fact that competition can no longer be narrowly viewed as consisting of only banks in a single local market (SMSA). Banks compete against other depository and nondepository institutions, and financial innovations and technology have already neutralized the difference between local and nonlocal vendors of saving and borrowing services for consumers and businesses.

Technical Efficiency and Technology

The most recent research on economies of scale in banking indicates diseconomies of scale. That is, operating costs for larger banks average more than those for smaller banks. Accordingly, the evidence provides no basis for fears that national or regional interstate banking would result in Florida banks being dominated by out-of-state banks (see chapter 6).

Since the evidence does not address consumer-borne costs, the research does not imply that consumers might not benefit from interstate banking. Interstate banking could benefit Florida citizens by resulting in broader product/service lines, more specialized services (such as international banking services, national cash management capabilities, or specific industry loan capabilities), and greater convenience in terms of outlets offered, including those in other states.

Although technological progress, along with deregulation and increased consumer sophistication, were not devised to circumvent restrictions on interstate banking, they combine to impinge on interstate banking significantly (see chapter 8). Automated tellers, point-of-sale systems, automated clearinghouses, credit cards, and home banking all tend to lessen the dependency of households and even small business firms on local banks. Thus, like the large corporation which has had nonlocal banking connections for years, individuals and small firms may increasingly turn to nonlocal vendors of financial services. As these trends continue, it will not be possible to prevent out-of-state financial institutions from providing credit, deposit, or payments services, even though it may be possible to prevent out-of-state banks from establishing banks in Florida for a considerable time period (see chapter 8).

Economic Development

Even though the South and Florida realize deposit growth rates higher than the national average, the state and the region remain net importers of capital. The region's shortfall is addressed presently through an already highly integrated national and international financial network. Capital flows to where it is most efficiently utilized in terms of prospective rates of return. The analysis on economic development (see chapter 5) indicated that Florida business borrowers are as likely to obtain credit from out-of-state sources as from in-state banks. Thus, the existing *de facto* interstate banking infrastructure is not only very large but is a major pillar of the present credit structure which supports economic activity in the state. Since it has taken a combination of in-state banks and out-of-state sources to generate the economic growth Florida has realized to date, it appears that the state's present ambitious economic growth plans will also require both sources to meet targets.

Legal and Public Policy Considerations

Florida does not face any constitutional difficulties related to a national reciprocal interstate banking statute. However, a regional reciprocal statute could be challenged three ways. Close analysis indicates that legal attacks based upon the commerce clause, the due process clause of the fourteenth amendment, and the interstate compacts clause would not likely succeed.[5]

Public policy considerations. What are the major public policy considerations that require evaluation when interstate banking proposals are put forth? This book has addressed several (see chapters 2 and 7) including (1) convenience and needs; (2) level and quality of services; (3) viability of small banks; (4) safety and soundness; (5) competition and concentration; (6) regulatory and supervisory impact. Policy considerations related to technology, technical efficiency and economic development are summarized above.

Interstate banking should result in more banking sites relative to population—in both rural and metropolitan areas. However, the number of banks per se would decrease as a result of mergers. It is important to note that financial services will increasingly include electronic options. Additionally, interstate banking should result in broader product and service offerings, i.e., greater convenience. Credit availability to all sizes of business, consumers, and municipalities would most likely be enhanced by interstate banking. Larger banks operate with higher lending limits, greater proportions of funds committed to risky assets (loans in particular), and higher gearing ratios (assets to equity). In this regard, it should be noted that Florida banks have often been net suppliers of funds to the national markets through their selling of federal funds.

Although smaller banking organizations face a number of challenges in the current environment, competing with larger organizations is not one of them. The evidence clearly indicates large banks have no scale or cost advantages vis-à-vis small banks. In fact, the small banks have outperformed large banks in recent years in terms of standard financial measures (return on assets and equity). Entry of large banks by acquisition of large banks within a market has resulted in declining market shares in entered markets rather than dominance. The specific competitive implications of various interstate banking alternatives are explored in more detail in the next two sections of this chapter.

Safety and soundness of banks does not appear to be a key determinant in assessing interstate bank expansion. The risk of banks involved in interstate acquisitions should increase due to the expected higher ratios of risky assets, leverage (assets to equity), and possibly greater competition. However, this risk is probably offset by the fact that interstate banks would gain better geographical and product (balance sheet and income statement) diversification. Also, larger organizations have increased capital raising and shifting capability to address financial strain. The Garn-St. Germain Act facilitates the takeover (rescue) of weak or failing institutions. Perhaps, these risk offsets account for the fact that fewer multi-office banks or BHCs than unit banks appear on the regulatory agencies problem bank lists.

Modification of interstate banking laws will most likely impact our nation's dual banking system and specifically Florida's regulatory authority versus that of federal agencies. Interstate bank expansion will probably tend to make the policies of the states more uniform and diminish the role of the state in banking supervision (see chapter 2).[6]

Summary of Arguments For and Against Liberalization of Geographical Restrictions

For

The arguments for liberalization of interstate banking restrictions derive from the following:

1. *Public policy considerations,* specifically the impact of interstate banking proposals on convenience and needs—level and quality of services, viability of small banks, safety and soundness, competition and concentration, and regulatory impact.
2. *Acknowledgment of reality.* Legislative action would recognize that interstate banking is already a reality. Impetus would be given to in-state banks to address present challenges and to make the strategic preparations necessary to adjust to the changing environment. Banks acting (or not acting) out of belief that they are still protected would realize their false sense of security.
3. *Larger banking organizations.* Larger banks result from interstate bank expansion. Size may prove to be strategically important to the ultimate success or failure of some Florida banks. Size does influence human resource, funding, investment, and lending capacities of banks.

Before discussing the most important factor, public policy considerations, items 2 and 3 are discussed.

To the extent that interstate banking already exists, legislative action liberalizing geographic restrictions is merely acknowledgment of reality. Some observers have argued that since so much *de facto* interstate banking exists that the issue should be more precisely labeled "interstate deposit taking." Of course, even now a significant amount of interstate deposit taking is being done and the future promises further increases in this activity. Acknowledging reality is not without important implications. To the extent that the incorrect views that out-of-state banks "are kept out" and Florida bank markets "are protected" by the state's present structure are maintained, in-state banks operate under a false sense of security. Moreover, if these banks postpone desirable organizational, investment, and other policy changes necessary to adjust to the challenges of deregulation, technology, and changing levels of consumer sophistication, they may operate in either a suboptimal fashion or possibly not survive.[7] Accordingly, lifting interstate banking barriers will force or encourage Florida institutions to get ready for the remaining challenges and opportunities in the financial services industry.

Larger banking organizations are the inevitable result of the current intrastate consolidation of Florida banks and permitted interstate banking expansion. Size may prove to be strategically crucial to success and/or survival in the emerging competitive environment. Higher caliber credit and noncredit personnel may be necessary to (1) effectively compete for loans and control credit risk, and (2) efficiently provide noncredit (fee based) services and system support. Size is essential to developing the required human resource base in terms of recruiting, training, and retention. Consumer banking is increasingly involving larger fixed investment. Again, size may be necessary either to make the required investment or to realize efficient per unit costs.[8]

Size can make further acquisitions easier. As banks necessarily get involved in new fixed investment, human resource programs, and new product lines to meet challenges, the ability to adjust size (by acquisition) to achieve cost efficiency and profitability could be important.[9] In sum, greater size tends to lead to modified organizations, up-graded human resources, increased fixed investment, and revised portfolio policies (higher risky asset ratios, greater leverage, and more funding capacity) for the banks modifying their size through interstate expansion. Loan ratios (consumer and commercial) would tend to be increased in the Florida banks involved in interstate acquisitions.

On balance, interstate banking proposals would be consistent with conventional public policy considerations. The public interest is certainly served by the greater number of bank sites, broader product and service lines, and the increased credit availability to businesses (of all sizes), consumers, and municipalities expected to result from liberalization of geographic restrictions.

The evidence indicates that small banks would not be endangered by interstate banking since they face no scale size cost disadvantages.[10] Moreover, the evidence indicates that larger banks entering markets by acquisition do not take market share at the expense of the small banks. The analysis suggests that bank safety and soundness (risk) would not be problematic in an interstate banking environment. Although the risks of affiliated interstate banks would increase, these risks would be offset by the benefits of geographic and product diversification as well as organizational (assist from within a multi-BHC) and institutional (Garn-St. Germain) factors.

The general effects of statewide banking (via holding company acquisition or branching) has been to deconcentrate local markets which otherwise would have been insulated from competition. Florida's statewide merging and branching structure is currently undergoing significant consolidation, especially among the state's largest BHCs (see chapter 1). A continuation of the status quo would result in further consolidation and concentration of banks in the state. Policies allowing interstate banking—regional or nationwide— would naturally lessen concentration and, thus, be more competitive than the existing bank structure. Out-of-state banks would enter local markets and change the set of major firms meeting in each of the state's major markets. These entrants bring qualitatively different competitive policies and/or tools and would tend to force a reexamination of the competitive "rules of the game."

The most recent evidence on competition between multi-market firms (multi-BHCs) suggests that as the number of links between firms increases the degree of competition between those firms increases (see 39). This research evidence (39) which is based upon Florida banking markets and banks suggests that the present links in the state—multi-market firms meeting each other in several or all major markets—is pro-competitive. This, of course, results in better prices, services, and/or greater credit availability for the public. These findings also suggest that policies maximizing multi-market meeting points in Florida is desirable. Whitehead (39) states:

> ...If geographic barriers to interstate banking are removed, this may serve to increase the links among banking organizations. To the extent that our finding in Florida may be applicable in the nation, this could serve to increase bank competition. Given that multi-market links are important and that interstate banking is a strong possibility in the near future, the impact of multi-market links may prove to be more important, not less, in the future.

In brief, Florida markets are rapidly consolidating. Proposals to permit interstate banking could tend to deconcentrate local bank markets. Further, the recent Florida evidence suggests that multi-market linkages that would result from interstate banking activity would be procompetitive; i.e., the public would realize better prices and/or greater services and/or increased output (credit).

Against

The arguments against liberalization of geographic restrictions on interstate banking involve the following:

1. Deposits (capital) will be drained from Florida communities by out-of-state banks who will redeploy funds elsewhere in the United States or abroad.
2. Florida banks would become controlled by large money center banks who will indirectly involve Florida banks in the risk emanating from foreign loan problems.
3. Interstate banking does not increase competition since it is accomplished by mere acquisition of existing banks. Thus, the number of banks is not increased.
4. Interstate banking results in economic concentration and power inconsistent with the nation's traditional policy against concentration of financial resources.
5. Out-of-state banks will control Florida bank structure. Florida banks will not have a role in the future bank structure.
6. Regional reciprocity and regional reciprocity not coupled with a "trigger" permitting nationwide reciprocity at a subsequent date may be illegal.

Each of the above arguments are addressed in the order listed.

The argument that interstate banking would lead to deposit drainage from Florida communities is analogous to the (earlier) traditional arguments made against liberalization of branching and BHC acquisition restrictions. Regarding these prior cases, it was subsequently found that credit in local communities was not only maintained but often increased; i.e., no deposit drains occurred. Entering banks had dual interests—deposit gathering and loan generation. Bankers have long recognized that these dual interests are highly interdependent in a given market. One could argue that a particular Florida deposit base would be valuable to an out-of-state bank in its efforts to penetrate local loan markets. And in the case of Florida these prospects may be deemed more desirable than redeployment elsewhere. Accordingly, a great deal of evidence and logic suggests that funds would not be drained from Florida. Previously, it was noted that Florida banks, ironically, do "drain deposits" to the extent that they sell federal funds on a net basis.

The transfer of foreign debt problems to Florida banks is not likely (see p. 49). It was previously explained that the responsible federal agency explicitly considers safety and soundness. Additionally, normal market behavior would discourage this via charging greater premiums to affiliate with entities that have notable risk exposure.

Entry into local markets by acquisition can be procompetitive even if no new producers are established. The conclusion that competition would not increase in an interstate banking setting derives from the supposition that competition is strictly a function of the number of competitors in a market. The empirical evidence suggests that market entry by acquisition generally leads to changes in the portfolio policies (assets and liabilities), prices, and services mostly along procompetitive lines. Additionally, it is observed that pre-existing banks in the entered market react or respond to match such procompetitive actions. Unfortunately this reaction function has not been well researched to date (see 18). Previously in this chapter, it was argued that banks affiliated on an interstate basis would have qualitatively different product and service competitive capability as a result of the size obtained or the affiliation with larger entities.[11] It should also be recalled that interstate banking would increase competitive linkages that, according to the most recent Florida evidence (39), would enhance competition.

The banking (and financial industry) is rapidly consolidating. Currently the focus is intra-state expansion and *de facto* interstate banking (including "when and if" agreements). Concentration is significantly increasing. Interstate banking may be necessary to stem this tide. Despite widespread consolidation, charges of unreasonable financial concentration and power in relationship to past bank structure and to structures of other countries are probably unwarranted. First, the competitive ability of small banks appears strong. Second, there is an abundance of cross-industry competition from S&Ls, security firms, insurance firms, and manufacturer/retailer nonbanks. Third, much banking activity has become national and international in nature.[12] Fourth, (regional) interstate banking may result in some large Florida institutions who might add to the competitive levels existing in the regional money center competitive category. To the extent that such entities survive in the long run, there is assurance that extreme concentration of financial power will not occur ultimately.

If an era of interstate banking evolves, out-of-state banks will gain significant control of the state's bank structure. However, it should be clear that well-managed small banks who do not have management succession problems can survive and do not have to sell out. Similarly, Florida BHCs can adopt strategies to survive and remain independent in the long run. Regional interstate banking would most likely preserve regional control over banking assets whereas nationwide interstate would lead to out-of-state banking dominance in Florida. Regional interstate banking followed by nationwide reciprocity (say 2, 3, or 5 years later) would have mixed effects. Some small and large Florida banking organizations would survive but state bank structure would have significant out-of-state participation.

The legal analysis (see chapter 9) indicates that attacks on regional reciprocity and/or regional reciprocity without a nationwide reciprocity "trigger" would most likely fail.

Appraisal of Possible Legislative Options

It appears that for the most part market forces and innovations have already involved Florida in interstate banking. The high degree of cross-industry competition with both depository and nondepository institutions has in effect already made interstate banking substantially a reality in Florida. From the public interest viewpoint, this reality has been advantageous to the state; i.e., these procompetitive developments have helped fuel the last several years' economic growth. The analysis presented in this chapter and throughout the entire report suggests that even further *de facto* interstate banking cannot be arrested. Interstate banking legislation most likely will be in the public interest, although its benefits will not be as great as they might if all the *de facto* interstate banking by banks and nonbanks were not already so prevalent. Fortunately, the resolution of this issue should not pit the public interest—in competition, greater credit availability and services, and lower prices—against Florida banks who would be affected by interstate banking legislation. That is, Florida banks could use such new legislation to join with out-of-state banks to further adjust and better compete in the present environment, particularly against less regulated competitors. Also, Florida bank shareholders could elect to sell out to the highest bidders. The public would stand to realize some gains from the reformulated bank structure.

The following section examines the implications of potential legislative actions. It should be pointed out that only the three interstate banking variations previously considered by the Florida legislature and expected to be explored in the future are discussed. These include nationwide reciprocity, regional reciprocity, or regional reciprocity transition to nationwide reciprocity (so-called regional with "trigger"). Before proceeding, it should be noted that other interstate banking variations such as those permitting *de novo* entry or implementing a nationwide unrestricted policy (see p. 52) would be in the public interest.

The analysis of the case for and against liberalization of geographic restrictions suggests that it is in the public interest to remove interstate banking restrictions. Public policy considerations would not be compromised by interstate banking proposals. Florida citizens could expect broader product and service offerings and increased credit availability. Although banking markets may become more competitive, small in-state banks would not be endangered and larger in-state banks could achieve further organizational restructuring that may improve their competitive capability. Arguments against geographical liberalization were found to be either invalid or of much less negative consequence than asserted. Accordingly, the maintenance of the status quo is not advised.

The status quo would result in a continuation of the present trends of intrastate consolidation and concentration. The prime beneficiary of this option would be the in-state and grandfathered banks who participate in this consolidation. These banks not only gain size and grow but face less competition in bidding for their acquisitions. The state would continue to witness the following:

1. Out-of-state banks will make "when and if" (interstate banking is legal) agreements to acquire Florida banks.
2. Out-of-country banks and individuals will make investments in or acquire Florida banks.
3. Out-of-state banks and nonbanks will expand their financial activities in Florida.

Nationwide Reciprocity Option (NRO)

The NRO would most likely lead to a banking structure that is less concentrated and, thus, more competitive than the more concentrated structure that is presently developing from the status quo competitive framework. Accordingly, the public should benefit from this more competitive structure in terms of greater credit availability, lower prices, and/or broader service offerings.

To the extent that out-of-state banks offer higher prices for acquisitions than in-state banks, Florida's structure would be controlled by out-of-state organizations. At the present, as a practical matter NRO would result in opportunities for New York banks to acquire Florida banks and vice-versa. However, most likely New York banks would acquire Florida banks. Florida banks would be less likely to survive and Florida would not realize benefits from diverse entry from out-of-state banks headquartered in other states since so few other states presently have reciprocity statutes with Florida. The fact that so few other states have reciprocity laws represents a significant limitation on Florida's ability to benefit from NRO.

The state could realize the maximum benefits from nationwide entry and avoid the more limited NRO arrangement which, at present, is primarily with New York by electing an unrestricted national policy (see p. 52). This policy would probably result in only a minor role for Florida banks in the long run. Since the legislature has not considered a bill without reciprocity it is not pursued further.

Regional Reciprocity Option (RRO)

The RRO is considered an intermediate step or adjustment to nationwide banking. It is generally put forth as an alternative that affords existing banks in the state and the region an opportunity to adapt to the changing financial environment. While in effect, the major beneficiaries of the RRO would be the major in-state bank organizations which expand by acquisition in the South. These organizations would grow, gain size, and establish networks at less expense than if they were forced to bid for acquisitions against banks headquartered outside the South.

The RRO would most likely preserve regional bank organizations. Such preservation could be important for various reasons. First, regional-based firms may tend to be more responsive to middle market firms, municipalities or regional industries. Second, the construction and survival of several larger regional organizations fosters competition in certain product and service categories limited to only the large money center (regional and national) institutions at the present time. Third, regional firms could expand their representation in natural markets which cross state lines. Similarly, some regional banks could further develop, expand or extend particular product (loan) expertise appropriate to the region. Although the RRO delays the implementation of nationwide banking, it does preserve the future option of national reciprocity.

Regional with Trigger Option (RWTO)

The RWTO would involve the legislature enacting a statute which allows regional reciprocity for a certain time period and then permits nationwide reciprocity (at the trigger point). Previously, proposals have included "triggers" permitting nationwide reciprocity after either 2, 3, or 5 years. The optimum "trigger" time period is conjectural. The period selected would allow time for the other states in the region to enact reciprocity laws and for the banks in the region to implement expansion plans.

This policy option would capture most of the potential benefits deriving from the NRO and the RRO and at the same time recognize the limitation(s) of each. By beginning with the RRO the state explicitly allows for an interim period which (1) allows in-state banks an opportunity to expand regionally; (2) allows the state, region, and nation to benefit from any real economic advantages alleged to result from the construction and preservation of large regional banks; and (3) allows time for other states both inside and outside the region to enact reciprocity laws.[13]

The "trigger" to nationwide reciprocity assures that some of the remaining geographical restrictions and any potential anti-competitive effects of the eventual consolidation and concentration of state and regional markets would be addressed. The public interest is best served when the state can achieve a more geographically diverse (national presence) representation in the various local Florida markets. Only nationwide interstate banking can provide this end result.

In-state banks would have considerable flexibility under the RWTO. Larger BHCs could elect an expansion strategy aimed at gaining size, growth, and multi-state presence. Other BHCs could elect to sell out and become part of larger in-state or regional entities or wait for nationwide bidders. Unit banks could elect to (1) remain independent (2) join regional entities or (3) wait for bids emanating from nationwide reciprocity.

Conclusions and Implications

This report provides abundant documentation and evidence that interstate banking already exists in Florida. Both out-of-state banks and nonbanks compete in Florida against in-state banks. Market forces, technology, and competitive realities assure the inevitability of interstate banking. Nevertheless the state has a definite role in shaping the unwinding process headed toward interstate banking, particularly since the Federal government has not aggressively pursued this issue.

The state faces two basic questions. First, should the state preserve the status quo or should the state pursue one of the various interstate banking policy options? Second, if the state pursues interstate banking, which policy option serves the public interest most?

The analysis of public policy considerations indicated that maintaining the status quo is not desirable. Removing the restrictions on interstate banking would be procompetitive and in the public interest. Liberalization of geographic restrictions would result in greater credit availability and/or better prices, broader and higher quality product/service offerings, and more efficient allocation of financial resources. Fortunately, the magnitude of *de facto* interstate banking in Florida along with the pressure of market forces innovations and technology have lessened the public policy costs of geographical restrictions to Florida citizens resulting from restrictive limitations on interstate banking. Additionally, Florida's economic development has been significantly enhanced in the past by the credit made available by out-of-state banks and nonbanks.

Although the focus of this study is the public interest, the findings are not at odds with the interests of Florida banks. Relaxation of interstate banking restrictions should enhance the ability of commercial banks to compete with less regulated competitors. Also, banks would be encouraged to take action that may be necessary to better compete in the evolving financial services industry. Despite the fact that Florida banking markets may become more competitive, small banks would still be viable and larger banks could achieve significant organizational restructuring to improve their chances for success and/or survival. The safety and soundness of the state's banks would not be threatened.

The conclusion that geographic restrictions on interstate banking should be removed is consistent with the public policy recommendations offered by the following: (see 9, 1, 37) (1) the Carter Administration; (2) the Graham Administration; (3) the Southern Growth Policy Board (Commission on the Future of the South); and (4) the *Sixty-Fourth American Assembly: The Future of American Financial Services Institutions.*

The analysis of policy options indicated that the nationwide reciprocity option would probably result in the most competitive structure in the long run. However, its immediate adoption would not result in diverse out-of-state bank entry into local markets since most other states do not have reciprocity statues in place. Most likely New York banks would gain control of Florida banking assets while Florida banks would not be expected to expand into New York. The ultimate bank structure would be dominated by out-of-state organizations.

Regional reciprocity involves a middle-of-the-road approach between the status quo and nationwide reciprocity. It most likely would lessen the trend toward concentration in Florida and would preserve some regional control of banking entities.

Another approach would involve regional reciprocity with a trigger allowing nationwide reciprocity after a certain time period (e.g., 2, 3 or 5 years). This approach permits regional reciprocity only as in interim step to allow Florida banks to acquire (or to be acquired by) banks in the region and make further strategic adjustments to address the changing financial environment. Additionally, more states throughout the nation would have an opportunity to pass reciprocity legislation which would result in a more geographically varied representation of out-of-state banks competing in local bank markets versus primarily New York banks. After an interim period, the implementation of nationwide reciprocity would serve to enhance competition in the state and the region. This probably would be quite timely since the state and region would be consolidating rapidly.

On balance the combination approach—regional reciprocity with a nationwide reciprocity trigger—would seem to allow for a short adjustment period culminating in a nationwide framework which promises to be the most competitive. The preservation of some large regional banking organizations would be a healthy by-product.

There are other policy options related to the interstate banking issue. Both *de novo* entry and unrestricted nationwide policies would be pro-competitive and superior to the status quo. These options were not pursued in detail since the legislature has not chosen to consider either in past deliberations.

Notes

1. See (14) and chapter 7 of this report for summarization of the empirical evidence related to the impact of bank expansion. Chapter 7 discusses the key public policy impact. The various portfolio impacts are examined in (14).

2. The reader should note that other commercial banks and investment banks (through their S&L affiliate) have attempted to use the Garn-St. Germain to acquire Florida S&Ls.

3. Money market mutual fund deposits emanating from Florida have been variously estimated to range between 10% and 13%.

4. Although data for the nonbank sample could not be disaggregated for a specific state, spot checks revealed that these companies were well represented in Florida.

5. The findings of this study are in agreement with those of John D. Hawke, Jr. as reported in the December 15, 1982, *American Banker*. However, for a counter viewpoint, see (21).

6. See (11) for greater insight into the political sensitivity of the division of regulatory authority between state and federal agencies.

7. See (8) for a rationale of one Florida BHC for electing an interstate bank acquisition. This rationale includes recognition of the changing market, realities and organizational and investment changes required to meet these realities.

8. See (16, 27) for further discussion of the importance of size and diversification to bank management in a changing environment.
   Other key factors such as marketing and regulatory compliance costs exist which involve increased overhead burden which ideally could be spread over a larger income base. See (27) for discussion of these points.

9. For additional insight into the financial rationale for BHC expansion, see (19). This study analyzes the seldom studied intra-organizational costs of BHCs.

10. Concern over the survival of small banks should focus on the problem of management succession and ownership transfer which historically have been major determinants of the sale of many small banks. This factor promises to be most important in the consolidation of banks nationally and in Florida. This will be the inevitable result of small bank ownership demographics. Because the age demographics of small bank owners is skewed to older age brackets, shareholders will seek to liquify their investments. The only matter left to assess is the *exact* timing and magnitude of this selling pressure. For an expanded discussion of the demographics "time bomb", see (26).

11. An example of competitive capabilities acquired through affiliation would be the business lending strengths developing at Exchange Banks as a result of their affiliation with NCNB. These capabilities are possible without affiliating with larger banks. Rather the benefits of size can obtain at a number of Florida Banks currently consolidating intrastate and potentially participants in interstate expansion; e.g., Barnett, Sun, Southeast, Florida National, and Landmark/Southwest Florida Bank.

12. Foreign competitors presently control over 20% of the United States Commercial and Industrial Loans.

13.   Recall that the fact that so few other states in the nation presently have reciprocity statutes severely limits the benefits Florida could obtain from the nationwide reciprocity option; i.e., the principal result would involve New York banks acquiring Florida banks. Also, recall that Florida could avoid this limitation and broaden the entry into Florida by adopting an unrestricted nationwide policy. Although such a policy has considerable merit, it has not to date been considered in the legislative arena.

References

1.   The American Assembly (64th), *The Future of American Financial Services Institutions,* Harriman, New York.

2.   Annual and quarterly reports of Barnett Banks, North Carolina National Bank, and Texas Commerce Bankshares.

3.   Annual Reports (Selected), Department of Banking, State of Florida.

4.   Benston, George J., "Economies of Scale of Financial Institutions," *Journal of Money, Credit, and Banking,* vol. 4, (May 1972), pp. 312-41.

5.   Benston, George J., "Economies of Scale and Marginal Costs in Banking Organizations," *National Banking Review,* vol. 2, (June 1965), pp. 507-49.

6.   Benston, George J., "The Optimal Banking Structure: Theory and Evidence," *Journal of Bank Research,* vol. 3, (Winter 1973), pp. 220-37.

7.   Benston, George J. and Gerald A. Hanweck, "A Summary Report on Bank Holding Company Affiliation and Economies of Scale," *Conference on Bank Structure and Competition,* Federal Reserve Bank of Chicago, April 1977, pp. 158-68.

8.   Campbell, Gordon W., "Mergers and NCNB," *Florida Banker,* September 1983.

9.   Department of Treasury, *The Report of the President on Geographic Restrictions on Commercial Banking in the United States,* Washington, D.C., January 1981.

10.   *Economic Review,* "Special Issue: Interstate Banking," Federal Reserve Bank of Atlanta, May 1983.

11.   Eisenbeis, Robert A., "Interstate Banking: Federal Perspectives and Prospects," *Proceedings of a Conference on Bank Structure and Competition,* Federal Reserve Bank of Chicago, May 1981.

12.   *Federal Reserve Bulletins:* Board of Governors, Federal Reserve System: Washington, D.C., various issues.

13.   Fraas, Arthur, "The Performance of Individual Bank Holding Companies," *Staff Economic Studies,* no. 84, Federal Reserve Board, 1974.

14.   Frieder, Larry A., *Commercial Banking and Holding Company Acquisitions: New Dimensions in Theory, Practice, and Evaluation,* UMI Research Press, Ann Arbor, Michigan (1981).

15.   Frieder, Larry A., "Orderly Transition to Interstate Banking," *Bankers Magazine*, Spring 1981, vol. 164, no. 2.

16.   Frieder, Larry A., "Banking's New Peer Group," *Bankers Magazine*, September-October 1983, vol. 166, no. 5.

17.   Frieder, Larry A. and Vincent P. Apilado, "The Performance of Multi-Bank Holding Companies in Light of Valuation Theory and Financial Regulation." *Proceedings of a Conference on Bank Structure and Competition* (1980), Chicago Federal Reserve Bank.

18.   Frieder, Larry A. and Vincent P. Apilado, "Bank Holding Company Research: Classification, Synthesis, and New Directions," *Journal of Bank Research*, Autumn 1982, pp. 80-95.

19.   Frieder, Larry A. and Vincent P. Apilado, "Bank Holding Company Expansion: A Refocus on its Financial Rationale," *Journal of Financial Research*, Spring 1983, pp. 67-81.

20.   Golembe, Carter H. (and Associates), *A Study of Interstate Banking By Bank Holding Companies*, Washington, D.C., May 25, 1979.

21.   Golembe, Carter H., "Massachusetts and Interstate Banking," *Banking Expansion Reporter*, January 17, 1983, volume 2, no. 2.

22.   Grunewald, Alan, "Economic Necessity for Interstate Banking," *Proceedings of a Conference on Bank Structure and Competition* (19/9), Chicago Federal Reserve Bank.

23.   Hawke, John D., Jr., "Comments on Douglas Amendment and Regional Reciprocity," *American Banker*, December 15, 1982 per 21 above.

24.   Johnson, Bradford M., "Converting an Unfriendly Target to a Willing Participant: Outline of Talking Points Favoring a Merger," *Takeovers of Banks*, Harcourt Brace Jovanovich, 1983.

25.   Johnson, Bradford M., "The Pros and Cons of a Minority Interest Investment Program," *American Banker*, June 3, 1981.

26.   Johnson, Bradford M., "The Bank Shareholder Demographics Time Bomb," *Banking Expansion Reporter*, vol. 2, no. 6, March 1983.

27.   Johnson, Bradford M., Allan I. Issaaeson, Robert B. Lochrie, *Takeover of Banks*, Harcourt Brace Jovanovich, New York, 1983.

28.   Lawrence, Robert J., "Operating Policies of Bank Holding Companies—Part I, " *Staff Economic Studies*, no. 59, Federal Reserve Board, 1971.

29.   Lawrence, Robert J., "Operating Policies of Bank Holding Companies—Part II," *Staff Economic Studies*, no. 81, 1974.

30.   Mayer, Thomas, "Competitive Equality as a Criterion for Financial Reform," *Journal of Banking and Finance* 4 (1980), North Holland Publishing Company.

31.   Mellon Bank, "Interstate Banking Legislation: A Need for Change," April 1979, Pittsburgh, PA.

32. McCord, Tom, "McFadden and the International Bank Act," *Issues in Bank Regulation,* Autumn 1979.

33. Rhoades, Stephen A., "Structure Performance Studies in Banking: A Summary and Evaluation," *Staff Economic Studies,* no. 92, Federal Reserve Board, 1977.

34. Rivard, Richard J., "An Independent Analysis of the Implications of Interstate Banking for Florida," *Florida Banker,* April 1983.

35. Rosenblum, Harvey and Diane Siegel, "Competition in Financial Services: The Impact of Nonbank Entry," Staff Study 83-1, Federal Reserve Bank of Chicago, 1983.

36. Savage, Donald T., "A Proposal for Managing a Transition to Interstate Banking," *Issues in Bank Regulation,* Winter 1980.

37. Southern Growth Policies Board, *Final Report: 1980 Commission on the Future of the South,* 1981.

38. Wells, Joel, "Wells Calls for Banks and SAL to Join Forces," *Florida Banker,* November 1983.

39. Whitehead, David D. and Jan Luytjes, "An Empirical Test of the Linked Oligopoly Theory: An Analysis of Florida Holding Companies Revisited," unpublished paper presented at Southern Economics meeting in Washington, D.C., November 20-23, 1983.

Index

REPORT

ON

"The Star-Spangled Banner"
"Hail Columbia"
"America"
"Yankee Doodle"

REPORT

ON

"The Star-Spangled Banner"
"Hail Columbia"
"America"
"Yankee Doodle"

BY

OSCAR GEORGE THEODORE SONNECK

LATE CHIEF OF THE MUSIC DIVISION,
LIBRARY OF CONGRESS

DOVER PUBLICATIONS, INC.
NEW YORK

42146

Published in Canada by General Publishing Company, Ltd., 30 Lesmill Road, Don Mills, Toronto, Ontario.

Published in the United Kingdom by Constable and Company, Ltd., 10 Orange Street, London WC 2.

This Dover edition, first published in 1972, is an unabridged republication of the work originally published by the Library of Congress (printed at the Government Printing Office, Washington, D. C.) in 1909.

International Standard Book Number: 0-486-22237-3
Library of Congress Catalog Card Number: 75-145993

Manufactured in the United States of America
Dover Publications, Inc.
180 Varick Street
New York, N. Y. 10014

CONTENTS

PREFATORY NOTE

In December, 1907, I received instructions from the Librarian of Congress to "bring together the various versions both of text and of music with notes as to the historical evolution" of "The Star-Spangled Banner," "Hail Columbia," "America," and "Yankee Doodle." The report was to be brief and light of touch, but accurate enough for practical purposes. This task would have been comparatively easy had the literature on the subject been reliable. Unfortunately it crumbled under the slightest critical pressure, and it became imperative to devote more research and more analytical and synthetic thought to the report than had seemed advisable at first. This and the fact that the report had to be compiled without neglect of current duties accounts for the delay in submitting it.

In form the report is frankly not a history of the subject, such as one would write for popular consumption. Rather, in this report data are collected, eliminated, or verified; popular theories founded on these data are analyzed, their refutation or acceptance is suggested, and, of course, some theories of my own are offered for critical consideration. All this is done in such a form that the reader is at no step supposed to find a locked door between himself and the argument. He is not supposed to accept a single statement of fact or argument unless the evidence submitted compels him to do so. This *plein air* treatment of a popular theme distinguishes the report somewhat from the bulk of the literature on the subject. In short, though not intended for popular consumption, it may be used for popular consumption with reasonable assurance of accuracy.

O. G. SONNECK

Chief, Music Division

HERBERT PUTNAM
 Librarian of Congress
  Washington, D. C., August, 1909

THE STAR-SPANGLED BANNER

Opinions differ widely on the merits of "The Star-Spangled Banner" as a national song. Some critics fail to see in Francis Scott Key's inspired lines poetry of more than patriotic value. Some look upon it merely as a flag song, a military song, but not as a national hymn. Some criticize the melody for its excessive range, but others see no defects in "The Star-Spangled Banner" and feel not less enthusiastic over its esthetic merits as a national song than over its sincere patriotic sentiment. This controversy will be decided, whether rightly or wrongly, by the American people regardless of critical analysis, legislative acts, or naïve efforts to create national songs by prize competition. This report does not concern itself at all with such quasi esthetic problems, nor is it here the place to trace the political history of "The Star-Spangled Banner" beyond what is necessary for the understanding of its history as a national song.

As has been well known for a long time, the first though brief account of the origin of "The Star-Spangled Banner" appeared in the Baltimore American on September 21, 1814, under the heading of:

DEFENCE OF FORT M'HENRY.

> The annexed song was composed under the following circumstances: A gentleman had left Baltimore, in a flag of truce for the purpose of getting released from the British fleet a friend of his who had been captured at Marlborough. He went as far as the mouth of the Patuxent, and was not permitted to return lest the intended attack on Baltimore should be disclosed. He was therefore brought up the Bay to the mouth of the Patapsco, where the flag vessel was kept under the guns of a frigate, and he was compelled to witness the bombardment of Fort M'Henry, which the Admiral had boasted that he would carry in a few hours, and that the city must fall. He watched the flag at the fort through the whole day with an anxiety that can be better felt than described, until the night prevented him from seeing it. In the night he watched the Bomb Shells, and at early dawn his eye was again greeted by the proudly waving flag of his country.

This account is followed by the text of Key's poem without special title, but with the indication: "Tune: Anacreon in Heaven."

As this account was printed almost immediately after the events therein described took place, and were in every reader's memory, the newspaper editor, of course, omitted specific dates, but it is a matter of history that the gallant defense of Fort McHenry under Major Armistead began on the morning of Tuesday, September 13, and lasted until the early hours of September 14, 1814. The *gentleman* is, of course, Francis Scott Key, and either his own modesty or an editorial whim kept his authorship from the public.

The first detailed and authentic account of the origin of "The Star-Spangled Banner" practically came from Francis Scott Key himself, who narrated it shortly after the British designs on Baltimore failed, to his brother-in-law, Mr. R. B. Taney, subsequently Chief Justice of our Supreme Court. When in 1856 Mr. Henry V. D. Jones edited the "Poems of the Late Francis S. Key, Esq. . . ." (New York, 1857), Chief Justice Taney contributed Key's version from memory, in an introductory "letter . . . narrating the incidents connected with the origin of the song 'The Star-Spangled Banner.'" This interesting narrative has been made the basis of all subsequent accounts. Its substance is this: When, after the battle of Bladensburg, the main body of the British army had passed through the town of Upper Marlborough, some stragglers, who had left the ranks to plunder or from some other motive, made their appearance from time to time, singly or in small squads, and a Doctor Beanes, who had previously been very hospitable to the British officers "put himself at the head of a small body of citizens to pursue and make prisoners" of the stragglers. Information of this proceeding reached the British and Doctor Beanes was promptly seized. The British "did not seem to regard him, and certainly did not treat him, as a prisoner of war, but as one who had deceived and broken his faith to them." Doctor Beanes was the leading physician of his town and so highly respected that the news of his imprisonment filled his friends with alarm. They "hastened to the head-quarters of the English army to solicit his release, but it was peremptorily refused," and they were informed that he had been carried as a prisoner on board the fleet. Francis Scott Key happened also to be one of the Doctor's intimate friends, and as Mr. Key, just then a volunteer in Major Peter's Light Artillery, but a lawyer by profession, was a resident of Georgetown, which means practically Washington, the other friends requested him—

to obtain the sanction of the government to his going on board the admiral's ship under a flag of truce and endeavoring to procure the release of Dr. Beanes, before the fleet sailed.

. . . Mr. Key readily agreed to undertake the mission in his favor, and the President [Madison] promptly gave his sanction to it. Orders were immediately issued to the vessel usually employed as a cartel [the *Minden*] in the communications with the fleet in the Chesapeake to be made ready without delay; and Mr. John S. Skinner, who was agent for the government for flags of truce and exchange of prisoners, and who was well known as such to the officers of the fleet, was directed to accompany Mr. Key. And as soon as the arrangements were made, he hastened to Baltimore, where the vessel was, to embark; . . .

We heard nothing from him until the enemy retreated from Baltimore, which, as well as I can now recollect, was a week or ten days after he left us; and we were becoming uneasy about him, when, to our great joy, he made his appearance at my house, on his way to join his family.

He told me that he found the British fleet, at the mouth of the Potomac, preparing for the expedition against Baltimore. He was courteously received by Admiral Cochrane, and the officers of the army, as well as the navy. But when he made known his business, his application was received so coldly, that he feared he would fail. General Ross and Admiral Cockburn—who accompanied the expedition to Washington—particularly the latter, spoke of Dr. Beanes, in very harsh terms, and seemed at first not disposed to release him. It, however, happened, fortunately, that Mr. Skinner carried letters from the wounded British officers left at Bladensburg; and in these letters to their friends on board the fleet, they all spoke of the humanity and kindness with which they had been treated after they had fallen into our hands. And after a good deal of conversation, and strong representations from Mr. Key, as to the character and standing of Dr. Beanes, and of the deep interest which the community in which he lived, took in his fate, General Ross said that Dr. Beanes deserved much more punishment than he had received; but that he felt himself bound to make a return for the kindness which had been shown to his wounded officers, whom he had been compelled to leave at Bladensburg; and upon that ground, and that only, he would release him. But Mr. Key was at the same time informed that neither he, nor any one else, would be permitted to leave the fleet for some days; and must be detained until the attack on Baltimore, which was then about to be made, was over. But he was assured that they would make him and Mr. Skinner, as comfortable as possible, while they detained him. Admiral Cochrane, with whom they dined on the day of their arrival, apologized for not accommodating them on his own ship, saying that it was crowded already with officers of the army; but that they would be well taken care of in the frigate *Surprise*, commanded by his son, Sir Thomas Cochrane. And to this frigate, they were accordingly transferred.

Mr. Key had an interview with Dr. Beanes, before General Ross consented to release him. I do not recollect whether he was on board the admiral's ship, or the *Surprise*, but I believe it was the former. He found him in the forward part of the ship, among the sailors and soldiers; he had not had a change of clothes from the time he was seized; was constantly treated with indignity by those around him, and no officer would speak to him. He was treated as a culprit, and not as a prisoner of war. And this harsh and humiliating treatment continued until he was placed on board the cartel . . .

Mr. Key and Mr. Skinner continued on board of the *Surprise*, where they were very kindly treated by Sir Thomas Cochrane, until the fleet reached the Patapsco, and preparations were making for landing the troops. Admiral Cochrane then shifted his flags to the frigate, in order that he might be able to move further up the river, and superintend in person, the attack by water, on the fort. And Mr. Key and Mr. Skinner were then sent on board their own vessel, with a guard of sailors, or marines, to prevent them from landing. They were permitted to take Dr. Beanes with them and they thought themselves fortunate in being anchored in a position which enabled them to see distinctly the flag of Fort M'Henry from the deck of the vessel. He proceeded then with much animation to describe the scene on the night of the bombardment. He and Mr. Skinner remained on deck during the night, watching every shell, from the moment it was fired, until it fell, listening with breathless interest to hear if an explosion followed. While the bombardment continued, it was sufficient proof that the fort had not surrendered. But it suddenly ceased some time before day; and as they had no communication with any of the enemy's ships, they did not know whether the fort had surrendered, or the attack upon it been abandoned. They paced the deck for the residue of the night in painful suspense, watching with intense anxiety for the return of day, and looking every few minutes at their watches, to see how long they must wait for it; and as soon as it dawned, and before it was light enough to see objects at a distance,

their glasses were turned to the fort, uncertain whether they should see there the
stars and stripes, or the flag of the enemy. At length the light came, and they saw
that "our flag was still there." And as the day advanced, they discovered, from
the movements of the boats between the shore and the fleet, that the troops had
been roughly handled, and that many wounded men were carried to the ships. At
length he was informed that the attack on Baltimore had failed, and the British
army was re-embarking, and that he and Mr. Skinner, and Dr. Beanes would be
permitted to leave them, and go where they pleased, as soon as the troops were on
board, and the fleet ready to sail.

He then told me that, under the excitement of the time, he had written a
song, and handed me a printed copy of "The Star Spangled Banner." When I
had read it, and expressed my admiration, I asked him how he found time, in
the scenes he had been passing through, to compose such a song? He said he
commenced it on the deck of their vessel, in the fervor of the moment, when he
saw the enemy hastily retreating to their ships, and looked at the flag he had
watched for so anxiously as the morning opened; that he had written some lines,
or brief notes that would aid him in calling them to mind, upon the back of a
letter which he happened to have in his pocket; and for some of the lines, as he
proceeded, he was obliged to rely altogether on his memory; and that he finished
it in the boat on his way to the shore, and wrote it out as it now stands, at the hotel,
on the night he reached Baltimore, and immediately after he arrived. He said
that on the next morning, he took it to Judge Nicholson, to ask him what he
thought of it, that he was so much pleased with it, that he immediately sent it
to a printer, and directed copies to be struck off in hand-bill form; and that he,
Mr. Key, believed it to have been favorably received by the Baltimore public.

More than forty years had elapsed since Chief Justice Taney had
heard this story for the first time from Francis Scott Key, and
though it probably was modified or embellished in course of time, yet
in substance it has the earmarks of authenticity. Exactly for this
reason, if for no other, Chief Justice Taney's account furnished the
foundation for all further accounts, but it should be noticed that the
Chief Justice does not tell us anything beyond how the words came
to be written, until struck off in handbill form. We do not learn
when and under what circumstances the broadside was printed,
how the poem was wedded to its music, or when and by whom the
song was first read or sung. If certain writers do include such statements in their quotations from Taney's account, they certainly did
not read Taney's introductory letter, but most probably copied
their quotations from Admiral Preble, who indeed but carelessly
attributes such statements to the Chief Justice. The data not contained in Taney's account had to be supplied by others, and it is
very curious that instantly this part of the history of "The Star-Spangled Banner" became confused, whereas Chief Justice Taney's
account remained unchallenged except in unimportant points, as
for instance, the reasons for Doctor Beanes's arrest. Under this
head Chief Justice Taney was rather vague; not so Mrs. Anna H.
Dorsey, who in the Washington Sunday Morning Chronicle added
some "lesser facts," which were reprinted in Dawson's Historical

Magazine, 1861, volume 5, pages 282–283. According to Mrs. Dorsey, Dr. William Beanes, the uncle of her mother, was celebrating with copious libations a rumored British defeat at Washington when "three foot-sore, dusty, and weary soldiers made their appearance on the scene in quest of water." Somewhat under the influence of the excellent punch, Doctor Beanes and his friends made them prisoners of war, and very naturally, the British resented this, to say the least, indiscreet act. The Beanes-Dorsey family tradition is given here for all it is worth, but if correct, then it would be a singular coincidence that an English drinking song called "To Anacreon in Heaven" furnished the melody for a poem which had its root in an event inspired by Bacchus. Indeed Doctor Beanes and his friends might have been voicing their sentiments "To Anacreon in Heaven."

Different is the account written by Mr. F. S. Key Smith for the Republic Magazine, 1908, April, pages 10–20, on "Fort McHenry and 'The Star-Spangled Banner.'" According to Mr. Smith, a party of marauding stragglers came into the Doctor's garden and intruded themselves upon him and his little company. "Elated over their supposed victory of the day previous, of which the Doctor and his friends had heard nothing," says Mr. Smith, "they were boisterous, disorderly, and insolent, and upon being ordered to leave the premises became threatening. Whereupon, at the instance of Doctor Beanes and his friends, they were arrested by the town authorities and lodged in the Marlborough jail."

This version, too, is quoted here for all it is worth; but it should be noted that throughout this article, dealing elaborately only with the political history of Key's poem, Mr. Smith is conspicuously silent about his authorities, thus preventing critical readers from accepting his statements without skepticism. A case in point is his continuation of Chief Justice Taney's narrative:

> He [Judge Nicholson, also Key's brother-in-law] took it [the draft of the song] to the printing office of Captain Benjamin Edes on North Street near the corner of Baltimore street, but the Captain not having returned from duty with the Twenty-Sixth Maryland Regiment, his office was closed, and Judge Nicholson proceeded to the newspaper office of the Baltimore American and Commercial Daily Advertiser, where the words were set in type by Samuel Sands, an apprentice at the time. . . . Copies of the song were struck off in handbill form, and promiscuously distributed on the street. Catching with popular favor like prairie fire it spread in every direction, was read and discussed, until, in less than an hour, the news was all over the city. Picked up by a crowd assembled about Captain McCauley's tavern, next to the Holiday Street Theater, where two brothers Charles and Ferdinand Durang, musicians and actors, were stopping, the latter mounted a chair, and rendered it in fine style to a large assemblage.
>
> On the evening of the same day that Mr. Charles [!!] Durang first sang "The Star Spangled Banner," it was again rendered upon the stage of the Holliday Street Theater by an actress, and the theater is said to have gained thereby a national reputation. In less than a week it had reached New Orleans [!] . . .

This is merely the hastily concocted and uncritically diluted essence of previous articles, including that by Taney. It will be more profitable to turn to the very few original accounts than to dissect or even pay much attention to the second-hand compilations from these original sources, no matter how spirited or otherwise attractive they may be.

One C. D., in the Historical Magazine of 1864, volume 8, pages 347–348, has this to say:

> One of your correspondents inquires in what form the song of the *Star Spangled Banner* was first printed? I think that in the *History of the Philadelphia Stage* you will find that subject clearly explained. The song was first printed and put upon the press by Captain Edes, of Baltimore, who belonged to Colonel Long's Twenty-Seventh Regiment of militia. He kept his printing office at the corner of Baltimore and Gay Streets. It was given him by the author, Mr. Key, of Washington, in its amended form, after the battle of North Point, about the latter end of September 1814. The original draft, with its interlineations and amendatory erasures, etc. was purchased by the late Gen. George Keim, of Reading, and I suppose his heirs have it now. It was printed on a small piece of paper in the style of our old ballads that were wont to be hawked about the streets in days of yore. It was first sung by about twenty volunteer soldiers in front of the Holliday Street Theater, who used to congregate at the adjoining tavern to get their early mint juleps. Ben. Edes brought it round to them on one of those libating mornings or matinees. I was one of the group. My brother sang it. We all formed the chorus. This is its history . . .

The reference to the "History of the Philadelphia Stage" and to "My brother" immediately implies the identity of this C. D. with Charles Durang, brother of Ferdinand Durang (both actors), and joint author, or, rather, editor of his father John's, "History of the Philadelphia Stage," published serially in the Philadelphia Sunday Dispatch, 1854–55. Consequently we have here the testimony of a contemporary earwitness. A few years later, in 1867, Col. John L. Warner read before the Pennsylvania Historical Society a paper on "The Origin of the American National Anthem called 'The Star-Spangled Banner,'" and this paper was printed in the Historical Magazine, 1867, Volume II, pages 279–280. As will be seen from the following quotation, it does not contradict Charles Durang's account, but merely supplements it. Says Colonel Warner:

> It was first sung when fresh from his [Captain Benjamin Edes'] press, at a small frame one-story house, occupied as a tavern next to the Holiday Street Theatre.
>
> This tavern had long been kept by the widow Berling, and then by a Colonel MacConkey, a house where the players "most did congregate," with the quid nuncs of that day, to do honor to, and to prepare for, the daily military drills in Gay Street, (for every able man was then a soldier;) and here came, also, Captain Benjamin Edes, of the Twenty-seventh Regiment; Captain Long and Captain Thomas Warner, of the Thirty-ninth Regiment, and Major Frailey. Warner was a silversmith of good repute in that neighborhood.
>
> It was the latter end of September, 1814, when a lot of the young volunteer defenders of the Monumental City was thus assembled. Captain Edes and Cap-

tain Thomas Warner came early along one morning and forthwith called the group (quite merry with the British defeat) to order, to listen to a patriotic song which the former had just struck off at his press. He then read it to all the young volunteers there assembled, who greeted each verse with hearty shouts. It was then suggested that it should be sung; but who was able to sing it? Ferdinand Durang, who was a soldier in the cause and known to be a vocalist, being among the group, was assigned the task of vocalising this truly inspired patriotic hymn of the lamented Key. The old air of "Anacreon in Heaven" had been adapted to it by the author, and Mr. Edes was desired so to print it on the top of the ballad.

Its solemn melody and impressive notes seem naturally allied to the poetry, and speak emphatically the musical taste and judgement of Mr. Key. Ferdinand Durang mounted an old-fashioned rush-bottomed chair, and sang this admirable national song for the first time in our Union, the chorus to each verse being re-echoed by those present with infinite harmony of voices. It was thus sung several times during the morning. When the theatre was opened by Warren and Wood, it was sung nightly, after the play, by Paddy McFarland and the company.

So far the historian would have plain sailing, but his troubles begin with an article written for Harper's Magazine, 1871, volume 43, pages 254–258, by Mrs. Nellie Eyster, as appears from the printed index. Under the title of "'The Star-Spangled Banner:' An hour with an octogenarian," she reports an interview held on November 20, 1870, with Mr. Hendon, of Frederick, Md., who knew Francis Scott Key personally as a boy and who moved in 1809 to Lancaster, Pa., whence both the Durangs hailed. Together with Charles and Ferdinand Durang he belonged to the Pennsylvania Volunteer Militia, which on August 1, 1814, left Harrisburg in defense of Baltimore, but, remembers Mr. Hendon, they "marched to the seat of war three days after the battle had been won," and with special reference to the defense of Fort McHenry he "was chafing like a caged tiger because [he] was not in it." He further says that "they remained upon Gallows Hill, near Baltimore, for three months, daily waiting for an enemy that never came. Then, for the first time since leaving York [Pa.], [they] took breathing time and looked about for amusement." Follows what Admiral George Henry Preble called a more fanciful version than Warner's account when he copied Mr. Hendon's words for a footnote (p. 494) in the chapter on "Our National Songs" (pp. 490–511) in the first edition (Albany, 1872) of his industrious and popular compilation, "Our Flag:"

"Have you heard Francis Key's poem?" said one of our men, coming in one evening, as we lay scattered over the green hill near the captain's marquee. It was a rude copy, and written in a scrawl which Horace Greeley might have mistaken for his own. He read it aloud, once, twice, three times, until the entire division seemed electrified by its pathetic eloquence.

An idea seized Ferd. Durang. Hunting up a volume of flute music, which was in somebody's tent, he impatiently whistled snatches of tune after tune, just as they caught his quick eye. One, called "Anacreon in Heaven", (I have played it often for it was in my book that he found it), struck his fancy and rivetted his attention. Note after note fell from his puckered lips until, with a leap and shout, he exclaimed "Boys, I've hit it!" and fitting the tune to the words, they sang out for the first time the song of the Star Spangled Banner. How the men shouted and clapped, for never was there a wedding of poetry to music made under such inspiring influences! Getting a brief furlough, the brothers [!!.] sang it in public soon after . . .

In the second edition of his work (1880), then called "History of the Flag of the United States of America," Admiral Preble reprinted this *fanciful* story, together with the Charles Durang and Colonel Warner account, but again without the slightest attempt at critical comparison and apparently without noticing that we do not have to deal here with more or less fanciful differences, but with reminiscent accounts that exclude each other. What subsequent writers contributed in this vein to the literature on "The Star-Spangled Banner" may be disregarded since they merely paraphrased with more or less accuracy what they found in Preble or in his sources, as for instance, when one writer in the American Historical Record, 1873, volume 2, pages 24–25, carelessly mentions Charles instead of Ferdinand Durang as the first singer of "The Star-Spangled Banner." However, a belated version with fanciful variations of the main theme should be noticed, as it was printed sometime in 1897 in the Philadelphia Ledger and from there reprinted in substance in the Iowa Historical Record, July, 1897, page 144. According to this, "the second day after the words were written, Ferdinand Durang was rummaging in his trunk in a tavern in Baltimore, where he had his baggage, for music to suit the words, and finally selected that of 'Anacreon in Heaven.' By the time he had sung the third verse, in trying the music to the words, the little tavern was full of people, who spontaneously joined in the chorus. The company was soon joined by the author of the words, Francis Scott Key, to whom the tune was submitted for approval, who also took up the refrain of the chorus, thus indorsing the music. A few nights afterward 'The Star-Spangled Banner' being called for by the audience at the Holliday Street Theater, in Baltimore, Ferdinand Durang sang it from the stage. Durang died in New York in 1832. Durang had a brother, Charles, also a soldier in the 'Blues,' who was likewise an actor, who died in Philadelphia in 1875. . . ."

Finally an account deserves to be reprinted here in part, because it mentioned the person who set Key's poem in type, though otherwise the lines quoted are not overly accurate, as the reader of the Taney letter will notice. It appeared in the Baltimore American on September 12, 1872, together with a facsimile of the article, etc., of September 21, 1814, and reads in part:

We have placed at the head of this article this now immortal national song just as it first saw the light in print fifty-eight years ago . . . This song, as the form in which it is given shows, was published anonymously. The poet, Francis Scott Key, was too modest to announce himself, and it was some time after its appearance that he became known as its author . . . Mr. Skinner chanced to meet Mr. Key on the flag-of-truce boat, obtained from him a copy of his song, and he furnished the manuscript to "The American" after the fight was over. It was at once put in type and published. It was also printed in slips and extensively circulated. The "printer's boy," then employed in the office of "The American," who put this song in type, survives in full vigor, our respected friend, the editor and publisher of the "American Farmer," Samuel Sands, Esq.

That to Ferdinand Durang belongs the honor of having first sung Key's poem is unanimously asserted (except by those who confuse him with his brother Charles), but it remains an open question when and where he might so have done. On this point, the two earwitnesses, Charles Durang and Mr. Hendon, disagree. According to the reminiscences of the latter, the event must have happened at least three months after September 14 in camp on Gallows Hill near Baltimore. Now, it has already been mentioned that the brief account of the circumstances leading to the writing of Key's poem printed in the Baltimore American on September 21, preceded the full text of the poem under the heading "Defence of Fort M'Henry" with the remark "Tune: Anacreon in Heaven." It may be that Mr. Hendon heard Ferdinand Durang sing the hymn in camp after September 21, but it stands to reason that at least as early as September 21 other vocally inclined readers of the Baltimore American enjoyed the combination of Key's "Defence of Fort M'Henry," and the tune "To Anacreon in Heaven." If we possessed no other contemporary evidence, Ferdinand Durang's claims would rest upon very shaky grounds indeed, nor is the rest of Mr. Hendon's story at all of a nature as to inspire reliance upon his memory. Mr. Elson in his "National Music of America" (p. 202) bluntly expressed his suspicion to the effect that "never was a bolder or more fantastical claim set up in musical history," and every musician will agree with him that the "puckered lips" and the frantic hunt for a suitable tune in a volume of flute music is sheer journalistic nonsense, which verdict applies also to the Philadelphia Ledger account. And his hunt for a melody happened three months after the tune, to which the words were to keep company, had been publicly announced!

The suspicious character of Mr. Hendon's long-distance reminiscences leaves those of Charles Durang to stand on their own merits, but unfortunately they do not help us in fixing the exact date of the first performance of "The Star-Spangled Banner." Charles Durang merely remembered having been one of the chorus when his brother Ferdinand and about twenty volunteer soldiers who used to congregate at the adjoining tavern in the morning first sang the song after Ben. Edes brought it round to them on *one* of those libating mornings. This may have been the morning of September 15, when Samuel Sands, the apprentice, is popularly supposed to have set the poem as a broadside, or any other morning, including a morning after September 21, when the poem had appeared with indication of the tune in the Baltimore American. Nor is Colonel Warner's account, who perhaps was a descendant of Capt. Thomas Warner, which possibility would give his account the strength of a family tradition, more explicit on this point. *At* this tavern, it being a southern September morning, may mean practically the same as in Charles Durang's version, in front of the adjoining Holliday Street Theater. There Captain Edes, in company of Capt. Thomas Warner, is said to have called the attention of the group of volunteers "to a patriotic song which [he] had *just* struck off at his press." Consequently, neither Durang nor Warner substantiate the popular version that Ferdinand Durang sang "The Star-Spangled Banner" for the first time on September 15, 1814. Nor do they even substantiate the universally accepted theory that the broadside was struck off Edes's press on September 15! Indeed, not even Key-Taney's report: "Judge Nicholson . . . immediately sent it [the manuscript] to a printer, and directed copies to be struck off in hand-bill form," necessarily implies the conclusion that they were struck off on the morning of September 15. At any rate, the story that Key's poem was taken to a printer, set as a broadside, distributed about town, read, discussed, sung with great gusto, etc., and all this on the morning of September 15, 1814, belongs to the realm of unwholesome fiction!

On the evening of September 15 "The Star-Spangled Banner," says Mr. F. S. Key Smith, was "rendered upon the stage of the Holliday Street Theater by an actress." Also Ferdinand Durang is mentioned in this connection by some writers, and others proffer other names. What are the facts? In the first place, the suspicions of the historians should have been aroused by the observation that the actor-manager, Wood, in his autobiography does not mention any theatrical performances at Baltimore in September, 1814. In the second place, if they had consulted the Baltimore papers of that period, such as the Federal Gazette, Baltimore Patriot, Baltimore American—none of which was published, by the way, by Benjamin Edes!—they would have found no theatrical performances announced in September, 1814, at all, but they would have found a notice in the Federal Gazette, September 20, to the effect that "about 600 Pennsylvania troops arrived yesterday," among them a Lancaster company, apparently the very militia troops to which Ferdinand Durang belonged. Not only this, the historians would further have found from the same source that the *theater was not opened until October 12, 1814.* No reference to "The Star-Spangled Banner" appears in the announcements of this evening or of the benefit performance on October 14 "to aid the fund for the defence of the city," unless hidden away on the benefit program as "a patriotic epilogue by Mrs. Mason." On this evening Ferdinand Durang *did* appear—dancing a "military horn-pipe." With a little patience the historians at last would have found in the announcement of the historical play "Count Benyowski" for Wednesday evening, October 19, 1814 (in the Baltimore American appears October 15 as a misprint), the following lines, which at last shed the light of fact on the whole matter:

> After the play, Mr. Harding [the Federal Gazette spells the name Hardinge] will sing a much admired *New Song*, written by a gentleman of Maryland, in commemoration of the GALLANT DEFENCE OF FORT M'HENRY, called, THE STAR SPANGLED BANNER. . . .

The rather immaterial question of whether or not and when and where Ferdinand Durang possibly sang "The Star-Spangled Banner" for the first time leads up to the much more important question: How came the tune of "To Anacreon in Heaven," and no other, to be wedded to Key's poem? Chief Justice Taney, as anybody can see and as all should have seen before rushing into print with their stories, is absolutely silent on this point. So is Charles Durang. Colonel Warner says:

> The old air of Anacreon in Heaven *had been adapted to it by the author*, and Mr. Edes was desired so to print it on to the top of the ballad.

The most reliable reports, therefore, do not mention Ferdinand Durang at all in this connection. He figures as musical godfather to "The Star-Spangled Banner" in the journalistic reports only and under rather suspicious circumstances. However, there exists another and different version. Mrs. Rebecca Lloyd Shippen, of Baltimore, a granddaughter of Judge Joseph Hopper Nicholson and a greatniece of Francis Scott Key, contributed to the Pennsylvania Magazine of History and Biography, 1901–2, volume 25, pages 427–428, an article on "The Original Manuscript of 'The Star-Spangled Banner,'" of which more will have to be said further on. In this article we read:

> Judge Nicholson wrote a little piece that appears at the heading of the lines, above which he also wrote the name of the tune "Anacreon in Heaven"—a tune which Mrs. Charles Howard, the daughter of Francis Scott Key, told me was a common one at that day—and Judge Nicholson, being a musician among his other accomplishments and something of a poet, no doubt took but a few minutes to see that the lines given him by Francis Scott Key could be sung to that tune, and, in all haste to give the lines as a song to the public, he thus marked it. I possess this rare original manuscript, kept carefully folded by his wife, Rebecca Lloyd Nicholson, and taken from her private papers by myself [Mrs. Shippen] and framed.

Judge Nicholson's part in the history of "The Star-Spangled Banner" was narrated in substantially the same manner in editorial footnotes to an article on "The Star-Spangled Banner," copied largely from Chief Justice Taney by Mrs. Shippen, for the Pennsylvania

Magazine of History and Biography, 1898–99, volume 22, pages 321–325. It follows that the editor was either inspired by Mrs. Shippen or Mrs. Shippen by the editor. Careful reading of this particular part of the article implies that we have to deal here with a personal opinion, not with contemporary evidence, or even with a family tradition. Waiving aside for the present some doubts as to the accuracy of the story as quoted above, the main contention appears to be that Judge Nicholson supplied the tune. Light is shed on the whole matter if the history of the tune "To Anacreon in Heaven" in England and America is briefly summarized.

For a long time the tune of "To Anacreon in Heaven" was attributed, if attributed to any composer at all, to Dr. Samuel Arnold (1740–1802). Of this opinion were J. C. (in Baltimore Clipper, 1841), Nason (1869), Salisbury (1872), and others. The general inability to substantiate this rumor finally led to one of the most grotesquely absurd articles in musical literature, namely that in the American Art Journal, 1896 (v. 68, pp. 194–195), by J. Fairfax McLaughlin, under the title "The Star-Spangled Banner! Who Composed the Music for It. It is American, not English." The Musical Times, of London, 1896 (pp. 516–519), immediately challenged Mr. McLaughlin's statements and elaborately buried his patriotic aspirations, though this service could have been rendered him just as neatly by a reference to Mr. William Chappell's article "The Star-Spangled Banner and To Anacreon in Heaven" in Notes and Queries, 1873, fourth series, volume 11, pages 50–51, or to the footnote on page 6 of Mr. Stephen Salisbury's "Essay on The Star-Spangled Banner," 1873, where the contents of a pertinent letter from Mr. William Chappell were made public.

In the following pages a combination is attempted of the data, so far as I could verify them in the articles by Chappell and X in the Musical Times with the data in Grove's Dictionary and elsewhere, adding to or deducting from this information the results of a correspondence with such esteemed British authors as Mr. Frank Kidson, Mr. William Barclay Squire, and Mr. W. H. Grattan Flood.

In his "Musical Memoirs" (1830, Vol. I, pp. 80–84) W. T. Parke entered under the year 1786 these entertaining lines:

> This season I became an honorary member of the Anacreontic Society, and at the first meeting played a concerto on the oboe, as did Cramer on the violin. The assemblage of subscribers was as usual very numerous, amongst whom were several noblemen and gentlemen of the first distinction. Sir Richard Hankey (the banker) was the chairman. This fashionable society consisted of a limited number of members, each of whom had the privilege of introducing a friend, for which he paid in his subscription accordingly. The meetings were held in the great ball-room of the Crown and Anchor Tavern in the Strand, once a fortnight during the season, and the entertainments of the evening consisted of a grand concert, in which all the flower of the musical profession assisted as honorary members. After the concert an elegant supper was served up; and when the

cloth was removed, the constitutional song, beginning, "To Anacreon in Heaven," was sung by the chairman or his deputy. This was followed by songs in all the varied styles, by theatrical singers and the members, and catches and glees were given by some of the first vocalists in the kingdom. The late chairman, Mr. Mulso, possessed a good tenor voice, and sang the song alluded to with great effect . . .

This society, to become members of which noblemen and gentlemen would wait a year for a vacancy, was by an act of gallantry brought to a premature dissolution. The Duchess of Devonshire, the great leader of the *haut ton*, having heard the Anacreontic highly extolled, expressed a particular wish to some of its members to be permitted to be privately present to hear the concert, &c., which being made known to the directors, they caused the elevated orchestra occupied by the musicians at balls to be fitted up, with a lattice affixed to the front of it, for the accommodation of her grace and party, so that they could see, without being seen; but, some of the comic songs, not being exactly calculated for the entertainment of ladies, the singers were restrained; which displeasing many of the members, they resigned one after another; and a general meeting being called, the society was dissolved.

Misreading slightly Mr. Parke's reminiscences, C. M. in Grove's Dictionary claimed that Parke wrote of the dissolution of the club in 1786, which he, of course, did not do. Nor would the year 1786 be tenable, since Pohl in his scholarly book on "Mozart and Haydn in London," 1867 (v. 2, p. 107), gleaned from the Gazetteer of January 14, 1791, that Haydn was the guest of honor at the society's concert on January 12. Nor is Mr. Grattan Flood correct if he, in some "Notes on the Origin of 'To Anacreon in Heaven,'" sent me in June, 1908, dates the dissolution of the society 1796. (While fully appreciating the courtesy of Mr. W. H. Grattan Flood in transmitting these notes, I regret the inadvisability of using them, except in connection with other sources, because these notes are singularly at variance with the contents of several letters sent me by Mr. Grattan Flood on the same subject, and because these notes contain certain positive statements without reference to source which it would be unmethodical to accept unreservedly.) The "Musical Directory for the Year 1794" in the "List of various musical societies" states distinctly: "The Anacreontic Society which *met* at the Crown and Anchor Tavern, in the Strand, the festivities of which *were* heightened by a very Select Band." Consequently the society no longer existed in 1794. This is not at all contradicted by the entry under Dr. Samuel Arnold "Conductor at Acad[emy of Ancient Music], Ana-[creontic Society]," because the title-page distinctly reads "musical societies of which they [the professors of music] are *or have been,* members." (To avoid confusion it may be here added that "To Anacreon in Heaven" is not contained in the "Anacreontic Songs for 1, 2, 3, & 4 voices composed and selected by Dr. Arnold and dedicated by permission to the Anacreontic Society," London, J. Bland, 1785.)

If it is now clear that the Anacreontic Society must have been dissolved between 1791 and 1794, the year of its foundation is not equally clear, and therefore it is a somewhat open question since when "To Anacreon in Heaven" can have been sung as the "constitutional" song of this society. Mr. Grattan Flood writes in his "Notes" mentioned above:

> The words and music of "To Anacreon" were published by Longman and Broderip in 1779–1780, and were reprinted by Anne Lee of Dublin (?1780) in 1781. Dr. Cummings says that he saw a copy printed by Henry Fought—at least it is made up with single sheet songs printed by Fought—but this is scarcely likely, as Fought did not print after 1770, and the song and music were not in existence till 1770–71 . . .

Mr. William Barclay Squire in a letter dated September 21, 1908, refers to the dates of these two publications, which contain both the words and the music, in the guarded sentence, "Both are about 1780, but it is quite impossible to tell the exact dates." The Longman & Broderip edition is the one the title of which Mr. William Chappell transcribed for Notes and Queries, 1873:

> The Anacreontic Song, as sung at the Crown and Anchor Tavern in the Strand, the words by Ralph Tomlinson, Esq. late President of that Society. Printed by Longman and Broderip, No. 26 Cheapside, and No. 13 Heymarket.

With reference to Dr. William Cummings's statement that he saw a copy printed by Fought, I have not found any such statement by Doctor Cummings in print. Apparently Mr. Grattan Flood reported part of a conversation with the distinguished English scholar, but in reply to a pertinent inquiry Doctor Cummings sent, under date of November 7, 1908, this brief note:

> I had a copy of Smith's "To Anacreon" pub.[lished] in 1771. I showed it at a public lecture, but cannot now find it. I have two copies of a little later date. The first named was a single sheet song.

Doctor Cummings evidently was not willing to commit his memory under the circumstances on the point of imprint, nor does he make it clear whether or no Smith's name appeared on the sheet song as that of the composer. Assuming that Doctor Cummings had every solid reason to date this, the earliest known issue, of "To Anacreon," 1771, it follows that words and music must have been written at the latest in 1771 and at the earliest in the year of foundation of the "Anacreontic Society," which is unfortunately unknown.

In 1786, according to Parke, the chairman of the society was Sir Richard Hankey, whose immediate predecessor seems to have been Mr. Mulso. About 1780 Ralph Tomlinson, esq., appears in the Longman & Broderip edition, as the "late President of the Society," and no other gentleman has yet been found to have preceded him in the chair. However, such biographical data are irrelevant for the present purpose, and attention might now profitably be called to "The Vocal

Magazine; or, British Songster's Miscellany" (London, 1778), in which are published on pages 147–148 as Song 566, without indication of the tune, as is the case with all the songs in the collection, the words of,

ANACREONTIC SOCIETY.

Written by Ralph Tomlinson, Esq.

To Anacreon, in Heav'n, where he sat in full glee,
 A few sons of harmony sent a petition,
That he their inspirer and patron would be;
  When this answer arriv'd from the jolly old Grecian—
    Voice, fiddle, and flute,
    No longer be mute;
   I'll lend ye my name, and inspire ye to boot:
  And, besides, I'll instruct ye, like me, to intwine
  The myrtle of Venus with Bacchus's vine.

The news through Olympus immediately flew;
 When old Thunder pretended to give himself airs—
If these mortals are suffer'd their scheme to pursue,
  The devil a goddess will stay above stairs.
    Hark! already they cry,
    In transports of joy,
   A fig for Parnassus! to Rowley's we'll fly;
  And there, my good fellows, we'll learn to intwine
  The myrtle of Venus with Bacchus's vine.

The yellow-hair'd god, and his nine fusty maids,
 To the hill of old Lud will incontinent flee,
Idalia will boast but of tenantless shades,
  And the biforked hill a mere desert will be.
    My thunder, no fear on't,
    Will soon do its errand,
   And, dam'me! I'll swinge the ringleaders, I warrant.
  I'll trim the young dogs, for thus daring to twine
  The myrtle of Venus with Bacchus's vine.

Apollo rose up; and said, Pr'ythee ne'er quarrel,
 Good king of the gods, with my vot'ries below!
Your thunder is useless—then, shewing his laurel,
  Cry'd, *Sic evitabile fulmen*, you know!
    Then over each head
    My laurels I'll spread;
   So my sons from your crackers no mischief shall dread,
  Whilst snug in their club-room, they jovially twine
  The myrtle of Venus with Bacchus's vine.

Next Momus got up, with his risible phiz,
 And swore with Apollo he'd chearfully join—
The full tide of harmony still shall be his,
  But the song, and the catch, and the laugh shall be mine:
    Then, Jove, be not jealous
    Of these honest fellows.
   Cry'd Jove, We relent, since the truth you now tell us;
  And swear, by Old Styx, that they long shall intwine
  The myrtle of Venus with Bacchus's vine.

Ye sons of Anacreon, then, join hand in hand;
 Preserve unanimity, friendship, and love.
'Tis your's to support what's so happily plan'd;
  You've the sanction of gods, and the fiat of Jove.
    While thus we agree,
    Our toast let it be.
   May our club flourish happy, united, and free!
  And long may the sons of Anacreon intwine
  The myrtle of Venus with Bacchus's vine.

About two years later, as has been stated above, Longman & Broderip, of London, and Anne Lee, of Dublin, published "To Anacreon in Heaven" as sheet song with music. It further appeared as Song CLXVII on pages 336–337 of "The Vocal Enchantress," London, J. Fielding [1783], and this being the earliest version of Tomlinson's words with their music in the Library of Congress, it is here reproduced in photographic facsimile. (*See* Appendix, Plate I.) The song received increased publicity as Song IV (p. 4) in "Calliope; or, the Musical Miscellany," London (C. Elliot and T. Kay), 1788, as Song I (pp. 1–4) "Sung by Mr. Bannister at the Anacreontic Society" in the "Edinburgh Musical Miscellany," 1792, and as Song LXXXVII in the first volume of Stewart's "Vocal Magazine," Edinburgh, 1797. In 1796 (Grattan Flood; Mr. Kidson prefers *ca. 1795*) Smollet Holden, of Dublin, made a curious use of the tune by including a "Masonic Ode, song and chorus, written by Mr. Connel, on behalf of the Masonic Orphan School," to the Anacreontic tune in his A Selection of Masonic Songs. A second edition bears the imprint "Dublin, A. L. 5802" (A. D. 1802), and Mr. Elson inserted a photographic facsimile of this Masonic Ode (first words: "To old Hiram, in Heav'n where he sat in full glee") from his copy of the second edition in his book on The National Music of America.

The inference to be drawn from the insertion of "To Anacreon in Heaven" in the quoted collections, not to mention many later collections, is plain. As those collections were among the most important and most popular of the time, "To Anacreon in Heaven" must have been familiar to all convivial souls in the British Isles toward 1800. Now it is a fact that with the possible exception of that mysterious sheet song of 1771, not one of these publications alludes to the composer of the tune. It was not the rule to do so in miscellaneous collections, yet it is a curious fact that, while contrary to custom, Stewart's Vocal Magazine, 1797, mentions in a separate index the composers of many of the airs, it leaves "To Anacreon in Heaven" without a composer. Possibly the editor doubted the now generally accepted authorship of John Stafford Smith, or he was still unaware of the peculiar form of entry (mentioned by Wm. Chappell as early as 1873!) of "To Anacreon in Heaven" in:

> The fifth book of canzonets, catches, canons & glees, sprightly and plaintive with a part for the piano-forte subjoined where necessary to melodize the score; dedicated by permission to Viscount Dudley and Ward, by John Stafford Smith, Gent. of His Majesty's Chapels Royal, author of the favorite glees, Blest pair of Syrens, Hark the hollow woods, etc. The Anacreontic, and other popular songs. Printed for the author. . . .

This collection was published between 1780 and 1790, the exact date being unknown. "To Anacreon in Heaven" appears on page

33, as reproduced here in facsimile. (Appendix, Plate II.) The words "harmonized by the author" may of course mean harmonized by the author of the collection and do not necessarily mean harmonized by the author of the air, but these words, together with the fact that the collection contains none but Smith's own glees, etc., and the wording of the title renders it probable that Smith refers to himself as the composer of the music. But why the words *"harmonized by the author?"* If one looks at the song in its garb as a glee, the bass starting out full of confidence, and the other voices continuing the melody and juggling with it, one is almost apt to see in this peculiar cooperation of the high and low male voices a plausible explanation of the notoriously wide range of "The Star-Spangled Banner," if sung by one voice. This explanation is possible only if the form of "To Anacreon in Heaven" in Smith's Fifth Book was the original form. That we do not know, yet the word "harmonized" renders it improbable. Furthermore, if that was the original form of the piece, then some very radical melodic changes must have taken place in the melody shortly afterwards, as a comparison of the two facsimiles will show. Probably Smith composed it, if he really did compose the tune, as a song for one voice, and in "harmonizing" it for several and different voices he felt obliged to wander away from the original. Of course, if the supposed 1771 sheet song was a sheet song for one voice, and if it contained Smith's name as composer, then all doubt as to original form and to the composer vanishes. We would still have a very simple explanation for the extensive range of the tune. Such a wide range was then (and still is, for that matter) considered the sine qua non of effective drinking songs. Two fine examples "Anacreon a poet of excellent skill" and "Ye mortals whom trouble & sorrow attend" may be found in the "Anacreontic Songs" of the very conductor of the Anacreontic Society, namely, Doctor Arnold, and after all, it should not be forgotten that John Stafford Smith could not possibly foresee that his anacreontic masterpiece would some day have to be sung by old and young of an entire nation.[a]

---

[a] John Stafford Smith was born 1750 at Gloucester and he died at London September 3, 1836. His principal teacher was Doctor Boyce. He became an "able organist, an efficient tenor singer, an excellent composer, and an accomplished antiquary." From 1773 on he won many prices of the Catch Club for catches, glees, etc., and his five books of glees contain, in the words of Grove, "compositions which place him in the foremost rank of English composers." His famous "Musica Antiqua" appeared in 1812, containing a selection of music "from the 12th to the beginning of the 18th century," for which simple reason it would be futile to look for "To Anacreon in Heaven" in Musica Antiqua.

Tracing the American history of the air, or rather the history of its use in America, one runs across these statements in Mr. Salisbury's "Essay on 'The Star-Spangled Banner,'" 1873, page 7:

> I do not discover that it was a favorite when Robert Treat Paine, Jr. used its measure in his spirited song entitled "Adams and Liberty" [1798]

p. 9:

> After sixteen years, in which the tune of the Anacreontic song was seldom heard in this country or in Europe, it was applied to the pathetic verses of Mr. Key.

The second of these statements is nonsensical, the first at least improbable, because it is now known that the musical intercourse between England and America was too lively in those days to have permitted such a well-known air as "To Anacreon in Heaven," published in the most popular collections, to have remained barred from our shores. The chances are entirely in favor of the possibility that the song had its votaries here in the seventies, the more so as Parke states Sir Richard Hankey, later on president of the Anacreontic Society, to have served in the British army during our war for independence. Nor would it be at all reasonable to assume that the "Columbian Anacreontic Society" founded in imitation of the London Society in 1795 at New York, the moving spirit of which was for years the great actor-vocalist and bon-vivant John Hodgkinson, should not have helped to spread a familiarity with "To Anacreon in Heaven." Indeed, at least one performance of it in public is reasonably certain, namely, when the "Anacreontic Song" was sung by Mr. J. West at a concert at Savannah, Ga., August 19, 1796. However, Mr. Salisbury himself assists in undermining his theory that "To Anacreon in Heaven" was little known in America before it was applied to Key's "pathetic verses." On page 5 of his essay he writes of having seen it in his copy of "The Vocal Companion, published in Philadelphia, by Matthew Carey in 1796." It matters little that no copy of such a collection is preserved at the Library of Congress, Boston Public, New York Public, Brown University, Philadelphia Library Company, Pennsylvania Historical Society, Princeton University, American Antiquarian Society, Worcester; Mr. Salisbury must have seen it in a copy of some collection in his possession. Then he mentions Robert Treat (scil. Thomas) Paine's spirited "Adams and Liberty" ("Ye Sons of Columbia who bravely have fought") written for and sung to the tune of "To Anacreon in Heaven" at the anniversary of the Massachusetts Charitable Fire Society in Boston on June 1, 1798. A photographic facsimile of this famous song is given here as it was published in the very popular "American Musical Miscellany" of 1798. (Appendix, Plate III.) Mr. Salisbury further mentions Paine's song "Spain" set to the same tune for a Boston festival in honor of the Spanish patriots, January 24, 1809. He also mentions (in footnote, p. 10) a "patriotic offshot" of the Anacreontic song, "perhaps as good as any other commonly known before 1814" [!] which appeared in The New York Remembrancer, Albany, 1802, with the first line "To the Gods who preside o'er the nation below," attributed by the Boston Daily Advertiser, May 1, 1873, to Jonathan Mitchell Sewall, of Portsmouth, N. H.

To these four instances of the use of "To Anacreon in Heaven" may be added these in the following collections:

1797. Columbian Songster, New York, p. 136. Song: For the glorious Fourteenth of July. ("The Genius of France from his star begem'd throne.")
1799. Columbian Songster, Wrentham, Mass. Song. 32: Union of the gods.
1799. A Collection of Songs selected from the works of Mr. Charles Dibdin, to which are added the newest and most favorite American Patriotic Songs, Philadelphia.
    p. 315. Boston Patriotic Song [Adams and Liberty].
    p. 326. Our Country's efficiency ("Ye sons of Columbia, determined to keep").
1800. American Songster, Baltimore:
    p. 9. "To Columbia, who gladly reclin'd at her ease . . .
    p. 13. "Ye Sons of Columbia, unite in the cause."
    No tunes are indicated for these two, but the metre plainly suggests "To Anacreon in Heav'n."
    p. 233. To Anacreon in Heav'n.
1802. Vocal companion, Boston. Song XVI. By J. F. Stanfield, Sunderland. ("Not the fictions of Greece, nor the dreams of old Rome.")
1803. The American Republican Harmonist:
    p. 4. "New Song sung at the celebration of the 4th of July, at Saratoga and Waterford, N. Y. By William Foster" (Brave sons of Columbia, your triumph behold).
    p. 30. Jefferson and Liberty. ("Ye sons of Columbia, who cherish the prize." Text merely altered from Adams and Liberty).
    p. 105. Song [for the fourth of July, 1803] ("In years which are past, when America fought).
    p. 111. Song. Sung on the 4th of March, at an entertainment given by the American Consul at London. ("Well met, fellow free men! lets cheerfully greet.")
    p. 126. Song for the anniversary festival of the Tammany Society, May 12, 1803. Written by Brother D. E.
1804. 'Nightingale,' selected by Samuel Larkin, Portsmouth.
    p. 69. Adams and Liberty.
    p. 188. To Anacreon in Heaven.

1804. Baltimore Musical Miscellany.
       v. 1, p. 26. Anacreon in Heaven (given in Appendix in facsimile, Pl. IV).
            p. 29. "When Bibo went down to the regions below."
            p. 121. Sons of Columbia [Adams and Liberty].
       v. 2, p. 158. The Social Club.
1811. Musical Repository, Augusta.
            p. 22. Young Bibo. ("For worms when old Bibo prov'd delicate fun.")
            p. 140. Adams and Liberty [without indication of the tune].
            p. 207. Union of the Gods. ("To Columbia, who gladly clined at her ease.")
1813. James J. Wilson, National Song Book, Trenton.
            p. 43. "For the Fourth of July" ("Columbians arise! let the cannon resound.")
            p. 66. "Embargo and Peace" ("When our sky was illuminated by freedom's bright dawn.")
            p. 68. "Union and Liberty." ("Hark! The Trumpet of war from the East sounds alarm.")
            p. 70. "Freedom." ("Of the victory won over tyrany's power.")
            p. 87. "The Fourth of July." ("O'er the forest crowned hills, the rich vallies and streams.")
            p. 88. "Jefferson's Election." Sung by the Americans in London, March 4, 1802. "Well met, fellow freemen! Let's cheerfully greet.")

This is not intended as an exhaustive attempt to trace the tune "To Anacreon in Heaven" in early American song collections, but merely to prove and to corroborate by facts that "the tune was a common one at that day," as Key's own daughter, Mrs. Howard, told Mrs. Shippen.

We have some further contemporary evidence in this communication sent by Mr. Charles V. Hagner to the American Historical Record, 1873, volume 2, page 129:

> At the time it was written by Mr. Key, during the attack on Fort McHenry, Sept., 1814, there was a very popular and fashionable new song in vogue, viz: "To Anacreon in Heaven," every one who could sing seemed to be singing it. The writer of this was at the time, (Sept. 1814) one of some three to four thousand men composing the advance Light Brigade, chiefly volunteers from Philadelphia, under the command of General John Cadwalader, then encamped in the state of Delaware. In the evenings before tattoo, many of the men would assemble in squads and sing this song, hundreds joining in the chorus. Mr. Key must have caught the infection and adapted his words to the same air.

Francis Scott Key simply can not have escaped "To Anacreon in Heaven"! Indeed so common was the tune that, after Thomas Paine had set the example with his "Adams and Liberty," the music and the rather involved form and meter of "To Anacreon in Heaven" were adopted as *standards* by poetically inclined patriots. This historical fact applies with all its force to Francis Scott Key. The form and meter of "To Anacreon in Heaven," "Adams and Liberty," and "The Star-Spangled Banner" are practically the same, as the juxtaposition of the first stanza will prove, if such proof be necessary.

TO ANACREON IN HEAVEN.

To Anacreon in heaven, where he sat in full glee,
    A few sons of Harmony sent a petition,
That he their inspirer and patron would be,
        When this answer arrived from the jolly old Grecian:
            "Voice, fiddle, and flute,
            "No longer be mute,
        "I'll lend ye my name, and inspire ye to boot:
            "And besides, I'll instruct you, like me, to entwine
            "The myrtle of Venus with Bacchus's vine."

THE STAR SPANGLED BANNER.

O say, can you see by the dawn's early light,
    What so proudly we hailed at the twilight's last gleaming?
Whose broad stripes and bright stars through the perilous fight,
    O'er the ramparts we watched, were so gallantly streaming!
        And the rocket's red glare,
        The bombs bursting in air
Gave proof through the night that our flag was still there;
    O say, does that star spangled banner yet wave
    O'er the land of the free and the home of the brave?

It is absurd to think that any poetically inclined patriot of those days like Key could have on the spur of the moment set himself to writing a poem of such involved meter and peculiar form as his is without using consciously or unconsciously a model. It is equally absurd under the circumstances to believe any story, tradition, or anecdote from whatever source to the effect that others, with more or less difficulty, supplied a tune which fits the words almost more smoothly than does John Stafford Smith's air the Anacreontic text of Ralph Tomlinson. Internal evidence proves that Francis Scott Key, when his imagination took fire from the bombardment of Fort McHenry, had either the meter and form of the words or words and air of "To Anacreon in Heaven" or one of its American offshoots in mind as a scaffold. If this be now taken for granted, two possibilities offer themselves: First, Key wrote his inspired lines as a poem without anticipating its musical use. When shortly afterwards a desire was felt to sing his poem, the identity of poetic meter and form of both poems necessarily, and, as it were, automatically, suggested to Key himself or any other person of culture the air of "To Anacreon in Heaven." The second possibility is that Key did anticipate the musical possibilities of his poem and intended it as a song to be sung. In that case the fact, as will be seen, that neither his so-called original manuscript nor the broadside contain any indication of the tune may be explained by assuming that Key, very much like the editor of the American Songster, Baltimore (1800), considered it unnecessary to mention what was self-evident to him as the author. The first possibility is really more plausible, but at any rate Colonel Warner's statement that "The old air of 'Anacreon in Heaven' had been adapted to it [the poem] by the author" seems to come nearest the truth, though if a very fine distinction were to be made we should rather say that the poem was adapted by the author to the air, or at least to its poetic mate.

One of the popular legends is that Key's poem with its music spread like wildfire beyond Baltimore, and in a short time became a national song. The popular mind seems to consider it a blemish, a reflection on the intrinsic merits of a song (or any other work of art) if it does not obtain immediate popularity, and writers who cater to the tastes and prejudices of the multitude do not hesitate to amputate the facts accordingly. "The Star-Spangled Banner" rather gains than loses in merit if the silly anecdotes of its wildfire progress are not heeded, and if we adhere to what is still common knowledge among the older generations, namely, that "The Star-Spangled Banner" was not rushed to the front of our national songs until the civil war. Before that time its progress as a national song had been steady, but comparatively slow, as anybody may see who follows its career through the American song collections. This statement in nowise interferes with the fact that Francis Scott Key put it too modestly if he "believed it to have been favorably received by the Baltimore public." It would be quite possible to trace with infinite patience the progress of "The Star-Spangled Banner" through the American song collections, but this report hardly calls for such a laborious undertaking. However, to illustrate the point raised above, one would find that "The Star-Spangled Banner" appears in such songsters as "The American Songster, New York," n. d.; "New American Songster, Philadelphia, 1817;" "Bird of Birds, New York, 1818;" "The Star-Spangled Banner, Wilmington, 1816;" "The Songster's Magazine, New York, 1820;" "American Naval and Patriotic Songster, Baltimore, 1831;" but not in such as "The Songster's Companion, Brattleborough, Vt., 1815;" "The Songster's Miscellany, Philadelphia, 1817;" "The Songster's Museum, Hartford, 1826." In other words, twenty years after its conception Key's "Star-Spangled Banner" was not yet so generally accepted as a national song as to necessitate insertion in *every* songster.

Key's poem was accessible to the public as a broadside possibly as early as September 15, 1814. Here must be quoted what Admiral Preble said on page 725 of the second edition of his "History of our Flag:"

The Song on this broadside was enclosed in an elliptical border composed of the common type ornament of the day. Around that border, and a little distance from it, on a line of the same are the words, "Bombardment of Fort McHenry." The letters of these words are wide apart, and each one surrounded by a circle of stars. Below the song and within the ellipsis, are the words "Written by Francis S. Key, of Georgetown, D. C."

This description applies to the "Fac-simile of broadside as the song first appeared in print," contained in L. H. Dielman's pamphlet "The Seventh Star," published at Baltimore by the board of public works for the Louisiana Purchase Exposition, 1904. However, it may be pointed out by way of correction that merely the initial "F" and not the full name of Francis is printed, that we read M'Henry, not McHenry, that a rather pretty and effective ornamental outer border follows the shape of the broadside, and that the four corners contain additional ornamental designs. What arouses the curiosity of the historian most is that Key's authorship is not withheld, that Admiral Preble does not mention this fact at all, that the title of the poem here is "The Star-Spangled Banner" and *that no tune is indicated*.

If Preble's description tallies with a broadside as facsimiled by Dielman, it absolutely differs from *"one of those first printed handbills"* which, so Mrs. Shippen stated in her article, first was in possession of her grandfather, Judge Joseph Hopper Nicholson, then of his wife, after that in Mrs. Shippen's possession, and recently was acquired together with a Star-Spangled Banner autograph by Mr. Henry Walters, of Baltimore. The latter courteously granted permission to examine these treasures, and I found that his broadside (about 6½ by 5½ inches) is without any ornamental design whatsoever, does not mention Key's name at all, and does not bear any title except "Defence of Fort M'Henry." This is followed by the same historical note as appeared in the Baltimore American of September 21, 1814, then by the indication "Tune: Anacreon in Heaven," and lastly by practically the same text of the poem as it appears in the Judge Nicholson–Widow Nicholson–Mrs. Shippen–Mr. Walters autograph. The only differences, apart from the differences in interpunctuation, etc., are these:

(1) In the first stanza was printed the "Bombs" instead of the bomb.

(2) In the second stanza the misprint "reflected *new* shines" instead of "reflected *now* shines."

(3) In the broadside capital letters frequently appear where they are not found in the autograph, f. i. "The Rocket's," "Land of the Free," "Home of the Brave." On the other hand, the autograph has "Country" whereas this broadside has "country."

Here then are *two* broadsides, both of which are claimed to have belonged to that edition set up on the morning of September 15,

1814. We are not permitted to accept Mrs. Shippen's claims for her broadside offhand, since her account is clearly a mixture of family tradition, personal opinion, and sediment from reading on the subject. The broadsides, to be authentic, must stand the test of analytical criticism, and if one, by this process, is eliminated then all reasonable scepticism will vanish from the other.

The three observations called forth by the broadside championed by Preble and Dielman are curious indeed in view of the fact that the Baltimore American, when publishing Key's poem on September 21, 1814, preceded by a brief historical note, did not print the title "The Star-Spangled Banner," but instead "Defence of Fort McHenry," did not mention Key by name at all, but added: "Tune: Anacreon in Heaven." Key's poem—and this is a fact hitherto rarely, if ever, pointed out—made its first appearance in an American songster in the very rare "National Songster, or, a collection of the most admired patriotic songs, on the brilliant victories achieved by the naval and military-heroes . . . First Hagerstown edition," Hagerstown [Md.], John Gruber and Daniel May, *1814* on p. 30–31 under the title of

"DEFENCE OF FORT M'HENRY.
Tune: Anacreon in Heaven.

Wrote by an American Gentleman [!], who was compelled to witness the bombardment of Fort M'Henry, on board of a flag vessel at the mouth of the Patapsco."

Evidently the compiler of the National Songster clipped Key's poem from the Baltimore American and did not use a copy of this broadside. If, as Mrs. Shippen insists (Pa. Mag. of Hist., 1901–2, pp. 427–428) her grandfather's broadside was "One of those first printed handbills," why was Key's name suppressed in the Baltimore American's account after Judge Nicholson had permitted it to go on the handbill which he himself had ordered at the printing office? One might suspect that in view of the vindicative nature of the British it was deemed safer for Mr. Key to suppress the name of the author of "Their foul footsteps' pollution" in a paper of fairly healthy circulation, but this explanation is not plausible, because the historical note in the Baltimore American could have left no doubt of the offender's identity in the minds of British officers should they have been in a position to catch Key. Possibly Key's modesty would not permit disclosure of his authorship, but what could his modesty avail him, if the broadside with his name had already been favorably received by the public of Baltimore? And not merely this, we have the words of Mrs. Shippen:

Judge Nicholson wrote a little piece that appears at the heading of the lines, above which he also wrote the "name of the tune Anacreon in Heaven."

Obviously this action of Judge Nicholson can not apply to the broadside which contains "no little piece" nor indication of the tune, but it does apply to the account in the Baltimore American. Hence it would have been Judge Nicholson himself who withheld Key's name from the newspapers after he had given it to the public in a broadside. Furthermore, the Baltimore American account was bodily reprinted in the National Intelligencer September 27, 1814, under the same title "Defence of Fort M'Henry," and at the bottom of the anonymous poem appears the editorial note: "Whoever is the author of those lines they do equal honor to his principles and his talent!" Consequently, not even the editor of a paper printed at Washington, D. C., practically Key's home, knew of his authorship as late as September 27. Indeed, the anonymous "gentleman" figures in the Baltimore American at least as late as October 19, 1814. There is another suspicious circumstance. It should have aroused surprise ere this that Samuel Sands, the apprentice, set up at a moment's notice such an elaborate ornamental handbill as described by Preble and facsimiled by Dielman. The boy must have had remarkably precocious artistic instincts indeed, and very rapid hands and eyes. But why did he refuse to follow copy; why are there several differences between his broadside and the so-called original manuscript? Thus one becomes convinced that this broadside is not and can not have been a copy of the one struck off before the publication in the Baltimore American, but a copy of a broadside published considerably after that date, when Key's authorship was no longer kept a secret, when his poem had changed—at least in print, the earliest manuscript extant has none—its title from "Defence of Fort McHenry" to "The Star-Spangled Banner," and when verbal differences in the text had commenced to be quite frequent. The Preble-Dielman broadside thus being eliminated, only the Nicholson-Shippen-Walters broadside remains for serious consideration, and as far as I can see, it contains absolutely nothing to arouse our suspicion. In absence of proof to the contrary, it may indeed be called a copy, perhaps a unique copy, of the original broadside edition.

We turn our attention to the whereabouts of the original manuscript of Key's poem.

Mrs. Shippen writes in the article already quoted:

> Having heard several times of late that there are in existence *several original* copies, of the lines written on the night of September 12 [sic!], 1814 . . . by Francis Scott Key . . . and as I am the fortunate possessor of the only document that could exist of these lines—the *original manuscript*—I will explain how it seems possible that there could be more than one . . . [follows a partly inaccurate account based on Taney] . . . *It is the back of that old letter, unsigned,* that Francis Scott Key (my great-uncle) gave to Judge Joseph Hopper Nicholson

(my grandfather) that I possess, together with one of those *first printed* handbills
. . . Judge Nicholson [seeing] that the lines given him by Francis Scott Key
could be sung to that tune [to Anacreon in Heaven] and in all haste to give the
lines as a song to the public, he thus marked it. I possess this rare original manuscript, kept carefully folded by his wife, Rebecca Lloyd Nicholson and taken
from her private papers by myself and framed. . . .

This is a clear-cut claim of possession of the original manuscript,
and yet Mrs. Shippen herself undermines the claim by closing her
interesting article thus:

. . . The first piece of paper on which the lines he composed were written on
the night of his arrival in Baltimore I have in my possession; the same that Mr.
Key himself gave to Judge Nicholson.

These statements slightly contradict each other, as a careful reading of Chief Justice Taney's account, on which Mrs. Shippen partly
bases her claim, will prove. According to Taney, Francis Scott Key
told him that—

(1) He commenced it [the poem] on the deck of their vessel . . .
that he had written *some lines or brief notes* that would aid him in
calling them to mind, upon the back of a letter which he happened
to have in his pocket; and for some of the lines, as he proceeded,
he was obliged to rely altogether on his memory.

(2) He finished it in the boat on his way to the shore.

(3) He *wrote it out as it now stands*, at the hotel, on the night he
reached Baltimore and immediately after he arrived.

(4) On the next morning he took it to Judge Nicholson.

Consequently, a distinction is here made between the autograph
sketch of the poem commenced on the cartel vessel and finished on
the back of a letter in the boat before reaching Baltimore, and a
written out autograph copy of the sketch. It is the latter which he
took to Judge Nicholson for his critical opinion, and, of course, not
the sketch on the back of the letter. In the first quotation from her
article Mrs. Shippen describes this sketch; in the second quotation,
the manuscript as written out after Key's arrival at Baltimore.
These two different manuscripts she confuses, not realizing the distinction implied in Chief Justice Taney's narrative. Hence she
considered herself Judge Nicholson's heir to the *original* manuscript
of "The Star-Spangled Banner," whereas *she really possessed, and
Mr. Henry Walters, of Baltimore, now possesses, not the original
manuscript, but Key's first clean copy of the original manuscript,*
sketched and finished under such peculiar circumstances. What
became of this sketch we do not know. The probabilities are that
Key destroyed it after he had neatly written out his poem at the hotel.
The Library of Congress is not in a position to inclose here for purpose
of comparison and analysis a photographic facsimile of Key's manuscript, as now possessed by Mr. Walters, but fortunately a facsimile

may be found in the Century Magazine, 1894, page 362, and in Diel-man's pamphlet "Maryland, the Seventh Star." Nobody looking at these facsimiles or the original can concede that the latter has the appearance of a filled-in sketch. It is too neatly written for that, the lines are too symmetrically spaced and the whole manuscript contains practically only two corrections: In the first stanza Key wrote and then crossed out *"through"* instead of *"by* the dawn's early light," and in the third, *" They have wash'd out"* instead of *" Their blood has wash'd out."* The manuscript contains no signature, no title, nor indication of tune. This is mentioned particularly because Mrs. Shippen's article might convey the impression that the manu-script is "thus marked." The visible effects of folding do not point at all to the "old letter" in Key's pocket, since Mrs. Shippen's manuscript had been "kept carefully folded" by Judge Nicholson's wife.

Unquestionably, the manuscript now at the Walters Gallery is the earliest extant of "The Star-Spangled Banner." In after years Key presented signed autograph copies to friends and others, but just how many such copies he made is not known. At any rate, it is not surprising that the existence of several autograph copies led to con-fusion as to the earliest, the incorrectly so-called original, copy. An attempt shall now be made to separate intelligently such copies as have come to my notice principally by way of Admiral Preble's several contradictory contributions to the subject.

Charles Durang, in the Historical Magazine, 1864, pages 347–348, claimed that "the original draft, with its interlinations and amend-atory erasures, etc. was purchased by the late Gen. George Keim, of Reading, and I suppose his heirs have it now."

Without the slightest hesitation Preble used this statement in his book "Our Flag" (1st ed., 1872, p. 495). In 1874 Preble wrote in his essay "Three Historical Flags" (New Engl. Hist. and Gen. Reg., pp. 39–40), that this particular copy was

> *Presented* by Mr. Key in 1842 to Gen. George Keim and is now in possession of his son Henry May Keim, Esq. of Reading, Penn. . . . I have a photo-graphic copy of the authograph in the possession of Mr. Keim.

Retracting his former statement about the original draft, with its erasures, in a footnote on the same page, Preble states that his pho-tograph shows it to be "a fair copy, written out by Mr. Key, and I learn from Gen. Keim's son that the autograph was presented to his father by Mr. Key."

A facsimile of this was made for the Baltimore Sanitary Fair in 1864, so Mr. Keim informed Admiral Preble January 8, 1874 (see New Engl. Hist. and Gen. Reg., 1877, pp. 29), but, if made, it cer-tainly was not included by Kennedy and Bliss in their "Autograph

Leaves," as the Library of Congress copy of this work proves. Preble gave the text of the Keim copy, though not in facsimile, in his essay, "Three Historic Flags" (1874). In the second edition of his "History of Our Flag" (1880) he then informed his readers that Gen. George Keim's copy had "since [been] presented to the Pennsylvania Historical Society by his son." This statement is somewhat puzzling, because the text of the Keim copy quoted by Preble, 1874, the dedication "To Gen. Keim," and the undated signature "F. S. Key" are identical with those of a supposed "Star-Spangled Banner" autograph in possession of Mr. Robert A. Dobbin, of Baltimore, Md. When generously loaning this to the Library of Congress for exhibition purposes and granting us the privilege to reproduce it in facsimile (see Appendix, Plate VII). Mr. Dobbin, under date of March 24, 1909, wrote:

> Mr. Key was an intimate friend of Gen. Keim of Pennsylvania. On account of this intimacy and as a mark of the friendship which existed between them, Mr. Key gave this copy, which I have loaned you, to General Keim. You will note that Gen. Keim's name is in Mr. Key's handwriting.
>
> Mr. Charles W. Keim, a son of General Keim, came into possession of this copy after the death of his father, and a few years before his own death presented it to my late wife, who was a granddaughter of Mr. Francis Scott Key.

Mr. Dobbin apparently was not aware of the fact that he possessed a photograph, not an original autograph, the photograph even showing the marks of thumb tacks. Consequently, not he but the Pennsylvania Historical Society is in the possession of the Keim copy, which, with its approximate date, 1842, is, of course, as far removed from the original draft with its erasures as is possible. It is here reproduced by permission of the society (see Appendix, Plate V).

Benson John Lossing wrote in footnote (p. 956), in his Pictorial Fieldbook of the War of 1812, first edition, 1868:

> The fac-simile of the original manuscript of the first stanza of the "Star Spangled Banner," given on the opposite page, was first published, by permission of its owner (Mrs. Howard) daughter of the author [Key], in "Autograph Leaves of our Country's Authors," a volume edited by John P. Kennedy and Alexander Bliss for the Baltimore Sanitary Fair, 1864.

Accepting Lossing's statement, Preble in his essay, "Three Historic Flags," 1874, credited Mrs. Charles Howard, of Baltimore, with the possession of this autograph. As the facsimile in the "Autograph Leaves" shows, it bears the title "The Star-Spangled Banner" and the signature "F. S. Key," but no dedication and no date. The handwriting has not the firmness of youth, and it stands to reason that Key wrote this manuscript in late life. Admiral Preble had occasion in his essay, "The Star-Spangled Banner," New England Historical and Genealogical Register, 1877, pages 28–31, to correct Lossing's statement of ownership, since Mrs. Howard wrote him under date of April 25, 1874:

> I do not think I ever had an autograph of The Star-Spangled Banner. My father [F. S. Key] gave his children from the time they could speak, the habit of committing poetry to memory, and in that way only has the song been preserved to me. Except in one or two words, Mr. Keim's version, as you have it, is the one I have ever remembered.

Though, therefore, Mrs. Howard disclaimed ownership of this particular autograph, yet it must have existed and is, to judge by the facsimile, genuine.

Another autograph of "The Star-Spangled Banner" was thus described by Preble in his book, "Our Flag," 1872:

> A copy of the poem in Key's own handwriting, a copy prepared many years after its composition, and evidently in the *exact* language intended by its author (as it was presented by him to James Mahar, who for thirty years was the gardener of the executive mansion), was a few years since, exhibited in the window of Messrs. Phillip & Solomons, on Pennsylvania avenue, Washington. The identity of the handwriting was certified to by Judge Dunlop, Nicholas Callen, Esq., Peter Force and others, all of whom were intimately acquainted with Mr. Key and perfectly familiar with his style of penmanship. In fact his style was so peculiar and uniform, that it would be almost impossible for anyone who had ever noticed it with ordinary care to be mistaken.

This report Preble evidently took from a copy of the National Intelligencer, from which he further quoted "verbatim" the text of the Mahar autograph which evidently bore the title: "The Star-Spangled Banner" and the signature "For Mr. Jas. Mahar, of Washington city, Washington, June 7, 1842. From F. S. Key."

In his essay, "Three Historic Flags," Preble merely added that the Mahar copy was exhibited at Washington "in 1843, after Mr. Key's death." The present whereabouts of the Mahar copy is unknown to me.

Finally, in his essay, "The Star-Spangled Banner," 1877 (already quoted above), Preble remarked of a copy, dated October 21, 1840:

> It was first published in fac-simile in the American Historical and Literary Curiosities (Pl. LV) by John Jay Smith [Sec. Ser. N. Y. 1860, pl. 55] who stated the original was in the possession of Louis J. Cist.

Preble enlivened his narrative by adding a reduced facsimile of this 1840 copy, and he again used it in the second edition of his "History of Our Flag," 1880. From there it was reproduced by Miss Mary L. D. Ferris in the New England Magazine, 1890, for her article on "Our national songs" (pp. 483–504). Another facsimile is in the possession of the American Antiquarian Society, Worcester, as Mr. E. M. Barton, the librarian, informed me. The American Antiquarian Society received it on October 21, 1875, from Maj. Albert H. Hoyt, then editor of the New England Historical and Genealogical Register. The original seems to have disappeared until offered for sale as No. 273 in Stan. V. Henkel's catalogue of the Rogers collection of autograph letters, etc., 1895. The added facsimile shows absolute identity in date, signature, orthography, appearance, and every other detail with the facsimile at Worcester.

To sum up, it appears that, not counting the original draft, at least five copies of "The Star-Spangled Banner" in Francis Scott Key's handwriting exist, or at least existed:

(1) The Judge Nicholson–Mrs. Shippen–Walters copy, 1814. (Walters.)
(2) The Louis J. Cist copy, 1840. (Cist, present whereabouts unknown.)
(3) The supposed Howard copy, ca. 1840. (Howard.)
(4) The Gen. Keim–Pennsylvania Historical Soc. copy. (Pa. Hist. Soc.)
(5) The Mahar copy, 1842. (Mahar.)

There may be other copies, but these five are sufficient for the purpose of showing the changes Francis Scott Key himself made in his poem. The different versions would, as often happens in such cases, be used by different compilers. In course of time verbal inaccuracies would creep from one song book into the other. Also the compilers themselves have sometimes felt justified in improving Key's text. The result of all this has been, of course, that gradually Key's text became unsettled. As early as 1872 Preble marked the verbal differences between certain different versions, and since then surely the confusion has not decreased. Hence, very properly, the cry for an authoritative text has been raised. What should constitute such a text, whether one of Key's own version, or a combination of them, or any later "improved" version, it is not for me to say, though I may be permitted to remark that in my opinion there is no reason for going outside of Key's own intentions. At any rate, I do not consider it my duty to wade through endless song books in order to trace all the verbal inaccuracies and alterations of the text of "The Star-Spangled Banner."[a] The comparison will be extensive enough for all practical purposes if it be limited to Key's own five versions, to the earliest printed versions, and to the one in his collected poems. They will be distinguished from each other, where necessary, by the words written in parenthesis. These printed texts here compared with the earliest manuscript extant are:

---

[a] In this connection part of the memorandum of Dr. A. R. Spofford, November 19, 1907, is very instructive. He wrote:

"A collation of this authentic copy [i. e., the Cist copy], with several widely circulated collections of songs, shows numerous variations and omissions: Following is a statement of a few of these, with the number of discrepancies found in each:

"Nason (E). A Monogram [!] on our National Songs. Albany, 1869. (11 variations from original, and one stanza omitted.)

"Higgins (Edwin). The Star-Spangled Banner. Baltimore, 1898. (7 variations.)

"Sousa (J. P.). National and Patriotic Airs of All Lands. Philadelphia, 1890. (14 variations, with a fifth stanza added, which was not written by Key.)

"Bryant (W. C.). Library of Poetry and Song. New York, 1880. (8 variations.)

"Dana (C. D.). Household Poetry. New York, 1859. (7 variations.)

"Coates (H. T.). Fireside Encyclopœdia of Poetry. Philadelphia, 1879. (9 variations.)

(6) The Walters Broadside. (Broadside I.)
(7) The Preble–Dielman Broadside. (Broadside II.)
(8) Baltimore American, 1814. (Baltimore American.)
(9) The " National Songster." (National Songster.)
(10) Key's Poems, publ. 1857. (Poems.)

The comparison is based on the Walters text, without esthetic comment and taking the title of "The Star-Spangled Banner" for granted. The words that differ are italicized. Differences in spelling and interpunctuation are disregarded.

O say can *you* see by the dawn's early light
    What so proudly we hail'd *at* the twilight's last gleaming,
Whose *broad stripes & bright stars* through the *perilous* fight
      O'er the ramparts we watch'd, were so gallantly streaming?
      And the rocket's red glare, the *bomb* bursting in air,
      Gave proof through the night that our flag was still there
O say does that star spangled banner yet wave
O'er the land of the free & the home of the brave?

On the shore dimly seen through the mists of the deep,
    Where the foe's haughty host in dread silence reposes,
What is that which the breeze, o'er the towering steep,
      As it fitfully blows, *half* conceals, *half* discloses?
      Now it catches the gleam of the morning's first beam
      In full glory reflected now shines *in* the stream
'Tis the star-spangled banner—O long may it wave
O'er the land of the free & the home of the brave!

And where *is that band who* so *vauntingly* swore,
    That the havoc of war & the battle's confusion
A home & a Country should leave us no more?
      Their blood has wash'd out *their* foul footstep's pollution
      No refuge could save the hireling & slave
      From the terror of flight or the gloom of the grave,
And the star-spangled banner in triumph doth wave
O'er the land of the free & the home of the brave.

O thus be it ever when *freemen* shall stand
    Between their lov'd *home* & *the war's* desolation!
Blest with vict'ry & peace may the heav'n rescued land
      Praise the power that hath made & preserv'd us a nation!
      Then conquer we must, when our cause it is just.
      And this be our motto—"In God is our Trust,"
And the star-spangled banner *in triumph shall* wave
O'er the land of the free & the home of the brave.

"Stedman (E. C.). American Anthology. Boston, 1900. (5 variations.)

"While some of these alterations from the author's manuscript may seem unimportant, others actually change the meaning of the lines, as in the second stanza, where Key wrote—

      " 'What is that which the breeze, o'er the towering steep
      "As it fitfully blows, half conceals, half discloses?'

"**The second line** is perverted into—

      " 'As it fitfully blows, now conceals, now discloses?'

"In all except three of the reprints before noted this change occurs.

"It is for the worse, for two reasons:

"(1) It destroys the fine image of the wind flapping the flag so as to show and conceal alternately parts of the stars and stripes; while the substitution makes the breeze sometimes conceal the whole star-spangled banner.

"(2) The substitution is bad literary form, since it twice uses the word 'now,' which the author has applied twice in the two lines immediately following."

Ye: Cist.
By: Cist.   *Bright stars & broad stripes:* Cist.
Clouds of the: Cist; Pa. Hist. Soc.; Howard; Mahar.
Bombs: Broadside I and II; Baltimore Am.; Poems.
From: Broadside II.
That: Cist; Pa. Hist. Soc.; Howard: Poems; *Now-now:* Poems.
On: Cist; Mahar.
{ *Are the foes that:* Pa. Hist. Soc.; Howard.
{ *Are the foes who:* Poems.
{ *That Host that:* Cist.
{ *The foe that:* Mahar.
Sweepingly: Mahar.
This: Mahar.
His: Mahar.
And: Broadside II.
Foemen: Mahar.
Homes: Baltimore Am.; Cist; Pa. Hist. Soc.; Howard; Mahar.
War's: Mahar.
O long may it: Broadside II.

Like other patriotic songs, "The Star-Spangled Banner" has had its share of additional stanzas; that is, of verses suggested by the changing times, the changing spirit of the times, and sectional antagonism. On the other hand, at least one stanza often came to be omitted. It is the third, undoubtedly expressive of bitter sentiment against the English, as was natural and logical in 1814, but rather unnatural and illogical after we were again the friends of England. This apparent defect of Key's text for a national hymn, which should stand above party feeling and chauvinism, led to the composition of one of the two additional stanzas, which shall here be briefly considered. Its origin was narrated to Preble in 1876 by Benjamin Rush in the following words printed by the Admiral in his essay on "The Star-Spangled Banner" (New Eng. Hist. and Gen. Reg., 1877, p. 31):

> The circumstances under which these additional stanzas to the Star-Spangled Banner first came to my hand were briefly adverted to in the Preface to my edition of my father's book, entitled "Recollections of the English and French Courts," published in London in 1871, where I then was. The stanzas were also published; but that need not interfere in the least with your desire to insert them in the second edition of your History of the Flag, wherein I should say they would appropriately come in. The name of the author by whom they were composed, was George Spowers, Esq., and this has never been published. I think it eminerítly due to him now that his name should be given to the public, considering not only the beauty but the admirable sentiments of the stanzas. He had seen in my hands a manuscript copy of the original song, and asked me to lend it to him, which I did. A day or two afterwards he returned it to me with these stanzas. I was quite a boy at the time, at school with my two brothers at Hampstead, near London, while my father was residing in London as minister of the United States. It must have been about the year 1824.

Mr. Spowers's well-meant but objectionable stanza, because it, too, drags our national hymn into foreign politics, reads:

> But hush'd be that strain! They our Foes are no longer;
>   Lo Britain the right hand of Friendship extends,
> And Albion's fair Isle we behold with affection
>   The land of our Fathers—the land of our Friends!
>   Long, long may we flourish, Columbia and Britain,
>   In amity still may your children be found,
> And the Star-Spangled Banner and Red Cross together
> Wave free and triumphant the wide world around!

The best known of the additional stanzas is the one written by Oliver Wendell Holmes, as he informed Admiral Preble, April 14, 1872, at the request of a lady during our civil war, there being no verse alluding to treasonable attempt against the flag. According to Preble the stanza was first published in the Boston Evening Transcript. Preble received a corrected and amended autograph of the stanza from Holmes, and this he reproduced in facsimile in the second edition of his famous work (p. 730). It reads:

> When our land is illumined with liberty's smile,
>   If a foe from within strikes a blow at her glory,
> Down, down with the traitor that dares to defile
>   The flag of the stars, and the page of her story!
>   By the millions unchained
>   Who their birth-right have gained,
>   We will keep her bright blazon forever unstained;
> And the star-spangled banner in triumph shall wave,
> While the land of the free is the home of the brave.

It has been noticed ere this that not only the text of The Star-Spangled Banner but its music is sung and played with noticeable differences. These occur both in the harmonization of the melody and in the melody itself. To trace the discrepancies in the harmonization would hardly be profitable, since the harmonization of any melody will always be to a certain degree a matter of individual taste. Often many ways are possible, several equally good—i. e., equally appropriate—and seldom one the only proper one. The harmonization depends, of course, largely on the bass, and since the harmonization of a national song should be simple and easily grasped by the popular mind, there can not be much variance of opinion as to the bass. However, historical considerations will hardly be helpful in this direction. An authoritative harmonization is less a problem of history than of musical grammar, and authoritative it can be only for those who accept the harmonization recommended by a jury of musicians as the authoritative one for the persons under their own musical jurisdiction. It is somewhat different with the melody. True, neither an act of Congress nor the recommendation of a board of musicians will stop the process of polishing and modification (either for better or worse) which takes place with all folk, traditional, and patriotic songs. Yet it is obviously imperative for musical and other

reasons that at least the melody of a national hymn have as much
stability and uniformity as can be forced through official channels on
the popular mind.   The most suitable form of the melody will again
be a matter of decision by a jury of musicians, yet it may be interesting and instructive to contrast "To Anacreon in Heaven," as used
and modified, partly for verbal reasons, about 1800, with the common
versions of its offshoot "The Star-Spangled Banner" of to-day, which
from the beginning must have slightly differed from "To Anacreon in
Heaven" by dint of the peculiarities of Key's poem.   First, the
melody as it appears in the Vocal Enchantress, 1783, the earliest
version in the Library of Congress, will be compared bar for bar with
"Adams and Liberty" in the American Musical Miscellany, 1798
(A. M. M.), and with the version in the Baltimore Musical Miscellany,
1804 (B. M. M.).   The facsimile of the "harmonized" version in
Smith's "Fifth Book" shows it to be too garbled for purposes of
melodic comparison.

VOCAL ENCHANTRESS, 1783.

DIFFERENCES

Thus the so-called polishing process had begun within one generation after the "Sons of Harmony" had adopted "To Anacreon in Heaven" as their constitutional song. How is their club melody sung to the words of "The Star-Spangled Banner" by Americans young and old at the beginning of the twentieth century? For the purpose of comparison I have selected at random 12 recent song books and John Philip Sousa's "National, patriotic, typical airs of all lands" (1890), compiled "by authority" for use in the United States Navy. (Sousa.) If these few differ so widely in single bars, what discrepancies could be revealed if all the song books used in our country were similarly compared!

1. W. H. Aiken, Part songs for mixed voices for high schools, 1908.
2. C. A. Boyle. School praise and song, 1903. (B)
3. C. H. Farnsworth, Songs for schools, 1906. (F)
4. A. J. Gantvoort. School music reader, 1907 (G)
5. B. Jepson's New Standard Music Readers, Seventh year, 1904 (J)
6. McLaughlin-Gilchrist, Fifth Music Reader, 1906. (M)
7. Ripley-Tapper, Harmonic Fifth Reader, 1904. (R)
8. E. Smith, Music Course, Book Four, 1908. (Sm)
9. J. B. Shirley, Part songs for girl's voices, 1908 (Sh.)
10. H. O. Siefert, Choice songs, 1902 (Si)
11. C. E. Whiting, The New public school music course, Third reader, 1909 (W)
12. E. J. A. Zeiner, The High school song book, 1908. (Z)

HAIL COLUMBIA.[a]

"Hail Columbia" was written in 1798 by Joseph Hopkinson (1770–1842), whose prominence as jurist, combined with his authorship of "Hail Columbia," has won him a place in biographical encyclopædias. The poet himself has described the circumstances which led to the composition of his poem in a letter written August 24, 1840, to Rev. Rufus W. Griswold and printed in The Wyoming Bard, Wilkesbarre, Pa.:

"Hail Columbia" was written in the summer of 1798, when war with France was thought to be inevitable. Congress was then in session in Philadelphia, debating upon that important subject, and acts of hostility had actually taken place. The contest between England and France was raging, and the people of the United States were divided into parties for the one side or the other, some thinking that policy and duty required us to espouse the cause of "republican France," as she was called, while others were for connecting ourselves with England, under the belief that she was the great preservative power of good principles and safe government. The violation of our rights by both belligerents was forcing us from the just and wise policy of President Washington, which was to do equal justice to both but to part with neither, and to preserve an honest and strict neutrality between them. The prospect of a rupture with France was exceedingly offensive to the portion of the people who espoused her cause, and the violence of the spirit of party has never risen higher, I think not so high, in our country, as it did at that time upon that question. The theatre was then open in our city. A young man belonging to it, whose talent was high as a singer, was about to take a benefit. I had known him when he was at school. On this acquaintance he called on me one Saturday afternoon, his benefit being announced for the following Monday. His prospects were very disheartening; but he said that if he could get a patriotic song adapted to "the President's March" he did not doubt of a full house; that the poets of the theatrical corps had been trying to accomplish it, but had not succeeded. I told him I would try what I could do for him. He came the next afternoon, and the song, such as it is, was ready for him. The object of the author was to get up an American spirit which should be independent of, and above the interests, passion and policy of both belligerents, and look and feel exclusively for our honour and rights. No allusion is made to France or England, or the quarrel between them, or to the question which was most in fault in their treatment of us. Of course the song found favour with both parties, for both were American, at least neither could disown the sentiments and feelings it indicated. Such is the history of this song, which has endured infinitely beyond the expectation of the author, as it is beyond any merit it can boast of except that of being truly and exclusively patriotic in its sentiment and spirit.

---

[a] Revised and enlarged from my essay "Critical notes on the origin of 'Hail Columbia,' " in the Sammelbände d. I. M. G., 1901, volume 3, p. 139–166.

The young man who was about to take a benefit was Gilbert Fox, to the talents of whom Charles Durang, the historian of the Philadelphia stage, does not pay a very high tribute. If we believe Durang, it was the misfortune of Fox to have "created Hail Columbia." His friends and admirers became so numerous that his health, and accordingly his career, were ruined by the excessive demands of conviviality.

The benefit with which the tragedy of his life began, but which made his name famous ever since, was thus advertised in the Porcupine Gazette, April 24, 1798:

> Mr. Fox's Night. On Wednesday Evening, April 25. By Desire will be presented (for the second time in America) a Play, interspersed with Songs, in three Acts, called *The Italian Monk* . . . . after which an entire *New Song* (written by a Citizen of Philadelphia) to the tune of the "President's March" will be sung by Mr. Fox; accompanied by the Full Band and the following *Grand Chorus:*
>
> > Firm united let us be
> > Rallying around our Liberty
> > As a band of brothers join'd
> > Peace and Safety we shall find!

It was a clever bit of advertising to have inserted the words of the "grand chorus." Containing no party allusions they aroused the public curiosity as to the tendency of the song, and consequently Mr. Fox reaped a golden harvest. The song met with immediate success. It was redemanded nearly a dozen times on that memorable evening and had to be sung by Mr. Fox "for the second time by particular desire" on Friday, the next play night, and again on Saturday under the name of a "New Federal Song." On Monday a Mr. Sully begged "leave to acquaint his friends and the public that the 'New Federal Song' to the tune of the President's March" would be given "among the Variety of Entertainments performed at Rickett's Circus this Evening for his Benefit."

The newspapers and magazines helped to spread the popularity of the song. It appeared, for instance, in the Porcupine Gazette for Saturday, April 28, as a "song," in the April number of the Philadelphia Magazine as a "patriotic song," and as early as May 7 in the Connecticut Courant as "song."

But it seemed at first as if "Hail Columbia," notwithstanding its neutral spirit, would become more a political than a national song, for Cobbett's Porcupine Gazette entered on its behalf into a passionate controversy with Bache and Callender's Aurora and General Advertiser. Thus Cobbett violently attacked his political antagonists on Friday, April 27, under the heading "Bache and Callender:"

> It is not often that I disgust my readers with extracts from the vile paper these fellows print, but that of this morning contains several things that merit to be recorded.

The Theatre. For some days past, the Anglo-Monarchical party have appeared at the theatre in full triumph — and the President's march and other aristocratic tunes have been loudly vociferated for, and vehemently applauded. On Wednesday evening the admirers of British tyranny assembled in consequence of the managers having announced in the bills of the day that there would be given a patriotic song to the tune of the President's March, all the British Merchants, British Agents, and many of our Congress tories, attended to do honour to the occasion. When the wished for song came, which contained, amidst the most ridiculous bombast, the vilest adulation to the anglo-monarchical party, and the two Presidents, the extacy of the party knew no bounds, they encored, they shouted, they became Mad as the Priestress of the Delphic God.

Cobbett adds:

This circumstance relative to the theatre, must have given a rude shock to the brain of the few remaining Democrats. It is a lie to say that the song is an eulogium on England or on Monarchy. It shall have a place in this Gazette to-morrow and in the meantime, to satisfy my distant readers that the charge of its being in praise of the English is false, I need only to observe, that it abounds in Eulogiums on the men, who planned and affected the American Revolution!

The public took Cobbett's side, and the song gained rapidly in favor. It was sung and whistled on the streets, and soon no public entertainment was considered as satisfactory without it. To quote from McKoy's reminiscences in Poulson's American Daily Advertiser for January 13, 1829: "Such was the popularity of this song that very frequently has Mr. Gillingham, leader of the band, been forced to come to a full stop in the foreign music he had arranged for the evening by the deafening calls for this march, or song to this march."

Hardly a week had passed since Mr. Fox's night, when another Thespian introduced the song in New York. But already the rather vague title of "New Federal Song" had been changed into that of "Hail Columbia."

Cobbett writes on Thursday, May 3:

The following is part of an advertisement of the Entertainment for the last Evening at the theatre New York.

End of the Play, Mr. Williamson will sing a new Patriotic Song, called "Hail Columbia:" Death or Liberty. Received in Philadelphia with more reiterated Plaudits than were perhaps ever witnessed in a theatre.

When Mr. Williamson again sang "Hail Columbia" "at the End of the Play" on May 18th [a] "Death or Liberty" was dropped, and ever since the song has been known as "Hail Columbia."

Mr. Williamson seems to have been much in vogue as a singer of patriotic songs. When assisting Mr. Chalmers in his "Readings and Recitations" at Oeller's Room in Philadelphia on June 15th [b], he entertained the audience with "The Boston Patriotic Song: Adams

---

[a] Advertisement in the New York Gazette May 15.

[b] Advertisement in Porcupine Gazette June 13.

and Liberty," the "New York Federal Song: Washington and the Constitution," and again "Hail Columbia." When engaged for the "Grand Concert" at Ranelagh Garden in New York for July 4th he sang the same three songs, and, we doubt not, much to the delight of a patriotic audience.

Indeed the success of "Hail Columbia" was "immediate and emphatic" (Elson). Far beyond the most sanguine expectations of Joseph Hopkinson! Including his song in a letter directed to George Washington under date of May 9, 1798, he wrote: [a]

> As to the song it was a hasty composition, and can pretend to very little extrinsic merit—yet I believe its public reception has at least equalled any thing of the kind. The theatres here [Phila.] and at New York have resounded with it night after night; and men and boys in the streets sing it as they go.

Evidently not much to the delight of some reporter who calls it (in the Centinel of Freedom, Newark, N. J., July 9, 1799) the "old threadworn song of Hail Columbia."

As might be expected, the words of "Hail Columbia," together with the music of the President's March, were published shortly after the first public performance of the song. In fact only two days had elapsed when Benjamin Carr inserted the following advertisement: [b]

> On Monday Afternoon will be published at Carr's Musical Repository, the very favourite New Federal Song, Written to the tune of the President's March, By J. Hopkinson, Esq. And sung by Mr. Fox, at the New Theatre with great applause, ornamented with a very elegant Portrait of the President [scil. John Adams].

No copy of this original edition of "Hail Columbia" has come to light. If Carr published it at all with Adams's portrait, he probably, according to his custom, added his imprint. This leads me to now believe, contrary to my remarks on former occasions, that the edition which is in Mr. Louis C. Elson's possession and which he reproduced in facsimile in his books "The National Music of America" (1900) and "History of American Music" (1904) is not identical with Carr's original edition, but of a trifle later date. Mr. Elson's unique copy shows the American eagle instead of Adams's portrait and it bears no imprint. These differences are, of course, not conclusive, since Carr may have been unable to secure a suitable picture, yet this difference, together with the fact that he must have had an edition in the press and that he was not in the habit of suppressing his imprint, compels us to assume Carr's edition and the one in Mr. Elson's possession not to have been identical until the identity is proven. The title of Mr. Elson's copy reads:

> "The Favorite New Federal Song [American eagle] Adopted to the Presidents March. Sung by Mr. Fox– Written by J. Hopkinson Esqr."

---

[a] Comp. William S. Baker's "Washington after the Revolution," 1898.
[b] Comp. Porcupine Gazette for Friday 27.

Filling two unpaged inside pages of a musical sheet, it was arranged in C major "for the voice, pianoforte, guittar and clarinett" and this arrangement was followed, as was customary, by an arrangement (in D major) for the flute or violin.   Among "new music.   Just published" the Federal Gazette, Baltimore, on June 25, 1798, advertised "The President's March," "Hail Columbia, happy land."   This may have been a special Baltimore edition by Joseph Carr, or it may simply have referred to Benjamin Carr's Philadelphia edition, or to the one in Mr. Elson's possession, or to:

The President's March, a new Federal Song.   Published by G. Willig, Marketstreet,
    No. 185.   Phila.

A copy of this is contained in a miscellaneous volume of "Battles and marches" at the Ridgway branch of the Library Company of Philadelphia, and is here reproduced in facsimile by permission.   (See Appendix, Plates VII–VIII.)   Willig published at the above address, as we know from the city directories, between 1798 and 1803, but the adjective *new* in the title surely suggests the year 1798.   Under the title of "Hail Columbia" the song was first advertised in August, 1798, among "patriotic and other favorite songs" as "just published and for sale at Wm. Howe's wholesale and retail warehouse, 320 Pearl street," New York, but as Howe is merely known as dealer in music, not as a music printer or music publisher, it stands to reason that he merely advertised for sale one or more of the editions so far published.

All these early editions contained the words and the music.   The text without music (8° 6 p.), of which a copy is in New York Public Library, was published at Philadelphia under the title of—

Song adapted to the President's march sung at the Theatre by Mr. Fox, at his benefit.
    Composed by Joseph Hopkinson, Esq.   Printed by J. Ormrod, 41, Chestnut
    street.

Thus "Hail Columbia" rapidly became a national song regardless of its bombastic and prosaic metaphors.   Patriotic songs had been written in America showing this prevailing fault of the times to a lesser degree, and better songs followed—among the latter, however, certainly not the "New Hail Columbia," which begins—

> Lo! I quit my native skies—
> To arms! my patriot sons arise

(see p. 45 of James J. Wilson's National Song Book, Trenton, 1813), but none, except Key's "Star-Spangled Banner" and Reverend Smith's "America" were destined to rival the popularity of "Hail Columbia" for almost a century.   But as "America" was written to the tune of "God Save the King" and the "Star-Spangled Banner" to the drinking song "To Anacreon in Heaven," at least "Hail Columbia" may claim the distinction in the history of our early national songs of being in poetry and music a product of our soil.

W. T. R. Saffell in his book "Hail Columbia, the Flag, and Yankee
Doodle Dandy," Baltimore, 1864, when describing the allegorical-
political musical entertainment of The Temple of Minerva, which was
performed at Philadelphia in 1781, points out the two lines: "Hail
Columbia's godlike son" and "Fill the golden trump of fame." He
adds: "Do not 'Hail Columbia,' the 'trump of fame,' and the measure
of the chorus, appear to carry Fayles back from 1789 to 1781, for his
music, and Hopkinson from 1798 to the same scene and the same year
for his words? Who can say but our immortal 'Hail Columbia' had
its real origin in 'The Temple of Minerva,' or in the surrender of Cornwallis, when 'Magog among the nations' arose from his lair at Yorktown and shook, in the fury of his power, the insurgent world beneath
him? May not Fayles have touched a key in the 'Temple of Minerva'
in 1781, and revived the sound in 1789? May not the eye of Hopkinson in 1798 have fallen upon the 'Columbian Parnassiad' of 1787,
when the 'Temple of Minerva' first entered the great highway of
history? But none the less glory for Mr. Hopkinson." The eye of
Joseph Hopkinson might indeed have fallen upon the Columbian
Parnassiad in the Columbian Magazine (Philadelphia) for April, 1787,
where the "Temple of Minerva" was printed, but "Fayles" certainly
did not "touch a key" in this little play. And this for the very
simple reason that the "Oratorio" (sic) "was composed and set to
Music by a gentleman" who signed himself *H.* With a little critical
thought Mr. Saffell might have suspected Francis Hopkinson to have
been the author and composer of "The Temple of Minerva," and so
he was indeed, as my monograph on "Francis Hopkinson and James
Lyon" (1905) has established beyond doubt. Consequently Mr. Saffell's effort to trace the "President's March" back to 1781, by way of
"The Temple of Minerva," if I understand his florid fantasies at all,
is demolished by plain historical facts. It is different with his suggestion that the author of "Hail Columbia" may have been influenced
by "The Temple of Minerva." Joseph Hopkinson of course knew
the poetry of his father and probably shared the admiration of many
contemporaries for it. Hence it was quite natural for him to remember the two lines quoted above and to unconsciously borrow from
them for his own poem. This process was quite probable in his own
peculiar case, yet we should be careful not to apply too zealously comparative philological text-criticism to the patriotic songs of those days
in order to trace the influence exercised by one poet upon the other.
Such apostrophes as "Hail Columbia" were frequently used by the
poet-politicians and indeed their patriotic effusions have many stock
phrases in common. Similar sentiments were then continually
expressed in similar methaphors just as they are to-day. Here, for
instance, is the first stanza of a poem which Joseph Hopkinson might

also have read in his youth and parts of which might have lingered in his memory. It was printed in the Federal Gazette, June 23, 1789, and reads:

A FEDERAL SONG

For the Anniversary of American Independence

To the tune of " Rule Britannia "

Ye Friends to this auspicious day!
   Come join the fed'ral, festive band
And all Columbia—homage pay
   To him who freed thy happy land.

Hail Columbia! Columbia! Genius hail!
Freedom ever shall prevail.

National songs are meant to be sung. The best and most heart-stirring patriotic poems will soon be forgotten if not supported by a melody which catches the public ear. It might be said that Hopkinson's "Hail Columbia" would have conquered the nation with any of the popular tunes of the time, but the fact remains that its immediate and lasting success was actually obtained with the aid of the "President's March." Not all the honor, therefore, is due to Joseph Hopkinson. We musicians are entitled to claim some of the laurels for the composer of the tune which, no matter how little its musical value may be, has become immortal together with the words of "Hail Columbia."

Until recently the musical origin of "Hail Columbia" was as obscure as its literary history was clear. Not that the composer had been treated unkindly by the historians. They tried to lift the veil which covered his name, but their accounts were so contradictory that one claim stood in the way of the other. A methodical analysis of the contradictory accounts left the problem open, and it became probable that merely an accidental find would enable us to solve it.

The reader will have noticed that Hopkinson mentions the "President's March" in his letter without any allusion to its composer. The same applies to Durang in his "History of the Philadelphia Stage" (1854–55) to Dunlap's "History of the American Theatre" (1823), to Wilson's "National Song Book" (1813), to McCarty's "Songs, Odes and other Poems on National Subjects" (1842), and to A. G. Emerick's "Songs for the People" (1848).

The critical investigations began 1859, with an anonymous article in Dawson's "Historical Magazine" (Vol. III, p. 23):

The President's March was composed by a Professor Pfyle, and was played at Trentonbridge when Washington passed over on his way to New York to his inauguration. This information I obtained from one of the performers, confirmed afterwards by a son of said Pfyle. The song "Hail Columbia" was written to the music during the elder Adam's administration, by Judge Hopkinson, and was first sung by Mr. Fox, a popular singer of the day. I well remember being present at the first introduction of it at the Holiday street theatre, amid the clapping of hands and hissings of the antagonistic parties. Black cockades were worn in those days.

I have also reason to believe that the "Washington March" generally known by that title—I mean the one in key of G major, was composed by the Hon. Francis Hopkinson, senior, having seen it in a manuscript book of his, in his own handwriting among others of his known compositions.

J. C.

The above was published in the "Baltimore Clipper" in 1841, by a person who well understood the subject.

Evidently this person was J. C., whose account was simply reprinted from the Baltimore Clipper.

A somewhat different version appears on page 368 of the "Recollections and Private Memoirs of Washington," by his adopted son George Washington Parke Custis, edited by Benson J. Lossing in 1860.

In New York the play bill was headed "By particular Desire" when it was announced that the president would attend. On those nights the house would be crowded from top to bottom, as many to see the hero as the play. Upon the president's entering the stage box with his family, the orchestra would strike up "The President's March" (now Hail Columbia) composed by a German named Feyles, in '89, in contradistinction, to the march of the Revolution, called "Washington's March".

The audience applauded on the entrance of the president, but the pit and gallery were so truly despotic in the early days of the republic, that so soon as "Hail Columbia" had ceased, "Washington's March" was called for by the deafening din of a hundred voices at once, and upon its being played, three hearty cheers would rock the building to its base.

In the following year, 1861, the "Historical Magazine," which took a vivid interest in the history of our national songs, brought out an article totally contradicting the two already quoted. The article—in Volume V, 280, page 281—is headed "Origin of Hail Columbia" and reads:

In 1829, William Mc Koy of Philadelphia, under the signature "Lang Syne", published in Poulson's Daily Advertiser an account of the origin of the song "Hail Columbia", which was set to the music of "The President's March" . . . Mr. Mc Koy's reminiscences have not, we believe, been reprinted since they were originally published. The article is as follows:

The seat of the Federal Government of the thirteen United States being removed to Philadelphia, and in honour of the new president, Washington, then residing at No. 190 High street, the march, ever since known as "the President's March", was composed by a German teacher of music, in this city, named Roth, or Roat, designated familiarly by those who knew him as "Old Roat". He taught those of his pupils who preferred the flute, to give to that instrument the additional sound of a drone, while playing in imitation of a bagpipe. His residence was at one time in that row of houses standing back from Fifth, above Race street, at the time known as "The Fourteen Chimneys", some of which are still visible in the rear ground, north eastward of Mayer's church. In his person he was of the middle size and height. His face was truly German in expression, dark grey eyes, and bushy eyebrows, round, pointed nose, prominent lips, and parted chin. He took snuff immoderately, having his vest and ruffles usually well sprinkled with grains of rappee. He was considered as excentric, and a kind of droll. He was well known traditionally, at the Samson and Lion, in Crown street, where it seems his company, in the olden time, was always a welcome to the pewter-pint customers, gathered there at their pipes and beer, while listening to his facetious tales and anecdotes, without number, of high-life about town, and of the players—Nick Hammond, Miss Tuke, Hodgkinson, Mrs. Pownall, and Jack Martin, of the old theatre in Southwark. This said "President's March" by Roat, the popular songs of Markoe, the "city poet," in particular the one called "The Tailor Done over" and the beautiful air of "Dans Votre Lit" which had been rendered popular by its being exquisitely sung at the time, by Wools, of the Old American Company, were sung and whistled by every one who felt freedom (of mind) to whistle and to sing . . .

Public opinion having . . . released itself suddenly from a passion for French Revolutionary music and song, experienced a vacuum in that particular, which was immediately supplied by the new national American song of "Hail Columbia happy Land" written in '98 by Joseph Hopkinson, Esq. of this city, and the measure adapted by him, very judiciously, to the almost forgotten "President's March". Ever since 1798, the song of "Hail Columbia" by Joseph Hopkinson, and the "President's March" by Johannes Roat, being indiscriminately called for, have become, in a manner, synonymous to the public ear and understanding when they are actually and totally distinct in their origin, as above mentioned.

Following the clue given in this reprint, I found the original article in Poulson's American Daily Advertiser for Tuesday, January 13, 1829, under the heading "President's March." Though this article appears anonymous, there can be no doubt of Mr. McKoy having been the author, for we know from "Watson's Annals of Philadelphia" that it was he who wrote the series of articles on olden times in Philadelphia, published in said paper during the years 1828 and 1829 and mostly signed "Auld Lang Syne."

In the same year that this gentleman's account was reprinted in the Historical Magazine, Richard Grant White's "National Hymns, How They Are Written and How They Are Not Written," left the press. What this author has to say on the origin of the "President's March" is contained in a footnote on page 22:

. . . The air to which Hopkinson wrote "Hail Columbia" was a march written by a German band master on occasion of a visit of Washington, when President, to the old John Street Theatre in New York.

A similar view as to the musical origin of the song is held by W. T. R. Saffell in his book "Hail Columbia, the Flag, and Yankee Doodle Dandy, Baltimore, 1864." He says, on page 53:

A piece of music set for the harpsichord, entitled the "President's March" was composed in 1789, by a German named Fayles, on the occasion of Washington's first visit to a theatre in New York.

Rev. Elias Nason, on page 33 of his monograph, "A Monogramm on Our National Song . . . 1869," is equally meager, equally omniscient, and equally opposed to giving authorities when he writes:

> . . . on Washington's first attendance at the theatre in New York, 1789, a German by the name of Fyles composed a tune to take place of "Washington's March," christening it with the name of "President's March."

Some years later, in 1872, Benson J. Lossing reprinted in Volume I (pp. 550–554) of his "American Historical Record" a paper on "The Star-Spangled Banner and National Airs," which the Hon. Stephan Salisbury had read before the American Antiquarian Society, October 21, 1872. In regard to "Hail Columbia" this author says:

> Poulson's Advertiser of 1829 mentions that this song was set to the music of "the President's March" by Johannes Roth, a German music teacher in that city. And the Historical Magazine, vol. 3, page 23, quotes from the Baltimore Clipper of 1841 that the "President's March" was composed by Professor Phyla of Philadelphia, and was played at Trenton in 1789, when Washington passed over to New York to be inaugurated, as it was stated by a son of Professor Phyla, who was one of the performers.

Rear-Admiral George Henry Preble, in his "History of the Flag of the United States; Boston, 1880," wrote:

> The "President's March" was a popular air, and the adaptation easy. It was composed in honour of President Washington, then residing at No. 190 High Street Philadelphia, by a teacher of music, named Roth, [a] or Roat, familiarly known as "Old Roat." He was considered as an excentric, and kind of a droll, and took snuff immoderately. Philip Roth, teacher of music, described as living at 25 Crown Street, whose name appears in all the Philadelphia directories from 1791 to 1799, inclusive, was probably the author of the march.
>
> According to his son, who asserted he was one of the performers, the march was composed by Professor Phyla, of Philadelphia, and was played at Trenton, in 1789, when Washington passed over to New York to be inaugurated.[b]
>
> [a] Poulson's Advertiser 1829.
> [b] Historical Magazine, Volume III, 23.
>   Baltimore Clipper, 1841.
>   American Historical Record Volume I, 53. Hon. S. Salisbury's paper before the American Antiquarian Society 1872.

John Bach McMaster, the celebrated author of "A History of the People of the United States; New York," has something to say on the subject in Volume I, on pages 564–565:

> At the John street theatre in New York, "in a box adorned with fitting emblems, the President was to be seen much oftener than many of the citizens approved. On such occasions the 'President's March' was always played. It had been composed by Phyles, the leader of the few violins and drums that passed for the orchestra, and played for the first time on Trenton Bridge as Washington rode over on his way to be inaugurated. The air had a martial ring that caught the ear of the multitude, soon became popular as Washington's March, and when Adams was President, in a moment of great party excitement Judge Hopkinson wrote and adapted to it the famous lines beginning 'Hail Columbia.'"

Mary L. D. Ferris, in a clever but superficial causerie on "Our National Songs" in the New England Magazine, new series, July, 1890 (pp. 483–504), expresses her opinion briefly, thus:

> The music of Hail Columbia was composed in 1789, one hundred years ago, by Professor Phylo of Philadelphia, and played at Trenton, when Washington was en route to New York to be inaugurated. The tune was originally called the President's March.

In the same year (1890) appeared John Philip Sousa's semiofficial work, "National, Patriotic, and Typical Airs of All Lands with Copious Notes, compiled by order and for use of the Navy Department." Of the "President's March" Sousa remarks:

> On the occasion of Gen. Washington's attendance at the John St. Theatre in New York, in 1789, a German named Fyles, who was leader of the orchestra, composed a piece in compliment of him and called it the "President's March," which soon became a popular favorite.

In the first of a series of articles on our national songs, published 1897, April 29, in the Independent, E. Irenaeus Stevenson maintains that "Hail Columbia" is rather a "personal" than a national song, having been, as he imagines, written in honor of George Washington. But this is not his only blunder, for he not even knew that the "Washington's March" and the "President's March" were two entirely different pieces.

> The very air to the words confirms one in wishing that "Hail Columbia" would remain solely an artless souvenir belonging to Washington. For the tune was not written to Judge Hopkinson's words. It was a little instrumental march, called "Washington's March," of vast vogue circa 1797, a march composed in honour of the first President by a German musician named Phazles, Phylz, Phyla, or Pfalz, of New York. Phazles looked after musical matters in the old theatre on John Street; and apparently he really wrote, not imported, the tune. Judge Hopkinson fitted to it the address to Washington, in 1798.

When George Washington, on Sunday, May 27, 1798, acknowledged the receipt of "Hail Columbia" sent to him by Joseph Hopkinson on May 9, he "offered an absence for more than eight days from home as an apology for . . . not giving . . . an earlier acknowledgment." The polite note has been reprinted by William S. Baker in his work already quoted. Baker adds the following editorial footnote:

> The song referred to in the above quoted letter was the national air, "Hail Columbia," the words of which were written by Joseph Hopkinson and adapted to the music of the "President's March" composed in 1789 by a German named Feyles, who at the time was the leader of the orchestra at the John Street Theatre in New York.

A similar version appears in S. J. Adair FitzGerald's Stories of Famous Songs. London, 1897, on page 100:

> The music was taken from a piece, called "The President's March," which had seen the light ten years previously. It was composed by a German named Fyles on some special visit of Washington's to the John Street Theatre, New York.

Col. Nicholas Smith in his "Stories of Great National Songs," Milwaukee, 1899, becomes involuntarily humorous, when saying (on p. 41):

> The "President's March" was composed in 1789 by a German professor in Philadelphia, named Phylo, alias Feyles, alias Thyla, alias Phyla, alias Roth, and was first played at Trenton when Washington was on his way to New York to be inaugurated president.

The few lines which Howard Futhey Brinton says to the subject in his "Patriotic Songs of the American People," New Haven, 1900, may also find a place here:

> Of the then current tunes none caught the popular fancy more than the "President's March," which had been composed in 1789 by a German named Feyles, in honour of General Washington.

Louis C. Elson is the last writer whom I have to quote. In his widespread work "The National Music of America and its Sources, Boston, 1900," we read (on pp. 157–159) a very much more elaborate account than the last ones mentioned:

> . . . it is definitely known that the composition was written in 1789, and that it was called "The President's March." Regarding its first performance and its composer there is some doubt. William Mc. Koy in "Poulson's Advertiser" for 1829 states that the march was composed by a German musician in Philadelphia, named Johannes Roth. He is also called "Roat" and "Old Roat" in some accounts. That there was a Philip Roth living in Philadelphia at about this time may be easily proved, for his name is found in the city directories from 1791 to 1799.[a] He appears as "Roth, Philip, teacher of music, 25 Crown St." Washington at this time was a fellow citizen of this musician for he lived at 190 High Street, Philadelphia.
>
> But there is another claimant to the work. There was also in Philadelphia at this time a German musician, whose name is spelled in many different ways by the commentators. He is called "Phyla", "Philo", "Pthylo" and "Pfyles" by various authors. None of these seems like a German name, but it is possible that the actual name may have been Pfeil.[b] This gentleman of doubtful cognomen claims the authorship of the march in question, or rather his son has claimed it for him. The march is also claimed by this son to have been first played on Trenton Bridge as Washington rode over, on his way to the New York inauguration. Richard Grant White, however, states, on what authority we know not, that the work was first played on the occasion of a visit of Washington to the old John Street Theatre in New York.

It is evident that all these different accounts are based directly or indirectly upon the three contradictory versions of William McKoy in Poulson's Advertiser, 1829, of J. C. in the Baltimore Clipper, 1841, and of George Washington Parke Custis, 1860. Later accounts con-

---

[a] History of the Flag of the United States, by Rear Admiral Geo. Henry Preble, p. 719.

[b] Through the courtesy of John W. Jordan, Esq., librarian of the Historical Society of Pennsylvania, we learn that the first Philadelphia "City Directory" was published in 1785, the second in 1791. In neither of these does the name of any musician bearing any ressemblance to the ones given above appear.

tain nothing substantially new except when confusing the problem by incorrect and uncritical quotations from unmentioned sources, as in the case of Rev. Elias Nason who inaccurately copied R. Grant White's superficial footnote.

If our problem can be solved, it will be possible only by critically investigating *pro et contra* the data given in the reports of 1829, 1841, and 1860.

These data are:

1. The march ever since known as the ''President's March'' was composed by a German teacher of music in Philadelphia, named Johannes Roat or Roth, ''the seat of the Federal Government of the thirteen United States being removed to Philadelphia and in honour of the new President Washington, then residing at No. 190 High street'' (Mc. Koy).

2) The President's March was composed by Professor Pfyle and was played at Trentonbridge when Washington passed over on his way to New York to his inauguration. (Information obtained by J. C. from ''one of the performers'' confirmed afterwards by a son of said Pfyle.)

3) The President's March was composed by a German, named Feyles in 1789 and was played upon President George Washington's entrance into the stage box with his family. (Recollections by George Washington Parke Custis.)

To begin with the first version: Who was this German teacher of music, by the name of Roth?

Even the most careful research in the old newspapers, magazines, directories, and in books relating to the early theatrical and musical life of the United States will add but very little to the following few items: I find Roth first mentioned in the year 1771. On December 5 a concert advertised in the Pennsylvania Gazette for November 28, by ''Mr. John M'Lean (Instructor of the German Flute)'' in Philadelphia, was to ''conclude with an *overture*, composed (for the occasion) by *Philip Roth*, master of the band belonging to his Majesty's Royal Regiment of British Fusiliers.''

Not until 1785 have I again found his name mentioned. But in this year we read his name in the first City Directory of Philadelphia, published by White. He appears there as *''Roots*, Philip, music maker, Sixth between Arch and Race streets.'' We next read his name in an advertisement in the Pennsylvania Journal (Phila.) for September 10, 1788.

> ''Mr. Roth, Music Master in Pennington Alley, running from Race to Vine Streets, between Fourth and Fifth Streets, teacher all kinds of Instrumental Music in the shortest manner, viz. Harpsichord or Piano Forte, Guitar, Flute, Hautboy, Clarinet, Bassoon, French Horn, Harp and Thorough Bass, which is the Ground of Music.''

The third item which I was able to trace shows Roth again as a composer.

The "Columbian Magazine" (Phila.) brought out in the April number of 1790 "A Hunting Song. Set to Music by Mr. Roth, of Philadelphia." It is written in E flat major and in the intentionally simple style of the German Volkslieder of that period, to the words: "Ye sluggards who murder your lifetime in bed, etc." Needless to say that the song is of little musical value.

The first directory for Philadelphia had been published in 1785. The second was issued in 1791, the third in 1793; after that the directory was issued annually. In all these, till 1805, we run across the "musician" or "teacher of music" or "music master" Philip Roth, his name being spelled from 1803–1805 "Rothe." He lived from 1791 to 1794 in 25 Crownst; from 1799–1803 in 33 Crownst, whereas for the years 1795–1798 his residence is given without a house number as in "Crownst." We find in the directory for 1806 "Rote, widow of Philip, music master, 94 N. Seventh." This would suggest 1805 as date of his death, but Mr. Drummond of the University of Pennsylvania informed me that the city records show Roth to have died in 1804.

That Philip Roth, besides teaching "all kinds of instrumental music in the shortest manner," played in the concert and opera orchestras of Philadelphia is highly probable, but he never appears as a soloist or as a composer in the many concerts given there till 1800, the programmes of which I have copied as far as I was able to trace them in the newspapers.

Of course, the last remark interferes in no way with the possibility of his having composed the "President's March." Mr. McKoy's claims must be considered as not contrary to chronology and circumstances in regard to Roth's person, and his misspelling the name and calling him Johannes instead of Philip matters very little. But otherwise his claims are suspicious, though he seems to have known Roth well.

The reader will have noticed that McKoy does not mention the year in which the "President's March" was composed. This is of importance, as his narrative excludes the years 1774–1788, during which we had fifteen presidents of the Continental Congress, and also the year 1789, when George Washington became President of the United States. The seat of government was not removed to Philadelphia until the fall of 1790. It had been, from 1789 to the date of removal, in New York and not in Philadelphia. If, therefore, McKoy's statement is correct the march was composed in 1790. In this case however the remark "in honour of the new President" loses its sense.

But the lines might represent an excusable slip of memory, and the march might have been written by Roth and played in honor of the President when passing through Philadelphia on his way to New York in 1789.

Washington left Mount Vernon on the 16th of April; reached Philadelphia on the 20th and continued his voyage the following day.[a] The Pennsylvania Journal (W., April 22), the Pennsylvania Mercury (T., April 21), the Independent Gazetteer (T., April 21), the Pennsylvania Packet (T., April 21), the Freeman's Journal (W., April 22), and the Pennsylvania Gazette (W., April 22) all give an account of the President's reception at Philadelphia, but none of these papers, except the Pennsylvania Gazette, refer to any music having been played at the entertainment and this paper only in a vague way:

"Philadelphia, April 22.

Monday last His Excellency George Washington, Esq., the President Elect of the United States, arrived in this city, about one o'clock, accompanied by the President of the State . . . troops . . . and a numerous concourse of citizens on horseback and foot.

His Excellency rode in front of the procession, on horseback . . . The bells were rung thro' the day and night, and a feu de joy was fired as he moved down Market and Second Street to the City Tavern . . . At three o'clock His Excellency sat down to an elegant Entertainment of 250 covers at the City Tavern, prepared for him by the citizens of Philadelphia. A band of music played during the entertainment and a discharge of artillery took place at every toast among which was, the State of Virginia."

This meager notice and the silence of the other papers in regard to music are significant. Had the band played a march composed in honor of the illustrious guest, the papers would have mentioned the fact, as it was their habit of doing on similar occasions. This statement can be proved over and over and will be supported by all who have had occasion to study our early newspapers and their habits.

For the same reasons, Mr. McKoy's claims, even if taken literally, which would imply that the President's March was written in 1790 when the seat of government was actually removed to Philadelphia, contain no evidential strength.

During the President's short stay in Philadelphia:

. . . an elegant Fête Champêtre was given to this illustrous personage, his amiable consort and family . . . [Sept. 4.] on the banks of the Schuylkill, in the highly improved grounds of the messrs. Gray, by a number of respectable citizens. . . A band of music played during the repast, and at the close of the repast several excellent songs were sung, and toasts were given.

Neither this account which appeared in the Pennsylvania Packet for Wednesday, September 8, 1790, nor any other, mentions a piece

---

[a] Comp. McMaster, I, 538 or Baker.

of music composed "for the occasion." It would have been quite contrary to the practice of our early newspapers to have omitted reference to a piece written and played in honor of the new president.

Consequently McKoy's version, in spite of the fact that he was a contemporary and fellow-citizen of Philip Roth, becomes very doubtful. Had he attributed the "President's March" to this musician without going into details, his case would have been much stronger. We then might have admitted the probability that he knew the history of the march either from Roth himself or from others conversant with the matter.

In its actual form, however, McKoy's statement not only contains a *contradictio in adjecto*, but it is contradicted moreover by two of his contemporaries, one of whom claimed to have been among the original performers of the march and the other to have been a son of the composer. If the claims made for Roth had been known to either of these two gentlemen, they emphatically would have denied their correctness, and at least a short reference to this protest would have slipped into J. C.'s account. Evidently Philip Roth was not generally considered outside of Philadelphia as author of the march, nay, not even in Philadelphia itself, for we shall see that "Professor Pfyle," too, resided for years in Philadelphia. Certainly his son would have heard of Roth's claims if such were made, and he would not have failed, in his conversation with J. C., to prove the fallacy of claims which unjustly robbed his father of the glory of having written the air to one of our national songs.

On what grounds Mr. McKoy attributes the piece to Roth we have no way of ascertaining. We have to content ourselves with the fact that chronology and circumstances command weight against his theory. Unless an early copy of the President's March is discovered, printed or in manuscript, bearing Roth's name as author, it would be uncritical to accept his authorship as a historical fact.

But who was "Professor Pfyle," alias Fayles, alias Feyles, alias Fyles, alias Pfalz, alias Pfazles, alias Pfeil, alias Pfyles, alias Philo, alias Phyla, alias Phyles, alias Phylo, alias Phylz, alias Thyla?

J. C.'s spelling seems to corroborate Elson's idea that the actual name was the German "Pfeil," anglicized later on into Ffyle. But the numerous instances in which the name of this "gentleman of doubtful cognomen" appears in newspaper advertisements, etc., leave no doubt that in America he spelled his name Phile. Only once is the name given with a different spelling. This name of Phile was not so uncommon after all in America, as I find five different "Phile's" in the two first Philadelphia city directories.

On Saturday, March 6, 1784, a concert was advertised at Philadelphia, in the Pennsylvania Packet, "For the Benefit of Mr. Phile," in which he and a Mr. Brown "for that night only" were to play "A

Double Concerto for the Violin and Flute." This concert was post-poned from March 18 to the following Tuesday, March 23. Previous to 1784 I have not found Phile mentioned.

He must have been an able violinist, for when the Old American Company of Comedians returned in 1785 to the Continent from the West Indies, where they had sought refuge in the fall of 1774, he was made leader of the orchestra. To quote Charles Durang, who in his rare and interesting "History of the Philadelphia Stage" (Ch. IX) throws "professional side lights" on the different performers in 1785:

> The orchestra was composed of the following musicians; Mr. Philo, leader; Mr. Bentley, harpsichord; Mr. Woolf, principal clarionet; Trimner, Hecker, and son, violoncello, violins etc. Some six or seven other names, now not remembered, constituted the musical force. The latter were all Germans.

On July 18, 1786, was to be performed in New York,[a] under the direction of Mr. Reinagle, the "vocal parts by Miss Maria Storer," "A Grand Concert of Vocal and Instrumental Music." The first part of the concert was to consist "chiefly of Handel's Sacred Music, as performed in Westminster Abbey. The Second Part miscellaneous." Phile was engaged as soloist in the first part, his name appearing thus in the program: "Concerto Violin . . . Mr. Phile," and Mr. Reinagle and Mr. Phile were to play a "Duett for Violin and Violoncello" in the second part.

We next find him at Philadelphia in 1787 [b] and again in connection with a concert. It was the one for Monday, January 15, at the Southwark Theater. The concert was interspersed with "Lectures Moral and Entertaining," and concluded with the "Grand Panto-mimical Finale. In two Acts called Robinson Crusoe." We read in the "First Act": "Rondeau—Mr. Phile."

He can not have remained very long in Philadelphia, because we find him a month after his concert engagement in Philadelphia at New York and offering his services as music teacher. The advertisement reads: [c]

> Music. Philip Phile, most respectfully offers his service to Lovers of Instrumental Musick, in Teaching the Violin and German Flute methodically. Attendance will be given at his Lodgings No. 82 *Chatham* Row, near Vande Waters. He will also wait on such Gentlemen, as would wish to take Lessons, at their own Houses.
>
> N. B. Musick copied at the above mentioned place. Feb. 20.

Not quite two months after this advertisement was inserted Phile reappeared in public in Philadelphia, and it seems as if he was expressly called from New York. The "Syllabus" of the magnificent "First Uranian Concert," which was performed at the German

---

[a] N. Y. Packet 1786, July 13.

[b] Pa. Packet, Jan. 13, 1787.

[c] N. Y. Daily Advertiser, Feb. 21, 1787.

Reformed Church on April 12, 1787, under the direction of the ambitious Andrew Adgate,[a] contains his name among the "Authors" in the following manner: "IV . . . Concerto Violino By Mr. Phile of New York."

In the following year "Mr. Rehine's Concert of Vocal and Instrumental Music," which was to have taken place on November 26 at the City Tavern in Philadelphia, was "postponed on account of the badness of the weather 'till Friday Evening the 29th.'" In this concert the restless Mr. Phile was to play "Solo Violino" in the first act.[b]

An entire "Amateurs Concert" was given "For the Benefit of Philip Phile" on January 29, 1789, "at the house of Henry Epple in Racestreet." The orchestral numbers were three "Grand Overtures" by Vanhall, Haydn, and Martini. As soloists we notice Reinagle with a pianoforte sonata, Wolf with a "Concerto Clarinetto," and Phile. The latter played in the first act a "Concerto Violino" and in the second a "Solo Violino."

It really seems as if Phile was the fashionable violin virtuoso of the day, constanly "on the road" between New York and Philadelphia, for again a "Violin Concerto by Phile" was to be performed at "A Concert of Sacred Music" which the recently founded "Musical Society of New York" gave on Thursday, June 18, 1789, at the Lutheran Church in order to cover the expenses resulting from the purchase of an organ by the Society.[c]

It may be that during all these years Phile remained the leader of the orchestra of the Old American Company, but it is by no means certain, as the fact is nowhere mentioned. We only know (from Durang) that he held this position about 1785. If some of the writers whom I have quoted claim that he was the leader of the orchestra in the John Street Theater at New York in 1789, they forgot to refer to their source of information, and therefore can not be considered as historically trustworthy.

Phile became tired of his erratic life and he decided to "continue his residence" in Philadelphia. Of this decision he gave public notice in the Pennsylvania Packet for December 16, 1789:

Mr. Phile most respectfully informs the citizens of Philadelphia, particularly those Gentlemen he had the honour to instruct formerly, that the unavoidable necessity which occasioned his abscence has now ceased, and that he is determined to continue his residence in this city.

He hopes from the many proofs he has afforded of his abilities as a Teacher of different Instruments of Music, to meet with the Patronage of a generous Public. He proposes to instruct Gentlemen on the Violin, Flute, Clarinet and Bassoon. Mr. Phile is willing to render every satisfaction; this, with a particular attention to those Gentlemen who may please to encourage him, will, he trusts, establish the Reputation he is desirous to merit.

---

[a] Pa. Packet, April 9.
[b] Federal Gazette, Nov. 26, 1788.
[c] N. Y. Daily Adv. and N. Y. Daily Gaz. for June 12, 1789.

Directions to Mr. Phile, living in Race street between Front and Second street, will be punctually attended to. N. B. Music copied. Philadelphia, Dec. 14.

Undoubtedly Phile resided at Philadelphia during the year 1790, as on March 18, 1790, "A Concert of Vocal and Instrumental Music for the Benefit of Mr. Phile" was to be given,[a] and as half a year later, on Saturday, October 16, he performed a "Flute Concert" at Messrs. Gray's Gardens, the entertainment concluding with "Harmony Music by Mr. Phile."[b]

These concerts at Gray's fashionable gardens were held regularly during the summer months and were by no means of the "roof garden" order. The best performers of Philadelphia were engaged for the instrumental and vocal solos, and music only of composers then considered as the best was played. The concert mentioned, for instance, comprised grand overtures by Haydn, Schmitt, Martini, and symphonies by Stamitz and Abel.

For the years 1791 and 1792 I have not been able to trace Phile's name, but I find him as "Phile Philip, music master, 207 Sassafrasst" in the Philadelphia directory for 1793. Then he disappears, and it is very likely that he died a victim of the yellow fever epidemic raging so terribly at Philadelphia during 1793, for we notice a "Phile, Susanna, widow, Washer, 86 No. Fourth st." in the directory for 1794.

This is a *curriculum vitæ* of Philip Phile, as far as I could glean it from newspapers and other sources. Not once is he mentioned as author of the "President's March." However, as he evidently was a composer besides being a violin virtuoso, so far neither chronology nor circumstances seriously weaken J. C.'s or Custis's claims in favor of Phile.

George Washington Parke Custis claimed that the march was composed by a German named Fyles in 1789, in contradistinction to [Francis Hopkinson's?] Washington's March, and that it was struck up when the President entered the stage box with his family. He does not state when the march was first played, far less does he claim that the march was composed for the occasion of Washington's first visit to the John Street Theater in New York. We have to examine his account as it stands and are not justified in embellishing it, as Saffell, Nason, and others have done.

I feel inclined to trust Custis's version neither as a solid basis for air castles, nor as a reflex of direct and authentic information bearing upon the subject, nor as a supplementary evidence in favor of J. C.'s Phile tradition.

It might be objected that Custis, having become a member of Washington's family a few months after his birth, ought to be considered a reliable witness and out of reach of historical skepticism.

Certainly, if it were evident that he visited the theater with the president on May 11, June 5, November 24 and 30, 1789, the only

---

[a] Pa. Packet, T. March 16, 1790.   [b] Federal Gazette, Fr. Oct. 15, 1790.

four times, according to Baker's "Washington after the Revolution,"
and Paul Leicester Ford's charming book, "Washington and the
theater," [a] that the president attended theatrical performances in
New York. This, however, is not the case, and we have no means
of ascertaining whether or not Custis himself heard the President's
March played on these occasions. In the second place, are the recollections of a boy of 8 years reliable? Certainly not; but this argument applies to Custis, who was born in 1781, on the 30th of April.[b]
Furthermore, the "Recollections" were written during a period of
thirty years, and their preface is dated by the author "Arlington
House Near Alexandria, Va. 1856." Is it not most likely that
Custis, when "recollecting" the events of the year 1789, was forced
to supplement his or his family's reminiscences with information
gained from other sources, in particular from tradition and the study
of books?

When a boy of 8 years George Washington Parke Custis probably
was not very much interested in the name of the composer of a march.
Even if he was, such early recollections can not be considered a safe
basis for critical history. If he learned the name later on, especially
after twenty or thirty years had elapsed, then his account has merely
the strength of hearsay. Neither the diary which Washington kept in
1789, nor the old newspapers, nor other contemporary sources mention
a performance of the President's March at the New York theater in
1789, nor have such lovers of historical minutiæ discovered any reference to that effect. Possibly the "President's March" was played
in 1789 on one or several occasions when George Washington visited
the theater, but we are not obliged nor even justified in admitting it,
and with the admission of this possibility as a fact we would still be
very distant from positive proof of the authenticity of Custis's statement that the "President's March" was *composed by Phile in 1789.*

"The President's March," said J. C., "was composed by a Professor
Pfyle, and was played at Trenton bridge when Washington passed
over on his way to New York to his inauguration."

It seems not to have entered the mind of any of the historians quoted,
except William S. Baker, to search for the contemporary accounts of
this occasion. The research would not have caused them very much
trouble, as quite a number of newspapers printed reports of the
"respectful ceremonies" at Trenton, among them the Pennsylvania
Mercury for Saturday, May 2, 1789; the Pennsylvania Packet for
M., April 27, and the New York Journal for April 30. By neglecting
the newspapers the writers missed a most important clue, as will
readily be seen from the report printed in the Pennsylvania Packet:

---

[a] Published in 1899 as No. 8 of the New Series of the Dunlap Society Publications.
[b] Comp. Appleton or the "Memoir of George Washington Parke Custis" prefixed
by his daughter to the "Recollections."

A Sonata Sung by a Number of young Girls, dressed in white and decked with Wreaths and Chaplets of Flowers, holding Baskets of Flowers in their Hands, as General Washington passed under the triumphal Arch, raised on the Bridge at Trenton, April 21, 1789.

> Welcome, mighty chief! once more,
> Welcome to this grateful shore
> Now no mercenary foe
> Aims again the fatal blow
> Aims at thee the fatal blow.
> Virgins fair and Matrons grave
> Those thy conquering arms did save—
> Build for thee triumphal bowers!
> Strew, ye fair, his way with flowers—
> Strew your Hero's way with flowers.

As they sung these Lines they strewed the Flowers before the General, who halted until the Sonata was finished. The General being presented with a Copy of the Sonata, was pleased to address the following Card to the Ladies.

To the Ladies of Trenton . . .

General Washington cannot leave this Place without expressing his Acknowledgments to the Matrons and Young Ladies who received him in so novel and graceful a Manner at the Triumphal Arch in Trenton, for the exquisite Sensations he experienced in that affecting moment.

The astonishing Contrast between his former and actual Situation at the same spot, the elegant Taste with which it was adorned for the present occasion—and the innocent Appearance of the White Robed Choir who met him with the gratulatory Song—have made such an impression on his Remembrance, as, he assures them, will never be effaced.

Trenton, April 21, 1789.

The other papers referred to brought similar reports, all printing sonata instead of cantata, with this important addition, however: "Sonata, composed [a] and set to music for the occasion." Of other music performed at Trenton bridge on this day, and especially of music composed for the occasion, not a syllable in any of the reports.

One is almost led to suppose that this "Sonata" was the piece alluded to by J. C. and attributed by one of the performers, and later by Phile's son, to Philip Phile as the "President's March."

At last the problem appears to approach solution. J. C.'s statement seems to be corroborated to the degree of circumstantial evidence by this account, and Philip Phile, indeed, seems to have been, beyond reasonable doubt, the author of the much-disputed march. Our joy is premature.

New Music. Just published (Price 3 S. 9) and to be Sold by Rice & Co. Booksellers; South side Market near Second Street.

A chorus, sung before General Washington, as he passed under the triumphal Arch raised on the Bridge at Trenton, April 21st. 1789; composed and dedicated by permission, to Mrs. Washington By A. Reinagle.

This advertisement was published in the Pennsylvania Packet, Tuesday, December 29, 1789. Therewith we have a third and formidable claimant in the person of one of the foremost musicians in the

---

[a] Mr. Baker attributes the words to Maj. Richard Howell, later on governor of New Jersey.

country, the composer of numerous operas, sonatas, songs, marches, in particular of the "Federal March," written for and performed at Philadelphia on July 4, 1788, in the grand procession in honor of the Constitution, the only known copy of which is now in the Library of Congress. If the music of the chorus sung on the bridge at Trenton was identical with that of the President's March, then, of course, Alexander Reinagle's music was wedded to "Hail Columbia," and not Philip Phile's. Fortunately a copy of the "Chorus" is still extant to throw light on the puzzling situation. In their pamphlet on "Washington's reception by the ladies of Trenton," the Society of Iconophiles published in 1903 a reduced facsimile in copper photogravure of the piece as once in possession of Maj. Richard Howell, supposed author of the poem in question. The extremely rare piece bears this title:

> Chorus sung before Gen. Washington as he passed under the Triumphal arch raised on the bridge at Trenton, April 21st, 1789. Set to music and dedicated by permission to Mrs. Washington by A. Reinagle. Price ½ dollar. Philadelphia. Printed for the author, and sold by H. Rice, Market Street.

The instrumental introduction and the first bars of the chorus may follow here to prove conclusively that Reinagle's chorus and the President's March are not identical.

Here, then, is a puzzling situation. Phile's son claimed that a march known as the President's March and composed by his father was played on the bridge at Trenton, and that he was one of the performers. On the other hand, there exists a composition by Reinagle, the title of which would seem to leave no doubt that it was played and sung on the same occasion to the words "Welcome, mighty chief! once more." If we were permitted to assume that *both* compositions figured on the programme of the festivities at Trenton, that would clear the situation somewhat, but no contemporary account mentions any music but the so-called "Sonata." Had the "President's March" been composed for the occasion the fact surely would have been mentioned in the newspapers. Even if "The President's March" was already so popular as to be played as a matter of course in the presence of the President, the probabilities are that the march would have been reported by name or at least that the contemporary reports would have alluded to the performance of other music besides the "Sonata." Such, however, is not the case, and the issue can not be avoided. Either Reinagle's chorus was sung or "The President's March" had been fitted to Major Howell's words. Under the circumstances it is fortunate that the rendition of Reinagle's chorus on the bridge at Trenton, all appearances to the contrary notwithstanding, is very doubtful for the following reasons:

(1) The printed title allows to read a distinction between *chorus sung*, which would then mean "words sung" and *set to music*.

(2) They must have been sung before Washington on April 21, whereas Reinagle's composition was advertised in the Pennsylvania Packet, Philadelphia, December 29, 1789, as *just published*. An unusual interval between performance and publication.

(3) Reinagle's piece is engraved for "2 voice. 1 voice. 3 voice" with pianoforte accompaniment apparently reduced from orchestral score. The 3. voice stands in the bass clef, and the whole is composed for either a mixed chorus or a 3-part male chorus. But the *Sonata* was sung "by a number of young girls," and of a band or orchestra assisting on the occasion and accompanying the singers no mention is made.

Any of these three observations alone might carry little weight. Together they do, and combined with a fourth they appear to bear out the doubt that Reinagle's chorus was not composed for April 21, 1789. The "Plan" (programme) of the "New York Subscription Concert" for Tuesday, September 15, 1789, as it appears in the Daily Advertiser for the same day, reads:

After the first act, will be performed a chorus, to the words that were sung, as Gen. Washington passed the Bridge at Trenton—The Music *now* composed by Mr. Reinagle.

This implies that Reinagle's setting, published in December, was *not* the one sung when General Washington passed the bridge. Consequently Reinagle no longer interferes with the Phile tradition. The claim put forth for Phile's authorship of the President's March is by no means yet proved, but it remains unshaken. It would be decidedly strengthened if it could be shown that the "Music of the Sonata" actually sung on April 21, 1789, and of the "President's March" were identical. As Reinagle did not compose the music for the occasion, and as Phile is the only other musician mentioned in connection with said occasion, appearances seem to be in his favor until counterbalanced by the observation that the claim for Phile is based upon the reminiscences of one of the original performers confirmed later by Phile's son. The term *performer* without the addition *vocal* generally applies to a performer on some instrument. To have been a *performer* on said occasion would infer that the "Sonata" was sung with instrumental accompaniment. To repeat it, nothing goes to show that such was the case. But in order not to push arguments too far, the possibility may be admitted either that the performer was a vocal performer, *scilicet*, one of the "young girls," or that the "Sonata" was really sung with instrumental accompaniment though not so described in any of the reports. We might even allow the combination of both possibilities for the simplification of matters. In that case the words of the "Sonata" were either fitted to the already popular "President's March," or this march was composed for the occasion and subsequently became popular under the name of "The President's March." However, all this seems to be impossible, for a very simple reason. In my opinion the *words of the "Sonata" can not have been sung to any of the versions of "The President's March."* Every attempt to fit the words of the "Sonata" to this march fails, even after the boldest surgical operations. Consequently, unless others succeed with such attempts, the conclusion·is inevitable that the *"Sonata" sung on the bridge at Trenton and the "President's March" were not identical.* It follows that J. C.'s statement of 1841, like McKoy's of 1829, contains a serious flaw. Therefore we are not justified in accepting it as authentic.

To prove the point just raised, some of the earliest versions of the "President's March" are here submitted either in facsimile or in transcript. At the same time these musical quotations will show the musical genesis and partial transformation of "Hail Columbia" about the year 1800.

(1) The arrangement for two flutes, on page 3, of the first number of R. Shaw's and B. Carr's "Gentleman's Amusement," Philadelphia, Carr, April, 1794. See facsimile of the copy at the Library of Congress (Appendix, Pl. IX). (This "Gentleman's Amusement" is

identical with the one advertised in the New York Daily Advertiser, May 8, 1794, as "Philadelphia printed for Shaw & Co.")

(2) "President's March." Philadelphia, G. Willig, Mark[et] street 185, and therefore published between 1798 and 1803. See facsimile of the copy at the Library of Congress in Appendix, Plate X.

(3)

The President's March as in Shaw's Flute Preceptor. Philadelphia, 1802.

(4)

The President's March as in the "Compleat Tutor for the Fife," Philadelphia, G. Willig, *ca.* 1805.

Now, it is a singular fact that, to my knowledge, "The President's March" is nowhere mentioned in contemporary sources before the year 1794. That it was popular about 1794 is clear, as it otherwise would hardly have been printed in Shaw and Carr's "Gentleman's Amusement." Some months later the Old American Company, then playing at the Cedar Street Theatre in Philadelphia, advertised in the American Daily Advertiser, September 22, for the same evening that—

. . . previous to the tragedy [the Grecian Daughter] the band will play a new Federal Overture, in which are introduced several popular airs; Marseilles hymn, Ça ira, O dear what can the matter be, Rose Tree, Carmagnole, "Presidents' March," Yankee Doodle, etc. Composed by Mr. Carr.

This "Federal Overture," by Benjamin Carr, was published 1795 in an arrangement for two flutes in the fifth number of Shaw and Carr's "Gentleman's Amusement." Had the march been well known as "The President's March" in 1789 and later, why should A. Reinagle's much less popular "Federal March" and Sicard's "New Constitutional March and Federal Minuet" (both 1788) and other patriotic pieces have been published and not "The President's March?" And if published, advertisements to that effect would have appeared before 1794 in the newspapers, as was the case with all early American musical publications, either sacred or secular. We must not forget that the demand for patriotic music was very eager in those days, and a march in honor of President Washington would have sold well. Furthermore, had the air been really popular during the years immediately following 1789, at least one of the innumerable political and patriotic songs which were to be sung to popular melodies (and the words with tune indication of most of these songs were printed in the newspapers or magazines) would show the indication: "Tune— President's March." Such is not the case, but it seems to be a fact that all songs, which, like "Hail Columbia," were fitted to this tune, appeared in print after 1794.

Therefore, while the analysis of traditions, reports, and contemporary evidence so far submitted permits us to concentrate our attention upon Phile more than on Roth as the possible author of the "President's March," it does not yet permit us, if at all interested in sound history, to attribute the "President's March" with something like certainty to Philip Phile, and most decidedly not to date the origin of the march 1789.

Here, then, the matter rested when recently the hoped-for accident helped to clear the situation still further. At the Governor Pennypacker sale the Library of Congress acquired a lot of miscellaneous early American musical publications. Among the fragments appears an unnumbered page, evidently torn from an engraved music collection for the pianoforte, bearing two marches, one,

THE PRESIDENTS MARCH, BY PHEIL,

the other, fortunately, "March, by Moller." Fortunately, because the reference to the name of John Christopher Moller proves that the page can not have been printed before his arrival in America in 1790, and that it most probably forms part of one of the publications issued by Moller and Henri Capron at Philadelphia in 1793. The importance of this page therefore lies in the fact that "The President's March" was attributed to Pheil and not to Roth as early as about 1793. Consequently this probably earliest edition of the march (see Appendix, Pl. XI), though it does not assist us in dating and locating the origin of "The President's March," removes all reasonable doubt from the tradition that the music of "Hail Columbia" was composed by Philip Phile.

A comparison of the "Hail Columbia" texts, as they appear in song books, is unnecessary, because practically no verbal differences have crept into Joseph Hopkinson's poem. It may be noticed, however, that the autograph which was formerly in possession of Mr. C. D. Hildebrand, of Philadelphia, and which Admiral Preble reproduced in facsimile in the second edition of his book on our flag,[a] has in the first stanza "war was *done*" instead of "war was *gone*." The latter version not only is the one now customary, but it appears in the two earliest printed versions of "Hail Columbia," described above. For this reason the Hildebrand autograph probably is not the earliest or even an early autograph copy. Two other copies in Joseph Hopkinson's hand are mentioned by Preble in this manner:

"During the centennial year an autograph copy of 'Hail Columbia' was displayed in the museum at Independence Hall, Philadelphia. This copy was written from memory Feb. 22, 1828, and presented to George M. Keim, esq., of Reading, in compliance with a request made by him. It has marginal notes, one of which informs us that the passage 'Behold the Chief' refers to John Adams, then President of the United States. Mr. Hopkinson also presented General Washington with a copy of his poem, and received from him a complimentary letter of thanks, which is now in the possession of his descendants."

An autograph copy signed and dated "Philadelphia, March 24, 1838" (4o, 3 p.) was offered for sale in Henkels's "Catalogue of Autograph Letters," 1895. The added facsimile showed that this 1838 copy has the marginal note about John Adams and *done* instead of *gone* in the first stanza, thereby corroborating the claim that the Hildebrand copy is of a comparatively late date. To whom this 1838 copy was sold, I do not know. Until recently the Pennsylvania Historical Society possessed *two* autograph copies of "Hail Columbia,"

---

[a] From there facsimiled by Mary L. D. Ferris for her article on "Our National Songs" in the New England Magazine, 1890, pp. 483–504.

one of them coming from the Hopkinson family papers, but the society has since disposed of one of the two.   The other is here reproduced in facsimile by permission of the society.   (See Appendix as Plates VIIIa–VIIIb.)

If a text comparison of "Hail Columbia" is unnecessary, not so a comparison of the musical settings, or rather arrangements.   First, in order to show the difference between the old and the new way of singing the "President's March" to the words of "Hail Columbia," the edition which Willig printed between 1798 and 1803 will be compared with the probably simultaneous edition of a copy which has been reproduced in facsimile by Mr. Elson in his books, as mentioned before.   From these early editions I turn immediately to current song books, selecting for the purpose the same as was done for "The Star-Spangled Banner" chapter (see p. 41).   Also the same principle and method of comparison will be adopted with this difference, that the text is added, since it is sometimes placed differently under the notes.

"The President's March.   A new Federal song," Philadelphia, G. Willig, between 1798 and 1803.

$\frac{2}{4}$ instead of *alla breve:* E.

E. E.

$\frac{4}{4}$: B; F; G; J; M; R; Si; W. (Hail Columbia is not in A.; Sh.; Sm.; Z.)

G; J.   F; W.   Who G; J.   Who M; R.   Who Si.   Who

fought and bled in   Free-dom's cause, Who fought and bled in   Free-dom's cause, And
F; G; J; M; R; Si; W.   F; M; R; Si; W.   F; G; J; M; R; Si; W.   F; M; R; Si; W.

The grace note *g* is discarded in modern editions.

And when the storm of val - or won; Let J   M
G;   J.   F; G; J: M; R; Si; W.G;   J.

F; M; R; Si; W.   G; J.   what it cost   J
F; M; R; W.

M; Si.   J   B; Si.   let its al - tar   W
F; M; R

F; R; Si; W   G; J.   B; F; G; J; M; R; Si; W.   F; G; J; R. W.   M

Si   Ral - ly - ing round our Ral - lying round our Ral - ly - ing round our
B   F; J; M; R; Si; W. G

F; G; J; R; W.   M   Si   B; Si   G; J

B; F; M; R: Si; W   G; J   F; W   G; J; Si.   M; R.

For eight song books, selected at random, to thus differ in the majority of bars of a national song of 28 bars, is a deplorable state of affairs. It means that if 8 children, each familiar with one of these song books, were to sing "Hail Columbia" together, not one would sing the melody exactly like any of the other 7 children. One is ashamed as an American to think of the result, if not 8, but 80 current song books were similarly examined! The discrepancies between current versions of "The Star-Spangled Banner" are regrettable enough, but those between current versions of "Hail Columbia" evidently are still worse.[a]

---

[a] This report was in proof sheets when Mr. Otto Hubach, financial editor of the New Yorker Staats-Zeitung and from 1876–1883 an officer in the Prussian army informed me of his recollection "that the march to which the text of 'Hail Columbia' is sung dates from the time of Frederick the Great and for more than one hundred years has been officially used in the Prussian army as '*Altpreussisches Rondo*' and that the infantry manual still in his time mentioned under accredited marches this rondo." I have not yet had occasion to verify this information. That the infantry manual contains a march at least similar to the "President's March" I have no reason to doubt, though the latter is by no means a rondo. Nor do I see how Mr. Hubach's recollections interfere at all with Philip Phile's authorship. Like many other foreign marches, his may have found its way to Prussia to be used on special official occasions. I suspect a slight error somewhere in Mr. Hubach's recollections. At any rate, neither Thouret nor Kalkbrenner ("Verzeichnis sämtlicher kgl. preussischen Armee-Märsche," 1896) substantiate Mr. Hubach's recollections so far as they affect place and date of origin of the "President's March," which may safely be attributed to Philip Phile, until facts render this impossible.

AMERICA.

Rev. Samuel F. Smith's (1808–1895) "America" does not call for elaborate treatment in a report like this. In the first place, words and tune show a praiseworthy uniformity in the song books. The only difference between the 12 song books selected, which is at all worth mentioning, is that Aiken, Gantvoort, Jepson, Ripley, Zeiner have in the forelast bar—

Let free-dom ring.

whereas Boyle, Farnsworth, McLaughlin, Shirley, Siefert, Smith, Whiting have—

Let free-dom ring.

No noteworthy discrepancies appear in the texts used in the song books. This has its simple explanation in the fact that Reverend Smith himself adhered to his original text whenever he was requested in later years to write autograph copies of "America."[a] Indeed, so numerous were these occasions that Mr. Benjamin in the Collector, July, 1908, expressed his willingness to supply autograph copies of "My country, 'tis of thee" at any time for $10. This is probably an

---

[a] The Chief Assistant Librarian, Mr. Griffin, then Chief of the Bibliography Division, in his memorandum of November 20, 1907, pointed out that in a version "published by D. Lothrop and company, Boston, 1884, there is an accompanying facsimile autograph copy in which, in the second stanza, there is a comma after the word *noble* changing somewhat the significance of the verse." Mr. Griffin also found in F. L. Knowles' "Poems of American patriotism" not less than four additional stanzas printed not to be found in the original. Mr. Kobbé included in his "Famous American Songs" the following stanza, believed to have been added, he says, by the author at the celebration of the Washington Inauguration Centennial:

> Our joyful hearts to-day,
> Their grateful tribute pay,
> Happy and free.
> After our toils and fears,
> After our blood and tears,
> Strong with our hundred years
> O God, to thee.

exaggeration, yet it is certain that more autograph copies exist than are referred to in the following.

In the clever chat on "Our national songs" in the New England Magazine (July, 1890, vol. 2, pp. 483–504) Mary L. D. Ferris has a facsimile of the original draft of "America" (on the margin of a printed subscription blank), then still in the possession of Reverend Smith. The text of this draft, which does not bear the title "America," nor any other title, reads:

My country 'tis of thee
Sweet land of liberty;
   Of thee I sing.
Land where my fathers died
Land of the pilgrims' pride
From every mountain side
   Let freedom ring.

My native country,—thee,
Land of the noble free
   Thy name I love;
I love thy—rocks & rills
Thy woods & templed hills
My heart with rapture thrills
   Like that above.

Let music swell the breeze
And ring from all the trees
   Sweet freedom's song
Let all that breathes partake
Let mortal tongues awake
Let rocks their silence break
   The sound prolong.

Our fathers' God to Thee
Author of liberty
   To Thee we sing
Long may our land be bright
With freedom's holy light
Protect us by Thy might
   Our God our King.

Between the second and fourth verse Reverend Smith sketched, but then crossed out, the following:

No more shall tyrants here
With haughty steps appear
   And soldier bands
No more shall tyrants tread
Above the patriot dead
No more our blood be shed
   By alien hands.

In the same article, Miss Ferris gives the facsimile of an autograph, apparently written for her by Reverend Smith and dated "Feb. 28, 1890." This has the title "America." In the third stanza the line "Let mortal tongues awake" precedes "Let all that breathe," and in the last line of the whole poem occurs the now current "Great God" instead of "Our God," but otherwise the texts are identical.

On April 4, 1893, Reverend Smith wrote a copy of his poem for the Outlook, where a facsimile appeared in 1898, volume 59, page 565.

The text is identical with that in the 1890 autograph, and also with that of a facsimile of an autograph copy sent Admiral Preble by Reverend Smith under date of "Boston, Mass., Sept. 12, 1872," and printed by the admiral in the 1880 edition of his book on our flag.

The autograph copy of "America" was accompanied by notes on the origin of the poem. Such historical notes the author was constantly, and until his death, requested to send to the admirers of "America." The version most frequently used by subsequent historians appears to be that in Admiral Preble's book. It reads:

> The origin of my hymn, "My Country 'tis of Thee", is briefly told. In the year 1831, Mr. William C. Woodbridge returned from Europe, bringing a quantity of German music-books, which he passed over to Lowell Mason. Mr. Mason, with whom I was on terms of friendship, one day turned them over to me, knowing that I was in the habit of reading German works, saying, "Here, I can't read these, but they contain good music, which I should be glad to use. Turn over the leaves, and if you find anything particularly good, give me a translation or imitation of it, or write a wholly original song,—anything, so I can use it."
>
> Accordingly, one leisure afternoon, I was looking over the books, and fell in with the tune of "God Save the King", and at once took up my pen and wrote the piece in question. It was struck out at a sitting, without the slightest idea that it would ever attain the popularity it has since enjoyed. I think it was written in the town of Andover, Mass., in February, 1832. The first time it was sung publicly was at a children's celebration of American independence, at the Park Street Church, Boston, I think July 4, 1832. If I had anticipated the future of it, doubtless I would have taken more pains with it. Such as it is, I am glad to have contributed this mite to the cause of American freedom.

These notes give substantially the same, though in some details not quite the full information as the letter Reverend Smith sent Miss Ferris from Newton Center, Mass., August 12, 1889, for her article "On our national songs" in the New England Magazine, 1890, and which is quoted here because it has not attracted the attention it deserved:

> The hymn, "My country,—'tis of thee,"—was written in February, 1832. As I was turning over the leaves of several books of music,—chiefly music for children's schools,—the words being in the German language,—the music, which I found later to be "God save the King", empressed me very favorably. I noticed at a glance that the German words were patriotic. But without attempting to translate or imitate them, I was led on the impulse of the moment to write the hymn now styled "America", which was the work of a brief period of time at the close of a dismal winter afternoon. I did not design it for a national hymn, nor did I think it would gain such notoriety. I dropped the MS., (which is still in my possession) into my portfolio, and thought no more of it for months. I had, however, once seen it, after writing it, & given a copy to Mr. Lowell Mason, with the music from the German pamphlet; and, much to my surprise, on the succeeding 4th July, he brought it out on occasion of a Sunday School celebration in Park St. church, Boston.

The story of the origin of "My country, 'tis of thee," as narrated at different times without conflicting variations by Reverend Smith, is generally accepted as authentic. As far as I can see, dissension of opinion has arisen only over the really unimportant question where, when, and by whom "My country, 'tis of thee," was first sung. In the Boston Evening Transcript of October 27, 1908, Mr. William Copley Winslow took Mr. Edwin D. Mead to task for having written in the same paper on October 19, 1908, that "America" was first sung on July 4, 1832, at Park Street Church. Mr. Winslow instead claimed:

> This hymn was first sung at the Bowdoin Street Church, of which Rev. Hubbard Winslow was then [1832] pastor and Lowell Mason the organist and conductor of the choir . . . The hymn with other selections, was sung by the Sunday school, aided by the choir before a large audience in the Bowdoin Street Church. Subsequently, at a combined service of Sunday schools, the hymn was sung in the Park Street Church . . .

This, if true, would interfere seriously with Edward Everett Hale's delightful little story, how he on the Fourth of July, 1832, after having spent all his holiday money on root beer, ginger snaps, and oysters at the celebration on Boston Common, on his way home marched with other children into Park Street Church and "thus by merest chance," as Mr. Kobbé retells the story, and because his money had been expended so rapidly, was present at the first singing of the hymn, which is national enough to be called "America." Mr. Winslow, whatever the merits of his claim may be, has not supported his statements with any evidence strong enough to undermine the fact, as Mr. Mead wrote in his rejoinder on October 27, 1908, that Reverend Smith "said it again and again in personal conversation, in public addresses, and in print" how "it was at the Park Street Church that the famous hymn was first sung" on July 4, 1832. To this the author adhered until his death without giving to any other account even the benefit of doubt. For instance, in an article in the New York World, January 20, 1895, reprinted from there in the Critic, 1895, he explicitly said:

> It was at this children's Fourth of July celebration that "America" was first sung.

"America" is perhaps too hymnlike and devotional in character for a national anthem, and possibly is pervaded too much by a peculiar New England flavor. It is also eminently peaceful and indeed so much so, as was remarked above, that the author deliberately crossed out the only verse with allusion to war. Yet, these can not really be considered shortcomings of "My country 'tis of thee" as a national song and would at all events be outweighed by the great advantage that "America" is appropriate for all occasions and professions, for old and young and for both sexes. It does not sound odd from the mouth of a woman as does, for instance, "The Star-Spangled Banner."

However, the main objection raised against "America" has been the union of the words with that foreign air of cosmopolitan usage "God save the King." Yet there is this difference, which should never be overlooked. If the Danes or the Prussians use "God save the King," they have deliberately borrowed it from the British. Not so with us. "God save the King" was, before 1776, as much our national anthem as that of the motherland. Being a British air it belonged to the British colonists just as much as it did to the Britons at home. When we gained national independence, did the Americans forthwith deprive themselves of the English language, of English literature, English tastes, of all the ties formed by an English ancestry? Why should, then, Americans renounce their original part-ownership of the air of "God save the King?" Why should it not be perfectly natural for them, in short, American, to use for their national anthem an air which, historically considered, they need not even borrow? Certain it is that after 1776 the air was not treated with this comparatively recent chauvinism. Young America sang patriotic songs like "God save America," "God save George Washington," "God save the President," and that "song made by a Dutch lady at the Hague for the sailors of the five American vessels at Amsterdam, June, 1779," printed in the Pennsylvania Packet and called "God save the thirteen States," without the slightest misgivings. Thomas Dawes, jr., used the air for his ode sung at the entertainment given on Bunker's Hill by the proprietors of Charles River bridge at the opening of the same in 1786 or 1787. It begins "Now let rich music sound," and may be found on pages 133–134 of the American Musical Miscellany, 1798. Indeed, this once standard collection included (on pp. 130–132) an "Ode for the Fourth of July," the words of which "Come all ye sons of song" were sung to the supposedly un-American air of "God save the King." The most curious use, however, was made of this air by an early American suffragette. In the Philadelphia Minerva, October 17, 1795, appeared in the "Court of Apollo" a poem under the title "Rights of Woman" by a lady, tune "God save America," and beginning:

> God save each Female's right
> Show to her ravish'd sight
> Woman is free.

To contribute to the discussion of the origin of "God save the King" from this side of the ocean would be preposterous. Whether Chappell, Chrysander, Cummings, etc., have exhausted the subject or not would be extremely difficult for any American to investigate. The literature mentioned in the appendix to this report will enable those interested in the problem to exercise their critical faculties, though it is very doubtful if they could sum up the whole matter more admirably than was done by Sir George Grove and Mr. Frank Kidson in the new edition of Grove's "Dictionary of Music & Musicians." Yet one remark I feel unable to repress. The efforts unreservedly to attribute the air of "God save the King" to Dr. John Bull (1619), merely because a few notes are similar, remind me of Mr. Elson's witty observation that with such arguments the main theme of the last movement of Beethoven's Ninth Symphony would come very close to being inspired by "Yankee Doodle."

YANKEE DOODLE

"Yankee Doodle" is sometimes called a national song—incorrectly so, because, with a now practically obsolete text or texts, it is hardly ever sung, but merely played as an instrumental piece. Though no longer a national song, it is still a national air and second only to "Dixie" in patriotic popularity. For one hundred and fifty years "Yankee Doodle" has appealed to our people, and the tune shows no sign of passing into oblivion. Surely, a tune of such vitality must have some redeeming features. This remark is directed against those who have ridiculed the musical merits of "Yankee Doodle" or treated it with contempt. That Schubert would not have composed such an air is obvious enough, and it is equally obvious that as a national air "Yankee Doodle" does not direct itself to our sense of majesty, solemnity, dignity. It frankly appeals to our sense of humor. Critics, pedantic or flippant, have overlooked the fact that every nation has its humorous, even burlesque, patriotic airs, and that these are just as natural and useful as solemn airs—indeed, more so, occasionally. As a specimen of burlesque, even "slangy," musical humor, "Yankee Doodle" may safely hold its own against any other patriotic air. But why apologize or explain, since the matter was summed up so neatly many years ago—at least as early as the Songster's Museum, Hartford, 1826, in the lines:

> Yankee Doodle is the tune
>   Americans delight in
> 'Twill do to whistle, sing or play,
>   And just the thing for fighting.

which apparently are the polished descendants of the lines in the Columbian Songster, 1799, under the title of "American Spirit:"

> Sing Yankee Doodle, that fine tune
>   Americans delight in.
> It suits for peace, it suits for fun,
>   It suits as well for fighting.

It may be added that the air has found its way with more or less effect into the works of modern composers, such as Rubinstein, Wieniawski, Schelling. However, be its esthetic appeal to musicians weak or strong, this much is certain: Exceedingly few airs have stirred antiquarians to pile a mass of literature around their origin as has "Yankee Doodle." But how grotesque, that the two most painstaking contributions to the subject of "Yankee Doodle" should have remained unpublished! I mean those by Mr. Moore and Mr. Matthews. Mr. George H. Moore's paper, called "Notes on the origin and history of Yankee Doodle," and read first before the New York Historical Society on December 1, 1885, acquired for its author the reputation of knowing more about our air than any other person then living; yet this famous paper was never printed. Indeed, even the manuscript disappeared in the fogs of mystery until Mr. Albert Matthews, of Boston, whose amazingly elaborate research in the history of Americanisms brought him into close contact with "Yankee Doodle," traced it to Doctor Moore's son. Mr. Matthews made extracts from the manuscript for his own purpose, and this purpose has been for many years to write an exhaustive history of "Yankee Doodle"—at any rate, as far as its literary history goes. Mr. Matthews contributed several papers on the subject to the Colonial Society of Massachusetts, but these papers, too, have remained unpublished and are not accessible to the public; nor have I seen them, but, after having collected the bulk of my data and having gained control over the subject in form and substance, I entered into a fruitful correspondence—mutually fruitful, I hope— with Mr. Matthews on "Yankee Doodle." His generosity in parting with data and information, patiently gathered for his own work and perhaps for theories differing from mine, has enabled me to polish this report and in many places to strengthen the line of argument where I felt dissatisfied with it.

YANKEE, A NICKNAME FOR NEW ENGLANDERS.

The nickname "Yankee" is usually and has so been applied by Europeans for a long time to citizens of the United States in general as distinguished from other Americans. In our own country the nickname still retains a New England flavor, in keeping with the history of the term. This statement seems to be contradicted by what Mr. Albert Matthews wrote to the author under date of November 30, 1908:

> It has been taken for granted by all writers that originally the word Yankee was applied to New Englanders only. My material shows that this is a mistake and that originally the word was applied by the British to any American colonist, and was applied by the American colonists themselves to the inhabitants of some colony other than their own. Thus, Pennsylvanians called the Connecticut settlers in the Wyoming Valley Yankees, but did not call themselves Yankees. Again, Virginians called Marylanders Yankees, but did not apply the term to themselves. I am speaking, you understand, of the decade between 1765 and 1775. Now as the year 1775 is approached, it is undoubtedly true that there was a tendency to locate the Yankees more especially in New England.

Mr. Matthews's material has not yet been published, and it is not yet necessary to accept his interpretation of reference to the early use of "Yankee" as the only correct one. Therefore, the author of this report still holds that the nickname, while perhaps originally not confined to New Englanders, was preferably applied to them by the colonists and that a Virginian, Marylander, Pennsylvanian, or New Yorker of colonial times, let us say after 1760, would hardly have considered it a compliment to be called "Yankee."

This does not argue that the British knew or always drew the local distinction, or that their use of the word always implied ridicule either of the Americans in general or the New Englanders in particular. At any rate, no satirical flavor attaches to the word when Gen. James Wolfe (see his "Life," 1864, p. 437, by R. Wright) wrote under date of June 19, 1758, "North East Harbour (Louisbourg) to General Amherst:"

> My posts are now so fortified that I can afford you the two companies of Yankees and the more as they are better for ranging and scouting than either work or vigilance.

How sectional the term still was shortly before our war for independence may be illustrated by a reference to J. H. T.'s communication to the Historical Magazine (1857, Vol. I, p. 375):

> In "*Oppression*," a Poem by an American with notes by a North Briton, . . . London, Printed; Boston, Reprinted . . . 1765, this word is introduced and explained as follows. The writer denounces Mr. Huske (then a member of the House of Commons, for Maldon in Essex), as the originator of the scheme for taxing the colonies;
>
> > "From meanness first, this *Portsmouth Yankey* rose
> > And still to meanness all his conduct flows;
> > This alien upstart, by obtaining friends,
> > From T-wn-nd's clerk, a M-ld-n member ends."
>
> [Note] "Portsmouth Yankey." It seems our hero being a new Englander by birth, has a right to the epithet of Yankey; a name of derision, I have been informed, given by the Southern people on the Continent, to those of New England: what meaning there is in the word, I never could learn." (p. 10).

In the same volume of the Historical Magazine (pp. 91–92) attention is drawn by B. H. H. to an unpublished letter which Robert Yates, the sheriff of Albany County, N. Y., wrote on July 20, 1771, on his return from an official visit to Bennington, Vt., and in which he refers to the inhabitants of this town, thus:

> We received an account from the *Yankies* that they would not give up the possession [of the farm] but would keep it at all events.

and again:

> We had discovered that the *Yankees* had made all the necessary preparations to give us the warmest reception.

In the extract of a letter dated Hartford and printed in the New York Journal, June 15, 1775, describing the capture of letters from the "high flying" Tory, Robert Temple, occurs this sentence:

> Other letters are full of invectives against the poor *Yankees*, as they call us.

In the "Journal of the most remarkable occurrences in Quebec, 1775–1776, by an officer of the garrison" (rep. by the N. Y. Hist. Soc. 1880, p. 222), we read:

> The New Yorkers look upon themselves as being far superior to what they call the *Yankies*, meaning the people of Connecticut, Massachusetts, Rhode-Island and New Hampshire, who effect a disgusting pre-eminence and take the lead in every thing.

Rev. Wm. Gordon, when describing the skirmishes at Concord and Lexington in the Pennsylvania Gazette, May 10, 1775, says:

> They [the British troops] were roughly handled by the *Yankees*, a term of reproach for the New Englanders, when applied by the regulars.

Silas Deane, when writing June 3, 1775 one of his characteristic letters from Philadelphia to his wife, after describing graphically the Continental Congress, remarks:

> . . . indeed, not only the name of a Yankee, but of a Connecticut man in particular, is become very respectable this way,

and James Thacher, in his Military Journal from 1775 to 1783 (p. 72), commenting on the difference "between troops from Southern States and those from New England," remarked:

> it could scarcely be expected that people from distant colonies, differing in manners and prejudices could at once harmonize in friendly intercourse. Hence we too frequently hear the burlesque epithet of Yankee from one party, and that of Buckskin, by way of retort, from the other.

These and other references would imply not only that the term was preferably used by New Yorkers and the British soldiers against New Englanders; that it was derisive, or at least not complimentary; that it was comparatively unfamiliar to the New Englanders; and that it had not yet been adopted by them for home use. They adopted it during the war, however, and took, as happens quite frequently to derisive nicknames, great pride in calling themselves, or being called, "Yankees." For instance, Anburey states in his "Travels," writing from Cambridge, 1777, "after the affair of Bunker's Hill the Americans gloried in it."

DERIVATION OF THE WORDS "YANKEE DOODLE."

The annotator of the poem "Oppression" expressed his inability in 1765 to explain the meaning of the word. To-day he would rather experience the difficulty of choosing between the various etymological explanations. The word "Yankee" gradually came to fascinate the historian of words until about 1850 this fascination reached its climax. Since then the craze has subsided, yet any number of explanations are still current and proffered as facts, merely on the presumption that embellished reiteration of statements correctly or incorrectly quoted produces facts. Without an attempt to be exhaustive, it will be well to bring some semblance of order into this literature by going back, as far as possible, to the form in which the different and sometimes fantastically developed theories originally appeared.

Possibly the first (in print) appeared in the Pennsylvania Evening Post, May 25, 1775, reprinted from there in the New York Gazetteer, June 1, 1775. It is in form of a short article:

ETYMOLOGY OF THE WORD YANKEE.

When the New England colonies were first settled, the inhabitants were obliged to fight their way against many nations of Indians. They found but little difficulty in subduing them at all, except one tribe, who were known by the name of the Yankoos, which signifies *invincible*. After the waste of much blood and treasure, the Yankoos were at last subdued by the New Englanders. The remains of this nation (agreeable to the Indian custom) transferred their name to their conquerors. For a while they were called Yankoos; but from a corruption, common to names in all languages, they got through time the name of Yankees. A name which we hope will soon be equal to that of a Roman, or an *ancient* Englishman.

It is a suspicious coincidence that the derivation of "Yankee" from Yankoo, meaning "invincible," should have been brought forward at the beginning of our hostilities with the English. Furthermore, it never has been the Indian custom to transfer their names to their conquerors, nor has it been the custom of the latter to acquiesce in such a transfer, though they adopted many Indian names for localities. Worst of all for this etymology, which has been accepted in all seriousness by several writers, an Indian tribe by the name of "Yankoos" is not known to have existed. To illustrate the extremes to which credulity in historical matters may lead, the following extraordinary yarn with reference to the "Yankoo" theory may be quoted from the Magazine of American History (1891, vol. 25, p. 256), where L. A. Alderman writes:

John Dresser Chamberlain, my grandfather, wrote in 1870: "According to tradition we descended from two brothers who came from England, one of whom settled in Massachusetts and the other in Connecticut. Benjamin Chamberlain, a descendant of the Massachusetts stock, was a great warrior against the Indians, and many of his exploits were printed in his biography. One was that he fought the Yankoo chief— *Yankoo* meaning 'conqueror' in English—and whipped him. Then the chief said: 'I no more Yankoo, *you* Yankoo,' and from that time and circumstance the name was transferred to the whites, now called Yankees. Benjamin Chamberlain lived at Southborough, Massachusetts, during the Revolutionary war." [!!]

A second theory of derivation was first printed in Gordon's History of the Rise, Progress, and Establishment of the Independence of the United States of America, (London, 1788, Vol. I, p. 481):

> You may wish to know the origin of the term Yankee. Take the best account of it which your friend can procure. It was a cant, favorite word with farmer Jonathan Hastings of Cambridge about 1713. Two aged ministers, who were at the college in that town, have told me, they remembered it to have been then in use among the students, but had no recollections of it before that period. The inventor used it to express excellency. A Yankee good horse, or Yankee cider and the like, were an excellent good horse, and excellent cider. The students used to hire horses of him; their intercourse with him, and his use of the term upon all occasions, led them to adopt it and they gave him the name of Yankee Jon. He was a worthy, honest man, but no conjurer. This could not escape the notice of the collegiates. Yankee probably became a by-word among them to express a weak, simple, outward person; was carried from the college with them when they left it and was in that way inculcated . . . till from its currency in New England, it was at length taken up and unjustly applied to the New Englanders in common, as a term of reproach.

This version, of course, depends on the actual existence of a farmer, Jonathan Hastings, about 1713. The assumption is corroborated by the "Proprietors's Records" of Cambridge, Mass., which prove a farmer and tanner, Jonathan Hastings, to have been quite prominent in the affairs of the town about this time. Page's History of Cambridge, 1877, further proves that Jonathan was born July 15, 1672, and died August 20, 1742. These facts do not yet establish a connection between Jonathan Hastings and the use of the term "Yankee" as maintained by Gordon, but the editor of the Massachusetts Magazine, 1795 (p. 301), while tracing the author of "Father Abdy's will," incidentally comes to our rescue. He writes that Rev. John Seccombe, the reputed author of "Father Abdy's will," in a letter (which the editor had before him) dated "Cambridge, Sept. 27, 1728," to his friend Thaddeus Mason, both Harvard men, gives a "most humorous narrative of the fate of a goose roasted at 'Yankey Hastings's,' " and it concludes with a poem on the occasion in the mock heroic.

Accordingly, Jonathan Hastings, of Cambridge, bore the nickname of "Yankey" in 1728 at Harvard. This may be considered an established fact, and though it does not necessarily follow that Gordon's account is based on equal facts, we may accept the reminiscences of the two aged ministers as substantially correct, however embellished in course of time. The objectionable feature of this account is that Hastings is called the inventor of the term. It is all the more objectionable in view of the following communication of J. T. F. to Notes and Queries, 1878 (5th ser., vol. 10, p. 467):

> The inventory of the effects of William Marr, formerly of Morpeth, and afterwards "of Carolina, in parts beyond the seas, but in the parish of St. Dunstan, Stepney" (*1725*), ends with, "Item one negro man named Yankee to be sold." Mr. W. Woodman, of Morpeth, has the document.

The natural inference from this is that Hastings did not invent the term. He bore it as a nickname about 1728, and probably came to it in the manner described by the tradition. Where he and from whom he borrowed it remains to be ascertained, and also whether he used the word in its original meaning or simply (though it may have had a totally different meaning originally) because he liked the sound of it. At any rate, the Jonathan Hastings theory leads merely to an early use of the word, but not to its origin. Nor is the process plausible that the term should have become so popular through the exertions of Jonathan Hastings and his Harvard friends that it spread from Cambridge, Mass., through the vast but thinly populated colonies and became, within fifty years, the reproachful nickname of the New Englanders in general, among whom the term "Yankee" does not appear to have been current.

A third derivation of the term "Yankee" is given by Anburey, who in 1777 wrote in a letter from Cambridge (Travels through . . . America," 1789, vol. 2, p. 50):

> . . . it is derived from a Cherokee word, *eankke*, which signifies coward and slave. This epithet of yankee was bestowed upon the inhabitants of New England by the Virginians, for not assisting them in a war with the Cherokees, and they have always been held in derision by it. But the name has been more prevalent since the commencement of hostilities . . .

This statement would be acceptable if it could be corroborated. A letter of inquiry addressed to the Bureau of American Ethnology brought this reply (August 18, 1908) from Mr. James Mooney, the eminent authority on the Cherokee Indians:

> The Cherokee words for *coward* and for *slave* (worker, or live stock property) respectively, are *udaskasti* and *atsinatlûni*.
> The Cherokee name for the "Yankees," *Ani-Yûngi*, is simply their form for "Yankee," in the plural . . .

In private conversation Mr. Mooney further expressed his opinion that no word like *eankke*, of whatever meaning, exists in the Cherokee language.

A third Indian derivation was advanced in "Diedrich Knickerbocker's History of New York" (1809 (First ed.), vol. 1, p. 169), in the chapter on "The ingenious people of Connecticut and thereabouts." Diedrich waxes eloquent over "that grand palladium of our country, the *liberty of speech*, or as it has been more vulgarly denominated the *gift of the gab*," and then proceeds:

> The simple aborigines of the land for a while contemplated these strange folk in utter astonishment, but discovering that they wielded harmless though noisy weapons, and were a lively, ingenious, good-humoured race of men, they became very friendly and sociable, and gave them the name of *Yanokies*, which in the Mais-Tschusaeg (or Massachusett) language signifies silent men—a waggish appellation, since shortened into the familiar epithet of *Yankees*, which they retain unto the present day.

This is in Washington Irving's best satirical vein. He makes his Diedrich Knickerbocker kill two birds with one stone, satirizing the New Englanders and at the same time those freak etymologies of the term "Yankee" that were just then beginning to attract public attention. Diedrich Knickerbocker's delightful narrative is full of such etymological pranks. Yet some people did not appreciate the joke nor see the point, but adduced in all seriousness Washington Irving's authority when further experimenting with the puzzling term.

The derivation of "Yankee" from the Indian language, which has attracted more attention than any other and is now current in the principal dictionaries, is presumably due to Heckewelder's "History, Manners, and Customs of the Indian Nations," Philadelphia, 1819. In the third chapter he writes of the "Indian relations and the conduct of the Europeans towards them," and while dealing with the Lenape, Mohicans, and kindred tribes, speaks of the Indian tradition surrounding the arrival first of the "Dutchemaan" at " *Manahachtanienk*" (Manhattan) and subsequently of the "*Yengeese.*" In a footnote he explains the latter term as being "an Indian corruption of the word English, whence probably the nickname *Yankees.*" This passing hint is elaborated by Heckewelder in the thirteenth chapter of his book (p. 130) as follows:

> The first name given by the Indians to the Europeans who landed in Virginia was *Wapsid Lenape* (white people), when, however, afterwards they began to commit murder on the red men, whom they pierced with swords, they gave to the Virginians the name *Mechanschican* (long knives) to distinguish them from others of the same colour.
>
> In New England, they at first endeavoured to imitate the sound of the national name of the *English*, which they pronounced *Yengees*. They also called them *Chauquaquock*, (men of knives) for having imported these instruments into the country, which they gave as presents to the natives.[a] The Mohicans of that country called them *Tschachgoos;* [later] they dropped that name, and called the whites by way of derision, *Schwannack*, which signifies *salt beings*, or *bitter things*.
>
> . . . They never apply it to the *Quakers*, whom they greatly love . . . they call them *Quaekels*, not having in their language the sound expressed by our letter R . . .
>
> These were the names which the Indians gave to the whites until the middle of the Revolutionary War, when they were reduced to the following three:
>
> 1. *Mechanschican* or *Chanschican* (long knives) [Virginians and Middle colonies].
>
> 2. *Yengees*. This name they now exclusively applied to the people of New England, who, indeed, appeared to have adopted it, and were, as they still are, generally through the country called *Yankees*, which is evidently the same name with a trifling alteration . . . The proper English they called *Saggenash*.
>
> 3. Quaeckels . . . Not only the Delawares, but all the nations round them make use of these names and with the same relative application.

---

a Rogers's Key into the language of the Indians of New England, ch. VI.

Before analyzing this theory of Rev. John Heckewelder, which has been adopted with more or less bold variations, one contemporaneous etymological attempt which runs in a similar vein may be mentioned. It appeared as a note to the appendix of John Trumbull's "Poetical works," Hartford, 1820:

> *Yankies.* The first settlers of New England were mostly emigrants from London and its vicinity, and exclusively styled themselves the English. The Indians, in attempting to utter the word *English*, with their broad guttural accent, gave it a sound which would be nearly represented in this way, *Yaunghees*, the letter *g* being pronounced hard, and approaching to the sound of *k* joined with a strong aspirate, like the Hebrew *chetz*, or the Greek *chi*, and the *l* suppressed, as almost impossible to be distinctly heard in that combination. The Dutch settlers on the river Hudson and the adjacent country, during their long contest concerning the right of territory, adopted the name, and applied it in contempt to the inhabitants of New England . . . This seems the most probable origin of the term. The pretended Indian tribe of Yankoos does not appear to have ever had an existence . . .

The sum and substance of these derivations is the supposed difficulty of the Indians in pronouncing the word "English" without corrupting it. The explanation seemed plausible, and it was adopted, mentioning Heckewelder as authority, by Webster in the first edition (1828) of his dictionary. By 1841 had been added "or more probably of the French word *Anglois*," but in 1848 the editor, not seeing the fine point of defense, changed *Anglois* into *Anglais*. In support of this corruption theory a passage in Hutchinson's "History of the Colony of Massachusetts-Bay," (1764, vol. 1, p. 479), was remembered:

> It was observed that without the greatest difficulty, they [the Indians] could not be brought to pronounce the letter *L* or *R*. For Lobster, they said Nobstan.

Having remembered this, one M. N. G., in Notes and Queries, 1877 (5th ser., vol. 7, p. 338), summed the whole theory up with all its virtues and defects in these words:

> They [the Indians] lengthened and softened the vowels; thus even a clever Indian could not pronounce *English* better than Eengeesh. Most Indians would be still wider off the mark and the common pronunciation was probably *Angees* (the *g* hard), or *Ankees.*

The trouble with this entire theory is that Rev. John Heckewelder (born 1743 at Bedford, England) did not begin his labors among the Indians until 1762. He abandoned the task before the expiration of the year. Between 1765 and 1771 he went on short missionary expeditions. His actual career as an important evangelist among the Indians began in 1771, his real services to Indian archeology, however, not until 1810, and his book on the Indians was not published until 1819. Sixty years are ample to form mental associations of disconnected data to amalgamate heterogeneous historical matter and traditions. Important as Heckewelder's "History" is, it is now reputed to suffer from too credulous an assimilation of fact and fancy, and while much of the book reads as if he had gathered the information at first hand, it may easily be proved that it frequently was of second hand and that previous books on the subject had been freely used. For instance, he says that the Englishmen were called "Chauquaquock (men of knives)" and he refers in a footnote to "Rogers's Key . . ." Such a book does not exist, but Heckewelder did mean and use Roger Williams's "Key into the language of America," London, 1643, and there may be found (see Reprint by the Rhode Island Hist. Soc., 1827, p. 51):

> Chauqock. A knife.
> Obs.: Whence they call *Englishmen* Chauquaquock, that is knivemen. . . .

To this he adds, on page 65:

> Waútacone-nûaog—Englishmen, men, that is, coat-men, or clothed.

and on page 116:

> Englishmánnuck—Englishmen.
> Dutchmnánuck—Dutchmen.

Though the absence of *R* and *L* in the Indian names of the Key is remarkable, not a word is said about the difficulty of pronouncing the word *English*, and not a single word even faintly resembling *Yankee* is mentioned in the whole Key. On the other hand, Roger Williams does say, when treating of the variety of aboriginal dialects, page 96:

> So that although some pronounce not *L* nor *R*, yet it is the most proper dialect of other places, contrary to many reports.

In the light of Roger Williams's Key, *1643*, Heckewelder's statement, *1819*, unsupported by contemporary evidence, that the "Indians at first endeavoured to imitate the sound of the national name of the *English*, which they pronounced *Yengees*," loses its authority. Secondly, the critical historical method would now demand that the tribes with or without the *L* and *R* be nicely separated, and that it be traced, how either fared with their supposed futile attempt to pronounce the word "English." Only by this process of investigation would we come nearer the Indian origin of the word "Yankee," if it really has an Indian origin. The manner in which this origin is developed backward does not appear to strengthen the theory. For instance, let it be supposed the word "Yankee" originated with the tribes who experienced no difficulty in pronouncing the letter *L*. Is it reasonable that then the word "English" could have become "Yankee," by changing the sound *e* into *a*, adding *y*, hardening *g*, dropping *i* and *sh?* If the word originated with tribes who did not enjoy the letters *l* and *r*, the objections become still more numer-

ous. We know from Hutchinson that such Indians liked to substitute *n* for *l* and *r* ("lobster" becoming "nobstan"), and we know
from Governor Edward Winslow's "Good news from England, Lond.
1624," that the Indians insisted on calling him Winsnow.   It follows
that the word "English," even if pronounced with a broad *E*, either
becomes "Engish" or "Engnish."   But the goal is "Yankee" and
can be reached only by subtle softenings, broadenings, clippings,
transformations, and additions of sound. The weakness of this
derivation could not escape the attention of the few, who are by
nature at all fitted to reason not only logically but methodically, and
efforts were made to substitute the word *Anglais* for *English*, thus
selecting the Indians of French Canada as possible godfathers of the
New England Yankees.   Brushing aside the Indians' preference for
substituting an *n* instead of dropping an *l* altogether, one could with
less difficulty arrive from *Anglais* at Yankee. Unfortunately for
this shift of responsibility from our to the Canadian Indians, the old
French word for Englishmen is *Anglois*, and therewith, of course,
the theory again drifts away from the word "Yankee."

It is, in view of these observations, not at all unlikely that Heckewelder's theory is one *a posteriori*, an afterthought, knowing, as he
plainly did, that the nickname of "Yankee" was confined in his
younger days more or less to the New Englanders, and having possibly heard it suspected that the word was of Indian provenience, he
combined fact and hypothesis without further analysis. He took
for granted what was merely a historical rumor, developed his story
from this artificial premise, and made the facts subservient to his
afterthought.

To-day our ethnologists, among them Mr. James Mooney, point to
other and even more grotesque corruptions of English words by the
Indians, and by subtle phililogical analysis they arrive at the conclusion that it was not impossible for the word English (with the
broad *E*) to have become Yankee in the mouths of the southern New
England Indians. However, they merely concede the *possibility*
from the standpoint of philology and do not positively commit themselves to Heckewelder's derivation. Nor would this be scientific,
since we have no evidence that the Indians actually used the word
"Yankee."

Simultaneously with the theory of Indian origin sprang up one
which carries us to the Orient, to Persia.   One B. H. H. in the Historical Magazine (1857, vol. 1, pp. 156–157), drew attention to an
article in the eighth volume of the Monthly Anthology, Boston,
1803–1811. This article, dated "New Haven, March 2, 1810," and
signed W, purports to have been copied from the Connecticut Herald,
New Haven, and the editor suspected N . . . W . . . jun., esq.,
to have been the author. This can but mean Noah Webster, and it

is significant in this connection that the Monthly Anthology was in the habit of attacking Webster's ponderous methods. The article is much too long for full quotation. It begins with the statement that—

> *Yankee* appears to have been used formerly by some of our common farmers in its genuine sense. It was an epithet descriptive of excellent qualities—as a *Yankee horse*, that is, a horse of *high spirit* and other good properties . . .

After this unmistakable allusion to farmer *Yankey Hastings* and some extraordinary feats of etymology of the type of Cicero's lucus a non lucendo, the author steers with full sails into a Persian origin of the word, as follows:

> Now in the Persian language, *Janghe* or *Jenghe* [that is Yankee] signifies a war-like man, a swift horse; also one who is prompt and ready in action, one who is magnanimous . . . The word Yankee claims a very honourable parentage, for it is the precise title assumed by the celebrated Mongolian Khan, Jenghis; and in our dialect, his titles literally translated would be *Yankee King*, that is, *War-like Chief*. . . .

The editor of the Monthly Anthology added that this article reads as if "intended for a buslesque upon those etymologists who are always forcing derivations beyond all bounds of probability." Notwithstanding these hints, this etymological hoax directed against Noah Webster, whose dictionary does not contain any such Persian definition, has been treated seriously. Its champions pointed to the supposed fact that Morier in his "Journey through Persia" said that the Persians of that day spoke of America as *Jenghee Duniah*, and a certain W. S. A., under the title of "Possible Eastern Origin of *Yankee Doodle*, had this to say in the New England Historical and Genealogical Register, volume 20, July, 1866:

> *A Possible Eastern Origin of Yankee Doodle.* I made the following extract from a volume printed in London about twenty-five years ago. It is the "Journal of Residence in England . . . originally written in Persian by H. R. H., Najaf Koolee Merza . . . London," without date. Vol. II, p. 146:
>
> "As to America, which is known in the Turkish language by the name of Yankee Dooniah, or the New World." On asking I found that this is generally correct, but the literal translation of the words is "End of the World."

More fantastic things have happened than the importation of an oriental word "Yanghee" to America. Simply because such a derivation appears to be fantastic, it must not be brushed aside without an effort to disprove it, for, after all, the derivations thus far criticised are not very much less fantastic. However, the oriental theory can be proved to be not only fantastic and extremely impossible, but incorrect.

In the first place, this gentleman surreptitiously, because he wanted to prove something, exchanged *Yengee* or *Yenghee* and *Yankee*, not aware of the fact that the discovery of a word in the language of some country other than the one where it is known to have been used for a century, proves nothing except its use. In the second place, Dooniah and Doodle are not even phonetically related. Thirdly, the words do not apply to North America, but to South America. Says James Morier in his "Second Journey through Persia between the years 1810 and 1816," London, 1818, when describing the return trip of the Persian ambassador from England to Asia by way of Cape Horn:

> On the 11th of September [1810] we made Cape Frio; and as we approached the shore we called the Persians to look at the *Yengee Duniah*, or the new world, of which in their country they had heard such wonders . . .

How far this is from "Yankee Doodle" is further illustrated by the attempt at a correct pronunciation in the German translation of Morier's book (1820): "*Jendschi Dunniah.*"

Different again is the derivation as suggested by *Salf* in Notes and Queries, 1879 (5th ser., vol. 11, p. 38):

> The word "Yanks" is always used in the east of Lincolnshire to describe the coarse, untanned leather gaiters worn by the country folk. There was a large exodus from this part of the country to America. Might not, therefore, the word "Yankee" have been used to distinguish those who wore these gaiters or "yanks", the incoming strangers, from the original inhabitants, who wore moccasins?

This is delightfully naïve. One naturally asks: Were these "yanks" used and known as such as far back as 1725? Were they worn in America, if at all, by New Englanders only? Were these gaiters known here as "yanks?" Who was it that thus distinguished between the immigrants from eastern Lincolnshire and the Indians?

With such fantastic and naïve methods the term *Yankee* may be traced to any desired language with more or less plausibility. For instance, Mr. Louis C. Elson hints at having read of a Norwegian derivation, and Mr. Nason, in a footnote to his "Monogram" (p. 21), says that some "deduce it from the old Scotch word *Yankie*, a sharp, clever woman."

It would be extraordinary if the fact that "Yankee Doodle" was applied to their New England neighbors, preferably by the people of New York, whose population in those days was largely of Dutch origin, had not invited the attempts to derive the term from the Dutch. Curiously enough, these attempts, though they all have the same object in view, weaken the Dutch theory somewhat by their contradictions.

One of the first, if not the first, attempt to derive the term from the Dutch was noted by George Ticknor. There is to be found in his "Life, Letters, and Journals" (vol. 2, p. 124), the following entry:

> *January 2, 1838.* I passed the evening with Thierry. . . . He is much skilled in etymology, and thinks our etymologies of the word *Yankee* are all wrong, and that, having arisen from the collision and jeerings of the Dutch and English in

New York and New England, it is from the Dutch *Jan*—pronounced *Yan*—John, with the very common diminutive *kee*, and *doodlen*, to quaver; which would make the whole "*quavering* or *psalm-singing Jacky* or *Johnny*." Doodle-sack means a bagpipe.

Johnny would refer to John Bull; and if, *doodlen* be made in the present tense, *Yankee-doodle* would be *Johnny that sings psalms*. *Hart-kee*—my little dear heart, and hundreds of other diminutives, both in endearment and in ridicule, are illustrations of the formation of the word. It amused me not a little, and seems probable enough as an etymology, better certainly than to bring it with Noah Webster from the Persian.

Somewhat similar is the derivation advanced by William Bell, in Notes and Queries, 1853 (vol. 7, p. 103), under the heading "Yankee, its origin and meaning:''

. . . the term is of Anglo-Saxon origin and of home-growth. . . . We may, of course, suppose that in the multitude of these Dutch settlers [of New Amsterdam, etc.] the names they carried over would be pretty nearly in the same proportion as at home. Both then and now the Dutch *Jan* (the *a* sounded very broad and long) . . . was the prevailing abbreviation appellative; and it even furnished, in *Jansen*, etc. (like our *Johnson*) frequent patronymics, particularly with the favour-ite diminutive *cke, Jancke;* and so common does it still remain as such, that it would be difficult to open the Directory of any decent sized Dutch or Northern German town without finding numerous instances, as *Jancke, Jaancke, Jahncke*, etc., according as custom has settled the orthography in each family. It is scarcely necessary to say that the soft *J* is frequently rendered by *Y* in our English reading and speaking foreign words . . . to show how easily and naturally the above names were transformed into *Yahnkee*. So far the name as an appellative; now for its appropriation as a generic. The prominent names of individuals are frequently seized upon by the vulgar as a designation of the people or party in which it most prevails . . . therefore, when English interests gained the upper hand, and the name of *New Amsterdam* succumbed to that of *New York*, the fresh comers, the English settlers, seized upon the most prominent name by which to designate its former masters, which extended to the whole of North America, as far as Canada: and the addition of *doodle*, twin brother to *noodle*, was intended to mark more strongly the contempt and mockery by the dominant party. . . . It is, however, to the credit of our transatlantic brethren and the best sign of their practical good sense, that they have turned the tables on the innuendo and by adopting, carried the term into repute by sheer resolution and determinate perseverance. . . .

There the matter rested for a while, except as it was made use of for secondhand articles, etc. Then the Notes and Queries, 1877 (5th ser., vol. 7, p. 338), printed a curiously illogical communication in which these words occur:

Doodle is surely only an imitation of the crowing of a cock—the meaning, if any, of *Yankee Doodle* is New Englanders, be on the alert; or, "show your spirit."

The absurdity of this apostrophe in the mouth of Dutchmen the correspondent does not see, and we may pass on to the reference in Notes and Queries, 1879 (p. 18), in which a reader of Smollett's novel "Sir Lancelot Greaves" (1760) called attention to Captain Crowe's words in third chapter:

> Proceed with the story in a direct course, without yawing like a Dutch *yanky*.

Here we evidently have a Dutch word which is almost identical with "yankee," but what sense can there possibly be in the combination of a Dutch ship with the word *doodle,* which either means fool or to bagpipe music?

Different again was Dr. George H. Moore's derivation, who read an (unfortunately unpublished) paper on the "Origin and history of Yankee Doodle" before the New York Historical Society, December, 1885. In the meager report of this paper in the Magazine of American History (1886, vol. 15, p. 99), we read:

> His theory of its derivation assigns the origin of the word to the Low-Dutch word janker, which signifies "a howling cur, a yelper, a growler, a grumbling person," and he formed in the history of relations existing between the English and Dutch sufficient reason for calling the English *dogs.*

This is driving the point home with a vengeance, and therein lies the weakness of the derivation. Different again, and assuming, as one naturally would, that "Yankee" has an ironical, sarcastic, but not brutally insulting flavor, is the derivation as given by G. W. V. S. in the Magazine of American History (1891, vol. 26, p. 236):

> When the Holland Society made its famous pilgrimage to Holland in 1888 . . . the Hon. H. D. Levyssohn-Norman . . . in the course of a very interesting speech, said: ": Yankee" is an alteration of the Dutch word Jantje (pronounced Yantyea), equivalent to Johnnie, a nickname of the Dutch people. In the days of the revolution of 1830, the Belgian insurgents gave often to a Dutchman the nickname of "Jantje Kaas (Johnnie Cheese)." So that Yankee is derived from Jan (John), Jantje being its diminutive.

But Jantje (Yantyea) and Yankee are not the same in sound, and if this be the correct derivation, it is difficult to see why Yankee should have been preferred to the equally easy Yantyea. If the Dutch, on the other hand, actually do use Jancke (pronounced Yankee) in the sense of little John or Johnnie, then this would be the most plausible derivation, and "Yankee Doodle" would be "Johnny Doodle."

To make sure of this point, a letter of inquiry was sent to the eminent Dutch musical scholar, D. F. Scheurleer, at The Hague, and he answered under date of October 7, 1908, as follows:

> . . . Merkwürdig genug hat man sich hier mit der Erörterung der Bedeutung des Wortes Yankee sehr wenig befasst. Ausgeschlossen ist es nicht, dass ein holländisches Wort zu Grunde liegt. Der sehr allgemein verbreitete Taufname Jan (so allgemein, dass früher jeder Kellner mit Jan angerufen wurde) hat viele Diminutiv-Formen je nach dem Dialekt. Jantje (spezial-Name für unsere Matrosen), Jannetje, Jannigie, Janke (nur an einzelnen Orten gebräuchlich). Ich weise darauf hin, ohne daraus eine Folgerung zu machen.

These, then, are some of the more or less ingenious attempts at the etymology of the word "Yankee," but not one of them exhibits as much learning as the eruditely witty mock derivation of "Porson Junior" from the Greek. This essay (in the Democratic Review, 1839, vol. 5, pp. 213–221) is by all odds one of the most brilliant contributions to the literature of parody.

Curiously enough the word "doodle" has almost escaped the onslaughts of etymologists, and yet this word and not "Yankee" may hold the key not only to the etymological problem but to that of the origin, or at least of the age of the tune "Yankee Doodle," as will be made clear later on.

One popular derivation of the word "doodle" is from the Scotch word *doudle*, used in the same sense as the German *dudeln*, the slang word for playing music. But the Oxford Dictionary does not trace *doudle* in print earlier than Sir Walter Scott, 1816. The Germans also use the word *Dudel-Sack* for bagpipe, and as the latter is also known in the English language as *doodle-sack*, it stands to reason that the Germans borrowed their Dudel-Sack and dudeln from the Scotch. Similarly the Dutch word *doedelzak* and similar words are not original with the Dutch, and as Weiland's Woordenboek, 1826, would allow us to infer, are of comparatively recent use with them. The Scotch derivation of the word "doodle" is at least plausible, whereas statements like this in Notes and Queries, 1877 (April 28), that "Doodle is surely only an imitation of a cock," may be relegated to the realm of etymological curiosities, inspired perhaps by the fact that in G. A. Stevens' Songs, 1772, and elsewhere, occurs the expression "cock a doodle do." However, still more acceptable than the Scotch, a derivation will appear to be which is based on the use of the word "Doodle" in English dramatic literature of the seventeenth and eighteenth centuries. It may be traced there with comparative ease as the following references, partly selected from Mr. Matthews' unpublished material, will prove:

> 1629. John Ford, "The Lover's Melancholy (act III, I): "Vanish, doodles, vanish."
>
> 1681. T. Otway's "The Soldier's Fortune" (act I, 2): *Sylvia* asks *Lady Dunce:* "Is your piece of mortality such a doting doodle"?"
>
> 1683. In Edward Ravenscroft's "London Cuckolds" "Doodle," and "Wiseacre" are the "Two aldermen of London."
>
> 1706. In E. Ward's "Humours of a Coffee House" (act II, 283) *Snarl* says: "Thou art the meerest *Tom Doodle* . . . sure *Nature* had too much work upon her hands when thou wer't making, and clos'd thy skull before she put the brains in."
>
> 1730. In H. Fielding's Tom Thumb "Noodle" and "Doodle" are "Courtiers in place, and consequently of that party that is uppermost!"
>
> 1731. Chetwood: "Generous Free Mason": or, the Constant lady with the humours of Squire Noodle, and his Man Doodle. A tragi-comi-farcical ballad opera . . . "

1731. In the cast of the Battle of the poets appear Noodle and Doodle as Judges of the Contention.
1733. In "Rome excis'd. A new tragi-comi ballad opera "Doodle" is "Brother to Cyrenaeus."

Whether or not Johnson in 1755 correctly saw in "doodle" a cant word possibly corrupted from *do little*, its meaning is clearly (see Oxford Dictionary) that of a "simpleton, noodle, silly, or foolish fellow," but generally of the rural type. If these derivations of "doodle" be adopted, all difficulties of explaining the meaning of "Yankee Doodle" vanish. Whatever the origin of "Yankee" might have been, after "Yankee" was preferably applied to the New Englanders, "Yankee Doodle" would simply mean a New England doodle, and it is not to be wondered at that the New Englanders did not take kindly to this nickname "Yankee," especially not if it meant "Johnny."

GENEALOGY OF THE THEORIES ON THE ORIGIN OF THE SONG "YANKEE DOODLE"

Though sometimes dragged into the discussion, the derivation of the word "Yankee" evidently furnishes no tangible clue to the origin of the *song* "Yankee Doodle." The etymological labyrinth merely leads to the probability that the words "Yankee Doodle" were not available for a song until after 1700. For the discovery of the origin of the melody, the first recorded use of the word "Yankee" is of absolutely no help, since melodies, from which certain words finally become inseparable, often precede these words by decades. The origin of the song must be traced in a totally different direction. As was the case with the derivation of the word "Yankee," numerous conflicting accounts of the origin of the song exist. Most of these, too, are merely inaccurate and uncritical reiterations, embellishments, combinations of previous theories. Only after the genealogy of these theories had been established, some main arteries became discernible in the confused mass of tradition. An attempt is here made to trace the original sources of the various theories, and as far as was possible, the original sources only, since all later reiterations, etc., contain nothing substantially new and merely cover the main paths with impenetrable underbrush and rubbish.

Possibly the earliest allusion to the origin of the song is contained in Gordon's "History of the Independence of the United States" (London, 1788, vol. 1, p. 481). This work is a collection of letters and the reference to "Yankee Doodle" is to be found in a letter dated "Roxbury, April 26, 1775:"

a song composed in derision of the New Englanders, scornfully called *Yankees*.

An entry to the same effect in James Thacher's "Military Journal, from 1775 to 1783," would appear to antedate Gordon, but the Journal was not published until 1823, and then with amendments and additions from other sources. Indeed, his references to "Yankee Doodle" are copied almost verbatim from Gordon. Much more substantial is the account given in Farmer & Moore's Collections, May, 1824 (p. 157–160), in an unsigned article on "Yankee Doodle:"

. . . The story runs that the song entitled *Yankee Doodle* was composed by a British officer of the Revolution with a view to ridicule the Americans, who by the English bloods of that time, by way of derision, were styled Yankees . . . it may possibly amuse some of your readers to see a copy of the song as it was printed thirty-five years since, and as it was troll'd in our Yankee circles of that day. What mutations it might have undergone previous to that time, or whether any additions or alterations have been made since, I know not; but I am, however, of the opinion, that it has had as many commentators and collators as the text of Shakespeare . . .

This anonymous article, together with the text of "Yankee Doodle," was printed in May. In July, 1824 (vol. 3, pp. 217–218), the editors published a totally different account of the "Origin of Yankee Doodle:"

In looking over an old file of the Albany Statesman, edited by N. H. Carter, Esq., we met with the following interesting note, respecting the origin of the tune Yankee Doodle—the words of which were published in the Collections for May:

"It is known as a matter of history, that in the early part of 1755, great exertions were made by the British ministry, at the head of which was the illustrious Earl of Chatham, for the reduction of the French power in the provinces of the Canadas. To carry the object into effect, General Amherst, referred to in the letters of Junius, was appointed to the command of the British army in North Western America; and the British colonies in America were called upon for assistance, who contributed with alacrity their several quotas of men, to effect the grand object of British enterprise. It is a fact still in the recollection of some of our oldest inhabitants, that the British army lay encamped, in the summer of 1755, on the eastern bank of the Hudson, a little south of the city of Albany, on the ground now belonging to John I. Van Rensselaer, Esq. To this day, vestiges of their encampment remain; and after a lapse of sixty years . . . the inquisitive traveller can observe the remains of the ashes . . . It was this army, that, under the command of Abercrombie, was foiled, with a severe loss, in the attack on Ticonderoga . . . In the early part of June, the eastern troops began to pour in, company after company, and such a motley assemblage of men never before thronged together on such an occasion, unless an example might be found in the ragged regiment of Sir John Falstaff, of right merry and facetious memory. It would, said my worthy ancestor, who relates to me the story, have relaxed the gravity of an anchorite, to have seen the descendants of the Puritans, marching through the streets of our ancient city, to take their station on the left of the British army—some with long coats, some with short coats, and others with no coats at all, in colours as varied as the rainbow, some with their hair cropped like the army of Cromwell, and others with wigs whose curls flowed with grace around their shoulders. Their march, their accoutrements, and the whole arrangement of the troops, furnished matter of amusement to the wits of the British army. The musick played the airs of two centuries ago, and the tout ensemble, upon the

whole, exhibited a sight to the wondering strangers that they had been unaccus-
tomed to in their own land. Among the club of wits that belonged to the British
army, there was a physician attached to the staff, by the name of Doctor Shackburg, who combined with the science of the surgeon, the skill and talents of a
musician. To please brother Jonathan, he composed a tune, and with much
gravity recommended it to the officers, as one of the most celebrated airs of martial
musick. The joke took to the no small amusement of the British corps. Brother
Jonathan exclaimed it was nation fine, and in a few days nothing was heard in the
provincial camp but the air of Yankee Doodle . . .''

This account was widely circulated, but soon other traditions and
theories began to demand recognition. One of the most perplexing
to all those who did not have access to its very scarce source appeared in an unsigned article on the "Origin of Yankee Doodle"
in the Musical Reporter (Boston, 1841, May, pp. 207–209):

It appears that, previous to the time of Charles I, an air somewhat similar to
the one in question, was common among the peasantry of England, of which
the following is a copy

This air during the time of Cromwell was set to various ditties in ridicule of
the Protector. One of these began with the words "The Roundheads and the
Cavaliers". Another set of words was called "Nankee Doodle", and has throughout a striking resemblance to some of the popular stanzas, which were common
in the American Colonies from the time of their origin to the Revolution, and in
some sections of the country, even to the present day. The song, "Lydia
Locket" or "Lucy Locket" has been sung to the same tune from time immemorial. This air seems to have been the foundation of Yankee Doodle.

The rest of the article is a more or less inaccurate repetition of
previous opinions.

This account was widely circulated, but apparently in the meantime other traditions had been clamoring for recognition. John W.
Watson, in his "Annals of Philadelphia," not in the first edition,
1830, but in the second, 1844 (vol. 2, pp. 333–335), hesitated not to
print this *bouquet* of historical gossip and blunder:

" *Yankee Doodle*". This tune so celebrated as a national air of the revolution,
has an origin almost unknown to the mass of the people in the present day. An
aged and respectable lady, born in New England, told me she remembered it
well, long before the revolution under an another name. It was then universally called "Lydia Fisher" and was a favourite New England jig. It was then

the practice with it, as with Yankee Doodle now, to sing it with various impromptu verses—such as

> Lydia Locket lost her pocket
> Lydia Fisher found it;
> Not a bit of money in it,
> Only binding round it.

The British, preceding the war, when disposed to ridicule the simplicity of Yankee manners and hilarity, were accustomed to sing airs of songs set to words, invented for the passing occasion, having for their object to satirize and sneer at the New Englanders. This, as I believe, they called Yankee Doodle, by way of reproach, and as a slur upon their favourite "Lydia Fisher".

. . . Judge Martin, in his History of North Carolina, has lately given another reason for the origin of "Yankee Doodle", saying, it was first formed at Albany, in 1755, by a British officer, then there, indulging his pleasantry on the homely array of the motley Americans, assembling to join the expedition of General Johnson and Governor Shirley. To ascertain the truth in the premises, both his and my accounts were published in the gazettes, to elicit, if possible, further information, and the additional facts ascertained, seem to corroborate the foregoing idea. The tune and quaint words, says a writer in the Columbian Gazette, at Washington, were known as early as the time of Cromwell, and were applied to him then, in a song called "Nankee Doodle", as ascertained from the collection he had seen of a gentleman at Cheltenham in England, called "Musical Antiquities of England", to wit:

> Nankee Doodle came to town
> Upon a little pony,
> With a feather in his hat,
> Upon a macaroni, &c.

The term feather, &c., alluded to Cromwell's going into Oxford on a small horse, with his single plume fastened in a sort of knot called a "macaroni". The idea that such an early origin may have existed seems strengthened by the fact communicated by an aged gentleman of Massachusetts, who well remembered that, about the time the strife was engendering at Boston, they sometimes conveyed muskets to the country concealed in their loads of manure, &c. Then came abroad verses, as if set forth from their military masters, saying:

> Yankee Doodle came to town
> For to buy a firelock:
> We will tar and feather him,
> And so we will John Hancock.

The similarity of the first lines of the above two examples, and the term "feather," in the third line, seem to mark, in the latter, some knowledge of the former precedent. As, however, other writers have confirmed their early knowledge of "Lydia Locket," such as

> Lucy Locket lost her pocket,
> In a rainy shower, &c.

we seem led to the choice of reconciling them severally with each other. We conclude therefore, that the cavaliers, when they originally composed "Nankee Doodle," may have set it to the jig tune of "Lydia Fisher," to make it the more offensive to the Puritans. Supposing it, therefore, remembered in succeeding times as a good hit on them, it was a matter of easy revival in New England, by royalists, against the people there, proverbially called by themselves, "Oliver Cromwell's children," in allusion both to their austere religion, and their free notions of government. In this view, it was even possible for the British officer at Albany, in 1755, as a man skilled in music, to have before heard of the old "Nankee Doodle," and to have renewed it on that occasion.

This was substantially the same story as the one which Watson wrote to the Massachusetts Historical Society, February 13, 1832, as Mr. Matthews discovered, but this letter was not published in their proceedings until 1861 (vol. 5, pp. 209–212), and therefore can not have had much influence before 1861.

Soon other compilers followed in Watson's footsteps, chief of whom the voluminous but unscrupulously inaccurate B. F. Lossing. In the first edition, 1851–52 (vol. 1, p. 81) of his "Pictorial Fieldbook of the Revolution" he claims that Thatcher [!] on page 19 of his Military Journal wrote:

> A song, called Yankee Doodle, was written by a British sergeant at Boston, in 1775, to ridicule the people there, when the American army, under Washington, was encamped at Cambridge and Roxburg.

It is characteristic of Lossing's methods that Thacher (comp., p. 95 of this report) never wrote these words, but that Lossing doctored the quotation to suit himself. It is equally characteristic of him that in the edition of 1859–60 the supposed quotation from Thacher is not canceled, though Lossing in the supplement of the second volume (p. 683) gives a totally different version. The latter is merely a confused conglomeration of previous accounts. About this time the columns of Notes and Queries were opened to a flood of communications on the subject of *Yankee* and *Yankee Doodle*. One of the longest was that by T. Westcott, dated Philadelphia, June 5, 1852, and printed 1852 in volume 6, page 57. It is merely an echo of previous accounts, principally of Watson, out of whose words he construes the claim that—

> The tune was known in New England before the Revolution as *Lydia Fisher's Jig*.

Mr. Westcott, however, took occasion to add this important observation:

> There is no song. The tune in the United States is a march; there are no words to it of a national character. The only words ever affixed to the air in this country is the following doggerel quatrain:

> > Yankee Doodle came to town
> > Upon a little pony,
> > He stuck a feather in his hat
> > And called it macaroni.

Duyckinck's Cyclopædia of American Literature, 1855, volume 1, page 463, helped to complicate matters still further. There we read:

> The tune was not original with Shackburg, as it has been traced back to the time of Charles I., in England. In the reign of his son we find it an accompaniment to a little song on a famous lady of easy virtue of that date, which has been perpetuated as a nursery rhyme—

> > Lucy Locket lost her pocket,
> > Kitty Fisher found it,
> > Nothing in it, nothing in it,
> > But the binding round it.

> A little later we have the first appearance of that redoubtable personage, Yankee Doodle. He seems even at that early stage of his career to have shown his characteristic trait of making the most of himself—

> > Yankee Doodle came to town,
> > Upon a Kentish pony;
> > He stuck a feather in his hat,
> > And called him Macaroni.

> It is not impossible, however, that Yankee Doodle may be from Holland. A song in use among the laborers, who in the time of harvest migrate from Germany to the Low Countries, where they receive for their work as much buttermilk as they can drink and a tenth of the grain secured by their exertions, has this burden—

> > Yanker didel, doodel down
> > Didel, dudel lanter,
> > Yanke viver, voover vown,
> > Botermilk and Tanther.

> That is, buttermilk and a tenth. This song our informant has heard repeated by a native of that country, who had often listened to it at harvest time in his youth.
> The precise date when

> > Father and I went down to camp—

> can not, we fear, be fixed with accuracy. But as the tune was sung at Bunker Hill, may be assumed to have been in 1775.
> Our copy of the words is from a broadside in a collection of "Songs, Ballads, etc., purchased from a ballad printer and seller in Boston in 1813" made by Isaiah Thomas. The variations and additional stanzas in the notes are from a version given in Farmer & Moore, III, 157.

A positive statement by F. B. N. S. appeared in the Historical Magazine (1857, vol. I, p. 92):

> The verses commencing 'Father and I went down to camp' were written by a gentleman of Connecticut, a short time after Gen. Washington's last visit to New England; as will be shown in a book of songs and ballads, soon to be issued in New York.

I have not been able to trace the proprietor of these initials nor the book he refers to in Roorbach's "Bibliotheca Americana," or in the catalogue of the famous Harris collection of American poetry.

A curious contribution to the "Yankee Doodle" literature found its place in the Historical Magazine, 1858 (vol. 2, pp. 214–215). One T. H. W. there reprinted an article clipped from the Press, Philadelphia, September, 1857. This, in turn, had been sent the Press by one Herman Leigh as the copy of the following letter, dated "London, July 21, 1854, 29 St. Mark's Crescent, Regent's Park:"

With respect to the air of Yankee Doodle, the earliest copy which Dr. Rimbault has found is in "Walsh's collection of Dances for the year 1750" where it is printed in 6/8 time, and called "Fisher's Jig." This is very interesting, because for more than half a century the air in question has been sung in our nurseries to the verse:

> Lucy Locket lost her pocket,
> Kitty Fisher found it,
> Not a bit of money in it,
> Only binding round it.

According to a set of old engravings of London characters (probably by Holler) published in the reign of Charles II, Kitty Fisher figures as a courtesan of that period. This seems to send the time back a long way.

It has been said that the air of Yankee Doodle dates still further back, and that the verse

> Yankee Doodle came to town,
> Upon a little pony;
> He stuck a feather on his hat,
> And called it macaroni.

relates (with the alteration of Nankee for Yankee) to Cromwell. The lines are said to allude to his going to Oxford with a single plume fastened in a knot, called a macaroni. But this is all conjecture; all we know for certain is, that the air in question was known in England the first half of the last century as "Kitty Fisher's Jig." Dr. Rimbault has all the popular music of England from the earliest time, but finds no trace of the air of Yankee Doodle (in print) before the year 1750.

This letter, which in the main merely reiterates a time-worn account, traces for the first time the earliest appearance of the tune "Yankee Doodle" in print. This reference has become one of the stumbling blocks in the controversy, and not in a manner as to bestow credit on the methods of the famous Doctor Rimbault. But who wrote the letter and sent it to the Historical Magazine? Doctor Rimbault is spoken of in the third person. This might lead to the impression that the letter merely gives to a third party the essence of a conversation between the writer and Doctor Rimbault. If this were the case, then Doctor Rimbault could not be held responsible for all the mischief done by the letter. I fear that nothing can exonerate him, since the responsibility rests with Doctor Rimbault and no one else. Says he in a contribution to the Historical Magazine, 1861, page 123: "When sending my communication to the H. M. in July, 1858 (vol. 2, p. 214)." This transaction throws a peculiar light on the methods of Dr. Edward F. Rimbault.

To the American, English, and Dutch the Historical Magazine now added a Biscay and Hungarian origin of the tune, 1858, volume 3, page 280:

The following letter, says the *National Intelligencer*, has been received by a gentleman of this city from our accomplished secretary of legation at Madrid:

MADRID, *June 3, 1858.*

MY DEAR SIR:

The tune Yankee Doodle, from the first of my showing it here, has been acknowledged by persons acquainted with music to bear a strong resemblance to the popular airs of Biscay; and yesterday a professor from the north recognized it as being much like the ancient sword dance played on solemn occasions by the people of San Sebastian. He says the tune varies in those provinces, and proposes in a couple of months to give me the changes as they are to be found in their different towns, that the matter may be judged of and fairly understood. Our national air certainly has its origin in the music of the free Pyrenees; the first strains are identically those of the heroic *Danza Esparta*, as it was played to me, of brave old Biscay.

Very truly yours,   BUCKINGHAM SMITH.

On the same page the Historical Magazine helped to circulate this story:

> Kossuth, says the Boston Post, informed us that the Hungarians with him in this country first heard Yankee Doodle on the Mississippi River, when they immediately recognized it as one of the old national airs of their native land— one played in the dances of that country—and they began immediately to caper and dance as they used to in Hungary.

Again it was the Historical Magazine, which in 1859 (vol. 3, pp. 22–23) printed an article signed J. C. with the editorial remark that it had been "Published in the Baltimore Clipper in 1841 by a person who well understood the subject:"

> In Burgh's Anecdotes of Music, vol. III, p. 405 [1814] after speaking of Dr. Arne and John Frederick Lampe, the author proceeds:
>
> Besides Lampe and Arne, there were at this time (1731) other candidates for musical fame of the same description. Among those were Dr. Christian Smith, who set two English operas for Lincoln's Inn Fields, *Teraminta* and *Ulysses*. . . .
>
> About the year 1797, after having become a tolerable proficient on the German flute, I took it into my head to learn the bassoon, and a book of instructions from the late Mr. Joseph Carr, who had then recently opened a music store in this city [Baltimore] being the first regular establishment of the kind in the country. In this book there was an *Air from Ulysses*, which was the identical air now called *Yankee Doodle*, with the exception of a few notes, which time and fancy may have added.

Benson J. Lossing again took part in the controversy in an article on "The Origin of Yankee Doodle" for the Poughkeepsie Eagle, which was reprinted in Littell's Living Age (1861, vol. 70, pp. 382–384). This article merely copies the accounts in "Notes and Queries," Duyckinck's Cyclopædia and other sources, without the slightest attempt at verification of the data except when he remarks of the "Botermilk and Tanther" refrain in Duyckinck:

> This account is apocryphal, to say the least, for the words in the above verses are neither German, Dutch, nor any other known language on the face of the earth.

To the theories of Yankee Doodle's origin thus far enumerated an anonymous writer in All the Year Round (1870, February, vol. 3, pp. 252–256), in an article "On a few old songs," added this:

> It seems on the authority of the late M. T. Moncrieff, the author of "Tom and Jerry" and countless other farces and plays, who made it his pleasure in the closing years of his life when afflicted with blindness, to investigate the history

and origin of old tunes, that the air was composed for the drum and fife about the middle of the eighteenth century by the Fife-Major of the Grenadier Guards. The air was not intended for a song, but for a march, and it was long after it had become familiar to the ears of the people in towns where British regiments were stationed, that words became associated with it.

Doctor Rimbault reappeared on the plan with an article on "American National Songs" in "Leisure Hour" (1876, vol. 25 pp. 90–92). This second account is not a repetition of what he had written in 1858. Indeed, without saying so, our author refutes most of his previous statements that had helped to make the origin of "Yankee Doodle" worse than a Chinese puzzle:

> There are no words to this tune in the United States of a national character; the tune is a march. The earliest words known there are this doggerel quatrain—
>
> > Yankee Doodle came to town
> > Upon a little pony,
> > He stuck a feather in his hat,
> > And called it Macaroni.

With the alteration of *N*ankee for *Y*ankee, a string of similar verses is said to exist, which were supposed to allude to the coming of Oliver Cromwell (on a small horse) into Oxford, with his single plume, which he wore fastened in a sort of knot, which the adherents of the royal party called "a macaroni" out of derision. We must own to an entire want of faith in this story. The probability is that the tune is not much older than the time of its introduction into America. We know that it was popular in England at that time, having been printed in one of Thomson's country dance books as "Kitty Fisher's Jig."

Kitty Fisher, as everybody knows, was a celebrated character in the middle of the last century. She was painted by Sir Joshua Reynolds more than once, and ultimately married Squire Norris of Bemmendon, in Kent. Lucy Lockit was also a well-known character in the gay world. She was not so fortunate as her friend in making a good marriage nor in having her face handed down to posterity by the Court painter.

The well-known rhymes to this tune, still sung by children—

> > Lucy Lockit lost her pocket
> > Kitty Fisher found it;
> > Not a bit of money in it,
> > Only binding round it.

have some covert allusion, understood at the time, but now forgotten.

We give a copy of Thomson's version of the tune, which is written in triple time. It was afterwards altered to common time, as now known:

KITTY FISHER'S JIG

Strange to say, this account appears to have escaped the atten-tion of Admiral George Henry Preble when he prepared the second edition (Boston, 1880) of his "History of the Flag of the United States." The admiral's article on "Yankee Doodle" (pp. 746–753, not in the first edition of 1872) does not pretend to be based on original research. It is merely a résumé of the various accounts thus far published. Yet it contains a few statements that call for consideration. He says:

> There is an earlier version of the words in England which I heard repeated by my father in my childhood days, which runs:
>
> > Nankee Doodle came to town
> > Upon a *Kentish* pony,
> > He stuck a feather in his hat,
> > And called him Macaroni.
>
> As I heard it repeated, the second line was, *Riding on a pony*, or, *Upon a little pony* . . .
> In the English opera written about the middle of the eighteenth century, by Dr. Arne, is the comic song of "Little Dickey," who resents the arrogance and attempted tyranny of some older boy. The last stanza runs thus:
>
> > Did little Dickey ever trick ye?
> > No, I'm always civil, etc.
>
> The air of the song is what we call "Yankee Doodle," but it is not so called in the opera. . . .
> Innumerable have been the verses that have been adapted to it [Yankee Doodle], but it is believed the following were those best known and oftenest repeated by our fathers during the war of 1776, and they are said to have been sung at the battle of Bunker's Hill in 1775. Words additional or similar were repeated to me by my father fifty years ago, as those familiar to him when a boy, during the revolutionary times. Perhaps their order of following is not correct.

Then follow 17 stanzas of "Yankee Doodle, or Father's return from Camp," in the main identical with the stanzas given in Farmer & Moore's Collections, but clearly accumulated from different versions.

The last few quotations illustrate that by 1880 the matter of "Yankee Doodle" had fallen entirely into the hands of compilers, whose sole object it seems to have been, and still seems to be, to accept more or less credulously the numerous conflicting statements and to weave them indiscriminately into a smooth, entertaining tissue of facts and fancy. The first to really analyze this ragout was Mr. William Barclay Squire, and he contributed to the first edition of Grove's Dictionary of Music (1879–1889) an article on "Yankee Doodle," which at that time was by far the best, and is still valu-able. Mr. Louis C. Elson, in his useful book on the "National Music of America," 1900, added in the main merely information received from Mr. Albert Matthews, of Boston. Nor does the amount of his original critical research rise above what may be expected from a book plainly designed and written in a style to satisfy the popular demand for more or less verified facts on our national songs. This applies even more strongly to Mr. Kobbé's chatty "Famous American Songs," 1906, who also caught a glimpse of Mr. Matthews's unpublished mine of data. From the same source come the following excerpts from Dr. George H. Moore's paper "Notes on the origin and history of Yankee Doodle," read before the New York Historical Society on December 1, 1885, and before the New England Historical and Genealogical Society on December 7, 1887. As was stated in the introduction to my report on "Yankee Doodle," Mr. Moore's paper was never printed, though it was mentioned in the Magazine of American History for January, 1886, in the Boston Post of December 8, 1887, and in the New England Historical and Genealogical Register for January, 1888. Mr. Albert Matthews, as he informed me under date of January 3, 1909, rediscovered the manuscript and copied long extracts. "Moore," says Mr. Matthews, "picked to pieces various theories about 'Yankee,' but accepted without criticism the Farmer & Moore version." Clearly Mr. Moore's unpublished paper can not have influenced subsequent writers very much, but it is essential that so much of it be printed here as was available through the courtesy of Mr. Albert Matthews:

Dr. Shuckburgh unquestionably played an important part in the proceedings which resulted in making Yankee Doodle a national tune. He took the initiative step. He married to verse, (not immortal, for not a line of it can be proved to exist to-day) but to a song sufficiently popular to be remembered for many years, the old fashioned jig which had charmed his childhood and lingered in his memory to become the (vehicle) inspiration of his comic muse in later years . . . Dr. Shuckburgh undoubtedly scored (achieved) a success in his Yankee Doodle Song, hitting off the men and events of the time, in a style which readily admitted additions and alterations to fit occasions. That song was a satire more or less clever of the New Englander and his ways—written originally from the point of view of an Englishman long domesticated in New York, and reflecting the prejudices of the British tory and the Albany Dutchman—the intellectual apparatus of that extraordinary mythical creature, the genuine Knickerbocker. What that first Yankee Doodle Song was is mainly left to conjecture . . . The only verses I have met with, which carry any appearance of having been a part of the original are the following:

> There is a man in our town,
>   I pity his condition,
> He sold his oxen and his sheep,
>   To buy him a commission—
>
> When his commission he had got,
>   He proved a nation coward
> He durst not go to Cape Breton
>   For fear he'd be devoured.

Another verse has less authority:

> Yankee Doodle came to town
>   Put on his strip'd trowse's
> And vow'd he could n't see the town (place)
>   There *was* so many houses.

So far the literature on the origin of "Yankee Doodle" moved in a few distinct channels, but in 1905 two theories were added that have very little in common with those previously advanced, combined, embellished. In the German magazine "Hessenland" (vol. 19, 1905, pp. 20–23), Mr. Johann Lewalter published an article under the title: "Der 'Yankee Doodle' ein Schwälmer Tanz?" In other words, the author endeavored to prove the probability of a Hessian origin, but his knowledge of the literature is very slight and he did not exercise discrimination in the use of his sources, so that most of his article is not worthy of consideration. As to his hypothetical question, it is sufficient to abstract from the article the following:

> In Langenscheidt's "Land und Leute in Amerika" it is said that probably the air of the folksong "Yankee Doodle" has its origin in a military march played by the Hessian soldiers in the War for Independence.
>
> The same origin is hinted at in the eighth volume (1880) of Spamer's "Illustriertes Konversationslexikon". Mr. Lewalter then calls attention to the fact that the principal recruiting station in 1776 was Ziegenhain in the Schwalm, the fertile province of Hesse, to the further fact that "Yankee Doodle" in form, musical spirit and rhythm bears a peculiar resemblance to the genuine dances and folksongs of the Schwalm region. Therefore, he concludes, it may be claimed that this song, played by the Hessian troops as a march, was imported by them to America in those days. Finally, the fact should be noted that during a country fair in the Schwalm in the fall of 1904 "Yankee Doodle" was played as a Schwalm dance, and men and women danced to it as they would to one of their own traditional airs without discovery of the substitution.

It will be seen later on how suddenly his Hessian theory collapses, if the historical test is applied. Much more complicated but much more fruitful in its application is a theory advanced by Mr. William H. Grattan Flood in the "Dolphin" (Philadelphia, 1905, vol. 8, pp. 187–193) under the title "The Irish origin of the tune of *Yankee Doodle.*" In this interesting article Mr. Grattan Flood, an enthusiastic student and champion of Irish music, first sets out to undermine principally the English origin. Then, in the footsteps of the eminent English folk-song collector, Mr. Frank Kidson, he refers to the "Earliest printed version" of "Yankee Doodle" in the first volume of James Aird's "Selection of Scotch, English, Irish, and Foreign Airs," printed at Glasgow in 1782. Without further preliminaries Mr. Grattan Flood then proceeds:

> The very structure of this tune is seen to be decidedly Irish and apart from any other argument intrinsic evidence should point to its Irish origin. . . . The above printed version by Aird in 1782, antedates the "Two to One" (1784) version by two years, and is much nearer the Irish original ['All the way to Galway'], with the strongly marked C natural (the so called "flat seventh") so characteristic of seventeenth century tunes in D major. However, the oldest form of the tune is also given here as it appears in a MS dated 1750, the authenticity of which is beyond question. The manuscript was written at different times between the years 1749 and 1750, and the owner's name is given, dated December 1, 1750.

By way of illustrating the changes which a tune undergoes in seventy or eighty years, I think it is well to give the version as noted by Dr. Petrie in 1840, but, as will be seen, the changes are unimportant.

Thus "Yankee Doodle" can rightfully be claimed as a product of Ireland. . . .

CRITICAL ANALYSIS OF THE THEORIES ON THE ORIGIN OF "YANKEE DOODLE"

The chronological enumeration of the theories on the origin of "Yankee Doodle" will have disclosed their genealogy and concatenation sufficiently to now warrant neglect of such dates, references, and inferences that are mere variations and aberrations from the original source. The examination of this amazing labyrinth of conjectures will be based entirely on such analytical data only as possess some real substance. The other data will be treated as not existing. Much of the analytical evidence has become quite familiar to historians, but much will have the flavor of novelty. However, no distinction will here be made between old and new data, except when necessary.

To sum up, since 1775, when the origin of "Yankee Doodle" began to arouse interest, it has been claimed that—

1. The song of "Yankee Doodle" was composed by a British officer of the Revolution.

2. The air had its origin in a military march "Schwälmer Tanz," introduced into this country by the Hessians during the war for Independence.

3. The first part of the tune is identical with the *Danza Esparta* and the tune had its origin in the Pyrenees.

4. The air is of Hungarian origin.

5. The tune was introduced by German harvest laborers into Holland.

6. The air was composed by the fife-major of the Grenadier Guards about 1750 as a march.

7a. The tune was founded on an English tune common among the peasantry of England previous to the time of Charles I.

7b. It was set during the time of Cromwell to various ditties in ridicule of the protector. One of these began with the words "The Roundheads and the Cavaliers;" another

> Nankee Doodle came to town
> Upon a Kentish pony [or Upon a little pony]
> He stuck a feather in his hat
> And called him Macaroni.

were known as early as Cromwell's time, and indeed applied to him.

8. In the reign of Charles II the tune was sung to the words, perpetuated as a nursery rhyme:

> Lucy Locket lost her pocket
> Kitty Fisher found it.
> Nothing in it, nothing in it
> But the binding round it.
> [or, Not a bit of money in it
> Only binding round it]

9. The air is the same as of the New England jig "Lydia Fisher," which was a favorite in New England long before the American Revolution.

10. The earliest printed version of the air "Yankee Doodle" appears in 6/8 time in "Walsh's collections of dances for the year 1750" under the title of "Fisher's Jig."

11. The air is identical with "Kitty Fisher's Jig" as printed in one of Thomson's country dance books in triple time.

12. "Yankee Doodle" is identical with an *"Air from Ulysses,"* opera by J. C. Smith.

13. The air "Did little Dickey ever trick ye" in an opera by Arne, composed about 1750, is the same as "Yankee Doodle."

14. Doctor Shackburg, wit and surgeon in the British army encamped in 1755 near Albany, composed a tune and recommended it to the provincial officers as one of the most celebrated airs of martial music and that this joke on the motley assemblage of provincials took immediately.

15. Doctor Shuckburgh wrote the Yankee Doodle verses to an old-fashioned jig.

16. The air is of Irish origin and is identical with "All the way to Galway."

These 16 theories have here been grouped not chronologically but amicably to a process of elimination. The majority of these theories, on close inspection, relate rather to the early use of than to the origin of the song. It will therefore facilitate the process of elimination if some consequential data on the use of the air in America until the time of our war for independence are here brought together.

In the New York Journal, October 13, 1768, we read in the "Journal of Transactions in Boston, Sept. 28, 1768:"

> *Sept. 29.* The Fleet was brought to Anchor near Castle William, that Evening there was throwing of Sky Rockets, and those passing in Boats observed great Rejoicings and that the Yankey Doodle Song was the Capital Piece in their Band of Music."

Writing of the events at Boston in 1769, the late Mr. Fiske in his work on the "American Revolution" (vol. 1, p. 65) says:

> On Sundays the soldiers would race horses on the Common, or play **Yankee Doodle** just outside the church-doors during the services.

Unfortunately Mr. Fiske did not refer to his authority for this almost incredible bit of information; nor did Mr. Elson, when he wrote in his book on our national music (p. 145):

> A little later [than 1769], when the camps were in the town of Boston, the British custom was to drum culprits out of camp to the tune of "Yankee Doodle," a decidedly jovial *Cantio in exitu.*

The next reference carries us to the commencement of hostilities. When the news of the affair at Lexington (Apr. 19, 1775) reached Lord Percy in Boston, says the Reverend Gordon in his History in a letter dated "Roxbury, April 26, 1775," he ordered out a reenforcement to support his troops.

> The brigade marched out playing, by way of contempt, *Yankee Doodle* . . .

James Thacher has almost literally the same in his Military Journal under date of April 21, 1775. A further contemporary reference is found in the "Travels (1st ed., vol. 2, p. 50) of Thomas Anburey, the British officer, who, under date of "Cambridge, in New England, Nov. 27, 1777," wrote as follows:

> . . . the name [of Yankee] has been more prevalent since the commencement of hostilities. The soldiers at Boston used it as a term of reproach, but after the affair at Bunker's Hill, the Americans gloried in it. *Yankee Doodle* is now their paean, a favorite of favorites, played in their army, esteemed as warlike as the Grenadier's March—it is the lover's spell, the nurse's lullaby. After our rapid successes, we held the Yankees in great contempt, but it was not a little mortifying to hear them play this tune, when their army marched down to our surrender.

Anburey, of course, alludes to General Burgoyne's surrender at Saratoga, October 17, 1777. Again the military bands of the Continental army are said to have used "Yankee Doodle" as their *paean* at the climax of the war when Lord Cornwallis surrendered at Yorktown, October 19, 1781, but Robin, Knox, Thacher, Anburey, Chastellux, Gordon, and Johnston do not confirm this popular legend. I distinctly recall having seen it told by a French memoir writer of the time, but unfortunately am unable to retrace my source.

On that occasion the British army marched out to the tune of "The World turned upside down." So it was in more than one respect. Clearly, before and during the first stages of the war, "Yankee Doodle" was considered a capital piece by the British soldiers to ridicule the New Englanders, but the latter blunted the point of the joke, and indeed used it in rebuttal by appropriating the tune with all its associations for their patriotic field music. This curious process found an echo in one of our very first by-products of the war. John Trumbull's "M'Fingal" was first published at Philadelphia in 1775.

In the first, original edition the first *canto* "The Town Meeting" begins:

> When Yankies skill'd in martial rule,
> First put the British troops to school;
> Instructed them in warlike trade,
> And new maneuvres of parade,
> The true war dance of Yanky-reels,
> And val'rous exercise of heels.

and later on the lines occur:

> Did not our troops show much discerning,
> And skill your various arts in learning?
> Outwent they not each native Noodle
> By far in playing *Yanky-doodle;*
> Which, as 'twas your New-England tune
> 'Twas marvellous they took so soon?

A New England tune or not, "Yankee Doodle" was common property in New England before the war for independence. Not alone this, it is easily proven that the tune was well known south of New England, too, at least nine years before the war. In my writings I have had repeated occasion to point to Andrew Barton's comic opera "The Disappointment, or The force of credulity," New York, 1767, in this connection. This, the first American opera libretto, unmistakably belongs to the class of ballad operas, that is, operas in which the airs were sung not to new music but to popular ballad tunes. Now, as Sabin, without attracting proper attention at the time, discovered as early as 1868, there appears in the 1767 edition, though not in the 1796 edition, of this coarse, yet witty, libretto, written in Philadelphia, but printed in New York:

AIR IV, YANKEE DOODLE.

> O! how joyful shall I be,
> When I get the money,
> I will bring it all to dee,
> O! my diddling honey.
> (Exit, singing the chorus, *yankee doodle,* etc.)

It follows conclusively that the air of "Yankee Doodle" was sufficiently popular in America in 1767, or more correctly, in Philadelphia, to be used in a ballad opera. It further follows from the above that the words of the chorus refrain were so well known in 1767 that it was sufficient to print: " *Yankee-doodle,* etc."

The fact that the air of "Yankee Doodle" was popular in America in 1767 renders it impossible for a "British officer of the Revolution" to have "composed" the song. If at all true, this tradition can only mean that he either added some verses to a current text or wrote an entirely new set of verses.

The second theory on the list collapses for the same reason. The Hessian military can not have introduced the tune to our country as it was popular in America long before their arrival here. On the contrary, it becomes probable that the Hessian bands exported the air from America. However, not chronology alone, but logic forbade the acceptance of the Hessian origin, since according to Mr. Lewalter's own account "Yankee Doodle" was merely grafted on the Schwalm peasants by way of experiment. They danced readily enough to the tune, but Mr. Lewalter's story clearly shows that they did not consider it one of their *traditional* dance tunes. This plain observation should discourage further efforts in this direction, which would presumably be based on the fact that the British military service included Hessians long before 1775, indeed before 1767.

Similar objections must be raised against the theories of the Biscay and Hungarian origin. They were advanced almost one hundred years after "Yankee Doodle" had become popular in America, time enough for any tune to find its way into any country and to be so assimilated that its foreign origin is entirely forgotten. That Hungarians danced to it fifty years ago proves absolutely nothing except that "Yankee Doodle" with its rhythmic accents appealed to them. Kossuth and his friends, experts in revolutions but not in musical history, recognized in "Yankee Doodle" one of the old national airs of Hungary; this also proves nothing except that they knew the air. It is the same with the Biscay origin advanced by Mr. Buckingham Smith in 1858. Had he contented himself with recording the use of the tune in Biscay, one may be puzzled by the coincidence that two Turanian nations were willing to naturalize "Yankee Doodle." But Mr. Smith goes further, and he claims that "the first strains are identically those of the heroic *Danza Esparta* [!] as it was played to me of brave old Biscay." Are they? I quote without comment the first bars of this "*Ezpata Dantza*" (sword-dance), as published by Charles Bordes in "Archives de la Tradition Basque," under title of "Dix danses . . . du Pays Basque Espagnol," 1908:

As a fifth theory we have that promulgated by Duyckinck's Cyclopædia in 1855:

> It is not impossible . . . that Yankee Doodle may be from Holland. A song in use among the laborers, who in time of harvest migrate from Germany to the Low Countries . . . has this burden—
>
> > Yanker didel, doodel down
> > Didel, dudel lanter,
> > Yanke viver, voover vown,
> > Botermilk and Tanther.

The Duyckincks received their information from a person who in turn relied on the memory of a Dutchman who "had listened to it at harvest time in his youth." This circuitous route may explain why the chorus refrain, as quoted above, belongs to no known language. In itself the fact that the words are neither German, Dutch, or English proves nothing and should not have been advanced so hastily by Lossing, Elson, and others, since such nonsense rhymes are common to all people. Here are a few examples taken at random from books in the English language. O'Keefe has this nonsense in one of his librettos:

> Ditherum, doodle adgety
> Nagity, tragedy rum,
> Goostnerum foodle nidgety
> Nidgety, nagety mum.

In the libretto to the "Castle of Andalusia" occurs this:

> A master I have, and I am his man,
>   Galloping dreary dun
> And he will get married, as fast as he can
>   With my haily, gaily, gambraily,
> Giggling, niggling, galoping,
>   Galloway, draggletail, dreary dun.

Finally, in the American songster "The Blackbird," New York, 1820, I noticed the refrain on page 39:

> With my titol teedle tum
>   Likewise fol lol feedle fum
> Not forgetting diderum hi,
>   And also teedle tweedle dum.

Sense there is not in these samples of nonsense rhymes, yet who would deny that they are based on the English language? Consequently, the "Yanker didel, doodel" lines with the one word Botermilk (buttermilk) as an anchor of sense may either have been intended as a Dutch nonsense rhyme, or they are the unintelligible Dutch corruption of a Low German (Plattdeutsch) chorus refrain, or they are merely the result of travel of the original English "Yankee Doodle" refrain corrupted more and more, as it passed from America into the German lowlands, thence to Holland, and from there back to America. I am inclined to think that this is the most plausible explanation, rather than to simply discredit, as has been done, the narrative in Duyckinck's Encyclopædia, and to accuse the editors of having invented the silly lines out of the whole cloth. After all, the substance of their statement is merely that during the first half of the nineteenth century harvest laborers from the German lowlands are known to have sung the air of "Yankee Doodle" in Holland. This implies early use, not origin, and even if it implied the latter, not the Dutch but the "Plattdeutsche" would be responsible for the melody.

We turn to Mr. Elson's book on the National Music of America and there find these interesting lines:

Just as this volume is going to press [1900] the author is enabled, through the kindness of M. Jules Koopman, traveling in Holland, to trace this theory of

Dutch origin more definitely. *The first period* of the melody is quite familiar to Dutch musicians, and has been used in Holland from time immemorial as a *children's song;* the second period is not known in Holland.

Again, this implies at the best merely early use and by no means a Dutch origin. If "Yankee Doodle" were a traditional Dutch air, it certainly would not have escaped the scrutinizing eye of the best authorities on Dutch folk songs, such as Van Duyse and D. F. Scheurleer. The story of a Dutch origin may be dropped, since Mr. D. F. Scheurleer, in a letter to me under date of October 7, 1908, remarks:

> Was die Melodie betrifft, muss ich gestehen in den Niederlanden *kein* Prototype zu kennen. Dieses war auch der Fall bei von mir befragten Sachverständigen.
>
> Das von Ihnen citierte *quasi* holländische Ernte-Lied ist mir völlig neu und ich wüsste daran keinen Sinn zu geben . . .
>
> Ich habe beim Yankee doodle öfters gedacht an hier im 18ten Jahrhundert sehr bekannte Savoyarden-Lieder, gesungen von Savoyarden-Knaben, die mit Drehleier und Meerschweinchen herumzogen. Diese Leierkastenlieder waren sehr geeignet um von Matrosen und Emigranten weiter befördert zu werden . . .

To avoid all possible confusion, it may be added that the air of the Dutch song "Pauwel Jonas" (Paul Jones) is not identical with "Yankee Doodle."

Somewhat more perplexing than the theory of Dutch origin is the one attributing "Yankee Doodle" to the fife-major of the Grenadier Guards about 1750, who is said to have composed the melody as a march for drum and fife. This statement rests on the authority of Mr. T. Moncrieff, but unfortunately no clue to his source is given. It is significant, however, that according to this theory words became associated with the air long after it had become familiar to the ears of the people in towns where British regiments were stationed. The weak point of this theory is its vagueness. The strong point that the air is attributed without circumlocution to a tangible author. "Yankee Doodle" must have had an origin. If we should be forced to admit that all other theories are inherently weak, then the fife-major of the Grenadier Guards would loom up as a very formidable candidate for the authorship of "Yankee Doodle." Not, of course, of a march by this title, but of a quick march, with some other or without title, which found its way shortly after 1750 to America, there became popular, was wedded to words dealing with the New England Yankees, and permanently retained the name of "Yankee Doodle." That the air was imported by the Grenadier Guards themselves is impossible, because Sir F. W. Hamilton's "History of the First or Grenadier Guards" proves that a detachment of the regiment, including seven drummers and two fifers, was not sent to

America until 1776. The whole fife-major theory, however, is considerably weakened by reference to these words in a letter written on December 22, 1908, to the Librarian of Congress by Major Montgomerie of the Grenadier Guards:

> . . . We cannot discover that the office of Fife-Major ever existed in this Regiment. We have had Drum-Majors since 1672, but their names we do not know.

The air of "Yankee Doodle" seems to have been founded, said our anonymous in the Musical Reporter, Boston, 1841, on an air somewhat similar which was common among the peasantry of England previous to the time of Charles I, 1600 (1625)–1649. On page 97 of this report the air in question is copied and it requires a very unmusical ear to detect beyond the rhythm and general character any telling similarity. Consequently, said air may have been common among the English peasantry of those days, but this fact would shed no light whatever on the origin of "Yankee Doodle," as the two airs are not related. Furthermore, if this air cited by our anonymous is the one that was set during Cromwell's time to various ditties, such as "The Roundheads and the Cavaliers," or "Nankee Doodle," then all protracted and painstaking controversy on this subject was unnecessary, since "Yankee Doodle" is not concerned. Indeed, the controversy could easily have been avoided ere this had the commentators found their way to a copy of the rather scarce Musical Reporter. The air there quoted and reprinted on page 97 of this report is but a version of "Nancy Dawson," and as such an eminent authority on folk songs as Mr. Frank Kidson expressed himself (Dec. 22, 1908), he "should very much be surprised to have proof of its existence before 1760 or thereabouts." As to the ditties beginning "The Roundheads and the Cavaliers" and "Nankee Doodle came to town," Rev. T. Woodfall Ebsworth, the eminent authority on English ballads, is quoted in the first edition of "Grove's Dictionary of Music" to this effect:

> I believe that I have seen and weighed, more or less every such ballad still remaining in print, and most of those in M.S. that search has detected: and I can declare unhesitatingly that I never came across any indication of such an anti-Cromwellian original as the apocryphal "Nankee Doodle came to town." I believe that none such is extant or ever appeared. . . There is no contemporary (*i. e.* 1640–1660 or, say 1648–1699) ballad specially entitled "The Roundheads and the Cavaliers."

The ante-Cromwellian origin of "Yankee Doodle" and its anti-Cromwellian use with all the embellishments that imaginative minds have added during the last seventy years may definitely be laid to rest. However, since the (slightly varying) lines—

> [Nankee] Yankee Doodle came to town
> Upon a Kentish pony.
> He stuck a feather in his hat
> And called him Macaroni

have actually been sung in America for generations to the tune of "Yankee Doodle," it will become necessary later on to approximately fix the date of these lines, and that is, to anticipate the third or even fourth quarter of the eighteenth century. Thus, Cromwell and "Yankee Doodle" are separated by at least a century.

Theories eighth to eleventh all have this in common, that they take as starting point the rhyme:

> Lucy Locket lost her pocket
> Kitty Fisher found it
> Not a bit of money in it
> [or, Nothing in it, nothing in it]
> Only binding round it.

For "Lucy Locket" Lydia Locket is sometimes substituted; for "Kitty Fisher," Lydia Fisher, and other slight verbal differences occur in the numerous citations of these lines.

With the exception of the theory of ante-Cromwellian origin, they have been chiefly responsible for the mass of confusion surrounding "Yankee Doodle," particularly after Doctor Rimbault threw the weight of his authority into the controversy.

From the perusal of the literature on the subject as gathered for this report, it appears conclusively that the lines were used as a nursery rhyme during the first half of the nineteenth century both in England and America, and were then always sung to the same air as "Yankee Doodle." Indeed, "two female relations" informed one G. A. G., for Notes and Queries, 1865 (vol. 8, p. 155), that the lines were "current some fifty years ago in the girls' schools" of the Isle of Wight and of Hampshire—that is, about 1810.

For the use of the lines during the eighteenth century we have, to my knowledge, the contemporary statement only of an aged and respectable lady born in New England, who remembered having heard the rhyme sung to the same tune long before the Revolution as a favorite jig, called "Lydia Fisher." (See on p. 98, Watson's account, 1844.) On the other hand, the anonymous author in the Musical Reporter, Boston 1841, gives

that is, "Nancy Dawson" as the air to which the song "Lydia Locket or Lucy Locket has been sung . . . from time immemorial." If we turn to page 98 and attempt to sing the rhyme to this melody, we find that this is easily done, even in the fourth bar, if the two words "found it" each get two of the four notes. Except for this fourth bar the traditional "Yankee Doodle" is not sung more readily. Here then would seem to be a conflict between the statement of an old lady relying on her memory and actual quotation of a melody by an equally anonymous writer who may have had an equally good memory. This difference of opinion is not vital, since often in folk music the same words are grafted on different melodies until the fittest survives. At any rate, we have no reason to doubt the possibility that "Lucy Locket" was sung also to the air of "Yankee Doodle" in New England previous to the American revolution.

For further data we must rely on internal evidence. "Lucy Locket," of course, points to "Lucy Lockit," one of the main characters in the famous "Beggar's Opera," first performed in 1728 and popular during the entire century. Possibly, "Lucy Locket" found her way into the rhyme only for reasons of sound. However, 1730 would appear to be about the earliest possible date for the rhyme unless Gay adopted "Lucy Locket" as an effective stage name from the popular rhyme. The presence of a Kitty Fisher in the rhyme would forbid this conjecture if we recognize in her with Rimbault the famous lady of easy virtue called "Kitty Fischer." What Rimbault wrote about her in the Historical Magazine (1858) is mostly nonsense, as he himself tacitly admitted by printing a totally different reference to this lady in the Leisure Hour (1876):

> Kitty Fisher, as everybody knows, was a celebrated character in the middle of the last century. She was painted by Sir Joshua Reynolds more than once, and ultimately married Squire Norris of Bemmendon [*recte* Benenden] in Kent.

This agrees with what one finds about her in "Notes and Queries" and Stephen's Dictionary of National Biography. The registers of Benenden give the date of her burial as March 23, 1767. It is not recorded when Catherine Marie Fischer, probably of German origin, was born, nor are such biographical details of much account for our argument. It stands to reason that Kitty Fischer was not made the heroine of such verses before she had become a really public character. Since she appears to have reached the height of her reputation as professional beauty about 1759, shortly before she became the second and exemplary wife of Mr. Norris, it would seem safe to conjecture that the "Lucy Locket" and "Kitty Fisher" rhyme did not originate many years before 1759. Therefore, the attempt to trace this rhyme, which only gradually can have become a *nursery*-rhyme, by way of this Kitty Fischer to the times of Charles II, 1630 (1660)–1685, was conspicuously absurd. On the other hand, nothing would prevent us from assuming that the rhyme, with whatever melody, may have found its way to America before our war for independence, that is, before 1775. In our country Kitty Fisher appears to have become Lydia Fisher. This modification may have been due to the natural desire to avoid the harsh verbal sound of "pocket—Kitty", and since our people probably took no special interest in the famous Kitty

Fischer's affairs, they substituted Lydia perhaps for some further local reason. But, after all, is it necessary to recognize in the Kitty Fisher of the rhyme the famous Kitty Fischer or any other particular Kitty Fisher? The name surely neither was nor is so uncommon as to compel this association. Indeed Mr. Matthews, following the same line of argument, has found two ladies of this name, contemporary with the beautiful courtesan. The one is "an eminently respectable young lady who is mentioned several times in letters written in 1743–1747 by Lieut. Colonel Charles Russell, of the British Army," the other a "Miss Kitty Fisher, a very young lady at boarding school at Leicester mentioned in the Oxford Magazine, April, 1771." It is entirely possible that "Kitty Fisher" was incorporated in the rhyme without the slightest intention of personal allusion, just because the name "Kitty Fisher" was common and popular, and because it sounds rather well in the rhyme and fits the tune. Should this have been the case, then the absence of real evidence to the effect that the lines were known long before 1800 would fortify the impression that they originated about 1800, and this again would explain nicely why they were sung to (the then already very popular) tune of "Yankee Doodle."

The "Lucy Locket" rhyme was clearly intended for singing, and it is the rule with such folk songs that the melody preceded the text. In other words, the earlier the rhyme is dated the older becomes the melody of "Yankee Doodle," unless the rhyme was sung originally to another tune, which was exchanged later on for the rhythmically similar and catchier "Yankee Doodle." Naturally the idea suggested itself to trace this tune in written or printed form as far back as possible. Here, again, Doctor Rimbault became responsible for much of the confusion surrounding our air. In the Historical Magazine (1858, vol. 2, p. 214), we read that Rimbault found the earliest copy of the tune in "Walsh's collection of dances for the year 1750 where it is printed in 6/8 time, and called *Fisher's Jig*," but in his article in Leisure Hour, 1876, Rimbault turns his back on his previous discoveries and says:

> The probability is that the tune is not much older than the time of its introduction into America. We know that it was popular in England at that time, having been printed in one of Thompson's country dance books as *Kitty Fisher's Jig*.

A few lines below Doctor Rimbault gives "a copy of Thompson's version of the tune which is written in triple time. It was afterwards altered to common time, as now known."

The contradictions between these statements are so flagrant that suspicions of Doctor Rimbault's methods not only, but of his veracity, are aroused. It is a disagreeable duty to attack a well-known and defunct scholar, yet Doctor Rimbault stands convicted by his own testimony. It may be after all that he saw our tune *somewhere,* but first he discovered a "Fisher's jig" in 6—8 time in Walsh, and then, forgetting all about this discovery, he finds it printed in triple time as "Kitty Fisher's Jig" in Thompson. Only if both statements are true, does Rimbault stand acquitted. Now, Mr. William Barclay Squire in the first edition of Grove's Dictionary, has already cast suspicions on Rimbault's statement of 1858 by the remark that "no copy of 'Fisher's Jig' has turned up," and he was repeatedly supported in this statement by Mr. Frank Kidson.

To make absolutely sure whether or no these two eminent authorities on English folk song had found in the meanwhile evidence to support Rimbault, carefully prepared letters of inquiry were addressed to them which they had the kindness to answer as follows:

Mr. Squire, August 5, 1908:

> We have [at the British Museum] a small collection of Country Dances published by Walsh in 1750, but no "Yankee Doodle" is in this.

Mr. Kidson, August 12, 1908:

> Dr. Rimbault's statements have never been proved. I have seen two copies of Walsh's Dances for 1750 and have seen those for 1742, 1745, 1748, 1765, and in fact have MS. copies of them all in full. I have many (very many) 18th century dance collections and four or five Caledonian Country Dances (Walsh) but nothing like Yankee Doodle in any of them. Kitty Fisher's Jig is also *non est.*

and previously Mr. Kidson had informed Mr. Albert Matthews that he had also examined Thompson's Dances from 1751 and 1765 in vain. Finally, Mr. Squire, September 21, 1908:

> "Kitty Fisher's Jig" has never turned up . . . he [Mr. Kidson] and I have both looked thro' endless dance books in vain.

Equally void of substance appears to be the claim presented by one J. C. in the Baltimore Clipper, 1841, that an *"Air from Ulysses,"* which he found "about the year 1797" in a book of instructions "for the bassoon" was the identical air now called *Yankee Doodle,* with the exception of a few notes."

A careful reader of these quotations from J. C.'s narrative (see p. 102) can not fail to notice that the air evidently was not really identical, that the author is contributing data to the controversy from memory after a lapse of forty years, that he did not have the book of instructions before him when he wrote his article. No methodically trained historian would accept such circumstantial evidence without serious scruples. A curious circumstance about J. C.'s statement is that he begins with a quotation from Burgh's Anecdotes, which has nothing to do with "Yankee Doodle," but merely acquaints the reader with the fact that John Christian Smith [*recte* John Christopher Smith, 1712–1795] composed an opera "Ulysses." Why this quotation? Apparently because J. C. desired to trace the composer of an *Air from*

Ulysses, whom he had either forgotten or who was not mentioned in his book of instructions. He remembered the word *Ulysses* in connection with a tune almost identical with "Yankee Doodle," and with the help of Burgh's Anecdotes he conjectured a bridge between the word *Ulysses* and the opera *Ulysses* by John Christopher Smith, which was performed at Lincoln's Inn Fields in 1733. It would seem an easy matter to verify J. C's conjecture by a reference to Smith's score, but unfortunately no copy of his opera has ever been discovered, nor is it certain that the music was ever published. However, if a tune like Yankee Doodle was in Smith's opera "Ulysses," then this jiglike tune, must of necessity fit words in the libretto of this mythological opera. Though such a combination appeared to be very improbable, Mr. William Barclay Squire of the British Museum was approached in the matter, and he wrote me under date of September 21, 1908:

Sam¹. Humphreys' Ulysses (libretto) is here, but contains nothing to which one can imagine Y. D. to have been sung. Here are some specimens:

> Balmy Slumbers, soft Repose,
>   Gently cull my lovely Fair;
> Send your solace to her Woes,
>   Ease her of said Despair, etc. etc.

Or,

> Now I die with joy, to be
> Chaste, and dutiful to thee;
> And resign my youthful Bloom,
> All untainted to the Tomb, etc. etc.

Not only this, Mr. Squire stated that he knows of no such book of instructions for the bassoon as alluded to by J. C.

Like so many other theories of the origin of "Yankee Doodle" the conjecture of a connection between the tune and John Christopher Smith's opera "Ulysses" may safely be dropped.

Ere this a flaw in the J. C. statement had been suspected, and Mr. William H. Grattan Flood in his article quoted on page 106, suggested that the error of asserting an air from *Ulysses* as the source of the tune might have arisen from a confusion of the designation *Ulysses* with a song of that name in Dibdin's Musical Tour, 1788, the full title of which is "The Return of Ulysses to Ithaca." As the analysis of J. C.'s statements leaves it open to doubt from where the "Yankee Doodle" melody in his book of instructions for the bassoon was taken, Mr. Grattan Flood's suggestion is as acceptable as any. The song in question accompanies "Letter LXXXIV" in Dibdin's Musical Tour, and is preceded on page 341 by this bit of explanatory monologue:

"Why," said the Poet, "you may remember Mr. O'Shoknesy, the other night, favoured us with the whole *siege of Troy* to an *Irish* tune—for my part, I felt my consequence as a poet a little touched at it—and so, not to be outdone, I have brought *Ulysses* back to *Ithaca* safely through all his perils, to the tune of— *Yankee Doodle.* . . ."

Omitting the prelude and postlude and the accompaniment, the first of Dibdin's eight burlesque stanzas reads:

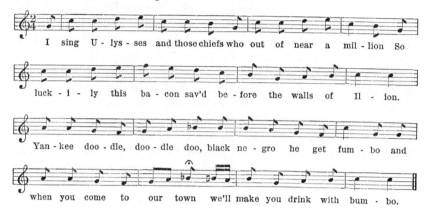

I sing U - lys - ses and those chiefs who out of near a mil - lion So
luck - i - ly this ba - con sav'd be - fore the walls of Il - ion.
Yan - kee doo - dle, doo - dle doo, black ne - gro he get fum - bo and
when you come to our town we'll make you drink with bum - bo.

A facsimile of the whole song appears in the Appendix as Pl. xlv-xv.

The burlesque song, by the way, was first used by Dibdin in this form for his puppet play "Reasonable Animals," 1780.

The statement in Admiral Preble's "History of the Flag," that the melody of "Yankee Doodle" occurs in an opera composed by Thomas Augustine Arne about 1750 to the words "Did little Dickey ever trick ye," was long ago discredited by Mr. William Barclay Squire in Grove's Dictionary. Mr. Squire called attention to the appearance of the air under its own title in the comic opera "Two to One," of which the libretto was written by George Colman the younger, the music selected, arranged, and composed by Dr. Samuel Arnold and the score published by Harrison & Co. in 1784. The song in question was sung by Mr. Edwin in the character of Dickey Ditto. Plate XVI shows the first stanza with the melody in facsimile.

At the time Mr. Squire held that this probably was the earliest appearance of Yankee Doodle in print, but Mr. Frank Kidson in his fine collection of "Old English Country Dances," 1890, pointed to an earlier version to be found in the first volume of James Aird's "A Selection of Scotch, English, Irish, and Foreign Airs," Glasgow. Since Mr. Kidson could not find "any air in it, which gives a later date than 1775 or 1776," he fixed (on p. 13) the date of publication at about that period, but the late Mr. Glen in his scholarly "Early Scottish Melodies" fixed the date of Aird's first volume as 1782, and Mr. Kidson, in a letter to me (Aug. 12, 1908), accepted this date as "all right." Aird's "Yankee Doodle" is reproduced in facsimile on Plate XVII of the appendix. No earlier appearance in print than this of 1782 has been discovered, and the fact that the same volume contains at least one negro jig and several "Virginian airs" would seem to prove a direct

American influence, probably called forth by the war.   Presumably "Yankee Doodle" came to Aird's notice by way of America.

If, then, the ascertained earliest appearances in print of Yankee Doodle in Europe have been traced to (1) James Aird's Selection . . . , first volume, Glasgow, 1782; (2) Samuel Arnold's Opera "Two to One," London, 1874; (3) Charles Dibdin's "Musical Tour," Sheffield, 1788, the question suggests itself, When and where was the tune first printed in America? In his valuable "Songs and Ballads of the American Revolution," 1855, Mr. Moore published a ballad of the title "The Recess."   This satire, he says, first appeared at London written by "a true friend of the King and the Colonies."   "It was reproduced in America, in 1779, on a music sheet adapted to the tune of *Yankee Doodle.*"

Mr. Moore does not mention publisher or place of publication of this music sheet, nor does he point to any library in which it may be found.   He may be correct in his statement.   In that case I failed to locate the piece when compiling material for my "Bibliography of Early Secular American Music."   Until actual proof of the piece's existence is given me, I prefer to suspect that "The Recess" was printed without music as a broadside, perhaps with the indication "To the tune of Yankee Doodle."   The first stanza as given by Mr. Moore reads:

> And now our Senators are gone
> To take their leave of London
> To mourn how little they have done
> How much they have left undone!

Of secular music very little was published in America before 1790, and according to my bibliography "Yankee Doodle" did not appear in print in America until Benjamin Carr's "Federal Overture," a medley of patriotic songs, including "Yankee Doddle," and composed in 1794, was published "adapted for the pianoforte" by B. Carr, New York, in January, 1795.   No copy of this appears to be extant, only a "medley duetto adapted for two German flutes" in the fifth number of Shaw and Carr's "Gentleman's amusement."   Unfortunately the copy of the Library of Congress, the only one that has come to my notice lacks the very pages where one could expect to find "Yankee Doodle" in the form given it by B. Carr.   Nor have I as yet found a copy of John Henry Schmidt's "Sonata for beginners," 1796, in which our air was "turned into a fashionable rondo," nor a copy of "*Yankee Doodle*, an original American air, arranged with variations for the pianoforte," as printed by J. Carr, Baltimore, in 1796.   Presumably in June, 1798, "Yankee Doodle" was "Published by G. Willig, Market street No. 185, Philadelphia," together with "The President's March.   A new Federal Song."   ("Hail Columbia."   For facsimile of both, see Pls. IX and X in Appendix.)   A copy of this extremely rare piece is preserved in a miscellaneous volume of "Marches and Battles" at the Ridgway branch of the Library Company of Philadelphia. The melody, sung to the words "Columbians all the present hour," has this form:

This version was composed or rather arranged by James Hewitt, since he advertised, probably between 1800 and 1802, the *"New Yankee Doodle"* beginning "Columbians all the present hour as Brothers should unite us," as "composed and published at his Musical Repository No. 59, Maidenlane, New York." A copy of this song is preserved at Harvard University. Some years later, Gottlieb Graupner, one of Boston's most important musicians, "printed and sold" at his "Musical Academy No. 6, Franklin Street, Franklin Place," "General Washington's March" together with "Yankee Doodle" in a simple arrangement for the pianoforte. Mr. Elson's "History of American Music" contains a facsimile, and from this the following version of the melody is quoted:

Different again is an earlier form of the tune in the "Compleat tutor for the fife," Philadelphia, George Willig [1805]. On page 28 of this curiously American reprint of a rare English publication, we find among the interpolations "Yankee Doodle:"

Another early form appears on page 8 of Raynor Taylor's "Martial music of Camp Dupont," Philadelphia, G. E. Blake [ca. 1818]:

Alexander Wheelock Thayer, the Beethoven biographer, communicated to the first edition of Grove "the following version as it was sung sixty years since, and as it has been handed down by tradition in his family from Revolutionary times:"

CHORUS, REFRAIN.

Yan - kee doo - dle, keep it up, Yan - kee doo - dle dan - dy,

Mind the mu - sic and the step, and with the girls be han - dy.

These early versions of the melody will be sufficient to demonstrate that "Yankee Doodle," whatever its original form might have been, passed through many hands before it became fixed in the popular mind in its present form. The semiofficial form now used in the United States is contained in John Philipp Sousa's "National Patriotic and Typical Airs of all Lands," Philadelphia, 1890:

This process of elimination and substitution of notes, and even bars is characteristic of many folk songs, and the "Folk" unconsciously adopts the same attitude of mind as does a composer who polishes and changes his melodic ideas until he feels satisfied with the result. But this process also explains, how imperfect rendition and local usage can produce such abortive and almost incredible versions as the one in James Hulbert's "Variety of Marches" (1803, p. 8) and in his "Complete Fifers' Museum" (Greenfield, Mass. [18–], p. 12):

or the one in Alvan Robinson's "Massachusetts Collection of Martial Musick" (2d. ed., Exeter, 1820, p. 58):

In addition to these early versions in print a few in manuscript are extant. For instance, the facsimile on Plate XVIII shows the form of "Yankey doodle" as it appears in "Whittier Perkins' Book 1790" of "A Collection of Dancing Tunes, Marches, & Song Tunes" now in possession of Mrs. Austin Holden, Boston, Mass. This is an exceedingly interesting collection of more than one hundred tunes, and its importance is increased by the fact that it was written by a person with a very neat hand not only, but a musical hand. Parts of a Boston newspaper of 1788 have been used for the inside of the leather binding, but this, of course, though original, may have been added any time after 1788. The earliest possible date of compilation is 1778, since in that year Francis Hopkinson wrote his "Battle of the Kegs," which figures in the collection. It furthermore looks as if the collection was complete before Whittier Perkins claimed it as his property in 1790. We are perfectly safe in dating this version of "Yankee Doodle" as it appears on the first page of the unpaged collection as "about 1790:"

YANKEE DOODLE

This last version is probably a few years earlier. It appears written in a collection of psalm and popular tunes attached to an incomplete copy of Thomas Walter's "Grounds and rules of musick," Boston, edition of 1760, as preserved under number of "G. 38. 23" at the Boston Public Library. As a matter of fact, the manuscript music forms two collections in two different hands. The psalm tunes are paged 26–46 in continuation of the engraved psalm tunes, and on page 42 we read "Wm. Cummingham, Esqr. 1765." These psalm tunes are followed by seventeen pages of such popular airs as "The Hero," "Lovely Nancy," "A trip to Halifax," "God save the King," "Prince Eugene's March," "Bellisle March," "Wild Irishman," "British Grenadiers," and "Yankee Doodle." The presence of so many marches and of a "Hessian Minuet" permits us to conjecture that the collection was written after 1765, either during the war or immediately after. It is therefore perhaps not unsafe to date this version of "Yankee Doodle" as "about 1780." It will be observed and the fact is noted here without an attempt to solve the puzzle, how strikingly these two early American manuscript versions differ from the early printed versions and how much more similarity exists between them and the printed New England versions of 1803 and 1820. *Indeed the assumption is not at all far fetched that Yankee Doodle in its modern form is a composite tune, formed out of at least two different tunes of different age.* Finally a version may here be recorded which Mr. Frank Kidson found in a manuscript book in his possession, the first date in which is 1790 and the last 1792:

"Yankee Doodle" has gradually become a national march, a national air. That its text is now more or less obsolete, is so evident as not to require proof. The only words current are with slight variations:

Yankee Doodle came to town
Riding on a pony,
Stuck a feather in his hat
And called it Macaroni.

These or similar words Admiral Preble, 1816–1885 in his childhood heard repeatedly (see p. 104) from his father, Capt. Enoch Preble, 1763–1842. As far as I can see, this is the only evidence we have that the words were known in America as early as about 1820. They may have originated much earlier. How much earlier, depends on the circumstancial evidence offered by the words "Yankee Doodle" and "Macaroni." The combination of "Yankee" and "Doodle" was, so Andrew Barton's "The Disappointment" proves, fairly current in 1767, at least in Philadelphia. Since no earlier reference to a tune "*Yankee* Doodle" has come to light, and since it is entirely possible that the tune under this title had rushed into popularity in the very year of publication of "The Disappointment," no earlier date for the use of the words "Yankee Doodle" would be safe than "at least as early as 1767." After that, the use of these two words in combination became, as we know, fairly frequent, at any rate in America, Doodle retaining its old meaning and "Yankee" becoming preferably a nickname for New Englanders. In England the combination "Yankee Doodle" probably was not used until about or after 1770.

As Mr. William Barclay Squire informed me, the British Museum [G. 310. (163)] preserves a single-sheet song, called "Yankee Doodle, or, the Negroes Farewell to America. The words and music by T. L." The sheet bears the initials C. & S., i. e., Charles and Samuel Thompson, who published music at London from 1764 to 1776 or 1778. (The music bears no relation to our "Yankee Doodle" tune. This is mentioned here because somebody in the ecstasy of discovery may claim that T. L. wrote and composed our "Yankee Doodle.") The publishers may have printed this sheet song as early as 1764 or as late as 1778. Consequently, it does not help us positively to trace the earliest known use of the words "Yankee Doodle" in England.

Attention had been drawn to this song in Notes and Queries as early as 1852, and by Doctor Rimbault in Notes and Queries December 1, 1860, and in the Historical Magazine, 1861, where he stated that the British Museum gave the song the conjectural date of 1775. Rimbault added the titles of two other "Yankee Doodle" songs printed in England and preserved at the British Museum, which are of interest in this connection:

(1) D'Estaing eclipsed, or Yankee Doodle's defeat. By T. Poynton.

(2) "Yankee Doodle, or (as now christened by the saints of New England), the *Lexington March.*"

Rimbault further stated that Poynton's song has its own melody, whereas the second song has the familiar "Yankee Doodle" music, a statement since verified by Mr. William Barclay Squire, Mr. Matthews, and others. Of the text of this particular "Yankee Doodle" song more will be said later on. Here it is sufficient to remark that Mr.

Albert Matthews discovered a copy of it in possession of Mr. John Ritchie, jr., of Boston. It bears the imprint of Thomas Skillern, London, and he is known, according to Mr. Frank Kidson's "British Music Publishers," to have printed music under his own name at 17 St. Martin's lane between 1777–78 and 1799. Therefore, this particular publication by Skillern can not have contributed to the circulation of the words "Yankee Doodle" in England before 1777.

With reference to "D'Estaing eclipsed, or Yankee Doodle's defeat," this quotation from the Gentleman's Magazine, 1783, by *Petersfield* in the Magazine of American History (1877, Vol. I, p. 452), will be of service:

> Your readers and the public must remember an object of compassion who used to sing ballads, about the streets and went by the vulgar appellation of *Yankee Doodle*, alluding to a song he sang about London, at the Commencement of the American War; his real name was Thomas Poynton.

Apparently he was identical with the author and composer of "D'Estaing eclipsed." In that case, he most probably sang his own "Yankee Doodle" words and tune about the streets and not our "Yankee Doodle." However, since D'Estaing was "eclipsed" in 1778 and 1779, T. Poynton can not have contributed to the circulation of the words "Yankee Doodle" in England until after 1778.

These data render it very improbable that lines containing the two words "Yankee Doodle" in this combination can have originated in England before 1764. This allows the widest possible margin (the beginning of C. and S. Thompson's activity as music publishers), whereas the probabilities are that the two words were not current in England until considerably after 1770.

Turning to the word "Macaroni" in our doggerel quatrain—

> Yankee Doodle came to town
> Riding on a pony
> Stuck a feather in his hat
> And called it Macaroni,

it may have been used as mere nonsense, the fun consisting in the in itself burlesque association of "feather in his hat" and "Macaroni" without any hidden meaning. In this case the word "Macaroni" would afford no tangible clue for tracing the earliest possible date of the verses. It is different if the prevailing and almost obviously correct impression be accepted that we have here an allusion to the London Macaronis imitated by a New England doodle with the aspirations of a dandy and a fop.

According to Doctor Murray's Oxford English Dictionary the word "Macaroni" as applied to a certain kind of burlesque poetry, dates back to 1638 and flourished between 1727 and 1741. In the sense of fop, dandy, it was the exquisite of a class which arose in England about 1760 and consisted of young men who had traveled and affected the taste and fashions prevalent in continental society. Again, according to Doctor Murray, this use seems to be from the name of the

"Macaroni Club," a designation probably adopted to indicate the preferences of the members for foreign cookery, macaroni still being at that time little eaten, though the dish was known in England as early as Ben Jonson's time (1599). Horace Walpole, on February 6, 1764, speaks of "the Macaroni Club, which is composed of all the traveled young men, who wear long curls and spying glasses." A few months later, on May 27, 1764, he writes: "Lady Falkener's daughter is to be married to a young rich Mr. Crewe, a Macarone, and of our Loo." Mr. Henry B. Wheatley in "London Past and Present" (1891, Vol. II, p. 453) states that the Macaroni Club was "instituted in 1764." As Mr. Wheatley does not allude to any authority for this definite date, I agree with Mr. Matthews that he ought rather to have stated "about 1764." Moreover, Mr. Matthews unearthed an important account of the origin of the word as applied to fops under the title "Macaroni explained" in the Scots Magazine for November, 1772:

> Macaroni is, in the Italian language, a word made use of to express a compound dish made of vermicelli and other pastes . . . This dish was far from being universally known in this country till the commencement of the last peace: when, like many other foreign fashions, it was imported by our *connoscenti* in eating, as an improvement to the subscription-table at Almack's. In time, the subscribers to those dinners became to be distinguished by the title of *Macaroni;* and as the meeting was composed of the younger and gayer part of our nobility and gentry, who, at the same time that they gave in to the luxuries of eating, went equally into the extravagances of dress, the word *Macaroni* changed its meaning to that of a person who exceeded the ordinary bounds of fashion, and is now justly used as a term of reproach to all ranks of people, indifferently, who fall into this absurdity.

The "last peace" was the Peace of Paris, 1763. This together with the fact that the statement was made less than a decade from that peace and that nobody has succeeded in unearthing a reference to "Macaroni" in the sense of fop earlier than 1764, leads to a very simple conclusion: If in our "Yankee Doodle" lines the word "Macaroni" is used in the sense of fop, then the lines almost with certainty had their origin *after 1764.* It is further significant that the Macaronis, who affected immense knots of artificial hair, ludicrously small cock-hats [!], enormous walking sticks with long tassels and jackets, waistcoats and breeches of very close cut (see Wright's Caricature History of the Georges, London [1868], p. 259), reached the height of their reign as arbiters of advanced fashion from about 1770 to 1775. All this direct and circumstantial evidence on the words "Yankee Doodle" and "Macaroni" leads to the conclusion that our doggerel quatrain did not originate until about or after 1764. Furthermore, it undermines the possibility that the verses were not written in America and since no reference is made in English sources to these lines until far into the nineteenth century, it may be taken for granted that indeed the lines originated in America. The question would still remain open, by whom were they written? By a city-bred Colonial, who merely desired to ridicule the rustic New Englanders, or by a Tory or by a Britisher? Had two or three verses, unmistakably belonging together, been preserved instead of one, the question would probably have been easy to answer. The stanza—

> Yankee Doodle came to town
> Riding on a pony, etc.

never appears with companion stanzas, and yet it is safe to say that such existed. Unless an authentic contemporary copy of the whole "poem" turns up, we, at this late date, can do no more than call attention to some verses which have survived, and which may have belonged to the original string of stanzas, or at least may have been inspired by them. Such verses are the following:

1. From Watson's "Annals of Philadelphia," 1844, contained also in his letter of February, 1832:

> Yankee Doodle came to town
> For to buy a firelock:
> We will tar and feather him
> And so we will John Hancock.

2. Samuel Breck in his "Recollections" (1877, p. 132), writing about 1830 and speaking of John Hancock, said:

> . . . This subject brings to my mind four verses to the tune of "Yankee Doodle" often sung by the British officers during the Revolution:

> Madam Hancock dreamt a dream;
> She dreamt she wanted something;
> She dreamt she wanted a Yankee King,
> To crown him with a pumpkin.

3. George H. Moore's manuscript on "Yankee Doodle" previously mentioned contains this stanza recorded by an "old gentleman who recalled [it] about 1830 as one of a ditty common in his own school days:"

> Yankee Doodle came to town
> Put on his strip'd trowse's
> And vow'd he could n't see the place (town)
> There *was* so many houses.

This last verse, just as the "Macaroni" verse, deals humorously with the personal appearance of Yankee Doodle, and while slightly satirical, might have been written not only by a Britisher, but by any American, Tory or Rebel, who desired to poke some fun at the New England country bumpkins. It is different with the first and second verse just quoted. They obviously can have been penned only by a Tory or a Britisher, and the question merely is what date of origin their contents suggest, though they do not seem to have appeared in print until far into the nineteenth century. A brief reference to the biography of so well known a historical figure as John Hancock will answer the question without much further comment:

> Born in 1737 at Quincy, Mass., John Hancock became one of the most active "Sons of Liberty" (after 1765), a representative of the Massachusetts Legislature, 1766–1772, and he was a member of the Committee to demand of the royal governor the removal of the British troops from Boston, 1770. The efforts of the governor to secure his and Samuel Adams's person, led to the Battle of Lexington April 18

and 19, 1775 and caused Gen. Gage to exclude both from the general pardon granted the rebels. Chosen President of the Provincial Congress in October, 1774, he became a delegate to the Continental Congress, 1775–1780, and its President from May, 1775, to October, 1777. He married Dorothy Quincy at Fairfield, Conn., August 28, 1775.

The "Madam Hancock" verse, therefore—so it may be argued— was not written before August 28, 1775, but a "Madam Hancock" may have been introduced for reasons of satire into this verse by its author without the slightest knowledge whether or not John Hancock was married. Nor do the words "Yankee King" necessarily point to the year 1775, when Hancock became President of the Continental Congress, because it appears from "A New Song" in the Boston Gazette of March 26, 1770 (to which Mr. Matthews called my attention) that the sobriquet "K—g H—k" was applied to him as early as 1770. However, "Madam Hancock" and "Yankee King" taken *together* would seem to lend force to the conjecture that this particular verse originated after August 28, 1775, rather than before. No such circumstantial evidence attaches to the "tar and feather" verse, except that from 1768 on the patriots delighted in inflicting this pastime on the Tories, and that John Hancock certainly was despised by Tory and Britisher alike after 1770 more than before.

The three verses beginning "Yankee Doodle came to town," it may safely be assumed, belong to the same breed of verses, though they and others may not have been written by one author or on the same occasion. The "Madam Hancock" verse surely had a source not very distant from that of the others, and as far as the date of origin of all four verses is concerned, everything seems to point to a date later than 1770. For practical purposes, indeed, these verses may be said to have been written probably about 1775.

On page 105 of this report George H. Moore's unpublished opinion of Doctor Shuckburgh's share in the fortunes of "Yankee Doodle" was quoted in part. He there mentions as "The only verses I have met with which carry any appearance of having been a part of the original."

> There is a man in our town
> I pity his condition,
> He sold his oxen and his sheep
> To buy him a commission—
>
> When his own commission he had got,
> He proved a nation coward
> He durst not go to Cape Breton
> For fear he'd be devoured.

Moore does not say that he got these verses from an "old gentleman" remembering them like the "Strip'd trowse's" verse about 1830, nor does he state who this old gentleman was, nor would a disclosure of identity help us much. Any attempt to date these two verses must take its cue from the allusion to Cape Breton: the author of the verses, clearly belonging together, referred either to the capture of Cape Breton on June 17, 1745, by the Americans, or by General Amherst on July 26, 1758 (Louisbourg).

Here the matter would have to rest, but for the "Yankee Doodle" song published by Thomas Skillern, of London, between 1777 and 1799, and preserved at the British Museum. As stated on page 177, Mr. Matthews discovered another copy at Boston in possession of Mr. Ritchie, jr., who allowed the Library of Congress to secure a facsimile. (See Appendix, Pl. XX.) The title and text read:

YANKEE DOODLE;

or,

(as now christened by the Saints of New England)

THE LEXINGTON MARCH.

N. B. The Words to be Sung throu' the Nose, & in the West
Country drawl & dialect.

[Here the music and first verse follow.]

1. Brother Ephraim sold his Cow
    And bought him a Commission,
    And then he went to Canada
    To fight for the Nation.
    But when Ephraim he came home
    He prov'd an arrant Coward,
    He wou'dn't fight the Frenchmen there,
    For fear of being devour'd.

2. Sheep's Head and Vinegar,
    ButterMilk and Tansy,
    Boston is a Yankee town,
    Sing Hey Doodle Dandy.
    First we'll take a Pinch of Snuff,
    And then a drink of Water,
    And then we'll say, How do you do,
    And that's a Yanky's Supper.

3. Aminidab is just come Home,
    His Eyes all greas'd with Bacon
    And all the news that he cou'd tell
    Is Cape Breton is taken.
    Stand up Jonathan
    Figure in by Neighbor,
    Nathan stand a little off
    And make the Room some wider.

4. Christmas is a coming Boys,
    We'll go to Mother Chases,
    And there we'll get a Sugar Dram,
    Sweeten'd with Melasses.
    Heigh ho for our Cape Cod,
    Heigh ho Nantasket,
    Do not let the Boston wags
    Feel your Oyster Basket.

5. Punk in Pye is very good,
    And so is Apple Lantern,
    Had you been whipp'd as oft as I
    You'd not have been so wanton.
    Uncle is a Yankee Man,
    I'faith he pays us all off,
    And he has got a Fiddle
    As big as Daddy's Hog's Trough.

Stanzas sixth and seventh are too obscene for quotation. The sixth, however, contains a reference to "Doctor Warren," and if the famous patriot Joseph Warren is meant, as is probable, then this stanza must have been written after 1764, when Warren began to practice medicine at Boston, and most likely before June 17, 1775, when he was killed at the Battle of Bunker Hill. If the whole song were known as a unit, and printed by Skillern in its original and complete form, then the allusion to Doctor Warren would also settle the approximately latest date of the text. In the absence of any such positive information, we are obliged to fall back on the single stanzas and on the title. Whatever the date of the text in part or as a whole may be, the title "Yankee Doodle *or* The Lexington March" clearly alludes to the momentous battle of Lexington and Concord April 18 and 19, 1775, and can not have been prefixed to the text before this date, though, of course, the text could have been written earlier without this particular title. The second and fifth stanza do not offer any clew except "Boston is a *Yankee* town" and "Uncle is a *Yankee* Man." The history of the use of the word as applied to New England, renders it probable that these stanzas were written after 1760. The third mentions the taking of Cape Breton as "news," but it is not at all necessary to date the stanza therefore as early as 1745 or 1758. The joke of the stanza may have consisted in this, to picture the Yankee Aminidab as such a country bumpkin and so absurdly behind the times, that "all the news that he cou'd tell" was the taking of Cape Breton. The more years had elapsed since that memorable event, the more effective the joke. Whether this was the intention of the author or not, we at least need not hesitate to date the stanza later than several months after July 26, 1758, because it would really be carrying historical accuracy too far to consider seriously the year 1745 in connection with any "Yankee Doodle" song.

The first stanza is still more puzzling. It may refer either to the French-Canadian war, and more particularly again to the year 1758, or to our own expedition to Canada in 1776. In the latter case the allusion to "The Frenchman" would be a little troublesome, though here again the joke may consist in ridiculing Brother Ephraim's anachronistic notions. That in older times the stanza was connected with the French-Canadian war rather than with the war of the Revolution may be argued from the fact that the two verses quoted on page 130 clearly refer to the expedition against Cape Breton in 1758, and these two verses, it will be noticed, are strikingly kin to the "Brother Ephraim" stanza. So kin indeed that one must have been evolved from the other. The two four liners, whatever their date of origin, were not recorded until far into the nineteenth century, whereas the "Brother Ephraim" stanza was published possibly as early as 1777. Consequently, in absence of proof to the contrary, the natural assumption must be that the "Brother Ephraim" stanza was the prototype.

The inferences to be drawn from this text interpretation are these:

(1) If the poem including the title was a unit, then it must have been written some time after April 18, 1775 (battle of Lexington and Concord), but not very much later than June 17, 1775 (Warren's death).

(2) If the poem was a unit, originally without the title "Yankee Doodle *or* the Lexington March," then it might have been written not much later than June 17, 1775, and not earlier than 1764.

(3) If the poem printed in this form, was a composite, then the single verses were written any time after July 26, 1758 (Amherst's victory at Cape Breton), and before the date of publication.

Whatever inference be preferred, with all its consequences, no disagreement seems possible on the point that this text was not written by a New Englander, but can only have been penned by either an American Tory or a Britisher. Here attention must be called to the statement of Reverend Gordon (see p. 95), who under date of "Roxbury, April 26, 1775," calls "Yankee Doodle" "a song composed in derision of the New Englanders." In view of such contemporary evidence it would be folly to deny the substantial correctness of this statement. Whether or not the story recorded by the anonymous author in Farmer & Moore's Collections, May, 1824, correctly adds the detail "composed by a British officer of the Revolution" is immaterial. The fact remains that verses composed, i. e., written in *derision* of the New Englanders must have existed before April 26, 1775, in form of a specific well-known song, to which, of course, any number of verses might have been added later on *ad libitum*. If the first of the three inferences enumerated above be adopted, then the shortness of the interval between April 18 and April 26, 1775, would seem to exclude the possibility that Reverend Gordon had "Yankee Doodle *or* the Battle of Lexington" in mind, and in that case the "Yankee Doodle came to town" verses would offer themselves more readily for a solution of the problem. If, on the other hand, inferences second or third be preferred, we would have our choice between *two* texts without much evidence in favor of either. However, there exists a *third* text, and the inability to keep the three asunder has caused much of the frightful confusion surrounding our "Yankee Doodle."

In the history of the American drama, Royall Tyler's comedy "The Contrast" holds the place of a pioneer work. Though not published until 1790, at Philadelphia, the play was acted as early as April, 1787, at New York, and performed there and elsewhere with more or less success. In "The Contrast" we find in Act III, scene 1, this amusing bit of dialogue. Jonathan, the first stage Yankee, when asked to sing a song, says:

all my tunes go to meeting tunes [psalm tunes], save one, and I count you won't altogether like that 'ere.

Jenny: What is it called?

Jonathan: I am sure you have heard folks talk about it, it is called Yankee Doodle.

Jenny: Oh! it is the tune I am fond of, and, if I know any thing of my mistress, she would be glad to dance to it. Pray, sing?

Jonathan [Sings]:

> Father and I went up to camp,
>   Along with Captain Goodwin;
> And there we saw the men and boys,
>   As thick as hasty-pudding.
>   Yankee doodle do, etc.
>
> And then we saw a swamping gun
>   Big as a log of maple,
> On a little deuced cart,
>   A load for father's cattle.
>   Yankee Doodle do, etc.
>
> And every time they fired it off
>   It took a horn of powder,
> It made a noise like father's gun,
>   Only a nation louder.
>   Yankee Doodle do, etc.
>
> There was a man in our town
>   His name was ———

No, no, that won't do. . . . [after some dialogue]

Jonathan: No, no, I can sing no more, some other time, when you and I are better acquainted, I'll sing the whole of it—no, no—that's a fib—I can't sing but a hundred and ninety-nine verses: Our Tabitha at home can sing it all—[Sings]

> Marblehead's a rocky place,
>   And Cape-Cod is sandy;
> Charlestown is burned down,
>   Boston is the dandy.
> Yankee doodle, doodle do, etc.

I vow my own town song has put me into such topping spirits, that I believe I'll begin to do a little, as Jessamy says we must when we go a courting— . . .

Enough of the dialogue has been quoted to make it self-evident that Royall Tyler did not write these verses himself, but merely borrowed them for his purposes from what the Germans so happily call the "Volksmund." Discounting some of the hundred and ninety-nine verses as part of Tyler's humorous poetic license, it is clear that many folk poets must have been at work to form such an endless chain of verses for Yankee Doodle, the single links of which would be left out or inserted according to local preferences, as is so often the case with folk songs. It is, furthermore, clear that the text, whole or in part, could not have become so well known and popular in one or two or three years in a country like America to make a reference to more than 199 ballad verses an effective bit of humorous exaggeration and comedy writing. Thus we seem to drift back toward Revolutionary times, but it is also significant that at least the verse "Marblehead's a rocky place" can not have been written before June 17, 1775, the day on which Charlestown was burned down by General Gage. Nor would there have been any sense in writing them after 1785, when the town was rapidly rising from the ashes.

Curiously enough, this verse, which seems to have been written between middle of June, 1775 and 1785, appears in none of the historically important sources of the publications of the "Yankee Doodle" text. No safe inference is to be drawn from this fact, but one is naturally inclined to believe that it was a local interpolation not belonging to the original text.

The publications of the text alluded to are the following:

(1) A broadside entitled "The Yankee's Return From Camp," containing fifteen stanzas and adorned in the upperhand corners by two grotesque woodcuts. This broadside is in the possession of the American Antiquarian Society, Worcester. The Library of Congress possesses, by courtesy of this institution, a photographic facsimile of this broadside (See Appendix, Pl. XXI), as also of the following broadside preserved at the American Antiquarian Society:

(2) "The Yankey's Return From Camp. Together with the favorite Song of the Black Bird." This version of "Yankee Doodle," too, has fifteen stanzas. (See Appendix, Pl. XXII.)

(3) "The Farmer and his Son's return from a visit to the Camp." The whereabouts of the original of this broadside are now unknown, but Mr. Worthington C. Ford, while still with the Boston Public Library, had a blueprint made of the original, and this blueprint he presented to Mr. Albert Matthews of Boston. Mr. Matthews, in turn, permitted the Library of Congress to photograph this doubly unique blueprint for this report. A description is unnecessary, as Plate XXIII shows this blueprint in facsimile.

(4) Under title of "Yankee Doodle" eleven stanzas contributed by an anonymous writer to Farmer and Moore's Collections (1824, vol. 3, p. 159-160), with five stanzas added by the editors:

YANKEE DOODLE.

1. Father and I went down to camp,
    Along with Captain Goodwin,
  Where we *see* the men and boys
    As thick as Hasty-*puddin.*

2. There was *captain* Washington
    Upon a *slapping* stallion,
  A giving orders to his men—
    I *guess* there was a million.

3. And then the feathers on his hat,
    They look'd so *tarnal fina,*
  I wanted *pockily* to get
    To give to my Jemima.

4. And there they had a *swampin* gun
   As large as log of maple,
On a *deuced* little cart—
   A load for father's cattle;

5. And every time they fired it off,
   It took a horn of powder;
It made a noise like father's gun,
   Only a *nation* louder.

6. I went as near to it myself
   As Jacob's *underpinnin,*
And father went *as near again*—
   I thought the *deuce* was in him.

7. And there I *see* a little keg,
   Its heads were made of leather—
They knock'd upon 't with little sticks
   To call the folks together.

8. And there they'd fife *away like fun,*
   And play on *cornstock* fiddles,
And some had *ribbonds* red as blood,
   All *wound* about their middles.

9. The troopers, too, would gallop up
   And fire right in our faces;
It scar'd me almost half to death
   To see them run such races.

10. Old uncle Sam. *come* there to change
   Some pancakes and some onions,
For *lasses-cakes,* to carry home
   To give his wife and young ones.

11. But I can't tell you half I *see*
   They kept up such a smother;
So I took my hat off—made a bow,
   And scamper'd home to mother.

[The editors are in possession of a copy of *Yankee Doodle* which contains several verses more than the foregoing. We will add them, though we are not certain but that they are interpolations.]

After verse 6:

Cousin Simon grew so bold,
   I thought he would have cock'd it,
It scar'd me so, I shrink'd it off,
   And hung by father's pocket.

And Captain Davis had a gun,
   He *kind* a clapt his hand on 't,
And stuck a crooked stabbing iron
   Upon the little end on 't.

And there I *see* a pumpkin shell,
   As big as mother's bason,
And every time they touch'd it off,
   They scamper'd *like the nation.*

After verse 10:

I *see* another *snarl* of men
   A digging graves, they told me,
So *tarnal* long, so *tarnal* deep,
   They *tended* they should hold me.

It scar'd me so, I *hook'd* it off
   Nor stopt as I remember,
Nor turn'd about till I got home,
   Lock'd up in mother's chamber.

A comparison of the three broadsides given in the Appendix in photographic facsimile proves that the texts are identical, though the titles and the orthography differ a little. Each broadside has fifteen stanzas in the same sequence, each has the spelling "Yankey Doodle" in the chorus, and what is not without importance, each has "Captain *Gooding*" in the second line of the first stanza. These three broadsides therefore represent three issues of one and the same poem not only, but of the poem in a concrete and accepted form.

The anonymous contributor to Farmer & Moore's Collections remarked that his was a "copy of the song as it was printed thirty-five years since, and as it was troll'd in our Yankee circles of that day." This would establish the year 1789 as approximate date of the original publication, but it does not follow that he actually copied the words from a printed broadside or page before him at the time of writing his article. He may have copied from memory, as it were, the song as printed and current about 1789. Though no broadside or sheet song appears to have come down to us with the unquestionable date of 1789, we are not justified in assuming that the anonymous invented the existence of a publication of the "Yankee Doodle" text about 1789, and in absence of negative proof are permitted only to regret that no copy of this publication is accessible.[a]

It is clear that this Yankee Doodle story lends itself to endless variation and expansion, and Royall Tyler's humorous "one hundred and ninety-nine verses" is an illusion to the fertility of the folk mind in inventing new stanzas with or without local flavor. Between 1789 and 1824 our anonymous therefore must have heard many stanzas not printed in the nonextant publication of 1789. If he then, in 1824, did not copy the text from a broadside before him, but from memory, very probably he no longer was able to distinguish such stanzas as actually occurred in the 1789 edition from those added later on. Nor would he be absolutely successful in adhering to the original order of the stanzas or in every instance to the original text. That this conjecture, and not the one which would imply actual copy of a broadside before the anonymous contributor to Farmer & Moore, comes nearer the truth may be inferred from the facts that the first seven stanzas of the eleven, though not in the same sequence, appear in the old broadsides, that the five stanzas added by Farmer & Moore appear in the same broadsides, and that only three of the fifteen stanzas in these broadsides do not appear in Farmer & Moore. Consequently Farmer & Moore used a copy of one of these three broad-

---

[a] This attitude involves certain consequences, for instance, as the tenth stanza contains a reference to "old Uncle Sam." This Americanism possibly was derived from Yankee Doodle verses current about 1789, and did not originate as late as about 1812.

sides, and since it will become clear that they contain in all probability the original text in an accepted form it follows that not the
five stanzas added by Farmer & Moore, but, on the contrary, the
stanzas eight to eleven in the version of our anonymous are interpolations. It will be further noticed that three of the stanzas appear
also in Royall Tyler's comedy. Consequently, everything tends to
safeguard the assumption that here we have the text of the "Yankee's
Return from Camp" in its best-known, oldest, and presumably original
form. The question now is whether or not the broadsides themselves help to trace the date of origin of this text. The "Yankee's
Return from Camp" has the imprint, "N. Coverly, jr., Printer, Milk-
Street, Boston." Reference to the Boston City Directories proves
that this printer flourished between 1810 and 1823, the "jr." disappear-
ing from the directory of 1818. However, the broadside can not
have been printed after 1813, since it forms part of the curious collection of songs, ballads, etc., in three volumes, presented to the American Antiquarian Society by Isaiah Thomas in 1814, with the statement that it was "purchased from a ballad printer and seller in
Boston, 1813. Bound up for preservation—to shew that the articles
of this kind are in vogue with the vulgar at this time, 1814." Consequently the date of this particular broadside is fixed as between
1810 and 1813.

No such definite clew is given in the broadside of "The Yankey's
Return from Camp. Together with the favorite Song of the Black
Bird." The spelling of *Yankey* instead of *Yankee* suggests the second half of the eighteenth century rather than the first half of the
nineteenth, but the argument is not a safe one, since the spelling
with *y* is easily traced in early nineteenth-century literature. Indeed,
it appears in the very chorus of Coverly's broadside, 1810–1813. In
his amazingly minute monograph on the Americanism "Uncle Sam"
(p. 61 of the reprint from Proceedings of the Am. Ant. Soc., 1908),
Mr. Matthews infers from Isaiah Thomas's dedicatory words accompanying the gift of this ballad collection that our anonymous broadside was "probably printed in 1813." In private correspondence
(November 30, 1908) Mr. Matthews asserts that "The burden of the
proof lies on him who asserts that the 'Yankey's Return' was printed
before 1813." I utterly fail to see how even a strictly literal interpretation leads to a definite year. Isaiah Thomas merely says that
he purchased the entire collection, not merely *this* broadside, from
a ballad printer and seller in 1813. Even without the fact that
some of the ballads were printed earlier, it would have been contrary
to common sense to assume that the three volumes of ballads were
actually printed in one and the same year, 1813. Thomas's words
do not really give any clew to the dates of publication of his ballads,

except that they can not have been later than 1813, and that they are somewhat limited by the remark "in vogue with the vulgar at this time, 1814." But if they were in vogue one year *after* the collection was purchased by him, they may, at the very least, have been in vogue one year *before*, 1812. But I doubt that Isaiah Thomas intended his remarks to be taken thus narrowly, and it will be methodically just as correct to give his words enough elasticity to prevent literal interpretations from ending unnecessarily in blind alleys. "At this time, 1814," may safely be taken to mean about this time, or, in round figures, as we are dealing with popular ballads more or less in vogue, the first quarter of the nineteenth century.

We also fail to find a definite clew to the date of publication of this particular broadside, if we turn our attention to "The favorite song of the Black Bird." All authorities (see f. i., Christie's Traditional ballad airs) agree that the song appears in the very earliest edition of Ramsay's Tea Table Miscellany, 1724–1727, and Mr. Grattan Flood, in his History of Irish Music, 1906, asserts that he found allusion to the song in 1709. Of course, the broadside can not have been published before "The Black Bird" became a favorite, and probably was not published after the song had ceased to be a favorite. Different melodies have been recorded for this song, but the texts preserved are practically identical and the text proves "The Black Bird" to be a Jacobite song. One version is given on page 68 of the second volume of Hogg's Jacobite Relics, 1821, and it is very significant that the author says in his note on the song (p. 288):

> The Blackbird, seems to have been one of the street songs of the day; at least, it is much in that style, and totally different from the manner of most Jacobite songs. It has had, however, considerable popularity. This copy was communicated by Mr. Fairley, schoolmaster in Tweedsmuir.

This surely does not read as if "the Blackbird" was still a favorite in Scotland in 1821. Furthermore, while it is claimed that the words appear in "The American Songster," Baltimore, 1830, it is a fact that most American songsters of the first quarter of the nineteenth century do not contain the song, nor can it be found in such standard collections of Scotch songs as Smith's "Scottish Minstrel" [182–]; Graham's "Songs of Scotland," 1848–1850; Johnson's "Scotish musical museum," 1859–; Johnson's "Scots Musical Museum" [1787]. There are still other reasons for holding that the song had passed its popularity in 1813. The words of "The Blackbird," as printed in the broadside and as anybody can see, clearly make veiled allusion to the Pretenders or their cause. The farther away from this time the song is removed chronologically the less popular it presumably was. Not only this, but the sentimental and once so popular song "The Maid's Lamentation," so the authorities in English folk song like

Baring-Gould and Chappell tell us, had one of its earliest appearances in print in the "Songster's Magazine," 1804, and this song has all the appearance of being a mere imitation and variation of "The Blackbird," or at least of having been poetically influenced by it. The "Maid's Lamentation" in its early form begins:

Early one morning, just as the sun was rising
I heard a young damsel sigh and complain
Oh gentle shepherd, why am I forsaken?
Oh why should I in sorrow remain!

After that the lines differ widely, yet the underlying poetic motive is the same—a lamentation on the loss of a beloved "blackbird," or sailor, or shepherd, etc.

All this seems to substantiate the impression that the broadside with "The favorite song of the Blackbird" should be dated away from the year 1813 rather than toward it. However, one part is undeniable: The Blackbird can not have been printed together with "The Yankey's return from Camp" before the words of the latter were written.

The mysterious F. B. N. S. wrote in 1857 and promised to prove in a book:

The verses commencing "Father and I went down to the camp" were written by a gentleman of Connecticut a short time after Gen. Washington's last visit to New England . . . .

This visit occurred in the fall of 1789, and therewith collapses the statement of F. B. N. S. In fact, in this form it is so absurd that one is almost led to suspect that he did not mean exactly what he wrote. The absurdity would disappear if F. B. N. S., either not knowing of or forgetting Washington's last visit, really alluded to his forelast visit. This would carry us to the so-called "Provincial Camp," Cambridge, Mass., where George Washington arrived on July 2, 1775, after his appointment as commander in chief of the American Army, and from where he removed headquarters after the evacuation of Boston on March 25, 1776. Unfortunately the book of ballads in which F. B. N. S. promised proof of his statement (see p. 100) has not been traced, and therefore we are also entirely in the dark as to the reasons for assigning the authorship of the text to a gentleman of Connecticut. Nor would this gentleman be without a competitor since Dr. Edward Everett Hale when printing the "Yankey's Return" in his "New England History in Ballads," 1903, remarked:

An autograph note of Judge Dawes, of the Harvard class of 1777, addressed to my father, says that the author of the well-known lines was Edward Bangs, who graduated with him.

The historian would have preferred to see the autograph note of Judge Dawes printed in full, as in this form it merely assigns the poem to a member of the Harvard class of 1777 without defining the date or place of Edward Bangs's poetic effusion. According to Doctor Hale's meager information, Edward Bangs might have written the lines any year between the time he was able to mount Pegasus and 1787, when part of the text was quoted in "The Contrast" written as Mr. Matthews suggestively pointed out in his monograph on "Uncle Sam" by a member of the Harvard class of 1776. In this connection it is also suggestive that Bangs had, as a college boy, joined the Middlesex farmers in the pursuit of April 19, 1775, that Harvard College was transferred from Cambridge to Concord in September, 1775, and returned to Cambridge in 1776. On the other hand there appears to exist no evidence, positive, circumstantial, or even traditional, that the words of the "Yankey's Return from Camp" were written or known before the war for independence, that is, before 1775.

If we turn to the text itself, it clearly reveals an American origin. It is so full of American provincialisms, slang expressions of the time, allusions to American habits, customs, that no Englishman could have penned these verses. Even if he could have done so, he would not have done so, because his poetic efforts in this form would largely have been a puzzle to his comrades. Had this text been a British production, it would have found its way to England, which apparently is not the case. To be a British satire on the unmilitary appearance of provincial American troops, as has been said, the verses would have to be derisively satirical, which they are not. They breathe good-natured humor and they deal not at all with the uncouth appearance of American soldiery, but with the experience of a Yankee greenhorn in matters military who went down to a military camp and upon his return narrates in his own naive style the impressions made on him by all the wonderful sights of military pomp and circumstance. But the text helps us beyond proving a mere American origin. Our Yankee clearly describes not an imaginary camp, but a particular camp, and part of the desired effect was calculated by the author from personal allusions: Captain Gooding, Squire David, Captain Davis, Captain Washington. These names were unmistakably borrowed from life. One need not go deeply into the military records of the several States to find captains by the name of Gooding and Davis. A perusal of Heitman's "Historical Register of Officers of the Continental Army" of "Massachusetts Soldiers and the Sailors of the Revolutionary War," etc., will bear out my statement abundantly, indeed confusingly. At any rate, the names of Gooding and Davis can not be used against the present network of argument, whereas the allusion to and description of a "Captain Washington and gentlefolks about him" who is "grown so tarnal proud, he will not ride without 'em," etc., as a bit of humorously twisted characterization, fits none so well as George Washington, commander in chief. Without this allusion to George Washington, the date of the text would be indefinite within certain limits. With this allusion the conjecture becomes fairly safe that *the text of "Father and I went down to camp" originated at or in the vicinity of the "Provincial Camp," Cambridge, Mass., in 1775 or 1776.*

This becomes an unavoidable conclusion, as much as anything can be conclusive in the absence of documentary evidence, if we now turn to the third broadside. (See facsimile Pl. XXIII.) The broadside is adorned by a crude woodcut of five soldiers, which suggests military times, but more suggestive is the fact that the title reads: "The Farmer and his Son's return from a visit to the Camp." Not *a* camp, but *the* camp, and since George Washington is one of the heroes of the text, the article *"the"* can not but refer to the provincial camp. The title of this broadside does not read so smooth and polished as that of "the Yankey's return from Camp," and for this reason, if for no other, we may conjecture that "The Yankey's" is an afterthought, not of the author, but of the folk, and that "The farmer and his son's return, etc.," antedates any version headed "The Yankey's return," indeed that the latter title did not appear in print before the New Englanders had proudly adopted for use amongst themselves this nickname "Yankee." Thus, to sum up, it would appear that the "Yankee Doodle" text "Father and I went down to camp" originated in 1775 or 1776, and that we have in this particular broadside its first and original edition printed presumably shortly after it had been written. Since the fifteen stanzas are identical in the three earliest known editions, they clearly represent an accepted form of the text not only, but a form attributable to a single author, and it would really seem as if the authorship of Edward Bangs in 1775 rather than in 1776, rests on something more than tradition.

An investigation of the "Yankee Doodle" text would not be complete without a brief consideration of the chorus refrain. Yet, strange to say, this appears not to have aroused any interest, though as a matter of fact the refrain may hold incidentally the key to the whole problem of the origin of the tune. As time went by, the refrain was altered and paraphrased to suit the merits and intentions of the occasion, but such versions are of no account historically in this particular connection. It is different, of course, with the text in Farmer & Moore and in the three broadsides analyzed above. No refrain appears in Farmer & Moore, but the three broadsides have:

> Yankey doodle, keep it up,
> Yankey doodle dandy,
> Mind the music and the step,
> And with the girls be handy.

Though conjectural analysis seems to force us to date the "Yankee Doodle" text beginning "Father and I went down to camp" either

1775 or 1776, yet this is after all a conjecture and all we positively know is that some of the verses appeared in print as early as 1790 in Tyler's "The Contrast." In this comedy, however, the full chorus refrain is not given, merely "Yankee doodle do, etc.," but it does appear in a song written by "A Yankee" in commemoration of the adoption of the Federal Constitution by Massachusetts, and this song was reprinted in the Independent Chronicle, Boston, March 6, 1788, from the Pennsylvania Mercury. The ballad "Yankee Doodle's Expedition to Rhode Island" in Rivington's Royal Gazette, October 3, 1778, has merely "Yankee Doodle, etc."

In Dibdin's "The Return of Ulysses to Ithaca" (1780), 1788, and in Andrew Barton's "The Disappointment," 1767, we have "Yankee Doodle, etc." The difference between these sources and Tyler is very slight, but it is also very suggestive, since the Dibdin and Barton refrain may have had the full text as given above, while the presence of the additional *do* in the Tyler refrain makes the use of this text at least doubtful. And this is not at all startling, but has a very obvious explanation if one reads the following references, some of which I owe to the courtesy of Mr. Matthews.

There appeared in the Royal Gazette, November 27, 1779,

A NEW SONG TO AN OLD TUNE.

Written by a Yankee, and sung to the tune of Doodle-doo:

The Frenchman came upon the coast
Our great allies, and they did boast
They soon would bang the British host.
Doodle, Doodle-doo, pa, pa, pa, pa, pa.

It should be borne in mind that this is a British satire, not really a patriotic Yankee song. Moving backwards, we find that in 1772 G. A. Stevens included in his "Songs, Comic and Satyrical."

DOODLE DOO.

Tune—Ev'ry where fine ladies flirting.

Younglings fond of Female Chaces,
Mount of Hopes in Wedlock's Races,
Some for Fortune, some for Faces.
Doodle, Doodle, Doo, etc.

The same refrain was used in "A Royal Love Song, 1770," in "A low Song upon a High Subject," 1769, and as printed in the Gazetteer and New Daily Advertiser, London, January 6, 1776 for—

A new Song, entitled and called, the Best exchange: The old fumblers for young lovers. *To the tune* of Doodle, Doodle, Doo.

Still earlier we have in the St. James Chronicle, February 3–5, 1763:

A new Song. Sung at a certain Theatre Royal in the character of a Frenchman. Tune—Doodle, Doodle, doo:

See me just arrived from France-e:
All de vay from dere I dance-e,
Vid my compliments I greet ye;
All de vile I mean to sheat ye.
Doodle, etc.

And in 1762, September 13 (reprinted in T. Wright's Caricature History of the Georges, 1868):

THE CONGRESS; OR, A DEVICE TO LOWER THE LAND TAX, TO THE TUNE OF DOODLE, DOODLE, DO.

> Here you may see the happy Congress
> All now is done with such a *bon-grace*,
> No English wight can surely grumble,
> Or cry, our treaty-makers fumble.
>   Doodle, doodle, do., etc.

The "Caricature History" also contains "The Motion" (p. 128) among verses clearly relating to the Duke of Argyle and to the year 1741, this one:

> Who de dat de box to sit on?
> 'Tis John, the hero of North Briton,
> Who, out of place, does place-men spit on,
>   Doodle, etc.

We are carried far into the seventeenth century by Edw. Ravenscroft's comedy after the Italian manner "Scaramouch a philosopher, Harlequin a School-boy," 1677. In the fifth act, first scene Harlequin sings "ridiculously" "Tricola, tracola" mixed with "Doodle-doodle-doo," and "Toodle-doodle-doo."

In "the Witch of Edmonston" by William Rowley, Thomas Dekker, John Ford, etc., 1658, Act IV, scene 1, occurs this interesting passage:

> *Enter* Anne Ratcliff *mad.*
>
> *Ratc.* Oh my Ribs are made of a payned Hose, and they break. There's a *Lancashire* hornpipe in my throat: hark how it tickles it, with Doodle, Doodle, Doodle, Doodle.

And finally in Middleton's & Rowley's "The Spanish Gipsy," 1653 (acted 1623 or 1624), Sancho sings a line with Doodle-doo.

What do these references prove? First, that a chorus refrain with "Doodle-doodle, do" existed as early as the middle of the seventeenth century. In America the word "Yankee" was grafted on to this not later than 1767 (Barton's Disappointment), and the form of "Yankee Doodle do" was used as late as 1787 or 1790 (Tyler's Contrast). If the internal and other evidence submitted led to the conclusion that the "Father and I" text originated 1775 or 1776, then the conjecture is fairly safe that the refrain "Yankee Doodle keep it up" is of the same date. This conclusion in turn would lead to the other that in Barton's "Disappointment" the older refrain "Yankee Doodle-doodle do" was used. But the references would appear to establish a very much more important point, namely, the existence of a tune called "Doodle, doodle, do" certainly as early as 1762 and probably as early as the seventeenth century. Indeed, we are almost compelled to assume that this tune was known as a *Lancashire* hornpipe as early as 1658. Since the texts mentioned lend themselves more or less smoothly to our "Yankee Doodle" melody, the latter may be suspected to be identical with the "Doodle, doo" tune, but it would not necessarily follow that words were sung to it except as chorus refrain. In 1772 Stevens' "Doodle Doo" was to be sung to the tune of "Ev'ry where fine ladies flirting." I have not yet traced a song with these first words, but it will be noticed that they lend themselves smoothly to the "Yankee Doodle" melody. This suggests the query: Were these perhaps the original words that went with the melody or were they grafted on the melody later, or do they, after all, represent a different melody? I am not in a position to give any answer to these questions which might solve the problem of "Yankee Doodle" in a manner heretofore hardly suspected. However, the existence of a "Doodle, doo" air before 1750 and possibly identical with the "Yankee Doodle" air has become so probable that this probability obliges the historian to move with caution and skepticism when examining the theories of the origin of "Yankee Doodle" not yet analyzed, namely, the Doctor Shuckburgh theory in Farmer and Moore's Collections, 1824, and the "All the way to Galway" theory of Mr. Grattan Flood, 1905.[a]

---

[a] This book was in proof sheets when at last Mr. Frank Kidson, having at first almost denied the existence of such a tune, was able to send the author the following under date of Leeds, May 11, 1909:

["Doodle Doo. No. 175, p. 88, Wright's 200 Choice Country Dances, vol. 2d, ca. 1750.]

In explanation Mr. Kidson, to whom again thanks are due for his professional courtesy, writes:

"I have great pleasure in sending you the Doodle Doo which you will see practically fits the words given in G. A. Steven's "Songs Comic and Satyrical," Oxford, 1772, p. 134, song 72.

I have copied the tune from a country dance book without title, but which I know for a *certainty* to be the second volume of Wright's 200 Country Dances, a later edition issued by John Johnson of Cheapside about 1750. Particulars are given in my British Music Publishers. . . Dan Wright first issued his two volumes, and then Johnson continued with his 3, 4, 5, & 6th, reprinting the 1st and 2d from his old plates with new plates substituted for certain cases. The

The latter does not call for a lengthy discussion, as the supposedly Irish origin of "Yankee Doodle" (see p. 106) is based simply on two assertions: First, that its structure is "decidedly Irish;" second, that it is identical with the Irish tune of "All the way to Galway" as it appears in a manuscript dated 1750, the authority of which Mr. Grattan Flood says to be beyond question.

Since the structure of the melody has been claimed with equal enthusiasm as decidedly Hessian, Hungarian, Scotch, English, etc.— indeed, in his letter quoted above, Mr. D. F. Scheurleer called my attention to the similarity of "Yankee Doodle" with the tunes of the itinerant Savoyards—Mr. Grattan Flood's manifestly sincere assertion can not be accepted without very careful proof as "intrinsic evidence." Mr. Grattan Flood's other assertion is somewhat strengthened by facts not mentioned in his interesting article. It appears from Sargent's "History of an expedition against Fort Du Quesne in 1755" (Philadelphia, 1855) that when Braddock's ill-fated campaign was being prepared drafts were made in Ireland "from the second battalion of the Royals, at Galway," besides from other Irish regiments. Furthermore, the "Orders for Foreign Service," quoted in Knox's "Historical Journal of the Campaignes in North America for the years 1757, 1758, 1759 and 1760," leave no doubt that Major-General Kennedy's regiment stationed at Galway, the Fifty-fifth Regiment stationed at Galway and two other Irish regiments, the First or Royal Regiment of Foot and the Seventeenth Regiment of Foot, received marching orders in February. In this connection it is also noteworthy that in 1758 the Fifty-fifth Regiment participated in General Abercrombie's unlucky Lake expedition (Ticonderoga!), the First and the Seventeenth regiments in General Amherst's siege of Louisburgh, whereas Kennedy's Forty-third Regiment all through 1758 was condemned to idleness in Nova Scotia. However these facts may fit into the historical argument, it is known that of the 8,000 regulars voted by Parliament in 1757 for reenforce-

---

old plates have the moons and half moons (as in the Dancing master), but the new plates have them not. *Doodle Doo* is from a new plate issued about 1750 . . .

I have some startling theories about Yankee Doodle name and tune, and one is that the first part is older than the 2d part. . . "

It is clear that our Yankee Doodle and this Doodle Doo are not identical or even similar and that the several Yankee Doodle texts can not have been sung to this Doodle Doo. It is equally clear that the Doodle Doo texts quoted on p. 143 fit our Yankee Doodle well, but this Doodle Doo very poorly, if at all. Here, then, is a new puzzle and a new obstacle in the path that seemed to lead easily out of the whole Yankee Doodle labyrinth. Personally, I still adhere to the belief that there must have been kinship between Yankee Doodle and Doodle Doo, and I am keenly interested in Mr. Kidson's startling theories in the desperate hope that he at last may be able to give a satisfactory solution of the Yankee Doodle puzzle.

ments, fully one-half were Irish. If then "Yankee Doodle" is of Irish origin and identical with "All the way to Galway," it is clear how this influx of Irish soldiers may have helped to spread the air in America, even had it not been known previously to the Irish then settled in America. But, has Mr. Grattan Flood succeeded in proving the identity, without which his theory of the Irish origin, of course, collapses? On pages 123–125 of this report some of the early printed and manuscript versions of "Yankee Doodle" are quoted, and here are two versions of "All the way to Galway" as given by Mr. Grattan Flood in his article:

ALL THE WAY TO GALWAY

Ms. 1750

ALL THE WAY TO GALWAY

PETRIE 184

To these may be added for more comprehensive comparison a manuscript version (ca. 1820) in possession of Mr. Frank Kidson:

and the version in Capt. Francis O'Neill's "Dance Music of Ireland" (Chicago, 1907, p. 172):

If Mr. Grattan Flood says that the C natural in the first half of "All the way to Galway," the so-called flat seventh, is unmistakably Irish, then the first half of "Yankee Doodle" is just as unmistakably not Irish. Though the eye may detect a similarity between the two first parts, to the musical ear they sound fundamentally unlike. Only the first, third, and fifth bars of the eight in the 1750 version of "All the way to Galway" could possibly be pressed into service for Mr. Grattan Flood's theory, which he bases, it should be kept in mind, on a comparison between Aird's "Yankee Doodle" of 1782 and a 1750 manuscript version of "All the way to Galway." This comparison becomes still more futile if the two second halves be contrasted. Only one bar, the last, is identical, and that bar, I trust, may be found in a million compositions. How weak the whole theory is appears convincingly if we figuratively try to cover one tune with the other and apply the numerical test of identity: "All the way to Galway" has 57 notes, "Yankee Doodle" 52. *Only 18 notes are identical!*

It is easily seen how Mr. Grattan Flood came to embrace the Irish theory. There is an obvious wholesale similarity in melodic structure, if considerations of key be discarded, between the secong halves of the earliest "All the way to Galway" and *some* of the "Yankee Doodle" versions—for instance, those of Willig (p. 122) and Sousa (p. 123). Approximate similarity, not approximate identity! This similarity in melodic patterns belongs to the chapter on "Thematic coincidences and common property" in the history of music. It is a fascinating but wholly unreliable and dangerous chapter. In the case of "Yankee Doodle" the wholesale similarity, as it was called above, may be admitted, but the moment deductions of identity are to be drawn from this similarity we are perfectly justified in claiming an equal share of similarity between "Yankee Doodle" and the Scotch air "Will ye go to Sheriff muir" as given, for instance, in Hogg's "Jacobite Relics" (1819, V. I, p. 149):

or, as in Gow's Third Repository (ca. 1806):

This version I owe to the courtesy of Mr. Frank Kidson, as also the much more important information that the "Sheriff Muir" air appears in Oswald's "Caledonian Pocket Companion" (Book 6, circa 1750–1760). Without this discovery it would merely be possible to state that the text of the air appears in Semple's "Poems and Songs of Robert Tannahill" (1876), among the "Unedited and unpublished pieces" (p. 354) of the poet (1774–1810), as doubtful, and that Hogg says "The air has long been popular." With Mr. Kidson's find, we would be able to offset the Irish claim for "All the Way to Galway" by a Scotch claim for "Will ye go to Sheriff Muir," since the proximity of the dates of first known appearance of both tunes would forbid to derive for the sake of argument "Will ye go to Sheriff Muir" and thus again incidentally "Yankee Doodle" from "All the Way to Galway." Should it be insisted that the Irish tune dates "from about the first quarter of the 18th century," as Mr. Grattan Flood suspects under date of July 23, 1908, equal emphasis might be laid on the probability that Oswald did not print a new tune, but a popular, that is, a fairly old one, and that there might be some connection between it and the battle of Sheriffmuir, 1715.

The probabilities are that neither "All the Way to Galway" nor "Will ye go Sheriffmuir" contributed anything to "Yankee Doodle." On the other hand, if mere similarity is to decide the origin of "Yankee Doodle," and if the latter's hypothetical prototype, the tune "Doodle, doodle, doo" (or perhaps "Everywhere fine ladies flirting") should be found to antedate "All the Way to Galway," what would prevent the argument that "All the Way to Galway" borrowed its better half from "Yankee Doodle" instead of *vice versa?* However, not to let my personal opinion enter too much into this report, it should be noted that Mr. Grattan Flood's theory is by no means accepted by other eminent authorities. For instance, Mr. Frank Kidson wrote me under date of August 12, 1908, this sweeping statement:

"All the Way to Galway" is *not* really like Yankee Doodle, and cannot be proved to be earlier in date even if it was like it.

And Captain Francis O'Neill under date of July 14, 1908, wrote:

> I agree with you in noting the dissimilarity of the first parts of the tunes under consideration, the style and composition of first part of Yankee Doodle is more modern. I must admit, no Irish tune, March or Air that I can remember, unmistakably resembles the first part of Yankee Doodle and I have an excellent memory in such matters.

The substance of the rather novelistic account (see pp. 96–97) which under the title of "Origin of Yankee Doodle" appeared in Farmer and Moore's Collections, 1824, is, to recapitulate, this:

In 1755 Doctor Shackburg[!], a physician attached to the staff of General Abercrombie's army, encamped a little south of Albany, N. Y., on the ground "now" belonging to John I. Van Rensselaer, esq., "*to please brother Jonathan composed a tune*" *and with much gravity recommended it to the officers as one of the most celebrated airs of martial music.* The provincial troops, whose march, accoutrements, arrangement, the narrator with great glee compares to that of Sir John Falstaff's ragged regiment, took the bait, and in a few days nothing was heard in the provincial camp but the air of *Yankee Doodle.*

By utilizing the data printed in the "Historical Magazine," in O'Callaghan's New York Colonial Documents, in the "Collections of the New York Historical Society," in the old British Army Lists, and combining them with the information contained in transcripts for the Library of Congress from the "Sir William Johnson Manuscripts of Letters, and passages relating to Dr. Richard Shuckburgh, 1745–1773," his life may be traced with sufficient clearness for the present purpose.

It is a curious coincidence that two Richard Shuckburghs appear about this time in the British army lists, but the Richard Shuckburgh whose commission in the army dates from March 18, 1755, who in December of the same year became a lieutenant in the First Regiment of Foot Guards, and in 1768 a captain, can not possibly be connected with "Yankee Doodle" in preference to the Dr. Richard Shuckburgh for the simple reason that this regiment, since 1815 commonly known as the Grenadier Guards, did not come to America before 1776. Dr. Richard Shuckburgh, on the other hand, was prospecting with a Captain Borrow as early as 1735 on the Delaware, and he held a commission as surgeon in the "Four Independent Companies of Foot at New York" since June 25, 1737. About 1748 Doctor Shuckburgh began to take a lively interest in the Indians, and as early as 1751 he speaks of his ambition to become secretary of indian affairs under Sir William Johnson, with whom he was on terms of friendship. When this position became vacant through the death of Captain Wraxall in July, 1759, Sir William immediately appointed Dr. Shuckburgh to this office for which he appears to have been eminently qualified, having in the words of Sir William Johnson, March 24, 1760, "recorded all my proceedings with the several nations of Indians since the opening of the last campaign," 1759. Unfortunately Sir William delayed the report of his action and recommendation to the board of trade. Consequently, when his letter finally reached London, a Mr. Marsh, in 1761, had already been selected as Wraxall's successor. If it was bad enough for Shuckburgh to be "elbowed out" of a position, as he put it, it was more unfortunate that the rules forbade him to hold two offices. In the firm expectation that his secretaryship would become permanent, he had in 1761 resigned his commission as surgeon in the Independent Companies, and of course now found himself without any position. His disappointment at these developments gives the keynote to his correspondence of the next few years, though on January 10, 1763, he is able to send Sir William the good news:

> I have compleated my Purchase with the Surgeon of the 17th Regt. and received my Commission from the General the 29th ult.

These facts explain why Shuckburgh suddenly disappears from the British army lists (carefully extracted for me by Mr. Lydenburg of the N. Y. Public Library), and just as suddenly reappears in 1764 as surgeon of the Seventeenth Regiment of Foot, stationed since 1758 in America. The most miserable year of his life Shuckburgh spent in 1765 at the military post of Detroit, separated for a full year from his family and for six months shut off from all communication. When he returned to New York at the end of 1765, the military service had lost its attraction for him, and he probably did not view the death of Mr. Marsh in the same year with much regret, since now the secretaryship of Indian affairs was again within reach. Sir William Johnson lost no time in repeating his former recommendation, but not until 1767 did Shuckburgh receive the place. This appointment explains why not Dr. Richard Shuckburgh, but a Thomas White, appears as surgeon in the 17th regiment from May 9, 1768, on.

Shuckburgh was not to enjoy his new office for many years. On December 26, 1772, Sir William Johnson wrote of him to the Earl of Dartmouth as "aged and of late very infirm," and on August 26, 1773, the New York Gazetter printed this obituary notice:

> Died, at Schenectady, last Monday, Dr. Richard Shuckburgh, a gentleman of very genteel family, and of infinite jest and humour.

Sir William Johnson was greatly shocked by this news, and from Johnson Hall, September 30, 1773, wrote to Mrs. Shuckburgh to assure her of his concern at her loss and of his great friendship for her husband. That he should, in the same letter, have called her attention to the fact that her husband had borrowed $100 from him shortly before his death was at least not tactful, and the fact is mentioned here merely to show that Shuckburgh, though quite a property holder in the colony, was frequently in financial trouble. However, he had at least the satisfaction of seeing his daughter well married to a British officer.

The obituary notice mentions Shuckburgh's "infinite jest and humour." His correspondence with Sir William Johnson would not permit this inference. It is of a serious turn and mainly expressive of his disappointment at not having received the secretaryship of Indian affairs. Yet one or two letters contain a few humorous remarks, and that Shuckburgh was conscious of his humorous talents appears from a letter to Sir William Johnson under date of April 18, 1763:

> I am apt to say somewhat like Scarron, when he was dying, that I may have made more People laugh in my lifetime in this World of America than will cry at my departure out of it . . .

When Dr. Richard Shuckburgh was born I am unable to tell, but it is fairly safe to conjecture that he was born in England about 1705. That Shuckburgh is a well-known Warwickshire name would not be conclusive, since there exist also Shuckburghs from Limerick, Ireland, but Sir William Johnson, in 1752, made some complimentary remarks to "Mr. Shuckburgh, stationer, in London," about his brother, the doctor. The latter, in one of his letters, speaks about his friends in England, and, indeed, in 1767 spends a few months in London. In view of this circumstantial evidence, O'Callaghan's statement in his New York Colonial Documents (vol. 8, p. 244, footnote) that Shuckburgh was of German origin may safely be said to be incorrect.

Farmer and Moore reprinted their article on the origin of Yankee Doodle from "an old file of the Albany Statesman, edited by N. H. Carter, Esq." Such a paper never existed. The facts are these: The "Albany Register" ran from 1788 to 1819, or the first months of 1820. In 1819, Nathaniel Hazeltine Carter had become the editor, and he became the sole proprietor of the Albany Register early in 1820. He changed its name into the New York Statesman for reasons given in the first issue, May 16, 1820. Since the New York Statesman was practically a continuation of the Albany Register some people, exactly as happens to-day in libraries in similar cases, would carelessly speak of the Albany Statesman, meaning either the Albany Register or the New York Statesman (printed at Albany). Farmer and Moore took their article from an *old* file of the "Albany Statesman," and the word *old* would suggest the Albany Register rather than the New York Statesman. The same account, as Mr. Matthews discovered, appeared in H. Niles's "Principles and Acts of the Revolution in America" (1822, p. 372), and there, too, the article was attributed to the "Albany Statesman." This would prove nothing, since the incorrect term "Albany Statesman" might have been the current one for the then defunct Albany Register, but in Niles's Register, November 11, 1826, the same story is actually attributed to the New York Statesman. This would suggest the inference that the story was printed at Albany in the New York Statesman between 1820 and 1822, but as a matter of fact the copy at the Library of Congress proves that the paper was not published between May, 1820, and end of November, 1821, and by 1822 the offices of the New York Statesman had been removed to New York City. Therefore, we have every reason to prefer the older Albany Register as source of the story. So did Mary L. D. Ferris in her article on "Our National Songs," New England Magazine, 1890 (vol 2, p. 483), but her statement that N. H. Carter himself wrote the article in 1797 for the "Albany Statesman" is woefully absurd, since Carter (1787–1830!) was then only 10 years of age. Furthermore, Mr. Frank L. Tolman, the reference librarian of the New York State Library, had the Albany Register for 1797 examined and reexamined for me without finding any article on the origin of Yankee Doodle. Finally, internal evidence absolutely forbids to date the article in question so early, because the author of the article distinctly writes of a "lapse of sixty years" since 1755, which would fix the date of publication of the article about 1815, and incidentally its source as the Albany Register. At any rate, two generations had passed before the tradition that Doctor Shuckburgh "composed the tune" of "Yankee Doodle" found its way into print. If such a tradition is to be accepted as history, its details must be above suspicion. The practical joke of composing a tune and then recommending it gravely as one of the most celebrated martial airs is at least plausible, since even great composers—for instance, Hector Berlioz—are known to have played such jokes on the unsuspecting. It is not plausible, however, that Shuckburgh would have blunted the point of his joke by calling the tune "Yankee Doodle." This name it can only have received after the novelty of the subterfuge had worn off, and the puzzle is, why just "Yankee Doodle?" Such impossibilities in the story, as General Amhert's presence at Albany in 1755 instead of 1758, may be here disregarded as pardonable historical inaccuracies, but the *sine qua non* is the presence of Dr. Richard Shuckburgh at Albany, N. Y., in the summer of 1755 on the Van Rensselaer estate. Now, it is a matter of history that in that year Doctor Shuckburgh was surgeon in the "Four Independent Companies of Foot" at New York, and it is also a matter of easily verified history (see f. i., Sargent's "History of an expedition against Fort Duquesne," Philadelphia, 1855) that at least two of these companies were ordered by Governor Dinwiddie in 1754 from New York to garrison the fort at Wills Creek, Va., where they still were in 1755, and exactly these troops George Washington had been so anxiously expecting. When the preparations for General Braddock's ill-fated expedition against Fort Duquesne had been completed, these companies, and more specifically Capt. Horatio Gates's company, to which Shuckburgh was attached as surgeon, participated in the campaign, and after Braddock's famous defeat, July 9, 1755, did not until well into October, 1755, reach the vicinity of Albany on their retreat. Now, it is of course possible that Shuckburgh was detailed to Albany and that only Alexander Colhoun, the other surgeon of the independents, was in the wilderness of Virginia in 1755, hundreds of miles away from Albany, but this possibility is far-fetched, and the burden of proof is on him who asserts Doctor Shuckburgh to have been at Albany in the summer of 1755. It may be well to add here that the only positive reference to Shuckburgh's whereabouts in 1755 is contained in one of his letters written from New York on November 27, 1755, to Sir William Johnson about the critical condition of Baron Dieskau, who had been taken prisoner by Johnson at the battle of Lake George.

Doctor Shuckburgh's case as *composer* of "Yankee Doodle" at Albany, N. Y., in the summer of 1755 is further weakened by the tradition in the very family on whose estate he is reported to have exercised his musical imagination. A granddaughter of Gen. Robert Van Rensselaer wrote to Mr. Albert Matthews (see Elson's National Music of America, p. 140):

> The story of "Yankee Doodle" is an authentic tradition in my family. My grandfather, Brig. Gen. Robert Van Rensselaer, born in the Green Bush Manor House, was a boy of seventeen at the time when Doctor Shackbergh, the *writer of the verses*, and General Abercrombie were guests of his father, Col. Johannes Van Rensselaer, *in June 1758*.
>
> We have a picture of the old well, with the high stone curb and well-sweep, which has always been associated with the lines written while the British surgeon sat upon the curb . . .

The contradiction between this tradition, which leaves us in the dark as to which verses are meant, and the account in Farmer & Moore is striking, and the confusion increases by a quotation of what a J. F. said in a note on Mrs. Volkert P. Douw in the Magazine of American History, 1884, v. 11, p. 176:

> . . . It was on the farm of the Douw family that the English army, and the sixteen Colonial regiments, were encamped in 1755, under General Abercrombie, previous to the attack on Fort Ticonderoga in the French and Indian war. And it was at this historical spot where "Yankee Doodle" was composed by Dr. Shackleferd, and sung in derision of the four Connecticut regiments, under the command of Col. Thomas Fitch, of Connecticut . . .

This belated tradition has been quoted merely as a matter of record. It is clumsily incorrect, because General Abercrombie's ill-advised attack on Fort Ticonderoga did not take place until 1758, because the general did not set foot on American soil until 1756, etc., etc. On the other hand, the Van Rensselaer tradition deserves serious attention, as General Abercrombie actually was at and near Albany in 1758 supervising the preparations for the attack on Fort Ticonderoga, as Doctor Shuckburgh had no known reason for being hundreds of miles away from Albany, and as it is much more plausible that a witty army surgeon from New York should have written humorous "Yankee Doodle" verses to an existing familiar and therefore effective tune, than to have composed such a tune himself.

Should the music of the old English tune "Doodle, doodle, doo" be discovered and found to be identical with our "Yankee Doodle," we might conjecture that the old tune, like so many other old English tunes, was well known in the colonies, and we might then feel inclined not to doubt the Van Rensselaer tradition that Dr. Richard Shuckburgh, in June, 1758, used this tune as an understructure for a humorous ballad on the Yankees. But the main problem would still remain unsolved, What verses did he write? Certainly not the verses, "Father and I went down to camp," certainly not the "Yankee Doodle came to town" verses with "Macaroni," "Madam Hancock," "John Hancock," certainly not any verses that allude to General Amherst's victory at Cape Breton on July 26, 1758, certainly not the "Doctor Warren" verse, and most assuredly not any verse full of insulting ill-humored satire against Americans or even New Englanders, since he would have a difficult task indeed who attempted to falsify history by asserting that about 1758 ill feeling beyond the proverbial, but harmless jealousy between regulars and militia, existed among the British and American troops fighting a common foe. These considerations narrow the possibilities of the Shuckburgh's authorship down either to verses unknown to us or to such "neutral" ones as—

> Brother Ephraim sold his cow
>   And bought him a Commission
> And then he went to Canada
>   To fight for the Nation.
> But when Ephraim he came home
>   He prov'd an arrant coward,
> He wou'dn't fight the Frenchmen there,
>   For fear of being devour'd.

But these belong to "Yankee Doodle, or (as now christened by the Saints of New England) the Lexington March," and were not published until anywhere from 1777 to 1799, and surely will be admitted to bear the earmarks of an origin later, at any rate, than June, 1758, and probably after 1770 rather than before.   Thus, to sum up, Dr. Richard Shuckburgh's connection with "Yankee Doodle" becomes doubtful again, and indeed the origin of "Yankee Doodle" remains as mysterious as ever, unless it be deemed a positive result to have eliminated definitely almost every theory thus far advanced and thus by the process of elimination to have paved the way for an eventual solution of the puzzle.

LITERATURE USED FOR THIS REPORT.

GENERAL.

BANKS, LOUIS ALBERT: Immortal songs of camp and field; the story of their inspiration, together with striking anecdotes connected with their history . . . Cleveland, The Burrows bros. co., 1899 [1898]. 298 p. illus. 8°.

BRINTON, HOWARD FUTHEY: Patriotic songs of the American people. New Haven, The Tuttle, Morehouse & Taylor co., 1900. 111 p. 12°.

BROWN, JAMES DUFF: Characteristic songs and dances of all nations. London, Beyley & Ferguson, c 1901. 276 p. 4°.

BUTTERWORTH, HEZEKIAH: The great composers. Rev. and enl. Boston, Lothrop publishing company, 1894. 5 p. l., 195 p. incl. plates. 18½ cm. pp. 124–160.

CELEBRATED FOLKSONGS AND THEIR TRUE HISTORY. Metronome, 1903, v. 19, no. 9, p. 9.

DANIELL, CARL A.: National airs and who wrote them. Current literature, 1896, vol. 20, pp. 453–454.

ELSON, LOUIS CHARLES: Folk songs of many nations, collected and ed., with preface and annotations. Cincinnati, Chicago [etc.] The J. Church company [1905]. 1 p. l., 171 p. 28 cm.

ELSON, LOUIS CHARLES: The national music of America and its sources. Boston, L. C. Page and company, 1900 [1899]. vi, v–viii, 9–326 p. 4 port. (incl. front.). 17½ cm. (See also his Hist. of Am. Music, 1904, pp. 140–164.)

FERRIS, MARY L. D.: Our national songs [illus. fac-similes, especially of letter by Rev. S. F. Smith, dated 1889 and narrating origin of "America"]. New England magazine, 1890. new ser. vol. 2, pp. 483–504.

FITZ-GERALD, S. J. ADAIR: Stories of famous songs. London, 1898.

JOHNSON, HELEN (KENDRICK) "Mrs. Rossiter Johnson:" Our familiar songs and those who made them. More than three hundred standard songs of the English-speaking race, arranged with piano accompaniment, and preceded by sketches of the writers and histories of the songs. New York, H. Holt and co. 1881. xiii, 660 p. 4°.

JOHNSON, HELEN (KENDRICK) "Mrs. Rossiter Johnson:" Our familiar songs and those who made them; three hundred standard songs of the English speaking race, arranged with piano accompaniment, and preceded by sketches of the writers and histories of the songs. New York, H. Holt and company, 1889. xiii, 660 p. 25½ cm.

JOHNSON, HELEN KENDRICK AND DEAN, FREDERIC: Famous songs and those who made them . . . New York, Bryan, Taylor & co. 1895. 2 v. 4°. [The American national songs here treated are contained in the first volume.]

KOBBÉ, GUSTAV.: Famous American songs. New York, T. Y. Crowell & co. [1906]. xvii, [1], 168, [1] p. incl. front. plates, ports., facsims. 20½ cm.

McCARTY, WILLIAM: Songs, odes, and other poems on national subjects. Philadelphia, 1842. 3v.

MEAD, LEON: The songs of freedom [includes M. Keller's "The American hymn" with music]. Chautauquan, 1900, vol. 31, p. p 574–584.

MOORE, FRANK: Songs and ballads of the American Revolution. New York. D. Appleton & co., 1856.

NASON, ELIAS: A monogram on our national song. Albany, J. Munsell, 1869. 69 p. 8°.

NATIONAL MELODIES OF AMERICA: The poetry by George P. Morris, esq., adapted and arranged by Chas. E. Horn. Part I. New York, 1839. [Review of the collection which does not deal with *national* melodies but rather with *folk* melodies with a leaning towards negro songs.] Southern literary messenger, 1839. vol. 5, pp. 770–773.

NATIONAL SONGS [merely reprint of two prize poems "Sons of America" and "Old Glory"]. Iowa historical record, 1895, vol. 11, pp. 329–331.

OUR NATIONAL SONGS; with numerous original illustrations by G. T. Tobin. New York, F. A. Stokes co. [1898]. 128 p. illust. 24° [words only.]

PREBLE, HENRY GEORGE: History of the flag of the United States of America. Second revised edition. Boston, A. Williams and co. 1880. 3 p. 715–768. [Chapter on "National and patriotic songs," also first edition, 1872, used.]

REDDALL, HENRY FREDERIC: Songs that never die . . . enriched with valuable historical and biographical sketches . . . Philadelphia National Publishing co. [c1892]. 615 p. 8°.

RIMBAULT, EDWARD F.: American national songs [with music]. Leisure hour,1876, vol. 25, pp. 90–92.

SAFFELL, W. T. R.: Hail Columbia, the Flag and Yankee Doodle Dandy. Baltimore, T. Newton Kurtz, 1864. 123 p. 8°.

SMITH, NICHOLAS: Stories of great national songs. Milwaukee, The Young churchman co. [etc. etc., 1899]. 238 p. 2 pl., 18 port. (incl. front.). 19½ cm.

SONNECK, O. G.: Bibliography of early secular American music. Washington, D. C. Printed for the author by H. L. McQueen, 1905. x, 194 p. 29 cm.

SPOFFORD, AINSWORTH R.: The lyric element in American history. Columbia Historical Society, Records, 1904, vol. 7. (Same printed separately.)

SOUSA, JOHN PHILIP: National, patriotic, and typical airs of all lands, with copious notes. Philadelphia, H. Coleman [c1890]. 283 p. 4°. [Compiled by authority of the Secretary of the Navy, 1889, for the use of the department.]

STEVENSON, E. IRENAEUS: Our "national" songs. Independent, 1897, vol. 49, nos. 2526–2561.

WAYNE, FLYNN: Our national songs and their writers. National magazine, 1899/1900, vol. 11, pp. 284–296.

WHITE, RICHARD GRANT: National hymns. How they are written and how they are not written. A lyric and national study for the times. New York, Rudd & Carleton [etc.], 1861. x, [11]–152 p. incl. front. 23 cm.

AMERICA.

THE AUTHOR OF "AMERICA": American notes and queries, 1889/90, vol. 4, pp. 283–284.

BATEMAN, STRINGER: The national anthem: A Jacobite hymn and rebel song [contains also references to earlier articles]. Gentleman's magazine, 1893, vol. 275, pp. 33–45.

BENSON, L. F.: America [and the Episcopal hymnal]. Independent, 1897, vol. 49, p. 51.

Boult, S. H.: God save the Queen. Good words, 1895, vol. 36, pp. 813–815.

Browne, C. A.: The story of "My country, 'tis of thee." Musician, 1908, vol. 13, p. 309.

Chappell, William: Old English popular music. A new ed. with a preface and notes and the earlier examples entirely revised by H. Ellis Wooldridge. London, Chappell & co. [etc.]; New York, Novello, Ewer & co., 1893. 2 v. front. (facsim.) 27 cm. First pub. 1838–40 as "A collection of national English airs" which was afterwards expanded into his "Popular music of the olden time." (1859. 2 v.) Part of the latter ed. was pub. under title "The ballad literature and popular music of the olden time." [God save our lord the King, vol. 2, pp. 194–200.]

Chrysander, Friedrich: Henry Carey und der Ursprung des Königsgesanges God save the King. Jahrbücher für musikalische Wissenschaft, 1863, vol. 1, pp. 287–407.

Clark, Richard. comp. and ed.: An account of the national anthem entitled God save the king! . . . Selected, edited, and arranged. London, Printed for W. Wright, 1822. 1 p. l., [vi–xxviii, 208 p. plates, ports. 23 cm. "Glees:" pp. 137–203.

C[rawford], G. A.: God save the King [excellent summing up in favor of the Jacobite origin]. Julian's dictionary of hymnology, 2d. ed., 1907, pp. 437–440.

Cummings, William H[ayman]: God save the king; the origin and history of the music and words of the national anthem. London, Novello and company, limited; New York, Novello, Ewer and co., 1902. v, 126 p.. incl. music, front., port. 20 cm.

Engel, Carl: An introduction to the study of national music; comprising researches into popular songs, traditions, and customs. London, Longmans, Green, Reader, and Dyer, 1866. [Pp. 13–18, instructive remarks on the origin, etc., of "God save the King."]

Gauntlett, H. J.: God save the King, a hymn of the Chapels Royal. Notes and queries, 1d ser., 1859, vol. 7, pp. 63–64.

God save the King. Gentleman's magazine, 1814, vol. 84, 2, p. 42, 99–100, 323–324, 339, 430, 552.

God save the King [on the origin]. Gentleman's magazine, 1836, new ser., vol. 6, pp. 141–142.

"God save the King," its authorship [communication from A. W. Thayer, John Moore, B. D. A., and editorial comment]. Dwight's journal of music, 1877, vol. 37, nos. 7, 9, 10.

God save the Queen [origin of the words]. Chambers's journal, 1867, 4th ser., no. 206, pp. 775–778.

God save the Queen. American notes and queries, 1889, vol. 3, pp. 1–3.

Gould, S. Baring: God save our gracious queen [Notes to songs, English Minstrelsie, vol. 1, pp. xxv–xxvii].

[Grove, Sir George and Kidson, Frank]: God save the King [résumé of the whole controversy]. Grove's dictionary of music and musicians, 2d. ed., 1906, vol. 2, pp. 188–191.

Hadden, J. Cuthbert.: The "God save the Queen myths." Argosy (Lond.), 1900, vol. 72, pp. 93–100.

The international patriotic air America—God save the Queen [with music and facsimile by Rev. S. F. Smith, 1893 of "America"]. Outlook, 1898, vol. 59, pp. 563–565.

MEAD, EDWIN D.: The hymn "America." Boston Evening Transcript, October 19, 1908, p. 10.

MOORE, AUBERTINE WOODWARD: Popular hymn claimed by all nations. Musical leader and concert goer, 1904, vol. 8, No. 8, pp. 6–8.

"MY COUNTRY, 'TIS OF THEE" [reprint of an account of its origin in the words of Rev. S. F. Smith]. Music, 1898, vol. 14, p. 107.

MYERS, A. WALLIS: God save the Queen. The story of our national hymn. The Ludgate, 1900/01, vol. 11, pp. 148–154.

N., J. G.: The history of "God save the King." Gentleman's magazine, 1836, new ser. vol. 6, pp. 369–374.

THE NATIONAL HYMN [inconsequential note on the origin of "God save the King"]. Atlantic monthly, 1896. vol. 77, p. 720.

THE STORY OF THE HYMN "AMERICA" [condensed from an article in the N. Y. World, Sunday Jan. 20, 1895]. The Critic, 1895, vol. 26, p. 69.

TAPPERT, WILHELM: Wandernde melodien. Eine musikalische Studie, 2. verm. und verb. aufl. Berlin, Brachvogel & Ranft, 1889 [contains interesting remarks on "God save the King"]. 2 p.l., 95, [1] p. 22½ cm.

W., J. R.: Origin of "God save the King." Gentleman's magazine, 1836, new ser. vol. 5. pp. 594–595.

WHAT IS OUR CLAIM TO "GOD SAVE THE KING?" Musical news, 1908, vol. 35, nos. 920–921.

WHERE "AMERICA" WAS FIRST SUNG [two communications from William Copley Winslow and Edwin D. Mead]. Boston Evening Transcript, 1908, Oct. 27, p. 11.

HAIL COLUMBIA

FACSIMILE OF "HAIL COLUMBIA" BY JOSEPH HOPKINSON [dated, March 24, 1838]. Henkels' Catalogue of autograph letters, etc., no. 738, p. 48.

HAIL COLUMBIA: Moore's complete encyclopaedia of music [1880], pp. 358–359.

HAIL COLUMBIA: American notes and queries, 1888/89, vol. 2, p. 18.

[KIDSON, FRANK]: Hail Columbia. Grove's dictionary of music and musicians, 2d. ed., 1906, vol. 2, pp. 271–272.

[McKOY, WILLIAM]: Origin of "Hail Columbia" [reprint from Poulson's *Daily Advertiser*, Phila., 1829, where article appeared under pseudonym "Lang Syne." (Dawson's) Historical magazine, 1861, vol. 5, pp. 280–282.

SONNECK, O. G.: Critical notes on the origin of "Hail Columbia." Sammelbände d. I. M. G. 1901, vol. 3, pp. 139–166.

STAR SPANGLED BANNER

APPLETON, NATHAN: The Star Spangled Banner. An address delivered at the Old South Meeting House, Boston . . . on June 14, 1877. Boston, Lockwood, Brooks & Co., 1877. 8°. 34p. [on the history of the flag, the song, etc.]

BROWNE, C. A.: The story of "The Star-Spangled Banner." Musician, 1907, v. 12, p. 541.

CARPENTER, JOHN C.: "The Star Spangled Banner" [with port. and facsimile]. Century magazine, 1894, vol. 48, pp. 358–363.

CHAPPELL, WM.: "The Star-Spangled Banner" and "To Anacreon in Heaven" [on the authorship of John Stafford Smith]. Notes and Queries (London), 1873, 4th ser., vol. 11, pp. 50–51.

DORSEY, MRS. ANNA H. Origin of the Star Spangled Banner [reprinted from Washington *Sunday Morning Chronicle*]. (Dawson's) Historical magazine, 1861, vol. 5, pp. 282–283.

FOR A NEW NATIONAL HYMN. North American review., 1906, vol. 183, pp. 947–948.

THE FRANCIS SCOTT KEY MEMORIAL. Munsey's magazine, 1898, vol. 20, pp. 325–326.

HIGGINS, EDWIN.: The national anthem "The Star Spangled Banner," Francis Scott Key, and patriotic lines. Baltimore, 1898 [illustrated reprint of the poem with a brief biographical sketch, 12 p. 16°].

HILL, MARION: The Star Spangled Banner. Does it get weighed? Or yet wade? Uncertainty of many school children on the subject. McClure's magazine, 1900, vol. 15, pp. 262–267 [not historical].

KEY, FRANCIS SCOTT: Poems . . . with an introductory letter by Chief Justice Taney. New York, R. Carter & Bros., 1857 [the letter narrates "the incidents connected with the origin of the song The Star Spangled Banner" as told the author by Key].

K[IDSON], FRANK: Star Spangled Banner. Grove's dictionary of music and musicians, 2d ed., 1908. vol. 4, pp. 674–675.

KING, HORATIO: The Star Spangled Banner. Magazine of American history, 1883. Vol. X, pp. 516–517.

LOSSING, BENSON JOHN: The pictorial field-book of the war of 1812. Facsimile of the original manuscript of the first stanza of "The Star Spangled Banner," reprinted from Kennedy and Bliss' "Autograph leaves of our country authors;" origin of the hymn narrated in footnote to pp. 956–958.

MCLAUGHLIN, J. FAIRFAX: "The Star-Spangled Banner!" who composed the music for it. It is American, not English. American Art Journal, 1896. vol. 68, No. 13, pp. 194–195.

MEAD, LUCIA AMES: Our National Anthem [against "The Star Spangled Banner"]. Outlook, 1903. vol. 75, p. 616.

MARYLAND, BOARD OF PUBLIC WORKS: The seventh star. Facts and figures about the State of Maryland. Her past greatness and her present prosperity . . . Pub. by the board of public works for the Louisiana purchase exposition. Maryland day, September 12th, 1904. Baltimore, Md. Press of Lucas brothers [1904]. [22] p. front., illus., ports., facsims. 23½ cm. Contains facsimiles. Compiled by [L. H. Dielman].

A MONUMENT TO FRANCIS SCOTT KEY [by Doyle and port. of K. on p. 128]. The Critic, 1898. new ser. vol. 30, p. 129.

THE NATIONAL ANTHEM [on the official adoption of "The Star Spangled Banner" by the Army and Navy]. Outlook, 1903. vol. 75, p. 245.

NATIONAL HYMNOLOGY [on our national anthem with special reference to "The Star Spangled Banner"]. Scribner's magazine, 1907. vol. 42, pp. 380–381.

PINKERTON, WILLIAM: The Star Spangled Banner. Notes & Queries, 1864. 3d ser. vol. 6, pp. 429–430.

PREBLE, GEORGE HENRY: The Star Spangled Banner, autographic copies, additional verses, etc. (8°. 7p.) published separately in ed. of 100 copies with facsimile. Boston, 1876.

PREBLE, GEO. HENRY: The Star Spangled Banner. Autograph copies, additional verses, etc. Communicated by Rear Admiral . . . [with facsimile of copy dated Oct. 21, 1840]. New England Historical and Genealogical register, 1877. vol. 31, pp. 28–31.

PREBLE, GEO. HENRY: Three historic flags and three September victories [contains important matter on "The Star Spangled Banner" especially the different autographs]. New England Historical and Genealogical Register, 1874. vol. 28, pp. 17–41.

SALISBURY, STEPHEN: The Star Spangled Banner and national songs [Read at a meeting of the American Antiquarian Society, in Worcester, Oct. 21]. Dwight's journal of music, 1872. vol. 32, pp. 332–333.

SALISBURY, STEPHEN: The Star Spangled Banner and national airs. [Read before the American Antiquarian Society, Oct. 21, 1872.] American Historical Record, 1872. vol. 1, pp. 550–554.

SALISBURY, STEPHEN: An essay on the Star Spangled Banner and national songs. Read before the Society, October 21, 1872. Worcester, 1873. 8°. 15 p. Reprinted from the Proceedings of the American Antiquarian Society.

—— Same [second ed.] with additional notes and songs. Worcester, 1873. 8°. 24 p. (ed. of 100).

SALISBURY, STEPHEN: The Star Spangled Banner and national songs. American Antiquarian Society, Proceedings, 1873, pp. 43–53.

SCHELL, FRANK H.: Our great national hymn "The Star Spangled Banner" and its origin [inconsequential note]. Leslie's weekly, 1898. vol. 87, p. 85.

[THE SELECTION OF THE MUSIC FOR THE "STAR SPANGLED BANNER" by Ferdinand Durang.] Iowa Historical Record, 1897. vol. 13, p. 144.

SHIPPEN, REBECCA LLOYD: The original manuscript of "The Star Spangled Banner." Pennsylvania Magazine of Hist. & Biogr., 1901. vol. 25, pp. 427–428.

SMITH, F. S. KEY: Fort McHenry and the "Star Spangled Banner" [with port. of Francis Scott Key]. The Republic magazine, 1908. vol. 1, No. 4, pp. 10–20.

THE STAR SPANGLED BANNER [facsimile of the handwriting of the author, Francis S. Key, dated Washington, October 21, 1840, formerly in possession of Lewis J. Cist]. Smith's American historical and literary curiosities, 2d ser. Philadelphia, Pl. LV.

THE STAR SPANGLED BANNER: Dwight's journal of music, 1861. vol. 19, pp. 37, 39, 46.

THE STAR SPANGLED BANNER: American Historical Record, 1873. vol. 2, pp. 24–25.

STAR SPANGLED BANNER [inconsequential note]. American notes and queries, 1888. vol. 1, pp. 199.

THE STAR SPANGLED BANNER. [Facsimile of four stanzas in autograph of F. S. Key, dated Oct. 21, 1840] Henkels' Catalogue of autograph letters, etc. No. 738, p. 50.

"TANEY, ROGER B.]: "The Star Spangled Banner" [extract from a letter dated 1856, written to her giving the origin of the words and] Contributed by Mrs. Rebecca Lloyd Shippen. Pennsylvania magazine of history and biography, 1898/99. Vol. 22, pp. 321–325.

WARNER, JOHN L.: The origin of the American National anthem called the Star Spangled Banner. [Read before the Pennsylvania Historical Society, at its meeting, 1867]. (Dawson's) Historical magazine, 1867. Vol. 11, pp. 279–280.

WILCOX, MARION: America's National song [The Star Spangled Banner] Harper's weekly, 1905. Vol. 49, p. 373.

X. The Star Spangled Banner . . . Musical times, 1896. Vol. 37, pp. 516–519.

YANKEE DOODLE.

BANSEMER, CAROLINE T.: Yankee Doodle. Lippincott's magazine, 1896. Vol. 58, pp. 138–140.

BELL, WILLIAM: Yankee, its origin and meaning. Notes and queries, 1853. 1st ser., vol. 7, p. 103.

BOOS, J. E.: Where "Yankee Doodle" was written. American music journal, 1907. Vol. 6, No. 8, pp. 30–32.

CARTER, N. H.: Origin of Yankee Doodle [repr. without date from the *Albany Register* or New York Statesman] Farmer & Moore's Collections, 1824. Vol. 3, pp. 217–218.

DEAR OLD YANKEE DOODLE! The song is seven centuries old and four great nations have owned it. Metronome, 1899. Vol. 15, No. 9, p. 10.

E. W. C.: YANKEE DOODLE. Lippincott's magazine, 1876. Vol. 18, pp. 126–128.

FLOOD, WM. H. GRATTAN: The Irish origin of the tune of "Yankee Doodle." [With music sheet containing the tune as printed by Aird, 1782, and the tune of "All the way to Galway" from a MSS. written 1750]. The Dolphin, 1905. Vol. 8, pp. 187–193.

J., G. W.: Kitty Fisher. Notes & Queries, 1865. 3d ser., vol. 8, pp. 81–82.

LOSSING, BENSON J.: The origin of Yankee Doodle [repr. from the Poughkeepsie Eagle]. Littell's Living age, 1861, vol. 70, pp. 382–384; Dwight's journal of music, 1861, vol. 19, p. 107.

LOSSING, BENSON JOHN. The pictorial field-book of the revolution. New York, Harper & brothers, 1860. [Yankee Doodle National Song of the Revolution] p. 683.

MOORE, AUBERTINE WOODWARD: Young America in musical tones [on origin of "Yankee Doodle"] Musical leader and concert goer, 1905. Vol. 10, Nos. 2–3.

ORIGIN OF YANKEE DOODLE. Musical reporter, Boston, 1841. Vol. 1, May, pp. 206–209.

THE ORIGIN OF YANKEE DOODLE. Various theories of the meaning of the words. Music and literature, 1898. Vol. I, No. 6, p. 10.

PORSON, JUNIOR. Original of the national melody "Yankee Doodle" [satire on the ethymological derivation of the words Yankee Doodle]. Democratic review, 1839. Vol. 5, pp. 213–221; repr. 1855, vol. 35, pp. 125–131.

RIMBAULT, EDWARD F. Kitty Fisher. Notes & Queries, 1870. 4th ser., vol. 5, pp. 319–320.

———— Yankee Doodle [note on 18th cent. broadsides]. Notes and queries (London), 1860. 2d. ed. vol. 10, pp. 426.

RYDER, JAMES F. The painter of "Yankee Doodle" [Archibald M. Willard]. New England magazine, 1895/96. New ser., vol. 13, pp. 483–494.

SONNECK, O. G. Yankee Doodle nicht "made in Germany." Allgemeine Musik Zeitung, 1907. Vol. 34, p. 381.

Sonneck, O. G. Yankee Doodle (article contributed to new ed. of Grove's Dictionary, 1909).

S[QUIRE], W. B. Yankee Doodle [comprehensive review of the different theories]. Grove's dictionary of music and musicians, 1st ed., vol. 4, pp. 493–495.

A VERY FUNNY OLD TUNE [Yankee Doodle]. Brainard's musical, 1901. Vol. 3, No. 1, p. 30.

WESTCOTT, T. Yankee and Yankee Doodle. Notes and queries, 1852. 1st ser., vol. 6, pp. 56–58.

YANKEE, DERIVATION OF. Notes and queries (Lon.), 1st ser., 1851, vol. 3, pp. 260, 437, 461; vol. 4, pp. 13, 344, 392–393; 1852, vol. 5, pp. 86, 258; 1852, vol. 6, pp. 56–58; 1853, vol. 7, pp. 103, 164.

YANKEE DOODLE [miscellaneous queries and answers as to derivation, origin, etc.] Historical magazine, 1857. Vol. I, pp. 26–27, 58–59, 86, 91–92, 124, 156–157, 189, 221, 279, 314, 375; 1858, vol. 2, pp. 214–215, 280; 1859, vol. 3, pp. 22–23, 189; 1861, vol. 5, p. 123.

YANKEE DOODLE [miscellaneous information on origin of the term, etc.] Magazine of American History, 1877. Vol. 1, pp. 390, 452, 576; 1879, vol. 3, p. 265; 1884, vol. 11, p. 176; 1886, vol. 15, p. 99; 1891, vol. 25, p. 256; 1891, vol. 26, pp. 75, 236.

YANKEE DOODLE [with the old text and additional stanzas] Farmer and Moore's Collection, historical and miscellaneous, 1824. Vol. 3, pp. 157–160.

YANKEE DOODLE. Dwight's journal of music, 1853/54. Vol. 4, p. 27.

YANKEE DOODLE [as a popular air of Biscay and Hungary]. Dwight's Journal of music, 1858. Vol. 13, p. 133.

YANKEE DOODLE [notes containing some curious etymological information, variants, etc]. American notes and queries, 1889, vol. 3, pp. 161–162; 1889/90, vol. 4, pp. 72, 142; 1890, vol. 5, p. 225.

YANKEE DOODLE [brief sketch with the supposed original text from Isaiah Thomas's collection of broadsides, 1813]. Duyckinck's cyclopædia of American literature. Philadelphia, 1875. I, pp. 463–464.

YANKEE, ITS ETYMOLOGY. Notes and queries, 5th ser., 1877, vol. 7, pp. 126, 337–338; 1878, vol. 10, p. 467; 1879, vol. 11, pp. 18, 38.

YANKEE [derivation of the words]. Webster's dictionary; Standard dictionary; Bartlett's dictionary of americanisms, etc.a

---

a These notes on the printed Yankee Doodle literature would be incomplete without reference to the important but unfortunately unprinted essays by Mr. George H. Moore and Mr. Albert Matthews mentioned throughout these pages.

ILLUSTRATIONS

PLATE I.—"TO ANACREON IN HEAVEN," FROM

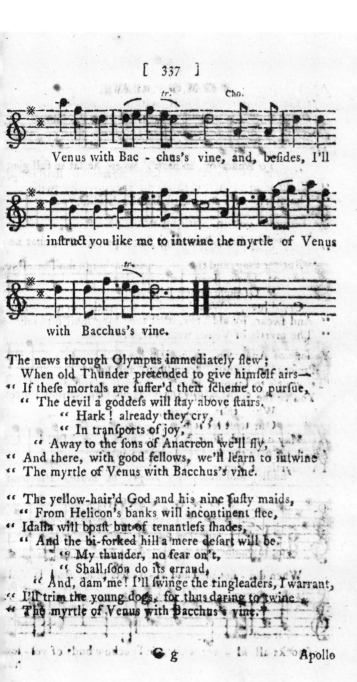

[337]

Venus with Bac - chus's vine, and, besides, I'll

instruct you like me to intwine the myrtle of Venus

with Bacchus's vine.

The news through Olympus immediately flew;
  When old Thunder pretended to give himself airs—
" If these mortals are suffer'd their scheme to pursue,
  " The devil a goddess will stay above stairs.
      " Hark! already they cry,
      " In transports of joy,
    " Away to the sons of Anacreon we'll fly,
  " And there, with good fellows, we'll learn to intwine
  " The myrtle of Venus with Bacchus's vine.

  " The yellow-hair'd God and his nine lusty maids,
    " From Helicon's banks will incontinent flee,
  " Idalia will boast but of tenantless shades,
    " And the bi-forked hill a mere desart will be.
      " My thunder, no fear on't,
      " Shall soon do its errand,
    " And, dam'me! I'll swinge the ringleaders, I warrant,
  " I'll trim the young dogs, for thus daring to twine
  " The myrtle of Venus with Bacchus's vine."

Gg

Apollo

"THE VOCAL ENCHANTRESS," LONDON, 1783.

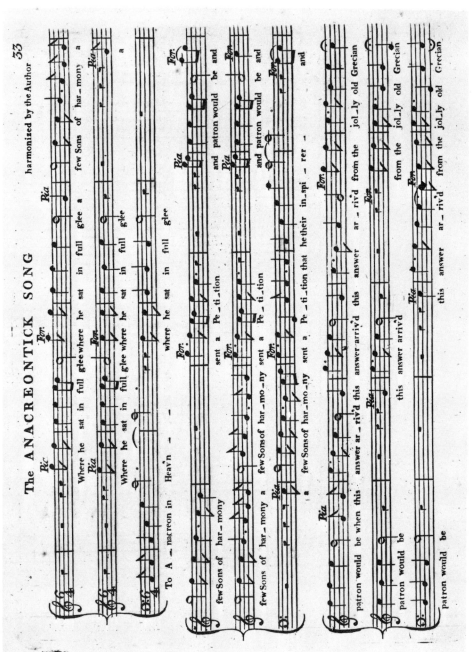

PLATE II.—FROM JOHN STAFFORD SMITH'S "FIFTH BOOK OF CANZONETS," LONDON, CA. 1785.

170

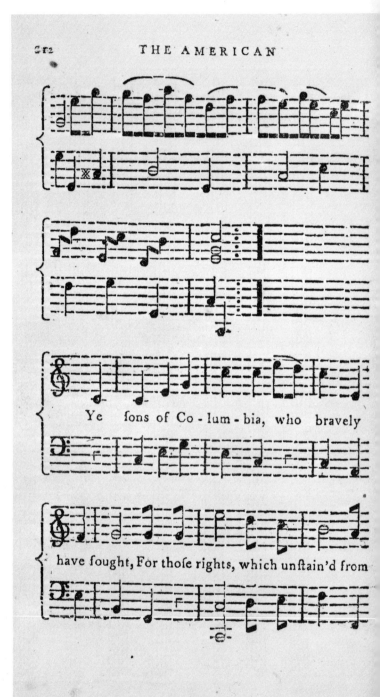

Ye   fons of Co - lum - bia, who   bravely

have fought, For thofe rights, which unftain'd from

PLATE III.—PAINE'S "ADAMS

your Sires had de-fcend-ed, May you

long tafte the bleffings your valour has

bought, And your fons reap the foil, which you

fathers defended, Mid the reign of

172

26

Hard, hard is my fate! oh, how galling my chain
    My life's steer'd by misery's chart—
And 'tho 'gainst my tyrants I scorn to complain,
    Tears gush forth to ease my sad heart:
I disdain e'en to shrink, tho' I feel the sharp lash;
    Yet my breast bleeds for her I adore:
While round me the unfeeling billows will dash,
    I sigh!—and still tug at the oar.

How fortune deceives!—I had pleasure in tow,
    The port where she dwelt we'd in view;
But the wish'd nuptial morn was o'erclouded with
    And, dear Anne, I hurried from you.   [woe,
Our shallop was boarded, and I borne away,
    To behold my lov'd Anne no more!
But dispair wastes my spirits, my form feels decay-
    He sigh'd—and expir'd at the oar!

· · · · · ·

ANACREON IN HEAVEN.

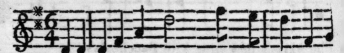

To Anacreon in Heav'n where he sat in ful

glee, A few sons of harmony sent a petition

PLATE IV.—FROM "BALTIMORE

27

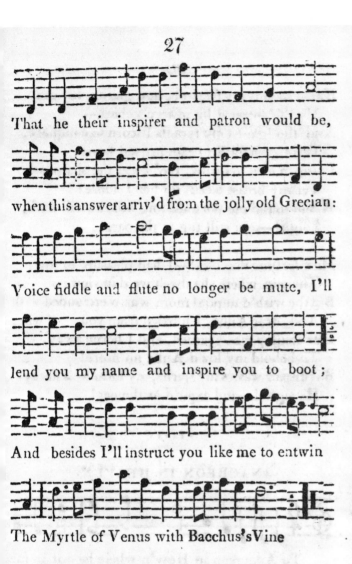

'That he their inspirer and patron would be,

when this answer arriv'd from the jolly old Grecian:

Voice fiddle and flute no longer be mute, I'll

lend you my name and inspire you to boot;

And besides I'll instruct you like me to entwin

The Myrtle of Venus with **Bacchus's Vine**

The news through Olympus immediately flew,
  When old Thunder pretented to give himself
        airs;

O Say. can you see by the dawn's early light
What so proudly we hail'd at the twilight's last gleaming
Whose broad stripes and bright stars, through the clouds of the fight
O'er the ramparts we watch'd were so gallantly streaming
And the rocket's red glare - the bomb bursting in air
Gave proof through the night that our flag was still there.
O Say, does that star-spangled banner yet wave
O'er the land of the free & the home of the brave? _

On that shore, dimly seen through the mists of the deep,
Where the foe's haughty host in dread silence reposes,
What is that, which the breeze, o'er the towering steep
As it fitfully blows, half conceals, half discloses?
Now it catches the gleam — of the morning's first beam,
In full glory reflected, now shines on the stream,
'Tis the Star-spangled banner — O long may it wave
O'er the land of the free & the home of the brave!

And where are the foes that so vauntingly swore
That the havoc of war & the battle's confusion
A home and a Country should leave us no more?
Their blood has wash'd out their foul footsteps pollution.
No refuge could save — the hireling & slave
From the terror of flight, or the gloom of the grave,
And the Star-spangled banner in triumph doth wave
O'er the land of the free & the home of the brave.

PLATES V–VI.—THE KEIM AUTOGRAPH (CA. 1842), IN POSSESSION

O' thus be it ever! when freemen shall stand
Between their lov'd homes & the war's desolation.
Blest with vict'ry & peace, may the heav'n-rescued land
Praise the power that hath made and preserved us a nation.
Then conquer we must – when our cause it is just
And this be our motto – in God is our trust –
And the star-spangled banner in triumph shall wave
O'er the land of the free & the home of the brave.

F S Key

To Gen Krin.

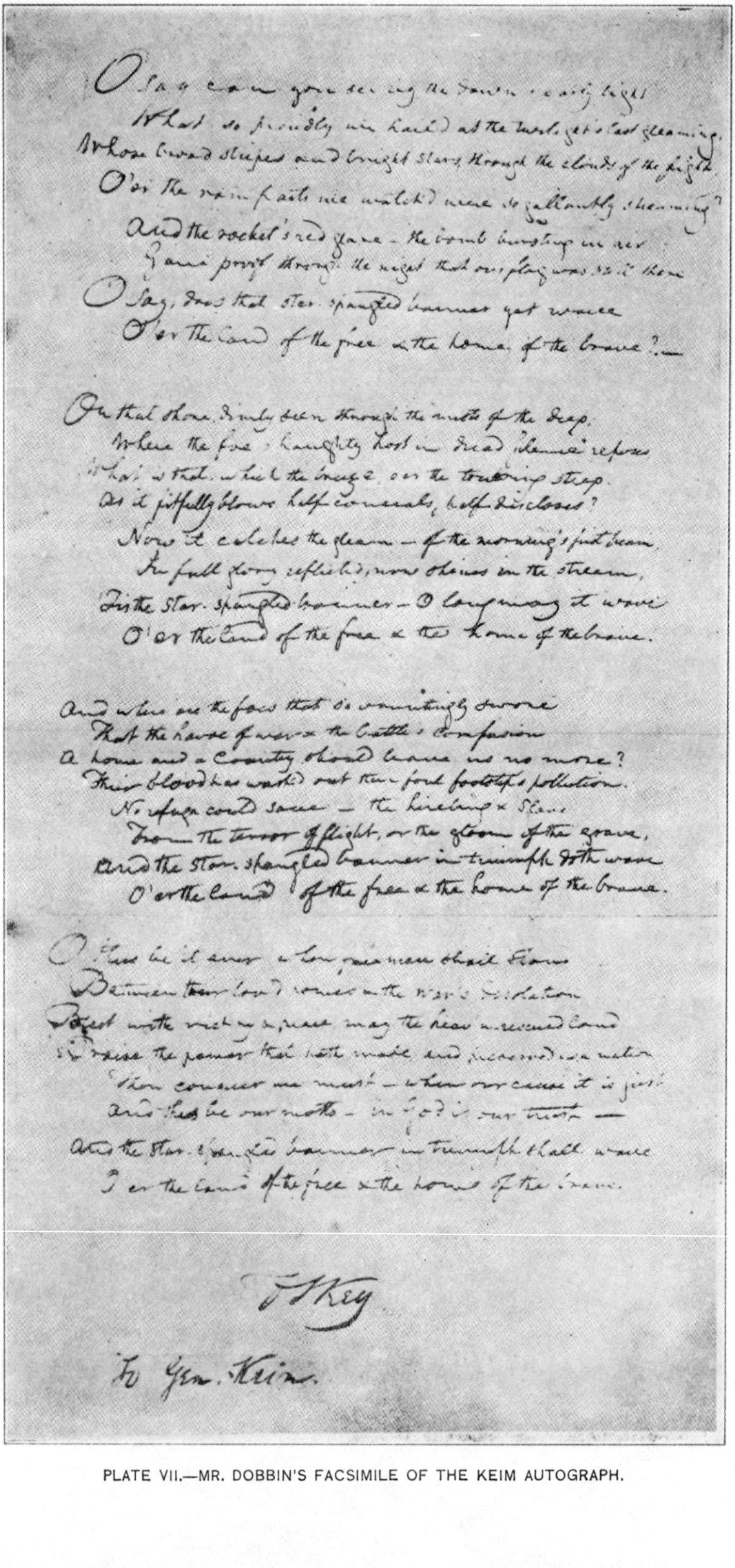

PLATE VII.—MR. DOBBIN'S FACSIMILE OF THE KEIM AUTOGRAPH.

Hail Columbia happy land,
Hail ye Heroes — heav'n born band,
Who fought and bled in Freedom's Cause,
Who fought and bled in Freedom's Cause,
And when the storm of war was done,
Enjoy'd the peace, your Valour won —
  Let Independence be our boast,
  Ever mindful what it cost;
  Ever grateful for the prize,
  Let its altars reach the Skies —
    Firm united let us be,
    Rallying round our Liberty,
    As a band of brothers join'd,
    Peace and Safety we shall find

Immortal Patriots rise once more,
Defend your rights, defend your Shore;
Let no rude foe with impious hand,
Let no rude foe with impious hand,
Invade the Shrine, where sacred lies,
Of toil and blood, the well earn'd prize —
  While off'ring Peace, sincere and just,
  In Heaven we place a manly trust,
  That Truth and Justice will prevail
  And every scheme of Bondage fail —
    Firm, united, let us be,
    Rallying round our Liberty,
    As a band of brothers join'd,
    Peace and Safety we shall find —

Found

PLATE VIIIa.—"HAIL COLUMBIA" AUTOGRAPH IN POSSESSION OF THE PENNSYLVANIA
HISTORICAL SOCIETY.

'ound, Sound the trump of Fame,
Let Washington's great name,
Ring through the world with loud applause,
Ring through the world with loud applause;
let every Clime to Freedom dear,
listen with a joyful ear;
 With equal skill, with godlike power,
 He governs in the fearful hour
 Of horrid war; or guides with ease,
 The happier times of honest peace.
  Firm, united, let us be,
  Rallying round our liberty;
  As a band of brothers join'd,
  Peace and safety we shall find —

Behold the Chief, who now commands,
Once more to serve his Country stands,
The rock on which the Storm will beat,
The rock on which the Storm will beat;
But arm'd in virtue, firm and true,
His hopes are fix'd on Heav'n and you —
 When hope was sinking in dismay,
 And clouds obscur'd Columbia's day,
 His steady mind, from changes free,
 Resolv'd on Death or liberty —
  Firm, united, let us be,
  Rallying round our liberty;
  As a band of brothers join'd,
  Peace and safety we shall find —
  —— " ——

PLATE VIIIb.—"HAIL COLUMBIA" AUTOGRAPH IN POSSESSION OF THE PENNSYLVANIA
HISTORICAL SOCIETY.

Immortal Patriots rife once more
Defend your rights defend your fhore
 Let no rude foe with impious hand
 Let no rude foe with impious hand
Invade the fhrine where facred lies
Of toil and blood the well earnd prize
 While offering peace fincere and juft
 In heav'n we place a manly truft
 That thruth and Juftice will prevail
And every fcheme of bondage fail
 Firm united ec:

Sound found the trump of fame
Let Wafhingtons great name
 Ring thro the world with loud applaufe
 Ring thro the world with loud applaufe
Let every clime to Freedom dear
Liften with a joyful ear
 With equal fkill with godlike pow'r
He governs in the fearful hour
Of horrid war or guides with eafe
The happier times of honeft peace
 Firm united ec:

PLATES IX–X.—"HAIL COLUMBIA," WILLIG'S

Behold the Chief who now commands
Once more to ferve his Country ftands
The rock on which the ftorm will beat
The rock on which the ftorm will beat
But arm'd in virtue firm and true
His hopes are fix'd on heav'n and you
When hope was finking in difmay
When glooms obfcur'd Columbias day
His fteady mind from changes free
Refolved on Death or Liberty   Firm united ec;

YANKEE DOODLE

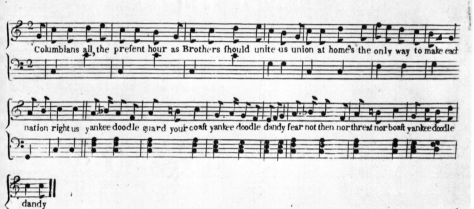

Columbians all, the prefent hour as Brothers fhould unite us union at home's the only way to make each

nation right us yankee doodle guard your coaft yankee doodle dandy fear not then nor threat nor boaft yankee doodle

dandy

2.

The only way to keep off war,
And guard'gainft perfecution,
Is always to be well prepar'd
  With hearts of refolution
    Yankee Doodle let's Unite,
    Yankee Doodle Dandy,
    As patriots, ftill maintain our right,
    Yankee Doodle Dandy,

3.

Great Wafhington, who led us on,
  And Liberty effected,
Shall fee we'll die, or elfe be free
  We will not be fubjected.
    Yankee Doodle, guard your coaft,
    Yankee Doodle Dandy
    Fear not then nor threat nor boaft,
    Yankee Doodle Dandy.

4.

A Band of Brothers let us be;
  While Adams guides the nation;
And ftill our dear bought Freedom guard,
  In every fituation.
    Yankee Doodle guard your coaft,
    Yankee Doodle Dandy
    Fear not then nor threat or boaft,
    Yankee Doodle Dandy.

5.

May foon the wifh'd for hour arrive,
  When Peace fhall rule the nations
And Commerce, free from fetters, prove
  Mankind are all relations.
    Then Yankee Doodle, be divine
    Yankee Doodle Dandy
    Beneath the Fig tree and the Vine,
    Sing Yankee Doodle Dandy.

EDITION, PUBLISHED BETWEEN 1798 AND 1803.

182

PLATE XI.—FROM SHAW AND CARR'S "GENTLEMAN'S AMUSEMENT."

PRESIDENTS MARCH.

PHILADELPHIA Printed and fold by G WILLIG Market Street Nº 185. [co. 1798]

For the Flute

PLATE XII.—WILLIG'S EDITION, PUBLISHED BETWEEN 1798 AND 1803.

185

PLATE XIII.—FRAGMENT OF A MUSIC COLLECTION IN THE LIBRARY OF
CONGRESS, PUBLISHED PROBABLY IN 1793.

186

The return of ULYSSES to ITHACA

Allegretto.

I sing U-lyf-fes and thofe chiefs who out of near a mil-lion So luck-i-ly their ba-con fav'd be--fore the walls of Il-ion Yankee doodle doodle doo black Negro he get fum-bo And when you come to our town we'll make you drink with

PLATES XIV–XV.—FROM CHARLES

bumbo

2
Who having taken fack'd and burnt that very firft of Cities,
Return'd in triumph while the Bards, all ftruck up amorous ditties.
    Such a Yankee doodle &c.

3
The Cyclops firft we vifited, Ulyfses made him cry out,
For he eat his mutton, drank his wine, and then   he pok'd his eye out.
    Yankee doodle &c.

4
From thence we went to Circe's land, who faith a girl of fpunk is,
For fhe made us drunk, an chang'd us all to afses goats and monkies.
    Yankee doodle &c.

5
And then to hell and back again, then   where the Syrens Cara
Swell cadence, tril and fhake, almoft as well as Madam Mara.
    Yankee doodle &c.

6
To fell Charybdis next, and then where yawning Scylla grapples,
Six men at once and eats them all, juft like fo many apples.
    Yankee doodle &c.

7
From thence to where Appollo's bulls and fheep all play and fkip fo,
From whence Ulyfses went alone to the Ifland of Calypfo.
    — Yankee doodle &c.

8
And there he kifs'd and toy'd and play'd, tis true upon my life Sir,
'Till having turn'd his miftrefs off   he's coming to his wife Sir.
Yankee doodle doodle doo black Negro he get fumbo,
And when you come to our town, we'll make you drunk with bumbo.

DIBDIN'S "MUSICAL TOUR," 1788.

188

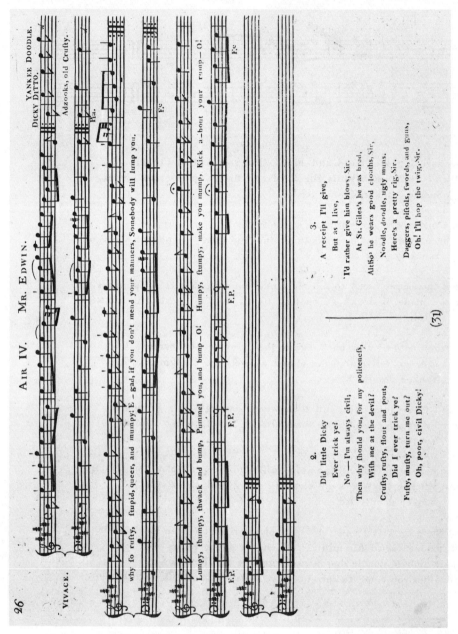

PLATE XVI.—FROM DR. ARNOLD'S OPERA "TWO TO ONE," 1784.

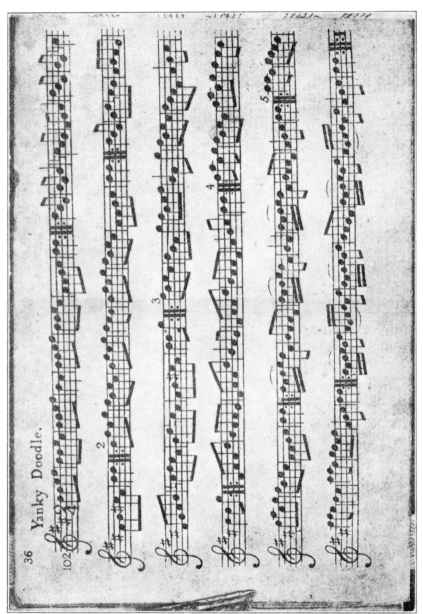

PLATE XVII.—FROM JAMES AIRD'S "SELECTION," 1782.

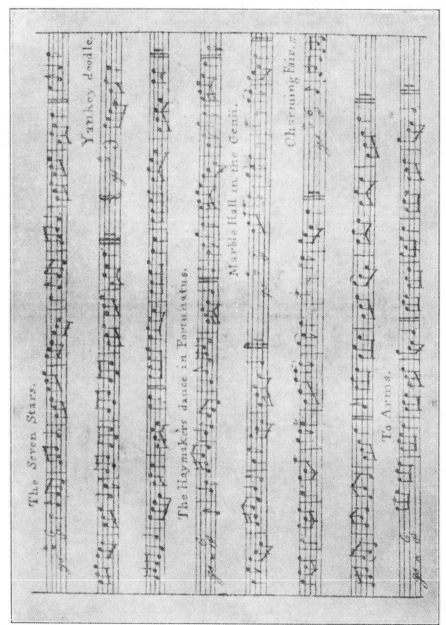

PLATE XVIII.—FROM "WHITTIER PERKINS' BOOK 1790."

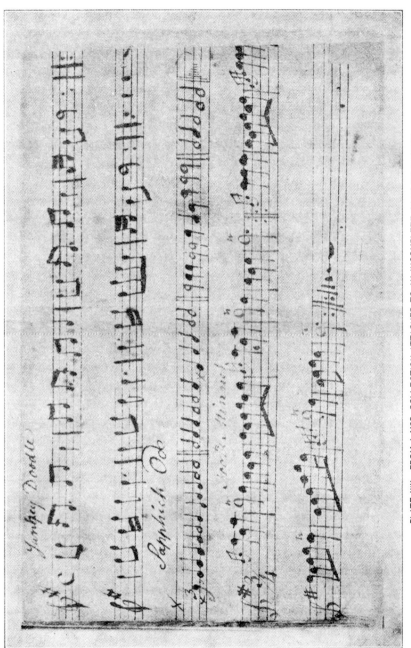

PLATE XIX.—FROM A MSS. COLLECTION ATTACHED TO AN INCOMPLETE COPY OF THOMAS
WALTER'S "GROUNDS AND RULES OF MUSICK," BOSTON, 1760.

192

PLATE XX.—BY PERMISSION OF MR. JOHN RITCHIE, JR., OF BOSTON, MASS.

 # THE YANKEES

RETURN FROM CAMP.

FATHER and I went down to camp,
  Along with captain Gooding,
There we see the men and boys,
  As thick as hasty pudding.
      Yankey doodle, keep it up,
        Yankey doodle, dandy ;
CHORUS. *Mind the music and the step,*
        And with the girls be handy.

And there we see a thousand men,
  As rich as 'Squire David ;
And what they wasted every day,
  I wish it could be saved.
          Yankey doodle, &c.

The 'lasses they eat every day,
  Would keep an house a winter ;
They have as much that I'll be bound
  They eat it when they're amind to.
          Yankey doodle, &c.

And there we see a swamping gun,
  Large as a log of maple,
Upon a deuced little cart,
  A load for father's cattle.
          Yankey doodle, &c.

And every time they shoot it off,
  It takes a horn of powder ;
It makes a noise like father's gun,
  Only a nation louder.
          Yankey doodle, &c.

I went as nigh to one myself,
  As 'Siah's underpining ;
And father went as nigh again,
  I thought the deuce was in him.
          Yankey doodle, &c.

Cousin Simon grew so bold,
  I thought he would have cock'd it :
It scar'd me so, I shrink'd it off,
  And hung by father's pocket.
          Yankey doodle, &c.

And Captain Davis had a gun,
  He kind of clap'd his hand on't,

And struck a crooked stabbing iron
  Upon the little end on't.
          Yankey doodle, &c.

And there I see a pumpkin shell
  As big as mother's bason,
And every time they touch'd it off,
  They scamper'd like the nation.
          Yankey doodle, &c.

I see a little barrel too,
  The heads were made of leather,
They knock'd upon't with little clubs,
  And call'd the folks together.
          Yankey doodle, &c.

And there was Captain Washington,
  And gentlefolks about him,
They say he's grown so tarnal proud,
  He will not ride without 'em.
          Yankey doodle, &c.

He got him on his meeting clothes,
  Upon a slapping stallion,
He set the world along in rows,
  In hundred and in millions.
          Yankey doodle, &c.

The flaming ribbons in their hats,
  They look'd so taring fine, ah,
I wanted pockily to get,
  To give to my Jemimah.
          Yankey doodle, &c.

I see another snarl of men
  A digging graves, they told me,
So tarnal long, so tarnal deep,
  They 'tended they should hold me.
          Yankee doodle, &c.

It scar'd me so, I hook'd it off,
  Nor stopt, as I remember,
Nor turn'd about till I got home,
  Lock'd up in mother's chamber.
          Yankey doodle, &c.

N. COVERLY, jr. Printer, *Milk-Street, Boston.*

PLATE XXI.—BROADSIDE IN POSSESSION OF THE A. A. S., WORCESTER, MASS.

194

THE YANKEY'S RETURN FROM CAMP.

Together with the favorite Song of the BLACK BIRD.

EARLY one morning for soft recreation,
I heard a young damsel a making her moan,
And sighing and sobbing with sad lamentation,
Crying, alas, my black bird is gone.
'Twas once in fair England my black bird did flourish,
He was the prime flower that in it did spring,
Prim ladies of honour his person did nourish,
Because that he was the true son of a king.
The birds of the forest do all flock together,
The turtle was chose to dwell with the dove,
And I am resolved come fair or foul weather,
Once in the spring for to seek out my love.
For he's my heart's treasure, my joy and my pleasure,
My heart is fixed on no one but he,
He's constant, he's kind, he's courageous in mind,
And deserving all blessing wherever he be.
It's not the wide ocean shall fright me with danger,
Although like a pilgrim I wander forlorn,
I might seek more friendship from one that's a stranger,
Than from any one that's a true Briton born.
But since cruel fortune has been so uncertain,
Has caused a parting between him and me,
May heaven so spacious to Britons be gracious,
Although some are odious to him and to me.
And if that my black bird proves false and inconstant,
Yet no one will I ever receive but he,
His name shall remain both in France and in Spain,
For I wish him all blessings wherever he be.
And if that the fowler my black bird has taken,
Sighing and sobbing shall be all my tune,
But if he's not taken, then I'm not forsaken,
Hoping to meet him in May or in June.
For him through the world undaunted with care,
I can go, for I love him to such a degree,
With fame and renown and laurel I'll crown
My true love with honour, wherever he be.

THE YANKEY's RETURN from CAMP.

FATHER and I went down to camp,
Along with Captain Gooding.
And there we see the men and boys,
As thick as hastypudding.
Chorus. Yankey doodle, keep it up,
Yankey doodle, dandy,
Mind the music and the step,
And with the girls be handy.

And there we see a thousand men,
As rich as 'Squire David ;
And what they wasted every day,
I wish it could be saved.
Yankey doodle, &c,
The 'lasses they eat every day,
Would keep an house a winter :
They have as much that I'll be bound
They eat it when they're a mind to.
Yankey doodle, &c,
And there we see a swamping gun,
Large as a log of maple,

Upon a deucid little cart,
A load for father's cattle.
Yankey doodle, &c,
And every time they shoot it off,
It takes a horn of powder,
And makes a noise like father's gun,
Only a nation louder.
Yankey doodle, &c,
I went as nigh to one myself,
As siah's underpinning ;
And father went as nigh again,
I thought the deuce was in him.
Yankey doodle, &c,
Cousin simon grew so bold,
I thought he would have cock'd it ;
It scar'd me so I shrink'd it off,
And hung by father's pocket.
Yankey doodle, &c,
And Captain Davis had a gun,
He kind of clap'd his hand on't,
And stuck a crooked stabbing Iron
Upon the little end on't.
Yankey doodle, &c,
And there I see a pumpkin shell
As big as mother's bason ;
And every time they touch'd it off,
They scamper'd like the nation.
Yankey doodle, &c,
I see a little barrel too,
The heads were made of leather,
They knock'd upon't with little clubs,
And call'd the folks together.
Yankey doodle, &c,
And there was Captain WASHINGTON,
And gentlefolks about him,
They say he's grown so tarnal proud,
He will not ride without 'em.
Yankey doodle, &c,
He got him on his meeting cloathes,
Upon a slapping stallion,
He set the world along in rows,
In hundreds and in millions.
Yankey doodle, &c,
The flaming ribbons in his hat,
They look'd so taring fine ah,
I wanted pockily to get,
To give to my Jemimah.
Yankey doodle, &c,
I see another snarl of men
A digging graves, they told me,
So tarnal long, so tarnal deep,
They 'tended they should hold me.
Yankey doodle, &c,
It scar'd me so, I hook'd it off,
Nor stop'd, as I remember,
Nor turn'd about 'till I got home,
Lock'd up in mother's chamber.

PLATE XXII.—BROADSIDE IN POSSESSION OF THE A. A. S., WORCESTER, MASS.

PLATE XXIII.—PROBABLY ORIGINAL EDITION OF "FATHER AND
I WENT DOWN TO CAMP," 1775 OR 1776.

INDEX.

I n d e x.

Chetwood, 94.

"Chorus, sung before General Washington," 63–65.

Cist, L. J., 35.

Columbian Anacreontic Society, 24.

Columbian songster (1797), 25; (1799), 25.

"Columbians all the present hour," 122.

"Columbians arise," 26.

"Come all ye sons of song," 77.

"Compleat Tutor for the Fife," 67, 122.

"Congress, the," 144.

Connel, 22.

Coverly, Jr., N., 138.

Cromwell and Yankee Doodle, 97, 100, 101, 103, 114–115.

Cummingham, Wm., 125.

Cummings, Wm., 20.

Custis, G. W. P., 50, 54, 61-62.

"Dans votre lit," 51.

Danza Esparta, 102, 111.

Dawes, Judge, 140.

Dawes, Th., 77.

Dawson's Hist. Mag., 49, 50.

"Death or liberty." See Hail Columbia.

Deane, Silas, 82.

"Defence of Fort McHenry." See "Star-Spangled Banner."

"D'Estaing eclipsed, or Yankee Doodle's defeat," 126, 127.

Dibdin's Return of Ulisses, 119.

Dibdin's songs (1799), 25.

"Did little Dickey," 104, 108, 120.

Dielman, L. H., 29–30.

"Disappointment, the," 110.

Dobbin, R. A., 34.

Doodle, derivation of the word, 89–94.

"Doodle doo," 143–145.

Dorsey, A. H., 10.

Douw, Mrs. V. P., 154.

Drummond, 56.

Dunlap, Wm., 49.

Durang (Charles and Ferdinand), 11–17, 33, 49, 59.

Dutch origin of the song "Yankee Doodle," 100, 107, 111–113.

Dutch origin of the words "Yankee Doodle," 91–93.

Dutch Yanky, 93.

Duyckinck, 100, 111.

Duyse, Van, 113.

"Early one morning," 140.

Ebsworth, T. W., 114.

Edes, Benj., 11–12, 13, 16.

Elson, Louis C., 15, 22, 46, 54, 58, 70, 78, 91, 104, 109, 112, 122, 154.

"Embargo and peace," 26.

Emerick, A. G., 49.

"Ev'rywhere fine ladies flirting," 143.

Eyster, Mrs. Nellie, 13.

Ezpata dantza, 111.

F., J. T., 84.

"Farmer (The) and his sons' return from a visit to the camp," 135, 141.

Farmer & Moore, 96, 133, 135, 150–156.

Farnsworth, C. H., 41, 71, 73.

"Father and I went down (up) to camp," 100, 104, 134–142.

Father's return from camp, 104.

Fayles. See Phile, Philipp.

"Federal March," 68.

"Federal Overture," 68.

Federal song for the anniversary of American independence, 49.

Ferris, Mary L. D., 35, 53, 69, 74, 75, 153.

Feyles. See Phile, Philipp.

Fielding, H., 94.

Fisher, Lydia (Kitty), 97, 100, 101, 103, 108, 115–117.

Fisher's jig, 101, 103, 117–118.

Fiske, 108.

Flood, W. H. Grattan, 18, 19, 20, 22, 106, 119, 139, 146–150.

"For the Fourth of July," 26.

"For worms when old," 26.

Ford, John, 94.

Ford, P. L., 62.

Ford, W. C., 135.

Foster, William, 25.

"Fourth of July," 26.

Fox, Gilbert, 44, 46, 47.

"Freedom," 26.

"From meanness first," 81.

Fyles. See Phile, Philipp.

G., G. A., 115.

G., M. N., 87.

Gantvoort, A. J., 41, 71, 73.

"General Washington's March," 122.

"Gentleman's Amusement," 66.

Gerald, S. J. A. Fitz, 53.

Glen, 120.

"God Save America," 77.

"God save each female's right," 77.

"God save George Washington," 77.

"God save the King," 75, 77, 78, 125, 157–160.

"God save the President," 77.

ML   Sonneck, Oscar
3551   George Theodore
.S6
              Report on The
           Star-spangled
           Banner, Hail

ML   Sonneck, Oscar
3551   George Theodore
.S6
              Report on The
           Star-spangled
           Banner, Hail

DATE	ISSUED TO
7 1980	B. Kilian ST 4 95